Academic Motivation
of Adolescents

Edited by

Frank Pajares
Emory University

and

Tim Urdan
Santa Clara University

INFORMATION AGE
PUBLISHING

80 Mason Street • Greenwich, Connecticut 06830 • www.infoagepub.com

Library of Congress Cataloging-in-Publication Data

Academic motivation of adolescence / edited by Frank Pajares and Tim Urdan.
    p. cm. – (Adolescence and education)
Includes bibliographical references.
  ISBN 1-931576-62-9 (pbk.) – ISBN 1-931576-63-7 (hard)
  1. Motivation in education. 2. High school teaching. 3. Middle
school teaching. I. Pajares, Frank. II. Urdan, Timothy C. III. Series.
  LB1065 .A23 2002
  370.15'4–dc21
                     2002011453

ISBN: 1-931576-62-9 (paper); 1-931576-63-7 (cloth)

Printed in the United States of America

For Afshin, whose love is a better fate than wisdom.
—Frank Pajares

For Carol Midgley, who continues to inspire and guide me.
—Tim Urdan

CONTENTS

FOREWORD

Few academic issues are of greater concern to teachers, parents, and school administrators than the academic motivation of the adolescents in their care. There are good reasons for this concern. Students who are academically motivated perform better in school, value their schooling, are future-oriented in their academic pursuits, and possess the academic confidence and positive feelings of self-worth so necessary to increasing academic achievement. Because academically motivated students engage their schoolwork with confidence and interest, they are less likely to drop out of school, suffer fewer disciplinary problems, and prove resilient in the face of setbacks and obstacles. It is precisely because academic motivation is so essential to academic achievement that motivation has taken a place along with cognition as one of the most followed lines of inquiry in educational psychology. In this volume, we are fortunate to gather together some of the most eminent scholars who have written extensively about the academic motivation of adolescents. We are fortunate also in that they represent the varied theories and lines of inquiry that currently dominate research in this area.

We begin the volume with a chapter by Barry Zimmerman, the leading theorist on academic self-regulation, a psychological process that is part and parcel of every motivation construct subsequently described and discussed in each chapter of the volume. As Zimmerman describes, self-regulation consists of the metacognitive processes, behavioral skills, and associated motivational beliefs that underlie youths' growing self-confidence and personal resourcefulness in acquiring the skills needed for adulthood. In his chapter, he discusses the attainment of self-regulation in terms of four levels of learning-specific skills: observation, emulation, self-control, and self-regulation. According to this formulation, socialization processes, such as modeling and social support, can greatly enhance youths' initiation and eventual regulation of their learning, especially during study or practice. In addition, Zimmerman analyzes the functioning of self-regulated learners in terms of a cyclical model of self-regulation that links metacognitive processes, behavioral performance, and motivational beliefs in three successive phases: forethought, performance, and self-reflection. Descriptive research regarding expert performance and experimental research in diverse areas of skill, such as academic writing, sports, music, and health, is discussed in terms of the two models of self-regulation. Finally, he considers the pedagogical implications of research on self-regulated learning.

The next three chapters focus on three theories that have explored academic self-beliefs highly prominent in the study of academic motivation. Dale Schunk and Sam Miller examine the academic self-efficacy beliefs of adolescents. Schunk and Miller trace current research findings on self-efficacy beliefs, and they explain how these judgments of capability for learning or performing behaviors at designated levels are powerfully related to the academic success that students experience, as well as to other motivation constructs and processes. Allan Wigfield and Stephen Tonks discuss the development of motivation during adolescence from the perspective of expectancy-value theory and explain how adolescents' expectancies for success and achievement values change during adolescence, particularly during educational transitions such as that from elementary to middle school and from middle to high school. These expectancies and values influence the choice of activities that adolescents pursue, as well as their performance in different academic areas. Herb Marsh and Rhonda Craven write on how adolescents' self-concept beliefs are powerfully influenced by frame of reference effects, which involve students' comparisons of their ability levels with those of other students in the immediate context as well as assessments of their own ability and academic accomplishments. They provide an overview of research findings and directions that extend theoretical predictions based on the "big fish–little pond" effect and elaborate the implications of this research for school policies and practices.

Avi Kaplan and Marty Maehr take an achievement goal theory perspective to show how the manner in which adolescents adopt differing achievement goal orientations provides a framework for understanding the processes that contribute to their adoption of adaptive motivational orientations. They review two decades of findings from this line of inquiry and trace the relationship between goal orientations and processes such as the use of effective and ineffective learning strategies, adoption of positive and negative attitudes toward school and learning, and engagement in cooperative and disruptive behavior. Of special interest, they show how adoption of mastery or performance goals may be viewed as aspects of the process of self-reconstruction in which adolescents engage, serving the development of their personal interests, establishing the basis of their self-worth, and forming desirable social relationships.

Martin Covington reframes the current debate over the presumed negative impact of extrinsic inducements such as praise, gold stars, and grades on such intrinsic educational objectives as subject-matter appreciation and creative expression from a developmental, self-worth perspective. He contends that, far from being disruptive, when properly employed by educators, tangible reinforcers can encourage adolescents' intrinsically-oriented goals.

From the perspective of self-determination theory, Jennifer La Guardia and Richard Ryan review research on how families, schools, and cultures influence adolescent motivation and well-being. They also examine the social-contextual factors that foster internalization of social goals and values, intrinsic motivation, and more secure attachments and identifications with adults. They dispute claims that adolescents need to "separate" from adults to individuate, and they review research showing that, contrary to several contemporary perspectives, support for adolescents' basic psychological needs fosters greater reliance on adults, security, and autonomy.

Willy Lens, Joke Simons, and Sigfried Dewitte further the discussion of intrinsic and extrinsic motivation by contending that learning and studying are multidetermined and that intrinsic motivation is typically accompanied by extrinsic motivation. Using what is described as "future-time perspective," they propose that, to the extent that learning is motivated by future goals (instrumental motivation), it is not rewarding in itself. Consequently, instrumental motivation can only be extrinsic, and they contend that instrumental motivation, as a type of extrinsic motivation, is not necessarily worse than intrinsic motivation.

More than 100 years ago, William James devoted an entire chapter in his *Talks to Teachers on Psychology* to describe the critical importance of interest in the motivation of students. In our next chapter, Suzanne Hidi and Mary Ainley examine the ways in which adolescents' interests develop, differ from those of younger children, and contribute to their developing sense of self. They help explain why many adolescents lack academic interests and how their interests can be related to antisocial behavior. The authors also describe how vocational interests may play critical roles in their lives, given that individuals are required to make career and lifestyle decisions during adolescence.

Jaana Juvonen and Jean Cardigan attempt to reconcile findings suggesting that early adolescence is, on the one hand, a time during which students' motivation declines and disciplinary problems increase while, on the other hand, it is also a time during which youngsters endorse attitudes and values that are consistent with those of their social structure. Their aim is to integrate some of the interpretations provided by scholars from differing disciplines, focusing their analysis on social norms and perceived values of school-based peer groups. In their chapter, they offer insights into why and how perceived peer group values, rather than personal values, may better explain the public behavior of early adolescents.

Joshua Aronson and Catherine Good describe stereotype threat as the social and psychological predicament that people face when they realize that they are the target of negative stereotypes and are at risk of confirming those stereotypes. When negative qualities are attached to a stereotype, as is the case with the stereotypes regarding the intellectual inferiority of certain minority groups, the consequences that result can be dramatically damaging. Aronson and Good trace research findings showing how these consequences can include lower academic performance both for minority groups on tests that include cognitive tasks and for women in male-oriented domains such as mathematics. The authors also describe research that examines the development of stereotype vulnerability in children and adolescents, as well as the various ways in which individuals can be affected by stereotypes alleging intellectual inferiority.

In our final chapter, Robert Roeser and Mollie Galloway show how integrating the study of motivation to learn with the issues of identity development during adolescence requires simultaneous attention to patterns of school functioning, peer relationships, and mental health at the level of the individual, and to patterns of developmental supports or risks at the level of the social contexts within which adolescents are developing. They contend that it is in the overall configuration of adolescents' personal and interpersonal resources and risk factors that researchers can best identify productive and more problematic pathways of holistic functioning during this period. Roeser and Galloway provide a conceptual architecture for studying adolescent development in the context of schools in particular, describe a methodological approach that emphasizes person-centered analysis of data, and illustrate their conceptualization with empirical results from a series of recent studies that they and their colleagues have been conducting employing person-centered analyses.

In all, we believe that in the dozen chapters that comprise this volume, the authors provide elegant insights regarding the academic and social motivation of adolescents that will prove of interest to researchers, students, teachers, school administrators, parents, policymakers, and all others who play a pivotal role or are otherwise invested in the lives of adolescents in today's society. It is our hope that these insights will not only further the conversation on adolescence and education, but will serve as the impetus for further research capable of generating the creative ideas, programs, and structures so necessary to better the lives of the young people in our care.

ADOLESCENCE AND EDUCATION, VOLUME II
LIST OF CONTRIBUTORS

Mary Ainley	*University of Melbourne, Australia*
Joshua Aronson	*New York University*
R. Jean Cadigan	*University of California at Los Angeles*
Martin V. Covington	*University of California at Berkeley*
Rhonda G. Craven	*University of Western Sydney*
Siegfried Dewitte	*University of Leuven, Belgium*
Mollie Galloway	*Stanford University*
Catherine Good	*Columbia University*
Suzanne Hidi	*University of Toronto*
Jaana Juvonen	*RAND Corporation*
Avi Kaplan	*Ben Gurion University of the Negev, Israel*
Jennifer G. La Guardia	*University of Wisconsin–Madison*
Willy Lens	*University of Leuven, Belgium*
Martin L. Maehr	*University of Michigan*
Herbert W. Marsh	*University of Western Sydney*
Samuel D. Miller	*The University of North Carolina at Greensboro*
Robert W. Roeser	*Stanford University*
Richard M. Ryan	*University of Rochester*
Dale H. Schunk	*The University of North Carolina at Greensboro*
Joke Simons	*University of Leuven, Belgium*
Stephen Tonks	*University of Maryland*
Allan Wigfield	*University of Maryland*
Barry J. Zimmerman	*City University of New York*

CHAPTER 1

ACHIEVING SELF-REGULATION

The Trial and Triumph of Adolescence[1]

Barry J. Zimmerman
City University of New York

Adolescence was envisioned at the dawn of the 20th century by G. Stanley Hall as a period of "storm and stress" and at mid-century by Erik Erikson as a period of "identity versus identity confusion" (Grinder, 1978). Although the hazards of the passage from childhood to adulthood have continued to grow for each subsequent generation, social cognitive psychologists at the turn of the 21st century now describe this pivotal developmental transition in terms of the attainment of self-regulation. Unlike personality trait or stage views of self-regulation, a social cognitive account focuses on the metacognitive processes, behavioral skills, and associated motivational beliefs that underlie youths' growing self-confidence and resourcefulness in acquiring the skills needed to succeed in adulthood. These include such self-regulatory techniques as goal setting, strategy use, time management, self-monitoring, self-evaluation, and self-reflection. Operational definitions for these and other self-regulatory techniques will be provided later. There is substantial evidence that experts in diverse areas of skill from academics to sports utilize these techniques to learn and perform at optimal levels (Zimmerman, 2001).

In this chapter, I discuss the role of school organization and students' development of self-regulation, distinctive levels in the development of self-regulation, the cyclical structure of self-regulation, and finally, interventions designed to overcome deficits in adolescents' self-regulation.

SCHOOL ORGANIZATION AND
THE DEVELOPMENT OF SELF-REGULATION

The organization of schools is predicated on developmental improvements in students' academic and personal self-regulation. Schools are organized to provide greater social assistance in the early grades and to reduce that support as students advance to higher grades. During the primary grades, teachers regulate student learning by setting explicit guidelines for classroom functioning. In these grades, students are not expected to engage in significant self-regulated learning experiences outside the classroom, such as homework or studying, but during later elementary school grades, teachers assign homework for completion outside of class. Many of these youngsters have difficulty completing these homework tasks and must turn to their parents for assistance (Hoover-Dempsey et al., 2001). However, preadolescent students have developmental limitations in their acquisition, self-evaluation, and transfer of learning strategies (Pressley & Dennis-Rounds, 1980). Thus, although teachers and parents seek to develop elementary school students' academic self-regulation via assigned homework, the transition from social to self-regulation is often unsuccessful.

Despite these limitations in self-regulatory development, students enter middle schools having more fluid classroom environments as well as increased expectations for personal responsibility than in elementary school. In middle school, students are often taught academic subjects, such as mathematics or English, by different teachers and are expected to manage multiple homework assignments on their own. To succeed in this more demanding academic setting, students must assume greater responsibility and display greater personal initiative. Wigfield, Eccles, and Pintrich (1996) have reported substantial increases in the difficulty and amount of assigned homework during the middle school years at a time when parental support declines. This can lead to significant self-esteem problems for students who have failed to become sufficiently self-regulatory to function on their own. In addition, many students confront negative academic influences among their peers, such as name calling or social exclusion as a "geek" or "nerd," if they devote outside time to academic matters (Steinberg, Brown, & Dornbusch, 1996). However, students with a strong sense of self-regulatory efficacy can resist adverse academic influences of low-achieving peers better than those with a weak sense of self-efficacy

(Bandura, Barbaranelli, Caprara, & Pastorelli, 1996b). Self-efficacy is defined as perceived capability to learn or perform at designated levels of skill (Bandura, 1986).

During the high school years, adolescents experience further decreases in the structure of their academic environment as well as further increases in the amount and difficulty of homework. These students are taught subject matter by different teachers in different classrooms with different classmates and are expected to manage these diverse requirements personally. High school students are expected to complete not only teacher-assigned work but also to engage in self-initiated forms of studying, such as preparation for tests. Often, these tests play a pivotal role in gaining access to further educational opportunities, such as placement in advanced classes and entrance into college. Frequently, out-of-school employment or extracurricular activities, such as music and sports, must be managed along with homework and studying (Steinberg et al., 1996). Students are expected to develop self-regulatory skills, such as goal setting, self-monitoring, and time management, as well as sources of motivation to self-initiate and sustain learning (Zimmerman, Greenberg, & Weinstein, 1994). Many students respond to these increasing demands for self-regulation by adopting effective learning strategies, but a significant number of students do not adopt them (Zimmerman & Martinez-Pons, 1986, 1988, 1990). Students need to self-monitor their academic progress and to seek out teachers and peers for help when it is needed (i.e., a help-seeking strategy), but poorly regulated students are reluctant to ask for help, often fearing exposure to criticism or ridicule (Newman, 1994).

In summary, educators seek to instill greater academic self-regulation as students progress from childhood to adolescence by initially introducing many social and physical curricular supports in the classroom and by gradually withdrawing them as students are expected to develop self-regulatory skill. However, there is seldom any instruction in methods of studying or other self-regulatory skills, and there is substantial evidence that many students fail to acquire these skills on their own. Social learning researchers have begun to investigate how the transition to academic self-sufficiency can be facilitated by teaching or otherwise optimizing social and self-sources of regulation (Schunk & Zimmerman, 1997; Zimmerman, 2000). These researchers have identified hierarchical levels in learners' development of self-regulated functioning. These levels represent regulatory milestones in an optimal educational path, and they provide an explanation for students' success in not only academic subjects but also in other nonacademic areas, such as sports and music (McPherson & Zimmerman, in press; Zimmerman, 1998).

DEVELOPMENT OF SELF-REGULATORY SKILL

A social cognitive perspective (Schunk & Zimmerman, 1997; Zimmerman, 2000) envisions academic self-regulation as having social origins but ultimately involves students' development of covert cognitive and emotional processes as well as overt behavioral skills to manage social and physical environmental tasks (Bandura, 1986; Zimmerman, 2000). What changes developmentally is students' capability to self-regulate both internal processes and external forces *proactively*. For example, young children initially lack the foresight to set appropriate goals and the behavioral skill to implement an effective strategy for writing an essay, but they can respond *reactively* to goal setting and strategy use by social models (Graham, Harris, & Troia, 1998). When these forms of self-regulation are internalized from a model, learners are empowered to respond proactively on their own.

As toddlers, children learn that they can master new skills easily by watching skilled adult or sibling models perform. Complex skills, such as using a remote control on a television set, involve underlying cognitive strategies that are often difficult to induce and integrate into performance on one's own because they are abstract, covert, and have subtle or delayed effects that are often difficult to discern. For children to develop advanced levels of strategic skill, they often require personal feedback and support, such as verbal tuition and encouragement, during efforts to emulate a model. Bandura (1986) and other social cognitive researchers have found modeling, emulation, and social feedback to be very effective in conveying diverse academic and nonacademic skills.

A critic might argue that social modeling is an unsuitable source of self-regulatory skill because it inherently fosters social dependency. However, there is extensive evidence (Rosenthal & Zimmerman, 1978) that adult models withdraw their support as observing youngsters display emulative accuracy. Reciprocally, these youngsters, seeing their increased proficiency, seek to perform on their own, such as when a young boy spurns further assistance from his mother when he feels he can tie his own shoelaces. At this point, the boy's reliance on his mother as a social model becomes selective, and he will seek assistance from her mainly when he encounters obstacles, such as a novel type of shoelace. When youngsters reach adolescence, socialization agents, such as teachers and parents, expect an adaptive level of functioning, such as modifying one's technique on the basis of self-monitored performance outcomes.

Four milestones have been discerned in this social cognitive path to self-regulatory skill. To acquire a skill at an *observational level*, learners must carefully watch a social model learn or perform. This initial form of learning involves discrimination of the correct form of the skill from a model's performance and descriptions, such as when a novice language learner can discern a difference between a native speaker's pronunciation of a word and second-language learner's (see Table 1.1). Complete induction of a skill seldom emerges from a single exposure to a model's performance, but rather, usually requires repeated observation, especially across variations in task, such as in hearing a word spoken in different sentences. Similarly, in the area of problem solving, learners who witness repeated variations in modeled examples learn more effectively (Rosenthal & Zimmerman, 1976). A novice's motivation to learn at an observational level can be greatly enhanced by positive vicarious consequences to the model, such as an audience's applause for a speaker. An observational level of skill has been acquired when a learner can discriminate qualitative levels in models' performances, such as discerning variations in the accuracy of a speaker's pronunciations.

Table 1.1.   Social and Self-Sources of Regulation

| | *Features of Regulations* | | | |
Levels of Regulation	*Sources of Regulation*	*Sources of Motivation*	*Task Conditions*	*Performance Indices*
Observation	Modeling	Vicarious reinforcement	Presence of models	Discrimination
Emulation	Performance and social feedback	Direct/social reinforcement	Correspond to models	Stylistic duplication
Self-control	Representation of process standards	Self-reinforcement	Structured	Automatization
Self-regulation	Performance/outcomes	Self-efficacy beliefs	Dynamic	Adaptation

Social cognitive researchers have studied observational learning of a wide variety of academic, sport, and work skills from both live and symbolic (recorded or described) models. One series of studies (Zimmerman & Rosenthal, 1974b) showed that observing models affected children's induction and use of a wide variety of skills, such as language syntax usage (Guess, Sailor, Rutherford, & Baer, 1968), concept formation (Zimmerman & Rosenthal, 1972), problem solving (Laughlin, Moss & Miller, 1969), information seeking (Rosenthal, Zimmerman, & Durning, 1970), creativity (Zimmerman & Dialessi, 1973), and moral judgments and reasoning (Bandura & McDonald, 1963; Brody & Henderson, 1977). By contrast, asocial learning methods, such as self-guided discovery, have proven to be far less effective (Zimmerman & Kitsantas, 1996).

In addition to conveying cognitive or motoric skill, models often display discernable self-regulatory processes, such as adherence to performance standards and motivational orientations and values. For example, a linguis-

tic model who self-corrects a mispronunciation helps observers to discriminate and rectify common errors. Motivationally, such a model also conveys
the high value placed on accurate speech and the need to persist in order
to improve one's pronunciation. There is evidence (Zimmerman & Ringle,
1981) that the persistence of a model during complex problem solving
affects the perseverance of observers, and there is evidence that models
who display a preference for a particular task will vicariously increase
observers' valuation of that activity (Zimmerman & Koussa, 1979). Observers' perception of similarity to a skilled model and perception of positive
consequences to a model will increase their motivation to develop the skill
further (Zimmerman & Rosenthal, 1974b).

To acquire skill at an *emulation level*, a learner must duplicate the general
form of a model's response on a correspondent task. Learners seldom copy
the exact actions of the model, but rather, they typically emulate the
model's general pattern or style of functioning. For example, when elementary school children observed a model ask causal questions such as
"What happens when you stick a pin in a balloon?" they subsequently emu-
lated the model's causal style of question rather than specific words
(Rosenthal et al., 1970). During efforts to emulate, learners can improve
their accuracy and motivation if a model provides them with guidance,
feedback, and social reinforcement (see Table 1.1). An emulative level of
skill is attained when observers' responses approximate the general form
or style of a model's on a similar task.

Although learners can induce the major features of a complex skill from
observation, they require performance experiences in order for the skill to
be incorporated into their behavioral repertoire. It is one thing to recognize the golf swing of a particular professional but quite another thing to
reproduce that swing oneself. Learners who emulate using a model's task
can master basic response elements before contending with new task variations. Emulation can be improved through individualized modeling and
social support. For example, during participant modeling (Bandura,
1986), a model repeats selected aspects of a skill based on a learner's emulative accuracy. As the learner acquires rudimentary aspects of a skill, the
model will introduce more difficult components. However, once an
advanced level of mastery is attained, the model's support will be reduced.

Some critics have decried the use of modeling as a form of instruction
because of fears that it fosters response mimicry during emulation. However, these fears are largely unwarranted because mimicry constitutes only
a small part of emulative learning (Zimmerman & Rosenthal, 1974).
Instead of duplicating a model's exact responses, observers primarily emulate the strategic features and blend them into their own repertoire of
responses (Rosenthal et al., 1970). This blending occurs even when learners are told to copy a model's performance exactly. However, mimicry can

be reduced even further when learners are exposed to multiple modeling experiences. Observers who see a model vary his or her response to differing stimuli, such as differing types of Piagetian conservation tasks, will discriminate essential strategic elements from inessential ones (Rosenthal & Zimmerman, 1974a). Similarly, observers who see multiple social models demonstrate the same pattern will discriminate it better than those who witness only a single model perform (Brody & Henderson, 1977). This reduces mimicry because these observers have abstracted the underlying strategy more completely and can blend it more broadly into their personal repertoire of responses.

To attain a *self-controlled level* of self-regulatory skill, learners must practice it in structured settings outside the presence of models, such as when aspiring language learners practice their pronunciation by reading from a prepared text (see Table 1.1). To optimize learning at this level, learners should regulate their practice using representational standards (e.g., verbal recollections) of an expert model's pronunciation rather than direct observation of that model (Bandura & Jeffery, 1973). Learners' success in matching a covert standard during practice will determine the amount of self-reinforcement they will experience. For example, students in a language learning laboratory may self-monitor their pronunciation from an audiotape and will be motivated by close approximations to the covert standard (Ellis & Zimmerman, 2001). According to Bandura (1986), "by making self-satisfaction conditional on a selected level of performance, individuals create their own incentives to persist in their efforts until their performances match internal standards" (p. 467).

Self-controlled use of a skill is sustained also by self-instruction, such as self-praise or self-critical statements (Bandura, Grusec, & Menlove, 1967). Self-instruction can help students encode and retrieve strategy sequences (Meichenbaum & Beimiller, 1990). For example, Schunk and Rice (1984) trained elementary school students who were poor listeners to verbalize a listening strategy for choosing a pictorial referent to a story. These students displayed greater self-efficacy and listening accuracy than did students who did not verbalize the strategy. Similar results were obtained when acquiring a reading comprehension strategy: Strategy verbalization enhanced students' perceptions of efficacy and their academic performance (Schunk & Rice, 1985). During level three practice sessions, learners who focus on fundamental processes or technique rather than on learning outcomes are more successful in achieving automaticity (Zimmerman & Kitsantas, 1997, 1999), which is defined as the internalization of a model's technique. This automatized quality of regulation is the most apparent behavioral manifestation of the attainment of the third level of regulatory control. Although a skill becomes internalized at this level, it remains dependent on a representation of an external model's standard.

To acquire a *self-regulated level* of task skill, learners should practice it in unstructured settings involving dynamic personal and contextual conditions (see Table 1.1). At this fourth level of skill, learners must learn to make adjustments in their skill based on the outcomes of practice, such as whether a strategy solves a particular problem. These adaptations are made on the basis of self-monitored outcomes rather than prior modeling experiences. Learners' perceived efficacy in making these adjustments influences their motivation to continue. At level four, learners can practice with minimal process monitoring, and their attention can be shifted toward performance outcomes without detrimental consequences. For instance, second-language learners who practice their pronunciation skills in natural settings can shift their attention from articulation technique to outcomes, such as audience reactions. A self-regulated level of skill is acquired when learners can adapt their performance to changing personal conditions and outcomes.

For learners to adapt their performance, they must discriminate key features of the transfer context, choose how to adapt their skill to that context, and monitor and evaluate the results. In terms of cognitive processing, it is important to note that when skill becomes automatized (i.e., level three is attained), learners' attention is freed to focus on response outcomes (LaBerge, 1981; Neves & Anderson, 1981). A behavioral manifestation of level four functioning is learners' development of their own distinctive styles of performing. However, whenever self-monitoring reveals unexpected outcomes, learners will redirect their attention quickly to the details of strategy execution (Bandura, 1986). Often, instructors prematurely end instruction before the fourth level of self-regulatory functioning is achieved. Simply transferring regulatory control of a method of learning from external agents to adolescent learners (i.e., level three competence) will not necessarily equip the latter to remain self-directed in the face of changing situations. This more demanding level of functioning represents the most advanced level of self-regulation.

Thus, a multilevel analysis of the development of self-regulatory competence begins with the most extensive social guidance at the first level, but this social support is systematically reduced as learners acquire underlying self-regulatory skill. However, level four functioning continues to depend on social resources on a self-initiated basis, such as when a novelist seeks advice from a confidant about whether a plot or character is compelling. Because self-regulatory skill depends on context and outcomes, new performance tasks can uncover limitations in existing skills and require additional social learning experiences. This multi-level formulation does not assume that learners must advance through the four levels in an invariant sequence as developmental stage models assume, or that once the highest level is attained, it will be used universally. Instead, a multi-level model assumes that students who master each skill level in sequence will learn more easily and effectively. Although level four learners have the competence to perform self-regulatively, they may not choose to do so because of low levels of motivation (Bandura, 1997). Various aspects of self-regulation, such as forethought planning, systematic self-monitoring, and intense self-reflection are mentally and physically demanding activities, and people may decide to forgo their use if they feel tired, disinterested, or uncommitted.

EVIDENCE OF LEVELS IN SELF-REGULATORY DEVELOPMENT OF SKILL

There is a growing body of evidence indicating that the speed and quality of learners' self-regulatory development and self-motivation are enhanced significantly if learners proceed according to a multilevel developmental hierarchy. To test the sequential validity of the first and second levels in the hierarchy, researchers compared the two primary sources of regulation for each level (i.e., modeling for observation level and performance and social feedback for the emulation level) in two studies (see column 2 in Table 1.1). The first study (Kitsantas, Zimmerman, & Cleary, 2000) involved the acquisition of dart-throwing skills by novice high school girls. Three observational learning groups were studied: a high-quality coping modeling group, a lower-quality mastery modeling group, and a no modeling (enactive learning) group. The mastery model performed flawlessly from the outset of the training, whereas the coping model initially made errors but gradually corrected them. Coping models are viewed as a qualitatively superior form of observational learning because they convey self-regulatory actions, such as self-monitoring and self-correction, as well as dart-throwing skills. By contrast, mastery models portray primarily dart-throwing skills. Both modeling groups learned initially by observing an adult demonstrate a multistep process dart throwing strategy, whereas the no modeling group learned only by hearing the multistep process described. Some members of each of the three experimental groups were given social feedback.

The results were supportive of a multilevel view of self-regulatory development. Adolescent girls in the two modeling groups significantly surpassed the dart skills of those who attempted to learn from only verbal description and performance outcomes. The coping model was significantly more effective than the mastery model, which indicates that the quality of the girls' observational learning experience influenced their development of skills. During emulation, girls who received social feedback learned better than those who practiced on their own. However, the impact of this social feedback was insufficient in the no modeling group to make up for the absence of vicarious experience. These results confirmed the sequential advantage of engaging in observational learning before engaging in enactive learning experiences. Finally, the girls exposed to observational learning from either form of modeling also showed higher levels of self-motivation, such as self-efficacy beliefs, than did the students in the control group.

A similar research design was used to study writing revision with college students (Zimmerman & Kitsantas, in press). The students were asked to revise a series of sentences from commercially available sentence-combining workbooks. These exercises involved transforming a series of simple and often redundant sentences into a single, nonredundant sentence. For example, the sentences: "It was a ball. The ball was striped. The ball rolled across the room" could be rewritten as "The striped ball rolled across the room." The students were taught a three-step strategy for revising these multisentence problems by using coping or mastery models or by verbal description and direct practice. Social feedback was given to some students in each experimental group.

Students in the two modeling groups, which had the benefit of some form of observational learning, significantly surpassed the revision skill of those who attempted to learn from only verbal description and performance outcomes. Students who observed the higher-quality coping model outperformed students who observed the lower-quality mastery model. As did the dart-throwing study, the writing study demonstrated that self-regulatory skills, such as self-monitoring and self-correcting actions of the coping model, were learned vicariously. As was found in the dart study during enactive learning, social feedback improved writing skills for both forms of modeling. Once again, social feedback was insufficient for students in the no modeling group to make up for their absence of vicarious experience. Finally, students exposed to both forms of modeling displayed higher levels of self-motivation, such as self-efficacy beliefs, than did students who relied on discovery and social feedback. These academic writing results confirmed the sequential advantages of engaging in observational learning before attempting enactive learning experiences.

To test the sequentiality of the third and fourth levels of skill (i.e., self-control and self-regulation) in the multilevel hierarchy, the two primary sources of regulation for these levels (i.e., process standards and outcomes) were compared in two studies (see column 2 in Table 1.1). Recall that process goals are hypothesized to be optimal during acquisition at the self-control level, but outcome goals are expected to be superior during the acquisition at the self-regulation level. Zimmerman and Kitsantas (1997) used the same dart throwing athletic task described above to examine the effectiveness of goal shifting during dart throwing practice with high school girls. A process goal group focused on practicing the strategy steps for acquiring dart-throwing technique, whereas an outcome goal group focused on improving their scores. The "bull's eye" on the target had the highest numerical value and the surrounding concentric circles gradually declined in value. An optimal goal-setting group from a multi-level perspective shifted from process goals to outcome goals when auto-maticity was achieved. Self-recording was taught to some girls in each goal group. Girls in the process-monitoring group recorded any strategy steps they may have missed on each practice throw, whereas girls in the outcome-monitoring group wrote down their target scores for each throw. Girls in the shifting goal group changed their method of self-monitoring when they shifted goals. Before being asked to practice on their own, all of the high school girls were taught strategic components of the skill through observation and emulation (levels one and two). The experiment com-pared the effects of process goals, outcome goals, and shifting goals as well as self-recording during self-controlled practice.

The results were consistent with a multilevel hierarchical view of goal setting: Girls who shifted goals developmentally from processes to out-comes surpassed classmates who adhered to only process goals or to only outcome goals in posttest dart throwing skills. Girls who focused on out-comes exclusively were the lowest in dart-throwing skills. Self-monitoring assisted learning for all goal-setting groups. In addition to their superior learning outcomes, students who shifted their goals displayed superior forms of self-motivation, such as self-efficacy beliefs.

A second study (Zimmerman & Kitsantas, 1999) that tested the sequenti-ality of the third and fourth levels (i.e., self-control and self-regulation) of skill was conducted with high school girls using the writing revision task described earlier. All of the adolescent girls in this study were initially taught the three steps of the revision strategy through observation and emulation (regulatory levels one and two) that was described previously. During a practice session following training, girls in the process goal group focused on strategic steps for revising each writing task, whereas girls in the outcome goal focused on decreasing the number of words in the revised passage. Some of the girls in each goal group were ask to self-record. Once again, the optimal group shifted from process goals to outcome goals when automaticity was achieved. Girls in the process-monitoring group recorded strategy steps they missed on each writing task, whereas girls in the out-come-monitoring group wrote down the number of words used in each writing task. Girls in the shifting goal group changed their method of self-monitoring when they shifted goals. Thus, the experiment compared the effects of process goals, outcome goals, and shifting goals as well as self-recording during self-directed practice.

The results were consistent with a multilevel hierarchical view of goal setting: Girls who shifted goals from processes to outcomes after reaching level four (i.e., having achieved automaticity) surpassed the writing-revision skills of girls who adhered exclusively to process goals or to outcome goals. Girls who focused on outcomes exclusively displayed the least writing skills, and self-recording enhanced writing acquisition for all goal setting groups. In addition to their superior writing-skill outcomes, girls who shifted their goals displayed advantageous forms of self-motivation, such as enhanced self-efficacy beliefs.

In summary, there is a growing body of evidence indicating that advanced levels of academic or athletic skills and motivation are readily attained when social learning experiences followed a multilevel regulatory training approach. These studies also indicated the importance of the various sources of self-regulatory development at each level in the hierarchy (see column 2 of Table 1.1), such as the quality of modeling, social feedback, process goals, and performance outcomes. In these studies, students were trained socially to use each of these key processes, and there was evidence that these processes not only enhanced acquisition of skill but also self-motivation. Next, I consider the issue of how goal setting, self-monitoring, and self-efficacy, as well as other self-regulatory processes and self-motivational beliefs, are interrelated and how they become self-sustaining.

A CYCLICAL VIEW OF SELF-REGULATION

There is growing evidence that students' self-regulatory processes and accompanying self-motivational beliefs influence learning in three successive phases: forethought, performance, and self-reflection. Forethought phase processes precede efforts to act in a self-regulated way and prepare the way for these efforts. Performance phase processes occur during motoric efforts and are designed to affect attention and action. Self-reflection phase processes occur after performance efforts and influence a person's response to those efforts. Finally, the latter phase processes influence forethought planning of subsequent performance efforts in cyclical fashion.

Forethought Phase

There are two major categories of forethought: task analysis and self-motivational beliefs (see Figure 1.1). A key form of task analysis, *goal setting*, is defined as specifying intended outcomes of learning or performance (Locke & Latham, 1990), such as memorizing a list of spelling words during a study session. Goals that are specific, proximal, and challenging are more effective than goals that are diffuse, delayed, and easily attained (Bandura & Schunk, 1981). Researchers, such as Bandura (1991) and Carver and Scheier (1981), have concluded that the goal systems of highly

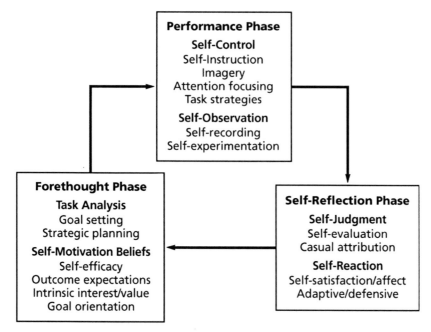

Figure 1.1.   Phases and subprocesses of self-regulation. From "Motivating self-regulated problem solvers" by B.J. Zimmerman & M. Campillo (in press). In J. E. Davidson & R. J. Sternberg (Eds.), *The nature of problem solving*, New York: Cambridge University Press. Copyright by Cambridge University Press. Reprinted with permission.

self-regulated individuals are organized hierarchically, with process goals operating as proximal regulators of more distal outcome goals. Hierarchical goals enable learners to guide their learning over longer time intervals without outside support because as one goal is accomplished, the learner can shift to the next goal in a hierarchy, such as the next item in a priority list of homework assignments.

A second form of task analysis is *strategic planning* (Weinstein & Mayer, 1986). Self-regulative strategies are defined as specific cognitive processes and associated actions designed to acquire or display skill (Zimmerman, 1989). When strategies are chosen and adapted to a specific task, they can enhance learners' cognition, affect, and motoric execution (Pressley, Woloshyn, & Associates, 1995). For example, imagistic or self-instruction strategies can enhance the recall on memory tasks (Bandura & Jeffery, 1973; Pressley, 1977). Strategies cannot be applied without planning and adjustments because of changing personal, behavioral, and environmental conditions. The effectiveness of a self-regulatory strategy will vary from person to person and will change during the course of acquisition. For example, an initial acquisition strategy often declines in usefulness as a person masters a skill, and another strategy should replace it, such as when a novice writer shifts from outlining strategy for generating text to a revision strategy for making literary corrections.

Because self-regulation of a skill involves self-initiative and persistence, it is essential to understand underlying sources of motivation. Goal setting and strategic planning have been linked in both theory and research to a number of key self-motivational beliefs, namely, self-efficacy, outcome expectations, intrinsic interest or valuing, and goal orientation. *Self-efficacy* refers to the beliefs about having the personal capability to learn or perform effectively, whereas *outcome expectations* refer to beliefs about the ultimate benefits or liabilities of performance (Bandura, 1997; Pajares, 1996). For example, self-efficacy may refer to students' belief that they can earn a grade of A in a writing course, and outcomes refer to beliefs about the likelihood that this grade in writing will help them gain an editorial position in a book publishing company. There is evidence that students' self-efficacy beliefs are very predictive of their goal setting and strategic planning (Bandura & Schunk, 1981; Zimmerman & Martinez-Pons, 1990). Self-efficacy beliefs influence goal setting because the more capable people believe themselves to be, the higher the goals they set for themselves and the more firmly committed they remain to those goals (Bandura, 1991; Locke & Latham, 1990). When students fall short of attaining their outcome goals, those who are self-efficacious increase their efforts, whereas those who are self-doubters withdraw (Bandura & Cervone, 1983). Goals also affect self-efficacy beliefs because self-regulated learners feel more self-efficacious when they choose goals that are specific and proximal. Attaining a proximal goal gives learners immediate satisfaction, whereas attaining distal goals delays satisfaction for long periods of time.

Two other beliefs have a self-motivational influence on self-regulation. *Intrinsic interest* refers to valuing an activity or skill for its inherent properties rather than for its ultimate external ends (Deci, 1975; Lepper & Hodell, 1989). Students with an intrinsic interest in a task are more motivated to plan and use learning strategies during efforts to study (Zimmerman & Kitsantas, 1997). A closely associated belief involves learners' *goal orientation*, which refers to their general reason for studying in school. The most advantageous goal orientation for initiating and sustaining academic study has been described as a learning, mastery, or task goal orientation, whereas the most disadvantageous belief has been referred to as a performance or ego goal orientation (see, e.g., Ames, 1992; Dweck, 1988; Nicholls, 1984). For example, a student who learns the piano for personal enjoyment will be better motivated than will a student who learns to avoid performing poorly during a competition. The distinction between learning and performance goals parallels the distinction between intrinsic and extrinsic interest (Pintrich & Schunk, 1996). There is evidence that students with a learning goal orientation display higher levels of cognitive strategies, such as elaboration and comprehension monitoring, than do students with a performance goal orientation (Pintrich & De Groot, 1990).

Performance Phase

Two major types of performance or volitional control processes have been studied to date: self-control and self-observation. Self-control processes enable learners, as well as performers, to optimize their perceptual and behavioral functioning. For example, *self-instruction* refers to overt or covert self-verbalization during execution of a task, such as counting musical notes aloud to help one learn a melody on the piano. Research shows that self-verbalizations, ranging from mnemonic rehearsal to self-praise statements, can improve students' learning (Schunk, 1982, 2001). Self-instruction has often been used with learning-disabled students to help them overcome hyperactivity or impulsivity (Meichenbaum, 1977). A second form of self-control, *imagery,* refers to the forming of mental pictures and is widely used to assist encoding and performance. Pressley, Levin, and colleagues (Pressley, 1977; Pressley & Levin, 1977) have conducted extensive research on the effectiveness of training youth to form mental images to assist representation and recall. Imagery has been used widely by sports psychologists to teach competitors, such as skaters, divers, or gymnasts to enhance their performance (Garfield & Bennett, 1985).

A third form of self-control, *attention focusing,* refers to methods designed to improve one's concentration and screen out other covert processes or external events, such as when a student turns off recorded music in order to memorize a list of foreign language words. Increasing one's concentration is often listed as the most difficult form of self-regulated learning—perhaps because so many distractions currently exist in adolescents' environments (Zimmerman & Bandura, 1994). In academic areas of functioning, Kuhl (1985) has studied dysfunctions in attention control, such as distractability and rumination about past mistakes. His research, along with that of others (Corno, 1993; Weinstein, Schulte, & Palmer, 1987), has demonstrated that strategies for focusing and screening out events are beneficial for effective studying. Expert performers on nonacademic tasks, such as music, have been found to use a wide variety of attention training techniques, ranging from ignoring the presence of an audience to slow-motion task execution (Mach, 1988). A fourth form of self-control, *task strategies,* refers to methods for reducing complex tasks to their essential parts and reorganizing them into a systematic performance sequence. For example, when students watch a teacher demonstrate an algebraic solution, they might identify key steps, record them in their notes, and create an acronym to guide their solutions. A wide variety of task strategies have been identified, and their effectiveness has been well documented (Pressley et al., 1995; Weinstein & Mayer, 1986). These include study strategies, such as note taking, test preparation, and reading for comprehension, as well as performance strategies for optimizing writing, speech elocution, and problem solving.

A second type of performance control process is self-observation, which refers to a person's self-monitoring or tracking of specific aspects of one's own performance, the conditions that surround it, and the effects that it produces (Zimmerman & Paulsen, 1995). Although the importance of this process may seem obvious, most learners and performers engage in self-observation in only the most cursory way. Self-monitoring is difficult because the amount of information involved in complex performances can easily overwhelm naive self-observers and can lead to disorganized or superficial self-monitoring. As a beginning tennis player once complained, "I have too much trouble watching the ball to worry about my footwork and racket preparation!" Experts are able to track themselves at a detailed level because they know how and when to be selective. Poorly hit tennis shots will be diagnosed by experts as involving breakdowns in a particular area, such as in footwork, and that will be the focus of experts' subsequent self-observation. Setting hierarchical process goals during forethought can facilitate selective self-observation because these goals direct attention to specific performance processes and associated external events.

In addition to selectivity, there are a number of other features of self-observation that influence its effectiveness. For example, the temporal proximity of one's self-observations is important because delayed self-feedback precludes a person from taking corrective action in a timely fashion (Bandura, 1986; Kazdin, 1974). When taking a timed test, students who monitor their use of time during a test can make important adjustments before adverse consequences can occur. A third feature of high quality self-observation is the informativeness of performance feedback. When learners practice a skill in a standardized or structured setting, they can derive more information from their results (Ericsson & Lehman, 1996). For example, when preparing for an entrance exam in writing, students will find practice tests that are identical in format to the exam are much more informative in judging writing progress than unstructured writing exercises. A fourth qualitative feature is the accuracy of self-observations. As was noted in the discussion of level-one regulation, accurate self-perception often depends on prior observational learning. Untrained individuals often misperceive or distort their self-observations. For example, there is evidence that speakers of minority dialects need special training to discriminate erroneous word pronunciations before they could practice in a self-corrective fashion on their own (Ellis & Zimmerman, 2001). A fifth qualitative feature of self-observation involves the valance of the behavior. It is often very depressing to self-monitor negative aspects of one's functioning, such as errors in grammar or spelling (Kirschenbaum & Karoly, 1977), but it is usually possible to shift to positive criteria, such as correctly written sentences or correctly spelled words.

One way to increase the proximity, informativeness, accuracy, and valence of feedback is to *self-record* it (Zimmerman & Kitsantas, 1996). Written records have many advantages, such as capturing personal information when it occurs, structuring it to be most meaningful, preserving its accuracy, and providing a longer database for discerning change. If self-recorded information is still ambiguous, learners can engage in *self-experimentation* by systematically varying aspects of their functioning that are in question (Bandura, 1991). For example, an aspiring adolescent novelist may be concerned about her lack of consistent progress in completing her first book. Her moments of inspiration and production of text have been sporadic and insufficient, and she urgently needs to increase her effectiveness. She can self-experiment by testing various hypotheses about her progress, such as her time, place, and method of writing. Which method or combination increases the quality and quantity of written text can be discerned from self-records (Zimmerman & Risemberg, 1997). In this way, systematic self-observation or self-monitoring can lead to greater personal understanding and to better performance control.

Self-Reflection Phase

There are two major types of self-reflection: self-judgment and self-reactions (Bandura, 1986). Self-judgment involves self-evaluating one's performance and attributing causal significance to the results. *Self-evaluation* refers to comparing self-monitored information with a standard or goal, such as when competitors in a national spelling bee compare their daily practice tests to their best previous effort, to the efforts of other competitors, or to published standards of word difficulty. Self-evaluations are not automatic outcomes of performance, but rather, depend on learners' selection and interpretation of an appropriate standard. Students who begin their preparation for a spelling competition by expecting to spell all the most difficult words correctly will be disappointed by their results. To be optimally effective, self-evaluative standards must be set at levels that are challenging for the learner (i.e., difficult but attainable). Setting standards that are too high will discourage, and setting standards that are too low will fail to produce progress. Optimal self-evaluation involves shifting one's goals based on learning progress. "Writer's block" is often due to setting unrealistic literary standards, and often it is preferable for writers to set a lower standard for generating text, then raising the standard during the revision process (Murray, 1984). Research on brainstorming has also revealed the advantage of separating the generation of ideas from their evaluation (Torrance, 1961).

There are advantages to using one's previous performance as a standard of comparison instead of the performance of others. Self-comparisons involve personal changes in functioning over time, and, as a result, they highlight learning progress, which typically improves with repeated practice. By contrast, social comparisons with the performance of others (who are simultaneously learning) diminishes awareness of personal improvements due to practice. Many athletic coaches are reluctant to place pupils in competitions (where social comparison is inevitable) until they are very likely to succeed at some level in order to ensure favorable self-evaluations.

Self-evaluative judgments are linked closely to *causal attributions* about the results, such as whether one's poor performance on a mathematics test is due to limited ability or to insufficient effort. These attributional judgments play a pivotal role in self-reflection: Attributions of error to fixed sources (i.e., ability) prompt learners to react negatively and discourage efforts to improve (Weiner, 1979). By contrast, attributions of error to controllable sources, such as learning strategies, will sustain motivation during periods of deficient performance because strategy attributions sustain perceptions of efficacy until all possible strategies have been tested (e.g., Zimmerman & Kitsantas, 1996, 1997). Attributions are not automatic outcomes of favorable or unfavorable self-evaluations, but rather, depend on cognitive appraisal of extenuating factors, such as perceptions of personal efficacy or mitigating environmental conditions (Bandura, 1991). For example, when students receive a low grade for an essay, those who are self-efficacious are more likely to attribute it to insufficient effort or a poor writing strategy than those who are self-doubters. By contrast, self-doubters are likely to interpret a low grade as further evidence of their lack of writing ability.

Self-evaluative and attributional self-judgments are closely linked to two key forms of self-reactions: self-satisfaction and adaptive inferences. *Self-satisfaction* refers to perceptions of satisfaction or dissatisfaction and associated emotional affect regarding one's performance, which is important because people pursue courses of action that result in satisfaction and positive affect and avoid courses that produce dissatisfaction and negative affect, such as anxiety (Bandura, 1991). Like other self-reflective processes, self-satisfaction is not an automatic outcome of performance, but rather, depends on learners' self-judgmental criteria as well as forethought goals and performance phase strategy use. When self-satisfaction is contingent upon reaching adopted goals, people give direction to their actions and motivate themselves to persist in their efforts to learn. Thus, a person's motivation does not stem directly from the goals per se but rather from self-satisfaction reactions to performance outcomes.

A person's level of self-satisfaction also depends on the intrinsic value or importance of the task. For example, students who greatly value a particular skill will experience severe dissatisfaction and anxiety if they obtain adverse outcomes. However, students who view a skill as peripheral to their interests will not be overly distressed by adverse outcomes. Students who feel highly self-efficacious about their capabilities to learn or perform a skill, such as playing a musical instrument, will also express greater satisfaction with the outcomes (Zimmerman & Kitsantas, 1997).

Adaptive or defensive inferences refer to self-reactive inferences by students about how to alter their self-regulatory approach during subsequent efforts to learn or perform. Adaptive inferences are important because they guide students to new and potentially more effective forms of performance self-regulation, whereas defensive inferences serve primarily to protect the person from future dissatisfaction and aversive affect. Defensive self-reactions, such as helplessness, procrastination, task avoidance, cognitive disengagement, and apathy, are self-handicapping because they ultimately limit personal growth (Garcia & Pintrich, 1994). These self-reactions affect forethought processes during additional efforts to learn. For example, self-satisfaction reactions strengthen self-efficacy beliefs about eventually mastering the academic skill, learning goal orientations (Schunk & Ertmer, 1999), and intrinsic interest in the task (Zimmerman & Kitsantas, 1997). These enhanced self-motivational beliefs form the basis for adolescents' sense of personal agency about continuing their cyclical self-regulatory efforts and eventually attaining their goals.

There is a growing body of experimental and descriptive evidence linking forethought, performance, and self-reflection phase processes and beliefs. For example, experimental manipulations of goal setting and self-recording has been shown to affect self-reflection phase processes and beliefs, such as self-evaluation, attributions, and changes in strategy choice. Those self-reflection processes were shown in turn to affect learners' intrinsic interest in the task and self-efficacy beliefs about further learning efforts (e.g., Zimmerman & Kitsantas, 1997, 1999). When experts and novices are compared in their forethought, performance, and self-reflection phase processes, significant differences were found in every phase (Cleary & Zimmerman, 2000).

OVERCOMING DEFICITS IN ADOLESCENTS'
SELF-REGULATION

The consequences of dysfunctions in personal regulation can be enormous for adolescents. For example, students who struggle to self-regulate their academic studying achieve more poorly in school (Zimmerman & Martinez-Pons, 1986, 1988) and display more deportment problems (Brody, Stoneman, & Flor, 1996). Furthermore, teenagers often are unable to regulate their health through proper diet, taking needed medicines, and avoiding exposure to disease. For example, people who cannot self-regulate the chronic disease of asthma display higher levels of symptoms, lower quality of life, and are hospitalized more frequently (Zimmerman, Bonner, Evans, & Mellins, 1999). Calamities such as death, injury, and sickness among youth and young adults can often be traced to a failure to self-regulate a variety of dangerous behaviors, such as drinking alcohol, taking recreational drugs, engaging in unprotected sex, and driving with excessive speed. There is evidence that the incidence of misbehavior, aggression, and crime of youth is associated with poor impulse control and disengagement of moral self-regulatory standards (Bandura, Barbaranelli, Caprara, & Pastorelli, 1996a). These self-regulatory problems of youth are not merely the result of misinformation about difficulties of adulthood; they entail developing appropriate skills, self-beliefs, habits, and styles of living (Prochaska, DiClemente, & Norcross, 1992). But how can these advantageous forms of self-regulation be developed among adolescents?

From cyclical phase perspective on self-regulation, dysfunctions are linked to ineffective forethought and performance phase techniques, such as absence of appropriate goal setting or strategy use (Bandura, 1991; Zimmerman, 1998). Instead of using these proactive methods, ineffective students rely primarily on reactive methods to manage their academic learning and health, such as responding to adverse grades or health outcomes. Unfortunately, reactive methods of self-regulation can lead to a *self-defeating cycle* of performance that is difficult to overcome. For example, because reactive self-regulators fail to set specific process goals, they are limited to self-monitoring performance outcomes. To self-evaluate their performance outcomes, reactive learners typically turn to the outcomes of others, but this social criterion can be daunting because other learners are improving as well. Furthermore, reactive learners' lack of strategic planning not only diminishes the quality of their performance, it prevents them from attributing unfavorable outcomes to strategy use, which can sustain motivation. Instead, reactive learners' reliance on social criteria for self-evaluation leads them to attribute their errors to fixed ability, to experience self-dissatisfaction, and to react defensively. Because of these adverse self-reactions to their task outcomes, reactive self-regulators experience not only a loss of self-efficacy about subsequent performance efforts but also a decline in intrinsic interest (Zimmerman & Kitsantas, 1996).

Fortunately, there is growing evidence that interventions that target specific deficits in self-regulatory processes in children and adolescents, such as the absence of forethought goal setting and strategic planning, can lead to *self-enhancing cycles* of learning and improved academic and nonacademic outcomes (Schunk & Zimmerman, 1998; Zimmerman & Schunk, 2001). For example, Graham and colleagues (1998) used modeling, emulation, and self-directed practice to teach learning-disabled (LD) students strategies to improve their writing skills. Lan (1998) taught college students in a statistics course to self-monitor their acquisition of and self-efficacy beliefs about key concepts in the discipline. Improved self-monitoring led to improved grades in the course. Butler (1998) taught LD collegiate students to analyze instructional tasks and select appropriate learning strategies through tutoring. She found that trained students displayed more positive perceptions of task-specific efficacy and were more likely to attribute successful performance to self-regulated sources, such as strategy use. In nonacademic areas of functioning, there is evidence that training mothers and their asthmatic children to self-regulate their youngster's symptoms using medicating strategies, self-monitoring, and self-reflective interpretation of outcomes can not only improve their level of self-regulation but also their lung functioning on a variety of measures (Bonner et al., in press).

CONCLUSION

Clearly, an essential aspect of passage from childhood to adulthood is adolescents' acquisition of self-regulatory skills. Although schools are organized on the assumption that students will develop increased self-regulation of their academic functioning, there is extensive evidence that many students fail to make this vital transition. Social cognitive researchers have identified four levels in the development of self-regulatory skill, beginning with social modeling and emulation and then shifting to self-control and self-regulation. There is evidence that students who master a skill, whether academic or nonacademic, according to this multilevel sequence display higher levels of acquisition as well as better motivation and greater self-regulation than students who use alternative methods or a different sequence.

In an effort to understand how self-regulatory processes become self-sustaining, social cognitive researchers have identified three key cyclical phases: forethought, performance, and self-reflection. These phases specify links between a person's use of self-regulatory processes, such as goal setting and strategy use, and self-motivational beliefs, such as self-efficacy and intrinsic interest. Advantageous self-motivational beliefs are essential because self-regulation involves self-initiation and self-sustained effort. When analyzing adolescents from a cyclical phase perspective, there is evidence that dysfunctions in achievement are linked to adolescents' use of reactive methods of self-regulation rather than proactive methods. Reactive learners fail to engage in effective forethought, such as setting specific process goals, but instead rely on reactions to performance outcomes, which are frequently adverse. However, when students who display low levels of self-regulation have been taught specific processes, such as learning strategies and self-monitoring techniques, there is evidence of impressive gains in functioning. These promising findings offer hope to educators and parents who have viewed poor self-regulation as an inevitable shortcoming of adolescence.

NOTE

1.   I would like to thank Frank Pajares and Tim Urdan for their helpful comments on an initial draft of this chapter. Correspondence regarding this chapter should be directed to Barry J. Zimmerman, Graduate School and University Center, City University of New York, PhD Program in Educational Psychology, 365 Fifth Ave., New York, NY 10016-4309, or bzimmerman@gc .cuny.edu.

REFERENCES

Ames, C. (1992). Achievement goals and the classroom motivational climate. In D. H. Schunk & J. L. Meece (Eds.), *Student perceptions in the classroom* (pp. 327–348). Hillsdale, NJ: Erlbaum.

Bandura, A. (1986). *Social foundations of thought and action: A social cognitive theory.* Englewood Cliffs, NJ: Prentice-Hall.

Bandura, A. (1991). Self-regulation of motivation through anticipatory and self-reactive mechanisms. In R. A. Dienstbier (Ed.), *Perspectives on motivation: Nebraska Symposium on Motivation* (Vol. 38, pp. 69–164). Lincoln: University of Nebraska Press.

Bandura, A. (1997). *Self-efficacy: The exercise of control.* New York: Freeman.

Bandura, A., Barbaranelli, C., Caprara, G. V., & Pastorelli, C. (1996a). Mechanisms of moral disengagement in the exercise of moral agency. *Journal of Personality and Social Psychology, 71*, 364–374.

Bandura, A., Barbaranelli, C., Caprara, G. V., & Pastorelli, C. (1996b). Multifaceted impact of self-efficacy beliefs on academic functioning. *Child Development, 67*, 1206–1222.

Bandura, A., & Cervone, D. (1983). Self-evaluative and self-efficacy mechanisms governing the motivational effects of goal systems. *Journal of Personality and Social Psychology, 45,* 1017–1028.

Bandura, A., Grusec, J. E., & Menlove, F. L. (1967). Some social determinants of self-monitoring reinforcement systems. *Journal of Personality and Social Psychology, 5,* 449–455.

Bandura, A., & Jeffery, R. W. (1973). Role of symbolic coding and rehearsal processes in observational learning. *Journal of Personality and Social Psychology, 26,* 122–130.

Bandura, A., & McDonald, F. J. (1963). Influence of social reinforcement and the behavior of models in shaping children's moral judgments. *Journal of Abnormal Social Psychology, 67,* 274–281.

Bandura, A., & Schunk, D. H. (1981). Cultivating competence, self-efficacy, and intrinsic interest through proximal self-motivation. *Journal of Personality and Social Psychology, 41,* 586–598.

Bonner, S., Zimmerman, B. J., Evans, D., Irigoyen, M., Mellins, R. B., & Resnick, D. (in press). A personalized intervention to improve asthma self-regulation among urban Latino and African-American families. *Journal of Asthma, 39.*

Brody, G. H., & Henderson, R. W. (1977). The effects of multiple modeled variations on the moral judgments and explanations of young children. *Child Development, 62,* 217–221.

Brody, G. H., Stoneman, Z., & Flor, D. (1996). Parental religiosity, family processes, and youth competence in rural, two-parent African American families. *Developmental Psychology, 32,* 696–706.

Butler, D. L. (1998). A strategic content learning approach to promoting self-regulated learning by students with learning disabilities. In D. H. Schunk & B. J. Zimmerman (Eds.), *Self-regulated learning: From teaching to self-reflective practice* (pp. 160–183). New York: Guilford Press.

Carver, C., & Scheier, M. (1981). *Attention and self-regulation: A control theory approach to human behavior.* New York: Springer.

Cleary, T., & Zimmerman, B. J. (2000). Self-regulation differences during athletic practice by experts, non-experts, and novices. *Journal of Applied Sport Psychology, 13,* 61–82.

Corno, L. (1993). The best laid plans: Modern conceptions of volition and educational research. *Educational Researcher, 22,* 14–22.

Deci, E. L. (1975). *Intrinsic motivation.* New York: Plenum Press.

Dweck, C. S. (1988). Motivational processes affecting learning. *American Psychologist, 41,* 1040–1048.

Ellis, D., & Zimmerman, B. J. (2001). Enhancing self-monitoring during self-regulated learning of speech. In H. Hartman (Ed.), *Metacognition in teaching and learning* (pp. 205–228). New York: Kluwer Academic.

Ericsson, A. K., & Lehman, A. C. (1996). Expert and exceptional performance: Evidence of maximal adaptation to task constraints. *Annual Review of Psychology, 47,* 273–305.

Garcia, T., & Pintrich, P. R. (1994). Regulating motivation and cognition in the classroom: The role of self-schemas and self-regulatory strategies. In D. H. Schunk & B. J. Zimmerman (Eds.), *Self-regulation of learning and performance: Issues and educational applications* (p. 127–53). Hillsdale, NJ: Erlbaum.

Garfield, C. A., & Bennett, Z. H. (1985). *Peak performance: Mental training techniques of the world's greatest athletes.* New York: Warner.

Graham, S., Harris, K. R., & Troia, G. A. (1998). Writing self-regulation: Cases from the self-regulated strategy development model. In D. H. Schunk & B. J. Zimmerman (Eds.), *Self-regulated learning: From teaching to self-reflective practice* (pp. 20–41). New York: Guilford Press.

Grinder, R. (1978). *Adolescence.* New York: Wiley.

Guess, D., Sailor, W., Rutherford, G., & Baer, D. M. (1968). An experimental analysis of linguistic development of the plural morpheme. *Journal of Applied Behavior Analysis, 1,* 297–306.

Hoover-Dempsey, K. V., Battiato, A. C., Walker, J. M. T., Reed, R. P., DeJong, J. M., & Jones, K. P. (2001). Parental involvement in homework. *Educational Psychologist, 36,* 575–209.

Kazdin, A. (1974). Self-monitoring and behavior changed. In M. J. Mahoney & C. E. Thoresen (Eds.), *Self-control: Power to the person* (pp. 218–246). Monterey, CA: Brooks/Cole.

Kirschenbaum, D. S., & Karoly, P. (1977). When self-regulation fails: Tests of some preliminary hypotheses. *Journal of Consulting and Clinical Psychology, 45,* 1116–1125.

Kitsantas, A., Zimmerman, B. J., & Cleary, T. (2000). The role of observation and emulation in the development of athletic self-regulation. *Journal of Educational Psychology, 91,* 241–250.

Kuhl, J. (1985). Volitional mediators of cognitive-behavior consistency: Self-regulatory processes and action versus state orientation. In J. Kuhl & J. Beckman (Eds.), *Action control* (pp. 101–128). New York: Springer.

LaBerge, D. (1981). Unitization and automaticity in perception. In J. H. Flowers (Ed.), *Nebraska Symposium on Motivation* (Vol. 28, pp. 53–71). Lincoln: University of Nebraska Press.

Lan, W. Y. (1998). Teaching self-monitoring skills in statistics. In D. H. Schunk & B. J. Zimmerman (Eds.), *Self-regulated learning: From teaching to self-reflective practice* (pp. 86–105). New York: Guilford Press.

Laughlin, P. R., Moss, L. L., & Miller, S. M. (1969). Information processing as a function of adult model, stimulus display, school grades and sex. *Journal of Educational Psychology, 60,* 188–193.

Lepper, M. R., & Hodell, M. (1989). Intrinsic motivation in the classroom. In C. Ames & R. Ames (Eds.), *Research on motivation in education* (Vol. E, pp. 255–296). Hillsdale, NJ: Erlbaum.

Locke, E. A., & Latham, G. P. (1990). *A theory of goal setting and task performance.* Englewood Cliffs, NJ: Prentice-Hall.

McPherson, G. E., & Zimmerman, B. J. (2002). Self-regulation of musical learning: A social cognitive perspective. In R. Colwell & C. Richardson (Eds.), *Second handbook on music teaching and learning* (pp. 327–347). New York: Oxford University Press.

Meichenbaum, D. (1977). *Cognitive-behavior modification: An integrative approach.* New York: Plenum Press.

Meichenbaum, D., & Beimiller, A. (1990). *In search of student expertise in the classroom: A metacognitive analysis.* Paper presented at the Conference on Cognitive Research for Instructional Innovation, University of Maryland, College Park, MD.

Murray, D. M. (1984). *Write to learn* (3rd ed.). Fort Worth, TX: Holt, Rinehart & Winston.

Neves, D. M., & Anderson, J. R. (1981). Knowledge compilation: Mechanisms for the automatization of cognitive skills. In J. R. Anderson (Ed.), *Cognitive skills and their acquisitions* (pp. 463–562). Hillsdale, NJ: Erlbaum.

Newman, R. (1994). Academic help-seeking: A strategy of self-regulated learning. In D. H. Schunk & B. J. Zimmerman (Eds.), *Self-regulation of learning and performance: Issues and educational applications* (pp. 283–301). Hillsdale, NJ: Erlbaum.

Nicholls, J. (1984). Achievement motivation: Conceptions of ability, subjective experience, task choice, and performance. *Psychological Review, 91,* 328–346.

Pajares, F. (1996). Self-efficacy beliefs in achievement settings. *Review of Educational Research, 66,* 543–578.

Pintrich, P. R., & De Groot, E. V. (1990). Motivational and self-regulated learning components of classroom academic performance. *Journal of Educational Psychology, 82,* 33–40.

Pintrich, P. R., & Schunk, D. H. (1996). *Motivation in education: Theory, research and applications.* Englewood Cliffs, NJ: Prentice-Hall.

Pressley, M. (1977). Imagery and children's learning: Putting the picture in developmental perspective. *Review of Educational Research, 47,* 586–622.

Pressley, M., & Dennis-Rounds, J. (1980). Transfer of a mnemonic keyword strategy at two age levels. *Journal of Educational Psychology, 72,* 575–582.

Pressley, M., & Levin, J. R. (1977). Task parameters affecting the efficacy of a visual imagery learning strategy in younger and older children. *Journal of Experimental Child Psychology, 24,* 53–59.

Pressley, M., Woloshyn, V., & Associates (Eds.). (1995). *Cognitive strategy instruction that really improves children's academic performance* (2nd ed.). Brookline: Cambridge, MA.

Prochaska, J. O., DiClemente, C. C., & Norcross, J. C. (1992). In search of how people change: Applications to addictive behaviors. *American Psychologist, 47,* 1102–1114.

Rosenthal, T. L., & Zimmerman, B. J. (1976). Organization and stability of transfer in vicarious concept attainment. *Child Development, 44,* 606–613.

Rosenthal, T. L., & Zimmerman, B. J. (1978). *Social learning and cognition.* New York: Academic Press.

Rosenthal, T. L, Zimmerman, B. J., & Durning, K. (1970). Observational induced changes in children's interrogative classes. *Journal of Personality and Social Psychology, 16,* 681–688.

Schunk, D. H. (1982). Verbal self-regulation as a facilitator of children's achievement and self-efficacy. *Human Learning, 1,* 265–277.

Schunk, D. H. (2001). Social cognitive theory and self-regulated learning. In B. J. Zimmerman & D. H. Schunk (Eds.), *Self-regulated learning and academic achievement: Theoretical perspectives* (2nd ed., pp. 125–151). Mahwah, NJ: Erlbaum.

Schunk, D. H., & Ertmer, P. A. (1999). Self-regulatory processes during computer skill acquisition: Goal and self-evaluative influences. *Journal of Educational Psychology, 91,* 251–160.

Schunk, D. H., & Rice, J. M. (1984). Strategy self-verbalization during remedial listening comprehension instruction. *Journal of Experimental Education, 53,* 49–54.

Schunk, D. H., & Rice, J. M. (1985). Verbalization of comprehension strategies: Effects on children's achievement outcomes. *Human Learning, 4*, 1–10.

Schunk, D. H., & Zimmerman, B. J. (1997). Social origins of self-regulatory competence. *Educational Psychologist, 32*, 195–208.

Schunk, D. H., & Zimmerman, B. J. (Eds.). (1998). *Self-regulated learning: From teaching to self-reflective practice.* New York: Guilford Press.

Steinberg, L., Brown, B. B., & Dornbusch, S. M. (1996). *Beyond the classroom.* New York: Simon & Schuster.

Torrance, E. P. (1961). Priming creative thinking in the primary grades. *Elementary School Journal, 42*, 34–41.

Weiner, B. (1979). A theory of motivation for some classroom experiences. *Journal of Educational Psychology, 71*, 3–25.

Weinstein, C. E., & Mayer, R. E. (1986). The teaching of learning strategies. In M. C. Wittrock (Ed.), *Handbook of research on teaching* (3rd ed., pp. 315–327). New York: Macmillan.

Weinstein, C. E., Schulte, A. C., & Palmer, D. R. (1987). *LASSI: Learning and Study Strategies Inventory.* Clearwater, FL: H & H Publishing.

Wigfield, A., Eccles, J., & Pintrich, P. R. (1996). Development between the ages 11 and 25. In D. Berliner & R. Calfee (Eds.), *Handbook of educational psychology* (pp. 148–185). New York: Macmillan.

Zimmerman, B. J. (1989). A social cognitive view of self-regulated academic learning. *Journal of Educational Psychology, 81*, 329–339.

Zimmerman, B. J. (1998). Academic studying and the development of personal skill: A self-regulatory perspective. *Educational Psychologist, 33*, 73–86.

Zimmerman, B. J. (2000). Attaining self-regulation: A social cognitive perspective. In M. Boekaerts, P. Pintrich, & M. Zeidner (Eds.), *Handbook of self-regulation* (pp.13–39). Orlando, FL: Academic Press.

Zimmerman B. J. (2001). Achieving academic excellence: A self-regulatory perspective. In M. Ferrari (Ed.), *Pursuit of excellence* (pp. 85–109). Mahwah, NJ: Erlbaum.

Zimmerman, B. J., & Bandura, A. (1994). Impact of self-regulatory influences on writing course attainment. *American Educational Research Journal, 31*, 845–862.

Zimmerman, B. J., Bonner, S., Evans, D., & Mellins, R. (1999). Self-regulating childhood asthma: A developmental model of family change. *Health Education & Behavior, 26*, 53–69.

Zimmerman, B. J., & Dialessi, F. (1973). Modeling influences on children's creative behavior. *Journal of Educational Psychology, 65*, 127–134.

Zimmerman, B. J., Greenberg, D., & Weinstein, C. E. (1994). Self-regulating academic study time: A strategy approach. In D. H. Schunk & B. J. Zimmerman (Eds.), *Self-regulation of learning and performance: Issues and educational application* (pp. 181–199). Hillsdale, NJ: Erlbaum.

Zimmerman, B. J., & Kitsantas, A. (1996). Self-regulated learning of a motoric skill: The role of goal setting and self-monitoring. *Journal of Applied Sport Psychology, 8*, 69–84.

Zimmerman, B. J., & Kitsantas, A. (1997). Developmental phases in self-regulation: Shifting from process to outcome goals. *Journal of Educational Psychology, 89*, 29–36.

Zimmerman, B. J., & Kitsantas, A. (1999). Acquiring writing revision skill: Shifting from process to outcome self-regulatory goals. *Journal of Educational Psychology, 91*, 1–10.

Zimmerman, B. J., & Kitsantas, A. (in press). Acquiring writing revision proficiency through observation and emulation. *Journal of Educational Psychology.*.

Zimmerman, B. J., & Koussa, R. (1979). Social influences on children's toy preferences: Effects of model rewardingness and affect. *Contemporary Educational Psychology, 4*, 55–66.

Zimmerman, B. J., & Martinez-Pons, M. (1986). Development of a structured interview for assessing student use of self-regulated learning strategies. *American Educational Research Journal, 23*, 614–628.

Zimmerman, B. J., & Martinez-Pons, M. (1988). Construct validation of a strategy model of student self-regulated learning. *Journal of Educational Psychology, 80*, 284–290.

Zimmerman, B. J., & Martinez-Pons, M. (1990). Student differences in self-regulated learning: Relating grade, sex, and giftedness to self-efficacy and strategy use. *Journal of Educational Psychology, 82*, 51–59.

Zimmerman, B. J., & Paulsen, A. S. (1995, Fall). Self-monitoring during collegiate studying: An invaluable tool for academic self-regulation. In P. Pintrich (Ed.), *New directions in college teaching and learning: Understanding self-regulated learning* (No. 63, pp. 13–27). San Francisco, CA: Jossey-Bass.

Zimmerman, B. J., & Ringle, J. (1981). Effects of model persistence and statements of confidence on children's self-efficacy and problem solving. *Journal of Educational Psychology, 73*, 485–493.

Zimmerman, B. J., & Risemberg, R. (1997). Becoming a self-regulated writer: A social cognitive perspective. *Contemporary Educational Psychology, 22*, 73–101.

Zimmerman, B. J., & Rosenthal, T. L. (1972). Concept attainment, transfer, and retention through observation and rule provision. *Journal of Experimental Child Psychology, 14*, 139–150.

Zimmerman, B. J., & Rosenthal, T. L. (1974a). Conserving and retaining equalities and inequalities through observation and correction. *Developmental Psychology, 10*, 260–268.

Zimmerman, B. J., & Rosenthal, T. L. (1974b). Observational learning of rule governed behavior by children. *Psychological Bulletin, 81*, 29–42.

Zimmerman, B.J., & Schunk, D.H. (Eds.). (2001). *Self-regulated learning and academic achievement: Theoretical perspectives* (2nd ed.). Mahwah, NJ: Erlbaum.

CHAPTER 2

SELF-EFFICACY AND ADOLESCENTS' MOTIVATION

Dale H. Schunk and Samuel D. Miller
University of North Carolina at Greensboro

Cedric, an African American adolescent at a lower-achieving high school, wants to do well in school so that he will be accepted to a prestigious university where he can study engineering. Overall, he has been able to get average grades by simply memorizing information, but he recently sensed a need to change his studying approach after he failed two quizzes in biology. With the help of his teacher, he now attempts to identify the most important course information and organize it by relating it to what he knows. Cedric informs his teacher how excited he is about his new approach and how interested he is in the course's content. For the first time, he feels challenged at school and wonders if he should switch his college major to biology. As Cedric studied for his final exam, he was confident that he would make at least a B+. He was shocked when he failed the exam with a score of 45. He quickly lost his confidence and enthusiasm for biology. As he reflected on his grade, he thought, "This course is getting old—I'm tired of it."

Adolescence—the period from puberty to the early twenties—is a time when individuals undergo many cognitive, social, emotional, and physical changes. There are multiple academic changes and increased challenges arising largely from the transitions from one school level to the next (e.g., elementary to middle/junior high school, high school to college). These transitions can have dramatic effects on student motivation and learning, as is seen in the opening scenario.

Current views conceptualize motivation as a dynamic and complex phenomenon comprising many cognitive, affective, and social processes that instigate, direct, and sustain action (Pintrich & Schunk, 2002). Key motivational processes include goals, expectations, attributions, values, emotions, and peer group dynamics. These processes, alone and in combination, influence students' perceptions of which academic disciplines are the most interesting and perhaps worthwhile studying. We see many of these processes at work in Cedric as he attempted to improve his biology grades.

In this chapter, we focus on the influence of one motivational process. *Perceived self-efficacy* refers to beliefs about one's capabilities to learn or perform behaviors at designated levels (Bandura, 1986, 1997). Much research shows that self-efficacy influences motivation across such varied domains as academics, sports, social relations, and health (Bandura, 1997).

We initially provide background information on self-efficacy to show its relation within a larger theoretical framework of human action: social cognitive theory. The bulk of the chapter discusses research on self-efficacy to include its operation in different contexts, developmental changes in self-efficacy, the key roles played by significant persons in adolescents' lives (parents, teachers, peers), and interventions designed to improve self-efficacy. The chapter concludes with suggestions for future research.

Throughout this chapter, we refer to the challenges to adolescents' self-efficacy that can negatively affect motivation, as exemplified in the scenario with Cedric. More specifically, we focus on how students like Cedric respond to failures and what teachers might do to help them "bounce back" from academic setbacks. Although a negative sense of self-efficacy affects behavior across the life span (Bandura, 1997), adolescents seem especially vulnerable given the constellation of academic, social, and physical changes. It is important that those who interact with adolescents recognize symptoms of low self-efficacy and work with students to strengthen their sense of competence.

THEORETICAL BACKGROUND

Social Cognitive Theory

Self-efficacy is a key mechanism in the framework of *social cognitive theory*. According to Bandura (1986, 1997), human achievement involves reciprocal interactions between one's behaviors, environmental variables, and cognitions and other personal factors (e.g., affects). In this view, self-efficacy (a personal factor) affects one's behaviors and the environments with which one interacts, and is itself influenced by actions and conditions.

For example, research shows that self-efficacy beliefs influence such student behaviors as task choice, persistence, effort, and achievement (Schunk, 2001). In turn, students' behaviors modify their self-efficacy beliefs. As students engage in tasks, they note progress toward learning goals. Perceptions of progress convey to students that they are capable of performing well, which enhances their self-efficacy for continued learning.

The interaction between self-efficacy and environmental conditions has been demonstrated in research on students with learning disabilities, many of whom lack self-efficacy for performing well (Licht & Kistner, 1986). As an example of how a personal factor (self-efficacy) can affect the environment, consider what happens when teachers believe that students lack skills and self-efficacy. They may give them easier tasks to work on or more assistance. In turn, teacher feedback (environmental condition) affects self-efficacy. A statement such as "I know that you can do this" can raise self-efficacy. The teacher in the opening scenario used such statements to counteract the negative effects on Cedric's self-efficacy of test feedback, an environmental variable.

Behaviors and environments influence each other. Cedric's teacher attempted to improve his self-efficacy by meeting with him to explain how to take lecture notes and how to improve his text understanding with a content area comprehension strategy. Her assistance had an immediate positive effect on his performance and attitude. He became more attentive in class and participated more frequently in class discussions. Based on his enthusiasm, the teacher demonstrated the strategy to her other students and posted its steps on a bulletin board for everyone to review. Both Cedric and his teacher were reinforced by each other's successes.

A major advance of social cognitive theory over earlier reinforcement theories is its emphasis on *vicarious learning.* Much human learning occurs without observers actually performing the behaviors learned, such as by observing others, attending to instruction, reading, watching television and videos, and networking via the Internet. Vicarious actions accelerate learning and save us from many unpleasant consequences. For example, Cedric does not have to drop out of school to appreciate the long-term career limitations of not having a college degree. He frequently receives this message verbally from his parents and older siblings.

By observing models (e.g., classmates, teachers, parents, siblings), students acquire knowledge that they may not demonstrate at the time of learning (Schunk, 2001). In our scenario, Cedric asked for assistance and then his teacher modeled a content area reading strategy for him to observe; he later watched the teacher demonstrate the same strategy to his classmates. Initially, Cedric and several of his friends were hesitant to try the strategy until they watched others use it. As he tried the strategy when reading a chapter in his text, he received feedback about his early attempts. While his early successes were encouraging, teachers need to understand how long it takes for students to acquire the ability to use any strategy (Miller & Meece, 1999; Schunk, 2001). Teachers need to check frequently through questioning and assignments (actual performances) to see how well their students understand course content and to gauge how independently they can use various reading strategies. Teachers then can intercede to provide corrective feedback.

Self-Efficacy

Self-efficacy refers to one's perceived capabilities for accomplishing a task. Self-efficacy is a situationally specific construct. It is meaningful to speak of self-efficacy for reading a textbook chapter, writing a lab report, solving an algebraic equation, learning to speak French, rebuilding automobile engines, high jumping, playing the saxophone, and so forth. Self-efficacy contrasts with more general measures such as self-concept and self-esteem, which involve general appraisals based on accumulated experiences across multiple sources (Pajares & Schunk, 2001).

Self-efficacy is hypothesized to affect task choice, effort, persistence, and achievement (Bandura, 1986, 1997; Schunk, 1995). Compared with students who doubt their learning capabilities, those who feel efficacious for learning or performing a task participate more readily, work harder, persist longer when they encounter difficulties, and achieve at a higher level. Self-efficacious students also bounce back more rapidly from failures, with corresponding benefits for motivation and achievement. Unfortunately, Cedric's self-efficacy has not reached a point where his teacher can expect him to recover quickly from a low test score.

Learners obtain information to appraise their self-efficacy from their actual performances, vicarious (observational) experiences, forms of persuasion, and physiological reactions. Students' own performances offer the most reliable guides for gauging self-efficacy; effects of the other sources are more variable. Successes raise self-efficacy and failures lower it, although an occasional failure is unlikely to have much impact on a strong sense of self-efficacy. Since Cedric did not have a strong history of prior successes in biology, his test failure immediately lowered his self-efficacy.

Learners acquire self-efficacy information from knowledge of others through social comparisons. Similar others offer the best basis for comparison. Students who observe similar peers learn a task are apt to believe that they also can learn it. This form of learning occurred when Cedric observed a friend using the content strategy with the teacher's guidance. He immediately said to himself, "If he can do it, I should be able to do the same." Vicariously derived information, however, typically has a weaker impact than does performance information because the effects of the former can be negated by actual performance failures. Thus, while teachers need to know how to select students to act as models in their classrooms, they must make sure that all students understand the course's content and are becoming independent learners.

Persuasive information often comes in the form of encouragement from others (e.g., "You can do it!"). Such feedback can affect self-efficacy, although the effect will be transitory if subsequent performance turns out differently. Students also acquire efficacy information from physiological indicators (e.g., heart rate, feelings of anxiety). Experiencing anxiety or trembling may signal that one lacks skills and thus negatively affect self-efficacy. Cedric's teacher needs to attend to such signs as she attempts to help him strengthen his self-efficacy.

The effects of these sources on self-efficacy do not occur automatically; rather, information is cognitively weighed and appraised. In forming self-efficacy beliefs learners may use multiple factors, including perceptions of their abilities, past successes, task difficulty, effort expended, time persisted, amount of help received, perceived similarity to models, credibility of persuaders, and the type and intensity of emotional symptoms. Cedric is evaluating many factors in reappraising his self-efficacy.

Self-efficacy is not the only influence on learning and achievement. No amount of self-efficacy will produce competent performance when requisite skills and knowledge are lacking. *Outcome expectations*, or beliefs about the anticipated consequences of actions, are important because students engage in activities they believe will lead to favorable outcomes and shun those they perceive will have negative outcomes. *Perceived value* refers to the importance that learners attach to activities or how badly they desire certain outcomes (Wigfield, 1994). When students value an activity or its perceived outcome, they are apt to work at it even when they feel inefficacious about succeeding. Cedric's poor exam grade led him to question the value of performing well in biology. His outcome expectations also may have changed. He expected to receive better grades because of his new study behaviors, but now he is less certain about this outcome.

Achievement in any domain requires resilient self-efficacy; that is, individuals continue to feel efficacious even when confronted with difficulties and failures (Bandura, 1997). The lives of many prominent individuals are filled with multiple setbacks, especially when they were younger and not yet established in their professions (White, 1982). The resiliency of self-efficacy beliefs depends on how they were acquired, their strength, and the potency of disconfirming experiences (Bandura, 1997). People are most resilient to failures when they have a strong sense of self-efficacy developed largely through personal mastery experiences and when the setbacks they experience are mild or occur infrequently. Hopefully, with his teacher's assistance, Cedric will be able to view this setback as temporary.

People with resilient self-efficacy are able to rebound quickly from difficulties and move forward. They assess the situation in which failure occurred and determine how they might perform better in the future, such as by changing strategies, seeking assistance, or altering dysfunctional environmental conditions. The *bounce-back* phenomenon is seen clearly in self-efficacious, high-achieving students who, after performing poorly on a test or assignment, redouble their efforts and again succeed. Conversely, when students like Cedric experience failure, they might expend less effort studying and their interest may recede. In such cases, teachers need to provide additional support and opportunities for success so that students might regain their confidence. Speed of bounce-back is one factor that distinguishes high achievers from low achievers.

RESEARCH EVIDENCE

Development of Self-Efficacy

Adolescents acquire much self-efficacy information from their homes, schools, and social environments. Home influences that promote effective interactions with the environment raise self-efficacy (Bandura, 1997; Meece, 1997). Parents who provide an environment that stimulates children's curiosity and allows for mastery experiences help to build their self-efficacy. These effects are reciprocal, because children who display more curiosity and exploration promote parental responsiveness (similar to what occurred between Cedric and his teacher).

Self-efficacy is aided when environments are rich in interesting activities that arouse their curiosity and offer reasonable challenges. There is much variability in home environments. Some contain computers, books, and puzzles that stimulate students' thinking. Parents heavily invested in their children's cognitive development spend time with them on learning. Parents also are key providers of self-efficacy information when they arrange for varied mastery experiences (Bandura, 1997). Other homes do not have these resources and adults may devote little time to the education of their daughters and sons.

With respect to nonperformance sources of self-efficacy information, parents who model effort, persistence, and ways to cope with difficulties strengthen children's self-efficacy. Parents who verbally encourage trying different activities and support these efforts develop children who feel more capable of meeting challenges (Bandura, 1997).

With development, peers become increasingly important (Steinberg, Brown, & Dornbusch, 1996). Parents who steer children toward efficacious peers increase the likelihood of vicarious boosts in self-efficacy. Peer influence on self-efficacy is enhanced by similarity. The effect of model similarity on observer self-efficacy is especially strong when observers encounter situations that demand new learning or behaviors. Similarity is potent among adolescents because peers are similar in many ways and teenagers are unfamiliar with many tasks.

Two important cognitive changes that occur with development are that capability self-beliefs become more specific and more accurate. Young students do not have differentiated conceptions of what they can and cannot do in various domains (Bandura, 1997). Depending on their early experiences, they may feel generally capable or incapable of accomplishing tasks. With development, students show less generality across domains and are able to make increasingly more accurate self-appraisals for learning or performing various tasks.

There are several reasons why self-appraisal skill improves. Young students have difficulty attending to models and tasks for long periods. With development, students are able to attend to multiple features of tasks simultaneously. They are less likely to be swayed by one distinguishing feature, such as how many numbers a problem contains or how many pages they have to read. They also are better able to derive cues about difficulty from models.

Cedric's ability and his classmates' abilities to appraise their learning have improved with development. They have the potential to use memory strategies, such as rehearsing and organizing information to be learned. Knowledge of strategies and when to employ them, and self-efficacy for working strategically, are key influences on learner's self-regulatory skill (Schunk, 2001). Moreover, students at this stage of development generally have a more extensive knowledge base to help them comprehend new information.

Students' ability to use social comparative information effectively depends on higher levels of cognitive development and experience in making comparative evaluations. Although students can evaluate themselves relative to others, they may not automatically do so and even when they do the comparisons may be based on superficial features rather than on those that determine performance (e.g., physical appearance rather than perceived skill). With development, comparisons shift from involving overt similarities and differences to a concern for factors that affect task performance (Ruble & Flett, 1988). For Cedric, the best comparisons are with peers he views as similar to himself in skill rather than ones based on ethnicity or gender.

Students also become more adept at discerning progress indicators. Most tasks involve multiple components, and it is common to learn some aspects but not others. Younger students can be easily misled into thinking they are efficacious when they can perform part of the task. In mathematics, for example, younger students may employ "buggy algorithms" that yield incorrect solutions (Brown & Burton, 1978). With development, self-assessment becomes more accurate as learners incorporate appraisals of their skills at performing multiple components.

The preceding paragraphs suggest that students like Cedric are at a stage in their development at which they have the potential to self-appraise their learning, to plan and study strategically, to use social comparison information effectively, and to discern improvements in their learning. What needs to be stressed, however, is how the potential for acquiring such skills does not develop in isolation. Unfortunately, in many schools, students have limited opportunities to acquire these cognitive skills because their teachers' instructional practices and curricular materials do not require such demonstrations (Bennett, DesForges, Cockburn, & Wilkinson, 1984; Goodlad, 1983; Miller, Adkins, & Hooper, 1993; Miller & Blumenfeld, 1993). Unless students have frequent opportunities to practice such skills, they cannot demonstrate the needed resiliency to overcome unavoidable academic failures.

Academic Self-Efficacy

Self-efficacy researchers have examined the relation of self-efficacy to academic motivation (effort, persistence) and achievement. Self-efficacy and its resiliency are related directly to the strength of a student's motivation and achievement. Significant and positive correlations have been obtained between students' self-efficacy for learning (assessed prior to instruction) and subsequent motivation during learning (Schunk, 1995). Judgments of self-efficacy for learning also correlate positively with post-instruction self-efficacy and skillful performance (Schunk, 1995). Studies across different domains and with children and adolescents have yielded significant and positive correlations between self-efficacy and academic achievement (Lent, Brown, & Larkin, 1986; Multon, Brown, & Lent, 1991; Pajares, 1996; Schunk, 1995).

Bouffard-Bouchard, Parent, and Parivee (1991) found that high school students with high self-efficacy for problem solving displayed greater performance monitoring and persistence than did students with lower self-efficacy. Zimmerman and Bandura (1994) obtained evidence among college students that self-efficacy for writing correlated positively with goals for course achievement, self-evaluative standards (satisfaction with potential grades), and actual achievement.

Multiple regression procedures have been employed to determine the percentage of variability in achievement accounted for by self-efficacy. Schunk (1982) found that self-efficacy and rate of problem solving during instruction (an index of motivation) accounted for significant increments in post-instruction academic achievement. Schunk and Swartz (1993a, 1993b) found that self-efficacy was the strongest predictor of children's writing performances. Pajares, Miller, and Johnson (1999) found that writing self-efficacy strongly predicted elementary children's writing performances; this finding also was obtained by Pajares and Valiante (1999) among middle school students. Shell, Murphy, and Bruning (1989) showed that self-efficacy predicted college students' reading and writing outcomes.

Several studies have tested causal models (Pajares, 1996). Using path analysis, Schunk (1981) showed that self-efficacy had a direct effect on mathematical achievement and persistence solving problems. Instruction had a direct effect on achievement and an indirect effect through persistence and self-efficacy. Instruction also had an indirect effect on persistence through self-efficacy. Schunk and Gunn (1986) also used path analysis and found that changes in students' mathematical achievement were due to use of effective learning strategies, self-efficacy, and attributions (perceived causes of outcomes).

Using path analysis, Pajares and Kranzler (1995) determined that mathematics self-efficacy has as powerful a direct effect on mathematics performance as does mental ability, a variable often presumed to be the strongest predictor of academic achievement. Pajares and Miller (1994) showed that mathematics self-efficacy was a better predictor of the mathematics performance of college undergraduates than were mathematics self-concept, perceived usefulness of mathematics, prior experience with mathematics, and gender. Using path analysis, Zimmerman and Bandura (1994) showed that self-efficacy affected achievement directly and indirectly through its influence on goals.

There is some research showing how students' perceptions of academic competence decline as they advance in school (Eccles, Wigfield, & Schiefele, 1998). This decline has been attributed to various factors including greater competition, more norm-referenced grading, less teacher attention to individual student progress, and stresses associated with school transitions (discussed below).

A different trend emerges for self-efficacy. Given its contextual sensitivity, we might expect that with development children's self-efficacy would increase. The standard school curriculum includes skills (e.g., reading, mathematical computations) that are taught and reintroduced in later grades and that serve as the building blocks for advanced skills. As children move through school they gain experience with these tasks, which should raise their self-efficacy. In support of this point, researchers have shown that older students judge self-efficacy higher than do younger ones (Shell, Colvin, & Bruning, 1995; Zimmerman & Martinez-Pons, 1990).

Nonetheless, there are school practices that can retard the development of academic self-efficacy, especially among students who are less academically prepared to cope with increasingly challenging academic tasks. For example, lock-step sequences of instruction frustrate some students who fail to grasp skills and increasingly fall behind their peers (Bandura, 1997). Ability groupings can hurt self-efficacy among those relegated to lower groups. Classrooms that allow for much social comparison tend to lower the self-efficacy of students who find their performances inferior to those of their peers. Some research shows that self-efficacy—like more general perceptions of academic competence—declines as students advance in school (Pajares & Valiante, in press). It would be useful to examine Cedric's school environment to determine whether students at this low-achieving school receive negative self-efficacy information about what they can accomplish.

Periods of transition in schooling can cause changes in self-efficacy (Schunk & Pajares, 2002). A large amount of research has investigated the transition from elementary school to junior high (Eccles & Midgley, 1989; Eccles, Midgley, & Adler, 1984). Elementary school children have the same teacher for most subjects and are grouped with the same peers. Children receive a lot of individual attention and progress feedback. The curriculum is focused heavily on basic skill acquisition and mastery is stressed. Although peer social comparisons occur, teachers employ criterion-referenced grading.

The transition results in changes in many areas. Several elementary schools may feed into one junior high, so students are exposed to many new peers. They may or may not have a homeroom, but regardless, they have different peers in their various classes—many of whom they do not know. Evaluation and grading become normative, and teachers are less concerned with individual progress. Adolescents may frequently reassess their self-efficacy in various subjects given this shift to normative grading among unfamiliar peers. Research shows that general perceptions of academic competence begin to decline in grade 7 or earlier (Harter, 1996; Midgley, Feldhaufer, & Eccles, 1989; Wigfield et al., 1997), and a similar decline may occur in academic self-efficacy (Pajares & Valiante, in press).

The transition from middle school or junior high to senior high brings more changes, although these may prove less disruptive because students are used to changing classes, unfamiliar peers, and norm-referenced grading. At the same time, high school classes are more difficult and there is an expanded pool of peers. In the face of these changes, adolescents like Cedric must reevaluate their self-efficacy in many domains and subject areas. We discuss the key roles played by peers in the next section.

Social and Peer Influence

Adolescents' self-efficacy is strongly influenced in social settings by peers. Vicarious observations of others performing a task can raise observers' self-efficacy and lead them to believe that they too can accomplish it, whereas observing others failing can lower self-efficacy vicariously.

The strongest vicarious influence comes from others we perceive as similar to ourselves in key characteristics. In school, similarity might be based on perceived ability, grades, and ease or difficulty in learning. Similarity is especially critical when observers are unfamiliar with tasks and therefore lack performance experiences. When Cedric's teacher used of one of his friends as a model, his confidence in his abilities increased as well.

Key social sources of self-efficacy information are friends and *peer networks*, or large groups of peers with whom students associate. Students in networks tend to be highly similar (Cairns, Cairns, & Neckerman, 1989), which enhances the likelihood of influence by modeling. Networks help define students' opportunities for interactions and observations of others' interactions (Dweck & Goetz, 1978). Discussions between friends influence their choices of activities and friends often make similar choices (Berndt & Keefe, 1992).

Peer groups promote motivational socialization. Kindermann, McCollam, and Gibson (1996) found that changes in children's motivational engagement across the school year were predicted accurately by their peer group membership at the start of the year. Children affiliated with highly motivated groups changed positively; those in less-motivated groups changed negatively. These results suggest that peer group academic socialization influences the group's academic self-efficacy and motivation (Schunk & Pajares, 2002). Unfortunately, many of the peers with whom Cedric associates do not share his academic aspirations.

Steinberg and colleagues (1996) tracked students from when they entered high school until their senior year and found developmental patterns in the influence of peer pressure on academic motivation and performance, as well as many other activities. Peer pressure rises during childhood and peaks around grade 8 or 9 but then declines through high school. A key period of influence is between ages 12 and 16, during which parental involvement in adolescents' activities often declines.

Steinberg and colleagues (1996) investigated whether students who began high school with similar grades, but who became affiliated with dif-

ferent peer crowds, remained academically similar. Students in academically oriented crowds achieved at a higher level during high school than
did students in less academically oriented crowds.

Another factor contributing to self-efficacy is how well students experience a sense of relatedness to the school environment. Hymel, Comfort,
Schonert-Reichl, and McDougall (1996) suggested that students' involvement and participation in school depend in part on how much the school
environment contributes to their perceptions of autonomy and relatedness, which in turn influence self-efficacy and academic achievement.
Although parents and teachers can develop autonomy and relatedness,
peers strongly affect adolescents' feelings of relatedness (i.e., belonging,
affiliation).

Interventions Affecting Self-Efficacy

Table 2.1 portrays a model of how self-efficacy operates in learning and
achievement situations (Schunk & Pajares, 2002). At the outset of an activity, students differ in their self-efficacy for learning as a function of their
prior experiences, personal qualities (e.g., abilities, attitudes), and social
supports. The latter includes the extent that parents and teachers encourage them to learn, facilitate their access to resources necessary for learning
(e.g., materials, facilities), and teach them self-regulatory strategies that
enhance skill acquisition and refinement. Bandura, Barbaranelli, Caprara,
and Pastorelli (1996) found that parents' academic aspirations for their
children affected children's academic achievements directly and indirectly
by influencing children's self-efficacy. This is a plus for Cedric, because his
parents believe strongly in education and support his academic pursuits.

**Table 2.1. Self-Efficacy for Learning and Achievement
(Schunk & Pajares, 2002)**

	Pretask	*Task Engagement*	*Posttask*
Personal qualitites		Personal influences	Motivation
Prior experience	Self-efficacy		
Social supports		Situational influences	Self-efficacy

As students engage in activities, they are affected by personal (e.g., goal
setting, information processing) and situational influences (e.g., rewards,
teacher feedback). These factors provide students with cues about how well
they are learning. Motivation and self-efficacy are enhanced when students
perceive they are performing well or becoming more skillful. Lack of success or slow progress will not necessarily lower self-efficacy and motivation

if learners believe they can perform better by adjusting their approach (e.g., expend more effort, use effective task strategies; Schunk, 1995). Cedric is giving serious thought to how he might adjust his studying based on the test feedback.

Research in diverse settings has explored the effects of instructional and other classroom processes on self-efficacy. There is strong evidence in support of the hypothesized relations shown in Table 2.1 across grade levels (e.g., elementary, middle/junior high, secondary, postsecondary), content areas (e.g., mathematics, writing, reading, computer applications), and types of students (e.g., regular, remedial, gifted) (Pajares, 1996; Schunk, 1995). Some instructional and other processes that are beneficial for developing self-efficacy are proximal and specific learning goals, strategy instruction and strategy verbalization, social models, performance and attributional feedback, and performance-contingent rewards (Schunk, 1983, 1984, 1995; Schunk, Hanson, & Cox, 1987; Zimmerman, Bandura, & Martinez-Pons, 1992). These different processes are hypothesized to affect self-efficacy and motivation through the common mechanism of informing students of their capabilities and progress in learning. We now illustrate some interventions designed to promote academic self-efficacy.

Goal setting is a key cognitive influence on self-efficacy (Bandura, 1997). When students set or adopt a goal they may experience a sense of self-efficacy for attaining it and make a commitment to try. They work at activities they believe will lead to goal attainment (e.g., attend to instruction, remember information, expend effort and persist). Self-efficacy is substantiated as they observe goal progress. Goals that are specific, close at hand, and moderately difficult enhance self-efficacy because motivation is higher and assessing progress is clearer than when goals are general (e.g., "Do your best"), temporally distant, and very easy or overly difficult. Cedric has a long-term goal of attending a university, and has broken this into subgoals of academic attainments needed for it. Providing students with feedback on goal progress also can raise self-efficacy, sustain motivation, and promote learning.

Most goal-setting research has employed product goals, such as number of pages to read, problems to solve, and time to complete a task. Goals also can be cast in the form of learning processes, such as learning to apply a method or strategy to aid skill acquisition. Research across domains shows that students who learn strategies improve their skills and that use of strategies relates positively to self-efficacy (Pintrich & De Groot, 1990; Zimmerman & Martinez-Pons, 1990).

Process goals (e.g., learn to use a strategy) may enhance self-efficacy and achievement better than product goals because process goals highlight strategy use as a means to improve skills. Students may experience a sense of self-efficacy for attaining the goal, which then is substantiated as they work on the task. Learners who believe they are learning a useful strategy feel efficacious and motivated to apply the strategy (Schunk, 1995). Cedric's teacher might help him to bounce back from his test failure by helping him to set several specific goals related to more consistent use of his new study strategies.

In a series of studies, Schunk and Swartz (1993a, 1993b) gave students instruction and practice over sessions on writing different types of paragraphs (e.g., informative, narrative). As part of the instruction, students were taught a paragraph-writing strategy. Some students were asked to adopt a product goal of writing paragraphs, others were given a general goal of doing their best, and those in a third condition received a process goal of learning to apply the strategy while writing paragraphs.

Some of the process-goal learners also periodically received feedback indicating their progress in using the strategy effectively. This condition was included because assessing progress toward a process goal can be difficult since the progress indicators for product goals (work completed, time spent) are not applicable.

Schunk and Swartz (1993a, 1993b) found that process goals and progress feedback promoted self-efficacy, achievement, strategy use, and maintenance and generalization of achievement outcomes more than did product and general goals, and that on some measures the combined condition performed better than the process goal condition. These results show the benefit of process goals and suggest that progress feedback may be important only when students have difficulty gauging progress on their own.

Models are an important source of self-efficacy information. Adolescents acquire much vicarious information from parents, teachers, and peers. Modeled displays can convey to observers that they are capable and can motivate them to attempt the task. Modeling is a common means of teaching skills in school; a teacher or peer may demonstrate and explain a skill, after which students practice and receive corrective feedback as needed (Schunk, 1987).

Research demonstrates the benefits of models on adolescents' self-efficacy, motivation, and achievement. Brown and Inouye (1978) asked college students to judge self-efficacy for solving anagrams, after which they attempted to solve them. Following the problem solving, students were told that they had performed better than or the same as a model. They then observed a model fail, judged self-efficacy, and again attempted to solve anagrams. Telling students they were more competent than the model led to higher self-efficacy and persistence than telling them they were as competent as the model.

Schunk and Hanson (1985) compared the effects on upper-elementary students of observing peer mastery and coping models with those due to showing adult teacher models and effects due to not observing models.

Peer mastery models solved math problems correctly and verbalized state- ments reflecting high self-efficacy and ability, low task difficulty, and posi- tive attitudes. Peer coping models initially made errors and verbalized negative statements, but then began verbalizing coping statements (e.g., "I need to pay attention to what I'm doing") and eventually verbalized and performed as well as mastery models. After observing models, students received instruction and practice solving problems over sessions. Following instruction, they judged self-efficacy and took an achievement test.

Peer models increased observers' self-efficacy and skill better than the teacher model and no model; teacher model students outperformed stu- dents not exposed to models. There were no differences between the mas- tery and coping conditions. Schunk and Hanson (1985) hypothesized that coping models would be more effective than mastery models because stu- dents had previously had difficulty with math and may have viewed the cop- ing models more similar to themselves than the mastery models. Students in this study had, however, experienced some prior successes in math, and may have based their efficacy beliefs on these previous successes.

A follow-up study used a similar methodology but a mathematical task at which students had previously experienced few successes (Schunk et al., 1987). This study also tested the idea that multiple models are better than a single model, because multiple models increase the likelihood that stu- dents will view themselves as similar to at least one model (Schunk, 1987). The results showed that multiple models—coping or mastery—promoted achievement outcomes as well as a single coping model and better than a single mastery model. Learners who observed a single coping model judged themselves more similar in competence to the model than did those who observed a single mastery model. Thus, similarity seems more important when students have few other cues for gauging self-efficacy.

Students learn from many models, including parents and teachers who are dissimilar in age, gender, competence, socioeconomic status, and other attributes. They also weigh and combine efficacy information from diverse sources. Multiple sources may yield conflicting information; for example, a student may be told by a teacher that "You can do it," but then observe a similar peer fail. The process by which students assimilate such conflicting information requires further research study.

We noted earlier that *feedback* can influence self-efficacy. Feedback is a persuasive source of self-efficacy information. Attributional feedback links students' successes and failures with one or more attributions (perceived causes of outcomes). Performance feedback informs students of how well they are doing. Progress feedback provides information about progress toward learning goals.

Research conducted with students of different ages and across content areas has yielded results that show beneficial effects of feedback on self-efficacy, motivation, and achievement (Schunk, 1995). In the absence of feedback, students may wonder whether they are becoming more capable, especially when it is difficult to obtain performance information on their own. Lack of feedback can retard the development of self-efficacy. Although Cedric's feedback was negative, it is information and he can use it to adjust his future studying.

Schunk and Lilly (1984) exposed middle school girls and boys to a novel mathematical task. Girls initially judged self-efficacy for learning lower than did boys, which is consistent with much research on gender differences in self-efficacy (Pajares, 1996; Schunk & Pajares, 2002). Following an instructional program that included performance feedback, girls and boys did not differ in actual achievement or in self-efficacy for solving problems. There also were no differences in male and female students' problem solving during the instructional program. The performance feedback indicated that learners were successfully acquiring skills, which was sufficient to override any preconceptions the girls might have had from prior experiences with mathematical tasks.

Feedback also is influential among students with learning difficulties. Schunk and Cox (1986) worked with students with learning disabilities during mathematics instruction. Some students received feedback linking their successes with effort ("You got it right; you've really been working hard."). Half of these students received effort feedback during the first half of the instructional program, whereas the other half received it during the second half. Schunk and Cox wanted to determine whether effort feedback becomes less credible—and therefore loses its effectiveness—as students developed skills and thus had to work less hard to succeed.

The results showed that each type of feedback promoted self-efficacy, motivation, and achievement better than no feedback. First-half feedback increased students' effort attributions for success and motivation during the first half of the program. Given students' learning disabilities, effort feedback for early or late achievement likely seemed credible because these students had to work diligently to succeed. Students may have interpreted the feedback as indicating that they were becoming skillful and capable of further learning. With students who learn more rapidly, shifting to feedback indicating developing skill or ability as instruction proceeds may be viewed as more credible and thus better promote achievement outcomes.

FUTURE RESEARCH

We have shown that self-efficacy is a key process among adolescents that affects motivation and achievement. At the same time, we sound the obvious call for more self-efficacy research with adolescents. In particular, we believe the following areas to be germane, and the results would have theoretical and practical significance.

Generality of Self-Efficacy

Research is needed on the extent to which self-efficacy beliefs generalize from one domain to another and whether such generalization varies as a function of adolescent development. Given that self-efficacy is conceptualized as a domain-specific construct (Bandura, 1997; Pajares, 1996), most self-efficacy researchers have not determined whether it generalizes across domains. There is limited evidence for generalization (Smith, 1989).

For any given content, students' self-efficacy for learning is affected by their aptitudes, prior experiences, and social supports (Schunk, 1995; see Table 2.1). Learners who typically perform well in a content area should have higher self-efficacy for learning new content than those who have had learning difficulties. Self-efficacy might generalize to the extent that the new domain builds on prior skills (e.g., self-efficacy for solving algebraic equations may affect self-efficacy for learning calculus).

Generalization also might occur across dissimilar domains if students believe that the domains share skills. For example, students who feel efficacious about writing term papers and believe that writing term papers and preparing science lab reports involve planning and organizing may have high self-efficacy for performing well on their first science lab report. We might expect that generalization would increase with cognitive development and experience because older students could determine the prerequisites of the new domain and draw on prior knowledge.

Researchers also need to examine the extent to which some academic tasks might facilitate generalization more so than do others. Miller and Meece (1997, 1999) found that students' confidence in their learning abilities and a preference for challenging academic tasks increased when they had frequent and regular opportunities across the entire school year to read and write complex prose while studying collaboratively with classmates over extended time periods. Students' self-efficacy might become more resilient and generalize to other domains more easily if students like Cedric are challenged by their teachers to achieve at their highest optimum levels.

Self-Efficacy Outcomes

Future research needs to investigate how well self-efficacy predicts achievement outcomes as a consequence of development. Bandura's (1986) contention that self-efficacy influences choice of activities, effort, and persistence is seen most clearly in contexts in which behavior reflects performance of learned skills (e.g., engaging in feared activities). In academic settings, the influence of self-efficacy on these indexes is complex.

Choice of activities often is not a good index because students do not choose many of the learning activities in which they engage. Persistence also presents problems. Students typically persist on activities not because of high self-efficacy, but rather, because the teacher keeps them on task. Educational research has yielded inconsistent results on the relation of self-efficacy to persistence (Schunk, 1995). A positive relation may be found in the early stages of learning when greater persistence leads to better performance. As skills develop, students should require less time to complete the same task, which means that self-efficacy will relate negatively to persistence. At higher grade levels, students often are required to complete tasks that take longer and require much persistence with minimal supervision (e.g., write a 10 page research paper), so we would expect that self-efficacy and persistence would relate directly. With development, adolescents are better able to determine how much persistence may be necessary to succeed. Thus, self-efficacy may predict persistence better at the higher grades, but this issue needs to be explored.

Research during learning also is needed on effort, which seems promising as a key motivational outcome linked to self-efficacy. Subject content increases in difficulty as students proceed through school, which means that greater effort is required to sustain the same level of success. Research has obtained positive relations between self-efficacy and cognitive effort (Corno, 1993; Salomon, 1984). We recommend that a longitudinal study be conducted during which students' careers are traced to determine how the self-efficacy/effort relation changes with development and with increased subject difficulty. Such an effort would help teachers to understand how they might promote self-efficacy and achievement with students, like Cedric, who lack the necessary persistence to recover from unexpected failures.

Multiple Influences on Self-Efficacy

We noted earlier that sources of self-efficacy often conflict. Students may work on a task and encounter difficulty, but observe peers succeeding and be encouraged by a teacher. In social settings, they may experience anxiety and doubt that they can interact effectively with peers, but observe peers mixing well. Clearly we need more research on how students weigh and combine sources of self-efficacy information, and how behavior varies when conflicts result. A longitudinal study would allow researchers to study how self-efficacy develops in actual classrooms where students constantly face many challenges. Certainly Cedric's self-efficacy did not develop incrementally in any predictable manner. Some days, he was at a loss for what he might do in a particular subject to improve his grades; at other times, he approached his studies with enthusiasm and confidence. We would think that his self-efficacy fluctuated as he experienced many successes and failures throughout his different classes. A longitudinal study would provide critical insights into how self-efficacy develops within and across various academic domains.

It is true that peer pressure or the overarching desire to do something can lead to action even in the face of low self-efficacy. Students may try out for sport teams not because they feel confident about performing well but rather because they want to be part of the athletic crowd. Students may take difficult courses not because they feel efficacious about succeeding, but rather because their parents are encouraging them to be on the college track and want them admitted to a prestigious university. Self-efficacy may bear little relation to behavior under these circumstances, but research is needed.

Self-Efficacy and Ethnicity

More self-efficacy research is needed on diverse ethnic populations. Graham (1994) found that African American students maintain optimism and positive self-regard in the face of social and economic disadvantage, and that the academic self-beliefs of African Americans are strong even in the face of achievement failure (and often stronger than those of their white peers). Similar findings have been reported with Hispanic American samples (Lay & Wakstein, 1985; Stevenson, Chen, & Uttal, 1990).

These findings are primarily from studies measuring generalized competence beliefs. When the belief assessed is task-specific self-efficacy, results can differ. Pajares and Kranzler (1995) found that mathematical self-efficacy of African American students was lower than that of whites; Pajares and Johnson (1996) showed that writing self-efficacy of Hispanic high school students was lower than that of white students. In each case, minority students reported positive math self-concepts. It may be that minority students hold different beliefs as a function of specificity of assessment (Edelin & Paris, 1995).

It is possible that socioeconomic conditions influence self-efficacy differently among ethnic groups. Bandura (1986, 1997) observed that when social and economic systems are prejudicial, students may find that no amount of effort will cause desired outcomes. Minority adolescents may possess the confidence and skill required to achieve but may choose not to because they lack the incentives (Ogbu, 1992; Steele, 1997). Self-efficacy may also be unrelated to achievement in schools where teachers, equipment, or resources required to help students perform academic tasks are inadequate (Schunk & Pajares, 2002). Studying Cedric's school environment would be useful to determine whether it is aiding or suppressing development of self-efficacy for learning.

Bandura (1997) also suggested that self-efficacy may exceed actual performance when social constraints and inadequate resources impede academic performances; students are unable to do what they know. This observation helps shed light on findings regarding the competence beliefs of minority students in some contexts. There is a need to explore the role that schools play as social systems in developing and cultivating self-efficacy as well as the effects of these systems' incentives on students' self-efficacy.

CONCLUSION

Adolescents' self-efficacy beliefs affect the instigation, direction, persistence, and outcomes of achievement-related actions. In this chapter, we traced how self-efficacy changes with development and elucidated variables that affect this change. We used Cedric as an example in the opening scenario to underscore the complexities associated with studying self-efficacy in classrooms in which the number of influential variables far exceeds those found in more structured research environments. Some of these variables may promote self-efficacy in some situations while undermining its development in others A greater understanding of how such variables operate in classrooms will help teachers to address the challenge of how to increase the learning and motivation of all students. Cedric's unique challenges call attention to the problems faced by students as they attempt to successfully negotiate obstacles to their successful classroom learning. Consistent with this focus, we suggested profitable areas of research. The future should provide greater clarification of the operation of self-efficacy in different domains and highlight ways that self-efficacy can be enhanced in learners across developmental levels.

REFERENCES

Bandura, A. (1986). *Social foundations of thought and action: A social cognitive theory.* Englewood Cliffs, NJ: Prentice-Hall.

Bandura, A. (1997). *Self-efficacy: The exercise of control.* New York: Freeman.

Bandura, A., Barbaranelli, C., Caprara, G. V., & Pastorelli, C. (1996). Multifacted impact of self-efficacy beliefs on academic functioning. *Child Development, 67,* 1206–1222.

Bennett, N., DesForges, C., Cockburn, A., & Wilkinson, B. (1984*). The quality of pupil learning experiences.* Hillsdale, NJ: Erlbaum.

Berndt, T. J., & Keefe, K. (1992). Friends' influence on adolescents' perceptions of themselves at school. In D. H. Schunk & J. L. Meece (Eds.), *Student perceptions in the classroom* (pp. 51–73). Hillsdale, NJ: Erlbaum.

Bouffard-Bouchard, T., Parent, S., & Parivee, S. (1991). Influence of self-efficacy on self-regulation and performance among junior and senior high-school age students. *International Journal of Behavioral Development, 14,* 153–164.

Brown, I., Jr., & Inouye, D. K. (1978). Learned helplessness through modeling: The role of perceived similarity in competence. *Journal of Personality and Social Psychology, 36,* 900–908.

Brown, J. S., & Burton, R. R. (1978). Diagnostic models for procedural bugs in basic mathematical skills. *Cognitive Science, 2,* 155–192.

Cairns, R. B., Cairns, B. D., & Neckerman, J. J. (1989). Early school dropout: Configurations and determinants. *Child Development, 60,* 1437–1452.

Corno, L. (1993). The best-laid plans: Modern conceptions of volition and educational research. *Educational Researcher, 22*(2), 14–22.

Dweck, C. S., & Goetz, T. (1978). Attributions and learned helplessness. In J. Harvey, W. Ickes, & R. Kidd (Eds.), *New directions in attribution research* (pp. 157–179). Hillsdale, NJ: Erlbaum.

Eccles, J. S., & Midgley, C. (1989). Stage-environment fit: Developmentally appropriate classrooms for young adolescents. In C. Ames & R. Ames (Eds.), *Research on motivation in education* (Vol. 3, pp. 139–186). San Diego, CA: Academic Press.

Eccles, J. S., Midgley, C., & Adler, T. (1984). Grade-related changes in the school environment: Effects on achievement motivation. In J. Nicholls (Ed.), *Advances in motivation and achievement: The development of achievement motivation* (Vol. 3, pp. 283–331). Greenwich, CT: JAI Press.

Eccles, J. S., Wigfield, A., & Schiefele, U. (1998). Motivation to succeed. In N. Eisenberg (Ed.), *Handbook of child psychology: Vol. 3. Social, emotional, and personality development* (pp. 1018–1095). New York: Wiley.

Edelin, K. C., & Paris, S. G. (1995, April). *African American students' efficacy beliefs and the match between beliefs and performance.* Paper presented at the Annual Meeting of the American Educational Research Association, San Francisco.

Goodlad, J. (1983). *A place called school.* New York: McGraw-Hill.

Graham, S. (1994). Motivation in African Americans. *Review of Educational Research, 64,* 55–117.

Harter, S. (1996). Teacher and classmate influences on scholastic motivation, self-esteem, and level of voice in adolescents. In J. Juvonen & K. R. Wentzel (Eds.),

Social motivation: Understanding children's school adjustment (pp. 11–42). Cambridge, UK: Cambridge University Press.

Hymel, S., Comfort, C., Schonert-Reichl, K., & McDougall, P. (1996). Academic failure and school dropout: The influence of peers. In J. Juvonen & K. R. Wentzel (Eds.), *Social motivation: Understanding children's school adjustment* (pp. 313–345). Cambridge, UK: Cambridge University Press.

Kindermann, T. A., McCollam, T. L., & Gibson, E., Jr. (1996). Peer networks and students' classroom engagement during childhood and adolescence. In J. Juvonen & K. R. Wentzel (Eds.), *Social motivation: Understanding children's school adjustment* (pp. 279–312). Cambridge, UK: Cambridge University Press.

Lay, R., & Wakstein, J. (1985). Race, academic achievement, and self-concept of ability. *Research in Higher Education, 22*, 43–64.

Lent, R. W., Brown, S. D., & Larkin, K. C. (1986). Self-efficacy in the prediction of academic performance and perceived career options. *Journal of Counseling Psychology, 33*, 265–269.

Licht, B. G., & Kistner, J. A. (1986). Motivational problems of learning-disabled children: Individual differences and their implications for treatment. In J. K. Torgesen & B. W. L. Wong (Eds.), *Psychological and educational perspectives on learning disabilities* (pp. 225–255). Orlando, FL: Academic Press.

Meece, J. L. (1997). *Child and adolescent development for educators.* New York: McGraw-Hill.

Midgley, C., Feldlaufer, H., & Eccles, J. (1989). Change in teacher efficacy and student self- and task-related beliefs in mathematics during the transition to junior high school. *Journal of Educational Psychology, 81*, 247–258.

Miller, S. D., Adkins, T., & Hooper, M. L. (1993). Why teachers select specific literacy assignments and students' reactions to them. *Journal of Reading Behavior, 25*, 69–95.

Miller, S. D., & Blumenfeld, P. C. (1993). Characteristics of tasks in basal skill instruction. *Elementary School Journal, 94*, 33–48.

Miller, S. D., & Meece, J. L. (1997). Enhancing elementary students' motivation to read and write: A classroom intervention study. *Journal of Educational Research, 89*, 1–11.

Miller, S. D., & Meece, J. L. (1999). Third graders preferences for reading and writing tasks. *Elementary School Journal, 100*, 19–36.

Multon, K. D., Brown, S. D., & Lent, R. W. (1991). Relation of self-efficacy beliefs to academic outcomes: A meta-analytic investigation. *Journal of Counseling Psychology, 38*, 30–38.

Ogbu, J. U. (1992) Understanding cultural diversity and learning. *Educational Researcher, 21*(8), 5–14.

Pajares, F. (1996). Self-efficacy beliefs in achievement settings. *Review of Educational Research, 66*, 543–578.

Pajares, F., & Johnson, M. J. (1996). Self-efficacy beliefs in the writing of high school students: A path analysis. *Psychology in the Schools, 33*, 163–175.

Pajares, F., & Kranzler, J. (1995). Self-efficacy beliefs and general mental ability in mathematical problem-solving. *Contemporary Educational Psychology, 20*, 426–443.

Pajares, F., & Miller, M. D. (1994). The role of self-efficacy and self-concept beliefs in mathematical problem-solving: A path analysis. *Journal of Educational Psychology, 86,* 193–203.

Pajares, F., Miller, M. D., & Johnson, M. J. (1999). Gender differences in writing self-beliefs of elementary school students. *Journal of Educational Psychology, 91,* 50–61.

Pajares, F., & Schunk, D. H. (2001). Self-beliefs and school success: Self-efficacy, self-concept, and school achievement. In R. J. Riding & S. G. Rayner (Eds.), *International perspectives on individual differences: Vol 2. Self-perception* (pp. 239–266). London: Ablex Publishing.

Pajares, F., & Valiante, G. (1999). Grade level and gender differences in the writing self-beliefs of middle school students. *Contemporary Educational Psychology, 24,* 390–405.

Pajares, F., & Valiante, G. (in press). Students' self-efficacy in their self-regulated learning strategies: A developmental perspective. *Psychologia.*

Pintrich, P. R., & De Groot, E. V. (1990). Motivational and self-regulated learning components of classroom academic performance. *Journal of Educational Psychology, 82,* 33–40.

Pintrich, P. R., & Schunk D. H. (2002). *Motivation in education: Theory, research, and applications* (2nd ed.). Upper Saddle River, NJ: Prentice-Hall.

Ruble, D. N., & Flett, G. L. (1988). Conflicting goals in self-evaluative information seeking: Developmental and ability level analysis. *Child Development, 59,* 97–106.

Salomon, G. (1984). Television is "easy" and print is "tough": The differential investment of mental effort in learning as a function of perceptions and attributions. *Journal of Educational Psychology, 76,* 647–658.

Schunk, D. H. (1981). Modeling and attributional effects on children's achievement: A self-efficacy analysis. *Journal of Educational Psychology, 73,* 93–105.

Schunk, D. H. (1982). Effects of effort attributional feedback on children's perceived self-efficacy and achievement. *Journal of Educational Psychology, 74,* 548–556.

Schunk, D. H. (1983). Ability versus effort attributional feedback: Differential effects on self-efficacy and achievement. *Journal of Educational Psychology, 75,* 848–856.

Schunk, D. H. (1984). Enhancing self-efficacy and achievement through rewards and goals: Motivational and informational effects. *Journal of Educational Research, 78,* 29–34.

Schunk, D. H. (1987). Peer models and children's behavioral change. *Review of Educational Research, 57,* 149–174.

Schunk, D. H. (1995). Self-efficacy and education and instruction. In J. E. Maddux (Ed.), *Self-efficacy, adaptation, and adjustment: Theory, research, and application* (pp. 281–303). New York: Plenum Press.

Schunk, D. H. (2001). Social cognitive theory and self-regulated learning. In B. J. Zimmerman & D. H. Schunk (Eds.), *Self-regulated learning and academic achievement: Theoretical perspectives* (2nd ed., pp. 125–151). Mahwah, NJ: Erlbaum.

Schunk, D. H., & Cox, P. D. (1986). Strategy training and attributional feedback with learning disabled students. *Journal of Educational Psychology, 78,* 201–209.

Schunk, D. H., & Gunn, T. P. (1986). Self-efficacy and skill development: Influence of task strategies and attributions. *Journal of Educational Research, 79,* 238–244.

Schunk, D. H., & Hanson, A. R. (1985). Peer models: Influence on children's self-efficacy and achievement. *Journal of Educational Psychology, 77,* 313–322.

Schunk, D. H., Hanson, A. R., & Cox, P. D. (1987). Peer-model attributes and children's achievement behaviors. *Journal of Educational Psychology, 79,* 54–61.

Schunk, D. H., & Lilly, M. W. (1984). Sex differences in self-efficacy and attributions: Influence of performance feedback. *Journal of Early Adolescence, 4,* 203–213.

Schunk, D. H., & Pajares, F. (2002). The development of academic self-efficacy. In A. Wigfield & J. Eccles (Eds.), *Development of achievement motivation* (pp. 15–31). San Diego, CA: Academic Press.

Schunk, D. H., & Swartz, C. W. (1993a). Goals and progress feedback: Effects on self-efficacy and writing achievement. *Contemporary Educational Psychology, 18,* 337–354.

Schunk, D. H., & Swartz, C. W. (1993b). Writing strategy instruction with gifted students: Effects of goals and feedback on self-efficacy and skills. *Roeper Review, 15,* 225–230.

Shell, D. F., Colvin, C., & Bruning, R. H. (1995). Self-efficacy, attributions, and outcome expectancy mechanisms in reading and writing achievement: Grade-level and achievement-level differences. *Journal of Educational Psychology, 87,* 386–398.

Shell, D. F., Murphy, C. C., & Bruning, R. H. (1989). Self-efficacy and outcome expectancy mechanisms in reading and writing achievement. *Journal of Educational Psychology, 81,* 91–100.

Smith, R. E. (1989). Effects of coping skills training on generalized self-efficacy and locus of control. *Journal of Personality and Social Psychology, 56,* 228–233.

Steele, C. M. (1997). A threat in the air: How stereotypes shape intellectual identity and performance. *American Psychologist, 52,* 613–6129

Steinberg, L., Brown, B. B., & Dornbusch, S. M. (1996). *Beyond the classroom: Why school reform has failed and what parents need to do.* New York: Simon & Schuster.

Stevenson, H. W., Chen, C., & Uttal, D. H. (1990). Beliefs and achievement: A study of black, white, and Hispanic children. *Child Development, 61,* 508–523.

White, J. (1982). *Rejection.* Reading, MA: Addison-Wesley.

Wigfield, A. (1994). The role of children's achievement values in the self-regulation of their learning outcomes. In D. H. Schunk & B. J. Zimmerman (Eds.), *Self-regulation of learning and performance: Issues and educational applications* (pp. 101–124). Hillsdale, NJ: Erlbaum.

Wigfield, A., Eccles, J. S., Yoon, K. S., Harold, R. D., Arbreton, A. J. A., Freedman-Doan, C., & Blumenfeld, P. C. (1997). Change in children's competence beliefs and subjective task values across the elementary school years: A 3-year study. *Journal of Educational Psychology, 89,* 451–469.

Zimmerman, B. J., & Bandura, A. (1994). Impact of self-regulatory influences on writing course attainment. *American Educational Research Journal, 31,* 845–862.

Zimmerman, B. J., Bandura, A., & Martinez-Pons, M. (1992). Self-motivation for academic attainment: The role of self-efficacy beliefs and personal goal-setting. *American Educational Research Journal, 29,* 663–676.

Zimmerman, B. J., & Martinez-Pons, M. (1990). Student differences in self-regulated learning: Relating grade, sex, and giftedness to self-efficacy and strategy use. *Journal of Educational Psychology, 82,* 51–59.

CHAPTER 3

ADOLESCENTS' EXPECTANCIES FOR SUCCESS AND ACHIEVEMENT TASK VALUES DURING THE MIDDLE AND HIGH SCHOOL YEARS

Allan Wigfield and Stephen Tonks
University of Maryland

Adolescence is a time in which individuals experience many changes, including the biological changes associated with puberty, changes in relations with family and peers, and the social and educational changes resulting from transitions from elementary to junior high school and junior high school to high school (see Eccles & Wigfield, 1997; Wigfield, Eccles, & Pintrich, 1996). Different theorists (e.g., Eccles & Midgley, 1989; Hill & Lynch, 1983; Midgley & Edelin, 1998) have proposed that these changes have significant impact on a variety of developmental outcomes. Many children make these changes relatively easily. Others, however, have difficulty with one or another of these changes and as a result are at risk for various negative outcomes. We focus in this chapter on the development of adolescents' achievement motivation. We take an expectancy-value approach to motivation, and so the particular focus of our chapter concerns the development during adolescence of expectancy-related beliefs and task values.

Expectancy-value theory has provided one of the most important views on the nature of achievement motivation, beginning with Atkinson's (1957) seminal work and continuing through the work of Battle (1965,

1966), the Crandalls (e.g., Crandall, 1969; Crandall, Katkovsky, & Crandall, 1965; Crandall, Dewey, Katkovsky, & Preston, 1964), Feather (1982, 1988, 1992), and Eccles, Wigfield, and their colleagues (e.g., Eccles, 1984, 1993; Eccles et al., 1983; Wigfield, 1994a; Wigfield & Eccles, 1992, 2000, 2002b). Theorists adopting this perspective posit that individuals' expectancies for success and the value they have for succeeding are important determinants of their motivation to perform different achievement tasks, and their choices of which tasks to pursue. Atkinson originally defined expectancies as individuals' anticipations that either success or failure will follow their performance. He defined value as the relative attractiveness of succeeding or failing at a task.

Eccles, Wigfield, and their colleagues have extended Atkinson's (1957) work in important ways. They expanded upon Atkinson's original definitions of expectancy for success and task value (Eccles, 1993; Eccles et al., 1983), discussed the nature of achievement values (Parsons & Goff, 1980; Wigfield & Eccles, 1992), focused on how expectancies and values develop during childhood and adolescence (Wigfield, 1994a; Wigfield & Eccles, 2002b), and compared the expectancy and value constructs to related constructs in the motivation literature (Wigfield & Eccles, 2000). In this chapter, we focus in particular on the development of children's expectancies and values during adolescence, as well as gender differences in these beliefs and values. We discuss how educational transitions and different educational environments influence adolescents' expectancies and values. We also discuss how children's expectancies and values relate to their achievement behaviors and activity choices. We begin the chapter with a brief consideration of some of the major changes that occur at adolescence.

BIOLOGICAL, PSYCHOLOGICAL, AND ENVIRONMENTAL CHANGES DURING ADOLESCENCE

The biological changes associated with puberty are among the most dramatic ones that individuals experience during their lifetimes. In part because of these dramatic biological changes, different theorists portray the early adolescent period as a period of "storm and stress," where there is a great deal of conflict between children, parents, and teachers (e.g., Blos, 1979; Hall, 1904). We have heard teachers (and parents) say, "If we could just lock kids up for those years, things would be fine!" With such prevailing sentiments, perhaps it is little wonder that early adolescents' motivation undergoes important changes. While it is undeniable that major physical changes occur during early adolescence, many researchers now believe that the characterization of this time period as one of storm and stress is an overstatement (see, e.g., Arnett, 1999; Dornbusch, Petersen, & Hetherington, 1991). Yet Lerner,

Entwisle, and Hauser (1994) again used the term "crisis" in their description of the state of contemporary American adolescents. Whether or not adolescents are in crisis, the biological changes they go through do have many influences on their thinking and behavior, and the adolescent time period does pose challenges for many adolescents (Arnett, 1999).

One important educational implication of the work on pubertal changes and their effects concerns the issue of timing for the transition from elementary to secondary school. Many researchers and educational policy analysts urged that middle school should begin earlier, so that students make the school transition before they enter puberty. The concern is that dealing both with puberty and school changes make both transitions more complex (see Wigfield et al., 1996). Many school districts have followed this advice. Middle school now often encompasses sixth through eighth grade, rather than seventh through ninth grade. Others have argued that a K–8 organizational structure may be most beneficial to early adolescents. There is increasing awareness among educators that this is a unique developmental phase that requires careful structuring of educational environments. This matter is further complicated by the fact that boys and girls go through puberty at different times, making it very difficult to time the school transition to avoid the pubertal transition.

Children's thinking also changes during the adolescent years (see, e.g., Byrnes, 1988; Keating, 1990; Moshman, 1999). For our purposes the most important changes to note are the increasing propensity of children to think abstractly, consider the hypothetical as well as the real, engage in more sophisticated and elaborate information-processing strategies, consider multiple dimensions of a problem at once, and reflect on oneself and on complicated problems (see Keating, 1990, and Moshman, 1999, for more complete discussion). Such changes have potentially important influences on children's learning. They also have important implications for individuals' self-concepts and motivation. Theorists such as Erikson (1963) and Harter (1990) view the adolescent years as a time of change in children's self-concepts, as young people consider what possibilities are available to them and try to come to a deeper understanding of themselves. These sorts of self-reflections require the kinds of higher-order cognitive processes just discussed. With motivation increasingly conceived in cognitive terms, these changes also have implications for early adolescents' motivation, and the relations of motivation to behavior.

Finally, many aspects of adolescents' social environments change. Most adolescents go through two school transitions, one from elementary to middle school, and one from middle to high school. The environments in these settings are quite different from one another, and so students have to adjust to them in many ways. These transitions, particularly the middle school transition, have a strong impact on many students' motivation.

Another crucial change in adolescents' social environments is the stronger influence of peers and amount of time spent with them, and the corresponding decrease in amount of time spent with parents. Students' social worlds thus change in many ways during this important time. With this information as a backdrop, we return to a consideration of the development of children's expectancies and values.

ECCLES, WIGFIELD AND COLLEAGUES' EXPECTANCY VALUE MODEL

Eccles and colleagues (1983) developed an expectancy-value model of achievement choice as a framework for understanding early adolescence and adolescents' performance and choice in the mathematics achievement domain. A recent version of the model is presented in Figure 3.1. Eccles and colleagues proposed that children's achievement performance, persistence, and choice of achievement tasks are most directly predicted by their expectancies for success on those tasks and the subjective value they attach to success on those tasks. Children's expectancies and values themselves are most directly determined by other achievement-related beliefs, including children's achievement goals and self-schemata, and their task-specific beliefs (defined as beliefs about ability or competence and task difficulty beliefs). Children's interpretations of their previous performance and their perceptions of socializers' attitudes and expectations influence their goals and task-specific beliefs. Aspects of children's cultural milieu, characteristics of the child such as their aptitude, their previous performance, and important socializers' beliefs and behaviors, influence children's perceptions and interpretations. Because the model is developmental, there is a feedback loop from current performance and choice back to the beginning of the model, showing the bidirectional influences of these different factors.

For theoretical clarity it is crucial to define the expectancy and value constructs in the model (see also Wigfield & Eccles, 2000). Expectancies for success are defined as children's beliefs about how well they will do on an upcoming task. Beliefs about competence refer to children's evaluations of their competence in different areas. Related constructs also are prominent in other motivation models, in particular Bandura's (1997) self-efficacy theory, Covington's (1984, 1992) self-worth approach, Dweck and her colleagues' work on perceptions of intelligence (Dweck & Leggett, 1988), Ryan and Deci's (2000) self-determination perspective, and Weiner's (1979, 1985) attribution theory; these related constructs are discussed in other chapters in this volume.

Wigfield and Eccles (2000) discussed how the definitions of the expectancy and ability belief constructs in our expectancy-value model differ

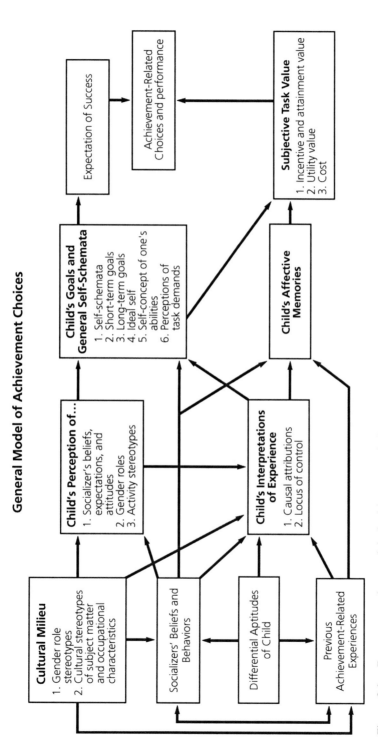

Figure 3.1.   Expectancy-value model of achievement choice.

57

from these other constructs (see also Pajares, 1996). Crucial differences include the level of specificity at which the constructs are defined and measured, and whether the focus primarily is on one's sense of one's own competence, or one's competence in comparison to that of others. For instance, Bandura's (1997) construct of self-efficacy usually is measured quite specifically and emphasizes individuals' own sense of whether they can accomplish a task. By contrast, other theorists often measure competence-related beliefs more generally (e.g., Dweck, 2002; Skinner, Zimmer-Gembeck, & Connell, 1998). We tend to measure these constructs at the domain-specific level (e.g., How good are you at math?), and to include individuals' comparative sense of competence along with their beliefs about their own ability. These are important differences, but a crucial similarity is that the individual's sense of competence is a key part of many models of motivation.

Values have both broad and more specific definitions. Rokeach (1973, 1979) broadly construed values as beliefs about desired end states. He identified a set of values that he believed were fundamental to human experience; some of these values concerned achievement. Schwartz (1992) also theorized about broad human values, listing 10 such values, with achievement included as one of them (see Rohan, 2000, for a review of these theories). In the achievement motivation literature, subjective task values have been defined more specifically as how a task meets the different needs of individuals (Eccles et al., 1983; Wigfield & Eccles, 1992). Task values are a crucial part of the model because they influence individuals' choices. Individuals may feel competent at a given activity but not engage in it because it has no value for them.

Eccles and colleagues (1983) proposed four major components of subjective values: attainment value or importance, intrinsic value, utility value or usefulness of the task, and cost (see Eccles et al., 1983, and Wigfield & Eccles, 1992, for more detailed discussion of these components). Building on Battle's (1965, 1966) work, Eccles and colleagues defined attainment value as the importance of doing well on a given task. More broadly, attainment value also deals with identity issues; tasks are important when individuals view them as central to their own sense of themselves. Intrinsic value is the enjoyment one gains from doing the task; this component is similar in certain respects to notions of intrinsic motivation (see Harter, 1978; Ryan & Deci, 2000). Utility value or usefulness refers to how a task fits into an individual's future plans, for instance, taking a math class to fulfill a requirement for a science degree. Cost refers to what the individual has to give up to do a task (e.g., Do I do my math homework or call my friend?), as well as the anticipated effort one will need to put into task completion. Sample items measuring these constructs can be found in Wigfield and Eccles (2000).

DEVELOPMENT OF CHILDREN'S COMPETENCE BELIEFS, EXPECTANCIES FOR SUCCESS, AND ACHIEVEMENT TASK VALUES

We and others have done extensive work on the development of children's competence beliefs, expectancies for success, and achievement values, examining change in the ways in which children and adolescents conceptualize different motivational constructs, change in the structure of children's motivational beliefs and values, and changes in the mean level of their beliefs and values (see Eccles, Wigfield, & Schiefele, 1998; Wigfield, 1994a; Wigfield & Eccles, 2002b, for review). We focus here on the latter two kinds of change.

The Structure of Children's Competence Beliefs and Values

In our expectancy-value model, children's competence beliefs, expectancies for success, and achievement values are proposed to be distinct constructs. We have empirically assessed whether this is the case by factor-analyzing children's responses to questionnaire measures of these constructs. We found that even during the early elementary school years, children have distinct beliefs about what they are *good* at and what they *value* in different domains (Eccles & Wigfield, 1995; Eccles, Wigfield, Harold, & Blumenfeld, 1993). This finding is crucial for the expectancy-value model.

Three other findings from this work are important to note. First, Eccles and Wigfield (1995) and Eccles and colleagues (1993) looked at whether children's competence beliefs and expectancies for success are distinct constructs, as is proposed in the Eccles and colleagues (1983) model. Children in their studies were in Grades 1 through 12. Results of confirmatory factor analyses showed that children's competence beliefs and expectancies for success load on the same factor; hence these components are not empirically distinct. Therefore, two of the constructs proposed as separate in the model (competence beliefs, expectancies for success) relate closely to one another. Second, these researchers also examined how distinct the different components of task value are, and found that they are less differentiated during the elementary school years and become differentiated during early adolescence (Eccles & Wigfield, 1995; Eccles et al., 1993). That is, by adolescence, children's attainment, interest, and utility value form distinct but related constructs.

Third, these researchers, and others doing work in the broader self-concept literature, have found that, even during the early elementary school years, children distinguish different domains of competence, including math, reading, general school, physical ability, physical appearance, peer relations, parent relations, and general self-concept (Bong, 2001; Eccles et al., 1993; Harter, 1982; Marsh, 1989; Marsh, Craven, & Debus, 1991, 1998). This is an important finding because it shows that children have a differentiated sense of their competence. Children's valuing of achievement also factors by domain, indicating that values are differentiated as well (Bong, 2001; Eccles et al., 1993). Recall that in the expectancy-value model, their expectancies and values most directly predict value model children's performance and choice. The findings that these beliefs and values are differentiated suggest that such relations need to be examined at relatively specific levels.

Changes in the Mean Level of Children's Expectancy-Related Beliefs and Values

Several researchers have found that children's competence beliefs and expectancies for success for different tasks decline across the elementary school years and into the middle school years (see Dweck & Elliott, 1983; Eccles et al., 1998; Stipek & Mac Iver, 1989, for review). To illustrate, Nicholls (1979) found that most first graders ranked themselves near the top of the class in reading ability, and there was no correlation between their ability ratings and their performance level. The 12-year-olds in his study had reading ability beliefs that were more dispersed and correlated highly with school grades. In a longitudinal study of elementary school-aged children's competence beliefs and values of math, reading, sports, and instrumental music, Wigfield and colleagues (1997) found that children's beliefs and values declined across age and also related more closely to parents' and teachers' ratings of their ability. Across the elementary school years, children's expectancies for success become more sensitive to both success and failure experiences and more accurate or realistic in terms of their relation to actual performance history (see Assor & Connell, 1992; Eccles, Wigfield, & Schiefele, 1998; Parsons & Ruble, 1977; Stipek, 1984).

What happens during adolescence? Wigfield, Eccles, Mac Iver, Reuman, and Midgley (1991) studied change in children's competence beliefs and values across the transition from elementary to junior high school. The questionnaire contained items assessing early adolescents' ability beliefs and values for math, English, social, and sports activities, as well as their general self-esteem. Students' general self-esteem was lowest in the fall of Grade 7, immediately after the school transition. Although students' self-esteem increased somewhat during Grade 7, it remained lower than self-esteem at Grade 6. Students' ability beliefs regarding math, English, and social activities showed the largest decreases between the spring of Grade 6 and fall of Grade 7, suggesting a transition effect.

The interest and importance aspects of task value were examined separately in this study. Early adolescents' liking of math was quite similar in the fall and spring of Grade 6 but declined across the transition. Students' liking of English and social activities was highest in the spring of Grade 6, declined across the transition, and then increased somewhat during Grade 7. Early adolescents' ratings of the importance of these activities also decreased between Grade 6 and Grade 7, with the largest differences for English and social activities occurring across the transition to junior high school.

One of the most striking findings was the strong differences in early adolescents' liking of academic and nonacademic activities. Perhaps not surprisingly, they greatly preferred the nonacademic activities (social and sports activities) to the academic activities (math and English), and they liked social activities more than any of the other activities. Early adolescents also rated social activities as most important to them. However, although sports was their second most *liked* activity, math was the activity rated second most *important* by early adolescents. In fact, participants rated sports as the least important of the four activities! The differences between liking and importance ratings illustrate the necessity of assessing different aspects of students' valuing of different activities.

Jacobs, Lanza, Osgood, Eccles, and Wigfield (2002) examined change in children's competence beliefs and valuing of math, language arts, and sports across grades 1 through 12, following the same sample that was studied by Wigfield and colleagues (1997). The overall pattern of change was a decline in each domain. There were some differences across domain with respect to when the strongest changes occurred, particularly in language arts and math. In language arts the strongest declines occurred during elementary school and then little change was observed after that. In sports, the change accelerated during the high school years. The declines in math competence beliefs were similar over time. Jacobs and colleagues found that children's valuing of the domains of math, language arts, and sports also declined. As was the case for competence beliefs, children's valuing of language arts declined most during elementary school and then leveled off. By contrast, children's valuing of math declined the most during high school.

The negative changes in children's competence-related beliefs and achievement values have been explained in two ways. The first concerns children's ability to process evaluative information. They become much better at understanding, interpreting, and integrating the evaluative feedback they receive, and of course they receive more extensive evaluative information from different academic and nonacademic activities they do in and out of school. They also engage in more social comparison with their peers. As a result of these changes, many children become more accurate or realistic in their self-assessments as they get older, with a corresponding drop in the initial optimism that characterizes many children's beliefs and values. (see Dweck & Elliott, 1983; Eccles et al., 1998; Nicholls, 1984; Parsons & Ruble, 1977; Ruble, 1983; Stipek & Mac Iver, 1989). Second, the environments children encounter change in ways that make evaluation more salient and competition between students more likely, with the result that some children's self-assessments will decline as they get older (see, e.g., Blumenfeld, Pintrich, Meece, & Wessels, 1982; Eccles & Midgley, 1989; Eccles, Midgley, & Adler, 1984; Wigfield, Eccles, & Pintrich, 1996).

Gender Differences in Competence-Related Beliefs and Expectancies for Success

Before discussing gender differences, some words of caution are in order. As other authors have pointed out, drawing conclusions about such differences must be done carefully (see Eisenberg, Martin, & Fabes, 1996; Ruble & Martin, 1998). Although such differences often are observed, in general they tend to be relatively small in terms of the amount of variance explained (e.g., Marsh, 1989). Thus there often is substantial overlap between different groups in the many different variables measured in studies of gender differences. Individual differences *within* groups typically are stronger than mean differences *between* groups. Even with these cautions in mind, there are reliable differences between various groups, and these differences are discussed in this section.

Gender Differences in Beliefs About Competence

Gender differences in competence-related beliefs during childhood and adolescence often are reported, particularly in gender-role stereotyped domains and on novel tasks (see Wigfield, Battle, Keller, & Eccles, 2002). For example, boys hold higher competence beliefs than do girls for math and sports, even after all relevant skill-level differences are controlled. By contrast, girls have higher competence beliefs than do boys for reading, English, and social activities (Eccles, 1984; Eccles et al., 1989; Huston, 1983; Marsh, 1989; Marsh et al., 1998; Wigfield et al., 1991; Wigfield et al., 1997). These differences emerge remarkably early. Wigfield and colleagues' (1997) longitudinal study of children's competence beliefs and valuing of different activities began when children were in Grade 1. Results showed that boys had higher competence beliefs for math and sports, and girls for English, even among the first graders. The age differences in beliefs did not change over time. Marsh and colleagues' (1998) study of self-concepts included kindergarteners, and results were similar to those of Wigfield and colleagues.

Few studies have looked at long-term change in children's competence beliefs. Jacobs and colleagues (2002) followed the children in the Wigfield and colleagues (1997) study through the end of high school, and found that gender differences in math competence beliefs narrowed by the end of high school. Gender differences in English competence beliefs are strongest at the end of elementary school and through middle school. Differences favoring girls remain at the end of high school, but also are smaller than during the earlier school years. In the sport domain, boys' competence beliefs are higher even at Grade 1, and the differences remain throughout the school years.

The extent to which children endorse the cultural stereotypes regarding which sex is likely to be most talented in each domain predicts the extent to which girls and boys distort their ability self-concepts and expectations in the gender stereotypic direction (Early, Belansky, & Eccles, 1992; Eccles & Harold, 1991). That is, boys who believe that in general boys are better in math are more likely to have more positive competence beliefs in math. However, these gender differences are not always found (e.g., Dauber & Benbow, 1990; Schunk & Lilly, 1982) and, when found, are generally quite small (Marsh, 1989; Marsh et al., 1998).

In sum, reliable gender differences in beliefs about competence for different activities have been found. One reason these differences are important is because competence-related beliefs are strong predictors of performance and task choice (Bandura, 1997; Eccles et al., 1983; Meece, Wigfield, & Eccles, 1990). Researchers looking at relations of competence beliefs to performance do not find sex differences in these relations; the links are as strong for girls as for boys (Meece et al., 1990). But given that the sexes differ in their level of competence beliefs for different activities, performance differences may in part reflect these beliefs. For instance, on average, girls doubt their competence in math more than boys do, and this likely influences their performance in math as well as their decisions about whether to continue doing math activities. Boys doubt their competence more in reading, again likely influencing their performance and choice.

Gender Differences in Achievement Task Values

Eccles, Wigfield, and their colleagues have found gender-role stereotypic differences in both children's and adolescents' valuing of mathematics, music, sports, social activities, and English/reading (e.g., Eccles et al., 1989, 1993; Wigfield et al., 1991, 1997). Across these studies, boys value sports activities more than girls do, although girls also value them highly. Relative to boys, girls value reading, English, and instrumental music more. Interestingly, recent work indicates that boys and girls value math equally (Eccles et al., 1993; Wigfield et al., 1997; Jacobs et al., 2002); in earlier work, gender differences in the value of math emerged in high school (Eccles, 1984). Jacobs and colleagues (2002) found that the differences in boys' and girls' valuing of sport activities narrowed by the end of high school.

Values also can be conceived more broadly to include things such as notions of what are appropriate activities for males and females to do. There is an extensive literature on gender differences in activities and interests (see Eisenberg et al., 1996; Ruble & Martin, 1998). Starting early on, boys and girls do very different activities and play with quite different toys. In research done prior to the 1980s, elementary school-aged children often classified school subjects as either masculine or feminine (see Huston, 1983). Math and science were viewed as masculine, and reading/English and the arts as feminine. This no longer appears to be the case, as gender stereotyping of school subjects now is less consistent (see Etaugh & Liss, 1992).

Although school subjects no longer appear to be clearly gender stereotyped, as just reviewed, boys' and girls' valuing of English, sports, and social activities differ in gender stereotypic ways, although they value math similarly. However, by adolescence, girls report less interest in science than do boys, and are much less likely to enroll in science and technically oriented classes or pursue these areas for their careers (see Gardner, 1998, for review). Explanations for these differences in interests and activity preferences have focused on several things, including children's understanding of what is appropriate for each sex to do. Children's understanding of stereotypes about what are gender-appropriate activities increase across the childhood years (see Eisenberg et al., 1996, and Ruble & Martin, 1998, for further discussion). From the perspective of the constructs discussed in this chapter, perhaps children develop more positive competence-related beliefs and values for activities they believe are appropriate for their gender, and thus engage more in those activities. Parents likely contribute to these differences through the toys they provide and activities they encourage children to do (see further discussion later). Peers have a strong role as well (Eisenberg et al., 1996).

During adolescence other values-related issues become crucial. One that is relevant to this chapter is the value young women place on family versus a career. Earlier work indicated that adolescent females often felt conflicts about whether to emphasize either family or career, and many young women chose to emphasize family at the expense of career. More recent studies indicate that young women perceive less conflict in these two roles, often believing that they can manage both successfully (see Battle & Wigfield, 2002). This likely is a positive change in many ways, but young women may underestimate the time and effort needed to perform competently in both roles. From the perspective of this chapter, the crucial point is that the stronger valuing of careers is likely something leading more women to pursue their careers avidly.

In summary, as with competence beliefs, there are gender differences in children's and adolescents' valuing of different activities, and their interest in them. These differences potentially have important implications for adolescents' choices of which activities to do, a point to which we return later.

EDUCATIONAL TRANSITIONS AND STUDENTS' EXPECTANCIES AND VALUES

We noted earlier how changes in school environments can influence the development of expectancies and values, and contribute to the decline in them that had been observed. Many adolescents make two major educational transitions, from elementary to middle school, and middle school to high school. How these transitions influence adolescents' expectancies and values is considered next.

The Transition to Traditional Middle School

Most children in this country go to elementary school from kindergarten through fifth or sixth grade, and then transition to middle school or junior high school. Such schools differ structurally in important ways from elementary schools (see Eccles & Midgley, 1989, and Wigfield & Eccles, 2002a, for a detailed review). Most are substantially larger than elementary schools because they draw students from several elementary schools. As a result, students' friendship networks often are disrupted as they attend classes with students from several different schools. Students also are likely to feel more anonymous because of the large size of many middle schools. Instruction is likely to be organized and taught departmentally. Thus middle school teachers typically teach several different groups of students each day and are unlikely to teach any particular students for more than one year. This departmental structure can create a number of difficulties for students. One is that the curriculum often is not integrated across different subjects. A second difficulty is that students typically have several teachers each day with little opportunity to interact with any one teacher on any dimension except the academic content of what is being taught and disciplinary issues. Finally, family involvement in school often declines during the middle school years.

Researchers also have discussed how instructional practices, and ways in which teachers and students relate to each other, can negatively impact students' motivation in traditional junior high and middle schools (Eccles & Midgley, 1989; Maehr & Midgley, 1996; Wigfield et al., 1996; see Wigfield & Eccles, 2002a, for a recent review). Changes in instructional practices include things such as an increase in the use of between-classroom ability grouping practices, as well as the use of more rigorous and rigid grading standards. Teacher–student relationships become more authority based and less personal, in large part because teachers have so many more students to deal with. Middle school teachers have a lower sense of teaching efficacy than do elementary school teachers. Finally, as noted above, peer networks are disrupted when children change schools. Many times friends are separated from one another, and it takes time for children to reestablish social networks. Wigfield and colleagues (1991) found that children's sense of social competence was lowest immediately after the transition to junior high school, in comparison to before the transition, or later in junior high school. Such disruptions could influence children's academic motivation as well.

Eccles and Midgley (1989) argued that a main reason these things have a negative impact is that they are developmentally inappropriate for early adolescents. At a time when the children are growing cognitively and emotionally, desiring greater freedom and autonomy, and focusing on social relations, they experience school environments that do not promote these things. Therefore, for many early adolescents these practices contribute to the negative change in students' motivation and achievement-related beliefs. What has been done about these problems? That is the topic of the next section.

Middle School Reform Efforts and Student Motivation

In response to the issues discussed above, many school districts have changed middle-grade schools in important ways. There is growing consensus about what kinds of changes should be made in middle-grade schools (Lipsitz, Mizell, Jackson, & Austin, 1997). One structural change adopted in many school districts has been to move the transition to middle school from after to before Grade 6. This change on its own accomplishes little; what is more important is changing school organization and instructional practices in systematic ways (Mac Iver & Epstein, 1993).

Various groups have recommended a number of important changes in school organization and instructional practices (see Mac Iver, Young, &

Washburn, 2002, and Wigfield & Eccles, 2002a, for review). One major change is replacing department structures with teams of teachers working with the same group of students. This practice allows groups of teachers to spend more time with the same group of adolescents, thus getting to know them better. It also allows for greater integration across the curriculum. A second change is having teachers serve as advisors and counselors so that adolescents can develop relationships with adults other than their parents. A third is to create smaller learning communities in often-large middle schools; "schools within schools" have been created in part through the teaming approach just discussed. This is particularly likely to occur for the youngest group in a middle school, be they fifth graders, sixth graders, or seventh graders. Cooperative learning practices are used more frequently, in part to reduce the use of ability grouping or tracking.

How many middle schools have adopted such changes? Mac Iver and Epstein (1993) reported results of a study of teaching practices in middle schools across the country. They found that many school districts have not adopted the "school within a school" approach for making middle schools seem smaller. Forty percent of middle schools use tracking for math and English, and 20% use it for all subjects. Seventy five percent of schools have advising periods for students, although Mac Iver and Epstein noted that many of these are used primarily for school business, such as attendance taking and announcements, rather than for "true" advising and counseling. Close to 40% of middle schools reported using some kind of interdisciplinary teaming, but few of these schools allowed for team planning periods. Only 10% of the schools have teaming programs that allow teachers regular times for planning their academic programs. It should be clear from these data that implementation of the recommendations is occurring slowly. Mac Iver and Epstein asked principals to forecast how their schools would change over the next few years. Principals were most likely to mention teaming with planning periods, students assigned to the same advisory teacher for the entire time they are in middle school, flexible scheduling, and greater use of cooperative learning.

What about students' motivation in reformed middle schools? Some evidence is beginning to be gathered. Maehr and Midgley (1996) presented an account of their collaborative effort to change the cultural organization of an elementary and a middle school using motivational principles stemming primarily from achievement goal theory. Through collaborations with teachers and school administrators, different practices in the school were changed in order to facilitate mastery rather than ability-focused goal orientations. They focused on creating teams of teachers, "schools within a school," and changing student recognition patterns so that student improvement rather than just ability were recognized. Other practices were changed as well. These changes were put in place in the schools, though the processes by which that occurred often were challenging (see Maehr & Midgley, 1996, for a detailed discussion of the challenges they faced).

Anderman, Maehr, and Midgley (1999) assessed students' motivation in an elementary school participating in the project, as well as in the collaborating middle school and a comparison middle school in which the changes did not occur. Indeed, in the comparison school, competition between students and ability grouping were emphasized. There were few differences in students' motivation during elementary school. Following the transition to middle school, students in the comparison school had stronger performance goals and extrinsic goals for learning. These students also perceived a stronger emphasis in their school on performance goals. These shifts in students' motivation did not occur for the students in the collaborating school.

Mac Iver and his colleagues began a middle school reform effort that they called Talent Development Middle Schools (see Mac Iver & Plank, 1997, and Mac Iver et al., 2002, for a summary). This project is focused on reforming middle schools that serve early adolescents who are at risk because of the backgrounds from which they come. The program involves the implementation of many of the recommendations discussed in this section: detracking the schools, using cooperative learning extensively, team teaching, offering a challenging core curriculum (including algebra) to all students, and providing advising services. The program began in a few schools in Philadelphia and is spreading to other areas of the country. Preliminary results for both achievement and motivation outcomes is encouraging. Mac Iver and colleagues measured several motivation outcomes, including students' perceptions of their effort, sense of ability, and valuing of school learning, and students in the Talent Development schools were more positive in these aspects of motivation.

Mac Iver and colleagues (2002) looked at how instructional practices in science in middle schools participating in this program influenced students' motivation for science. The science instructional practices included an emphasis on hands-on science activities as well as opportunities to engage in higher-order thinking about the science activities (called a "minds-on" approach by Mac Iver and colleagues). The "minds-on" opportunities predicted students' value of learning science, expectancies for success, reported effort, and sense that the teacher cared about them. The hands-on activities predicted students' interest in science and perceptions of teacher caring. The researchers also looked at change in motivation over a school year in these students and found no evidence of a decline. Thus, when middle school students experience instructional practices that engage them, their motivation does not decline.

In summary, middle school reform efforts organized by a guiding set of principles are under way in middle schools across the country. However, despite the call for these changes and agreement on the principles to guide change, many middle schools have been slow to adopt them, or have not changed at all. Evidence from schools adopting the recommended changes suggests that students' motivation is enhanced in these middle schools; thus, the decline in student motivation that we have been discussing is not inevitable. This evidence is still sketchy, however; much more work is needed on how middle school reform efforts are influencing students' motivation along with their achievement. Following middle school, students face another important school transition. What happens during that transition?

The Transition to High School

There is less work on the transition to high school. In certain respects the transition from middle to high school may be easier than that from elementary to middle school, in part because the organizational structure of the two kinds of secondary schools is more similar. However, there are important challenges associated with this transition. High schools are typically even larger and more bureaucratic than are junior high schools and middle schools. Bryk, Lee, and Holland (1993) provided numerous examples of how the sense of community among teachers and students is undermined by the size and bureaucratic structure of most high schools. There is little opportunity for students and teachers to get to know each other, and, likely as a consequence, there is distrust between them and little attachment to a common set of goals and values. In many schools there is also little opportunity for the students to form mentor-like relationships with a nonfamilial adult, although this is beginning to change across the country. Such environments are likely to further undermine the motivation and involvement of many students, especially those not doing particularly well academically, those not enrolled in the favored classes, and those who are alienated from the values of the adults in the high school.

Academic pressure increases in high school (Newman, Lehman, Newman, Myers, & Smith, 2000). For the first time, grades matter in concrete ways to the future success of the students. If students plan on working full time after high school, then having a high school diploma is key to their future success. If students plan on continuing their education, then grades and test scores earned in high school are a large determinant of the kind of higher education they can pursue. Such pressures may increase the value that some students attach to doing well in school. For others, especially for those doing poorly, valuing of school activities likely decreases.

In high school, students' social worlds also change dramatically. As was the case during the transition to middle school, students' social worlds may be disrupted in important ways. In one sense, middle school can be seen as a bridge between a more innocent world of elementary school children and the more real-world setting of high school. For example, high school is the first place that many students encounter (either personally or vicariously) alcohol, drugs, gangs, and sex. These new social challenges combine with challenges familiar to middle school students to form a complicated setting for new high school students, which can make the already tougher academic workload even more difficult. These changes also can have strong influences on students' motivation.

Interviews with students after they enter high school confirm that they are concerned with many of the difficulties listed above. Newman and colleagues (2000) found that 55% of ninth graders mentioned that ninth grade was harder, and over 30% made negative comments about their teachers. That same percentage stated concerns about adjusting to a new school, attending a bigger school, and meeting new people.

Much of the research that has been done on the transition to high school has included measures of achievement in the analyses. A number of researchers have found declines in achievement after students move from a junior high or middle school to a high school (Alspaugh, 1998; Barone, Aguirre-Deandreis, & Trickett, 1991; Blyth, Simmons, & Carlton-Ford, 1983; Felner, Primavera, & Cauce, 1981; Isakson & Jarvis, 1999; Seidman, Aber, Allen, & French, 1996). Schiller (1999) found that the relationship between academic achievement before and after the transition to high school depended on the number of fellow eighth graders who attended the same high school. Students who were high achievers in Grade 8 benefited from attending a school with a majority of their fellow eighth graders, whereas low-achieving eighth-graders benefited from attending a high school different from those of most of their middle school classmates. However, these findings should be viewed with caution, as finding a comparable measure of achievement across a grade and school transition is a difficult task. When comparing GPA between Grades 8 and 9 or 9 and 10, and between schools, one must consider that the students are being rated by different teachers, being held to different standards, and being compared to different students. Another decline after the high school transition that has been noted in the literature is in school attendance (Barone et al., 1991; Felner et al., 1981; Isakson & Jarvis, 1999).

From the above findings it seems likely that adolescents' motivation would change in a negative direction across the high school transition. Murdock, Anderman, and Hodge (2000) measured aspects of students' motivation that are related to the expectancy and value constructs we are discussing, as well as students' perceptions of school context in Grades 7 and 9 in a system where students transitioned to high school after Grade 8. They found that students' academic self-concepts increased, as did the economic value they placed on education. Also, perceptions of teacher support and encouragement increased, whereas perceptions of teacher disrespect and criticism decreased, which indicates that students on average perceived their teachers in a more positive light after the transition to high school. The authors suggested that these positive changes could be due to a better match between high school teachers' treatment of students and students' developmental level, in contrast to the mismatch of these two things that has been proposed to occur during middle school (Eccles & Midgley, 1989).

In another study of high school students' motivation, Seidman and colleagues (1996) found an increase in academic self-efficacy and social self-efficacy over the transition. However, these researchers also found an increase in students' reported daily hassles and decreases in reported social support and involvement in extracurricular activities after the transition, perhaps reflective of the different structural environment of high school.

In summary, the transition to high school is potentially a crucial time for adolescents due to developmental changes and various changes in the school, academics, and social networks. Researchers have theorized that these changes could have profound effects on the achievement, motivation, and self-esteem of students. Findings show that, indeed, achievement and attendance do decline, along with some other negative outcomes such as a reported increase in daily hassles. Although the research is sparse, the transition does not appear to be related to negative motivation outcomes. Taken together, these findings paint a complex picture of the high school transition. The relationship between the negative achievement findings and the more positive motivation and self-esteem findings is not easily explained. Clearly, more research is warranted to clarify the sparse and somewhat confusing results.

Easing the Transition to High School

As has been the case with elementary to middle school, there have been efforts to ease the middle to high school transition. A complete review of this work is beyond the scope of this chapter; we highlight some relevant findings. Smith (1997) used national data to compare students who had access to different kinds of transition programs. She found that higher grades and a lower dropout rate were present in students who had access to "full" transition programs, which include programs targeting students, staff, and parents, as opposed to programs that target only one or two of these groups. Felner, Ginter, and Primavera (1982) added counseling and liaison duties to homeroom teachers' responsibilities and also reorganized class schedules so that students and teachers had more classes together. When they compared this group to a control group, they found that students in this program had higher GPA, better attendance, and more stable self-concepts. Thus, easing the high school transition has positive impacts on various student outcomes. Few studies have examined how such efforts influence students' expectancies and values, however.

One possible reason that work on the high school transition is sparse is that the middle school transition remains the larger concern. As is evident from this chapter, more research has focused on the earlier transition. Nevertheless, we believe a more thorough examination of how the organization and structure of our high schools influences cognitive, motivational, and achievement outcomes is sorely needed.

EXPECTANCIES, VALUES, AND ACADEMIC OUTCOMES

Performance and Choice of Achievement Activities

A crucial part of our expectancy-value model is the predicted links of expectancies for success and achievement values to children's and adolescents' achievement outcomes, including their performance, persistence, and choices of which activities to undertake (e.g., Eccles, 1993; Eccles et al., 1983; Eccles, Wigfield, & Schiefele, 1998). We have obtained empirical support for these proposed links in longitudinal studies of children ranging from ages 6 to 18. The major findings from these studies are that even when levels of previous performance are controlled, students' competence beliefs strongly predict their performance in different domains, including math, reading, and sports. Students' achievement task values predict both intentions and actual decisions to keep taking mathematics and English and to engage in sports. Because expectancy beliefs and values relate positively to one another (Wigfield et al., 1997), it is important to note that competence-related beliefs have indirect effects on choice, whereas values have indirect effects on performance.

The relations just noted are evident in children as early as first grade, although the relations strengthen across age (Eccles, 1984; Eccles et al., 1983; Eccles & Harold, 1991; Meece et al., 1990). The relations become particularly strong during adolescence. For instance, Eccles (1984) showed that 5th- through 12th-grade students' expectancies for success predicted subsequent performance in math more strongly than did their achievement values. Students' valuing of math predicted their intentions to keep taking math more strongly than did their expectancies for success. Meece and colleagues (1990) looked at these relations longitudinally and found similar results with respect to the prediction of performance and intentions. Eccles (1984) and Eccles, Adler, and Meece (1984) showed that 8th- through 10th-grade students' valuing of math strongly predicted their actual decisions to continue taking math later in their high school careers, whereas their self-concepts of ability in math did not predict enrollment decisions.

Eccles, Barber, Updegraff, and O'Brien (1998) extended these findings to other achievement domains, utilizing data from the Michigan Study of Adolescent Transitions (MSALT). They examined how adolescents' ability beliefs and values predicted their choices of participation in team sports in high school, taking honors math classes, and taking physical science classes. A particular focus of their work was on explaining gender differences in these choices; in each case boys chose to participate in these activities more than did girls. Adolescents' valuing of the activity, particularly their utility value, was the strongest predictor of student choice. Students' math ability beliefs predicted choice of honors math classes and participation in team sports, but the predictive relations were weaker than those for utility value and choice. Inclusion of the value and ability belief variables in the path models mediated the gender effect; the direct path from gender to choice no longer was significant when the value and ability belief variables were included.

Expectancies, Values, and the Self-Regulation of Behavior

Most of our empirical work to date has examined how children's competence beliefs and values relate to course grades and course enrollment decisions. In this empirical work we have not examined processes that could explain the relations obtained. Wigfield (1994b) provided a micro-level analysis of the relations of children's achievement values and their achievement behaviors that suggests the kinds of processes that could be involved. Among other things, he suggested that students who value different academic activities likely will study harder and more effectively. They also should continue to pursue goals they have set even if they encounter difficulties.

More recently, Wigfield and Eccles (2002b) expanded on this analysis by discussing potential links between children's expectancies and values and the specific ways they regulate their achievement behaviors. They suggested that the work on how expectancies and values influence performance and choice could be integrated with recent theoretical models of the self-regulation process (see Boekaerts, Pintrich, & Zeidner, 2000, for review of the work on self-regulation). One essential part of behavioral regulation is choice of whether or not to continue to do different activities. Such choices can be complex in real-world achievement situations where there are many uncertainties about probable outcomes (see Busemyer & Townsend, 1993, and Byrnes, 1998, for discussion of complex decision making under uncertainty). Theorists who have developed models of self-regulation argue that the decision about whether to continue or discontinue an activity often comes as individuals reflect back on their performance and evaluate the outcomes they attained (see Scheier & Carver, 2000; Schunk & Ertmer, 2000; Zimmerman, 2000). A number of self-regulation theorists discuss how such evaluations can influence individuals' perceptions of competence regarding the activity, and that competence beliefs themselves can influence the evaluations. We believe also that students' values play a strong role in students' reflections about their performance and in their choices of activities. When an activity is valued, students likely attend more carefully to how they are doing, invest more time, and try to understand why they obtained the outcome that they did. Such elaborate processing may be less likely for activities that are valued less. The mediating role of values on the regulation of behavior deserves further study (see Wigfield & Eccles, 2002b).

Expectancies, Values, and the Decision to Stay in School

We have focused so far in this section on relatively narrow educational choices, such as how much to study or which course to take. How do adolescents' expectancies and values relate to their broader educational choices? Feather (1988) found that college students' valuing of math (and math ability beliefs) predicted choice of science-related majors, with ability beliefs having a stronger predictive link than values. English values predicted strongly the students' choice to enroll in humanities courses. Feather also found that students' broader values related to the kinds of educational experiences students enjoyed having.

One essential question for researchers interested in adolescents' expectancies and values is how those beliefs relate to the decisions students make to stay in or drop out of school. Most researchers examining how students' beliefs relate to dropping out of school have focused on students' general self-esteem, a construct that can be ill-defined and is influenced by so many factors that it might not have much predictive utility in explaining specific decisions like dropping out of school (see Finn, 1989, for a critique of the self-esteem explanation of dropping out of school). In one step toward greater specificity of measurement in this area, Vallerand, Fortier, and Guay (1997) measured adolescents' perceived competence and intrinsic motivation in school, and related these to the decision to stay in school or drop out. They found that high school students who eventually dropped out had lower perceived academic competence than did those who persisted in school. Dropouts also had lower scores on measures of intrinsic and extrinsic motivation, as well as perceived social support and autonomy, showing the complexity of the issue.

We would argue that students' valuing of achievement likely has an important influence on this decision. From our research we know that students who do not value math will be more likely to opt out of math when they no longer have to take it. It may be the case that students who begin to have difficulties in middle school and high school could initially come to devalue individual school subjects. If they continue to struggle they may begin to devalue school in general, which could lead them to drop out when that option becomes available to them. For children who never did well, their valuing of specific subject areas and school likely never was high, or dropped very quickly across the school years, again leading them to devalue the whole educational enterprise.

Certainly, other factors besides achievement beliefs and values, such as the economic pressure many poor students face, discrimination, and bad schools, play a major role in the decision to drop out (see Finn, 1989; Rumberger, 1987). Yet the relative contribution of both specific achievement values and more general valuing of education also are likely to play a significant role, one that has not been addressed sufficiently.

CONCLUSION

We have reviewed work on adolescents' competence-related beliefs, expectancies for success, and achievement values in this chapter. We discussed how adolescents' beliefs and values change, and gender differences in these beliefs and values. We also discussed the impact of school transitions on adolescents' competence-related beliefs and values, and how middle school reform efforts are focusing on enhancing these aspects of children's motivation. We hope readers can see that much has been learned both about the nature of children's competence-related beliefs and values and how they are influenced by the educational experiences students have. Yet much remains to be done, particularly with respect to better understanding how educational reform efforts at middle and high school are influencing not only adolescents' achievement but also their beliefs and values about their achievement. We look forward to learning about and participating in the next generation of research on these important topics.

REFERENCES

Alspaugh, J. W. (1998). Achievement loss associated with the transition to middle school and high school. *Journal of Educational Research, 92,* 20–25.

Anderman, E. M., Maehr, M. L., & Midgley, C. (1999). Declining motivation after the transition to middle school: Schools can make a difference. *Journal of Research and Development in Education, 32,* 131–147.

Arnett, J. J. (1999). Adolescent storm and stress, reconsidered. *American Psychologist, 54,* 317–326.

Assor, A., & Connell, J. P. (1992). The validity of students' self-reports as measures of performance affecting self-appraisals. In D. H. Schunk & J. L. Meece (Eds.), *Student self-perceptions in the classroom* (pp. 25–47). Hillsdale, NJ: Erlbaum.

Atkinson, J. W. (1957). Motivational determinants of risk taking behavior. *Psychological Review, 64,* 359–372.

Bandura, A. (1997). *Self-efficacy: The exercise of control.* New York: Freeman.

Barone, C., Aguirre-Deandreis, A. I., & Trickett, E. J. (1991). Growing up the hard way: Pathways of urban adolescents. *American Journal of Community Psychology, 19,* 207–225.

Battle, A., & Wigfield, A. (in press). College women's value orientations toward family, career, and the pursuit of graduate school. *Journal of Vocational Behavior.*

Battle, E. (1965). Motivational determinants of academic task persistence. *Journal of Personality and Social Psychology, 2,* 209–218.

Battle, E. (1966). Motivational determinants of academic competence. *Journal of Personality and Social Psychology, 4,* 534–642.

Blos, P. (1979). *The adolescent passage.* New York: International Universities Press.

Blumenfeld, P., Pintrich, P. R., Meece, J., & Wessels, K. (1982). The formation and role of self-perceptions of ability in elementary school classrooms. *Elementary School Journal, 82,* 401–420.

Blyth, D. A., Simmons, R. G., & Carlton-Ford, S. (1983) The adjustment of early adolescents to school transitions. *Journal of Early Adolescence, 3,* 105–120.

Boekaerts, M., Pintrich, P. R., & Zeidner, M. (2000). Self-regulation: An introductory overview. In M. Boekaerts, P. R, Pintrich, & M. Zeidner (Eds.), *Handbook of self-regulation* (pp. 1–9). San Diego: Academic Press.

Bong, M. (2001). Between- and within-domain relations of academic motivation among middle and high school students: Self-efficacy, task value, and achievement goals. *Journal of Educational Psychology, 93,* 23–34,

Bryk, A. S., Lee, V. E., & Holland, P. B. (1993). *Catholic schools and the common good.* Cambridge, MA: Harvard University Press.

Busemeyer, J. R., & Townsend, J. T. (1993). Decision field theory: A dynamic-cognitive approach to decision making in an uncertain environment. *Psychological Review, 100,* 432–459.

Byrnes, J. B. (1988). Formal operations: A systematic reformulation. *Developmental Review, 8,* 1–22.

Byrnes, J. B. (1998). *The nature and development of self-regulated decision making.* Mahwah, NJ: Erlbaum.

Covington, M. V. (1984). The self-worth theory of achievement motivation: Findings and implications. *Elementary School Journal, 85,* 5–20.

Covington, M. V. (1992). *Making the grade: A self-worth perspective on motivation and school reform.* New York: Cambridge University Press.

Crandall, V. C. (1969). Sex differences in expectancy of intellectual and academic reinforcement. In C. P. Smith (Ed.), *Achievement-related motives in children* (pp. 11–45). New York: Russell Sage Foundation.

Crandall, V. C., Katkovsky, W., & Crandall, V. J. (1965). Children's beliefs in their own control of reinforcements in intellectual-academic achievement situations. *Child Development, 36,* 91–109.

Crandall, V. J., Dewey, R., Katkovsky, W., & Preston, A. (1964). Parents' attitudes and behaviors and grade school children's academic achievements. *Journal of Genetic Psychology, 104,* 53–66.

Dauber, S. L., & Benbow, C. P. (1990). Aspects of personality and peer relations of extremely talented adolescents. *Gifted Child Quarterly, 34,* 10–15.

Dornbusch, S. M., Petersen, A. C., & Hetherington, E. M. (1991). Projecting the future of research on adolescence. *Journal of Research on Adolescence, 1,* 7–18.

Dweck, C. S. (2002). The development of ability conceptions. In A. Wigfield & J. S. Eccles (Eds.), *The development of achievement motivation.* San Diego, CA: Academic Press.

Dweck, C. S., & Elliott, E. S. (1983). Achievement motivation. In P. H. Mussen (Ed.), *Handbook of child psychology* (3rd ed., Vol. 4, pp. 643–691). New York: Wiley.

Dweck, C. S., & Leggett, E. (1988). A social-cognitive approach to motivation and personality. *Psychological Review, 95,* 256–273.

Early, D. M., Belansky, E., & Eccles, J. S. (1992, March). *The impact of gender stereotypes on perceived ability and attributions for success.* Poster presented at the Biennial Meeting of the Society for Research on Adolescence, Washington DC.

Eccles, J. S. (1984). Sex differences in achievement patterns. In T. Sonderegger (Ed.), *Nebraska Symposium on Motivation* (Vol. 32, pp. 97–132). Lincoln: University of Nebraska Press.

Eccles, J. S. (1993). School and family effects on the ontogeny of children's interests, self-perceptions, and activity choice. In J. Jacobs (Ed.), *Nebraska Symposium on Motivation, 1992: Developmental perspectives on motivation* (pp. 145–208). Lincoln: University of Nebraska Press.

Eccles, J. S., Adler, T. F., Futterman, R., Goff, S. B., Kaczala, C. M., Meece, J., & Midgley, C. (1983). Expectancies, values and academic behaviors. In J. T. Spence (Ed.), *Achievement and achievement motives* (pp. 75–146). San Francisco: Freeman.

Eccles, J. S., Adler, T. F., & Meece, J. L. (1984). Sex differences in achievement: A test of alternate theories. *Journal of Personality and Social Psychology, 46,* 26–43.

Eccles, J. S., Barber, B. L., Updegraff, K., & O'Brien, K. M.. (1998). An expectancy-value model of achievement choices: The role of ability self-concepts, perceived task utility and interest in predicting activity choice and course enrollment. In L. Hoffman, A. Krapp, & K. A. Renninger (Eds.), *Interest and learning: Proceedings of the Seeon conference on interest and gender.* Kiel, Germany: Institute for Science Education, University of Kiel.

Eccles, J. S., & Harold, R. D. (1991). Gender differences in sport involvement: Applying the Eccles' expectancy-value model. *Journal of Applied Sport Psychology, 3,* 7–35.

Eccles, J. S., & Midgley, C. (1989). Stage/environment fit: Developmentally appropriate classrooms for early adolescents. In R. Ames & C. Ames (Eds.), *Research on motivation in education* (Vol. 3, pp. 139–181). New York: Academic Press.

Eccles, J., Midgley, C., & Adler, T. (1984). Grade-related changes in the school environment: Effects on achievement motivation. In J. G. Nicholls (Ed.), *The development of achievement motivation* (pp. 283–331). Greenwich, CT: JAI Press.

Eccles, J. S., & Wigfield, A. (1995). In the mind of the achiever: The structure of adolescents' academic achievement related-beliefs and self-perceptions. *Personality and Social Psychology Bulletin, 21*, 215–225.

Eccles, J. S., & Wigfield, A. (1997). Young adolescent development. In J. L. Irvin (Ed.), *What current research says to the middle level practitioner.* Columbus, OH: National Middle School Association.

Eccles, J. S., Wigfield, A., Flanagan, C., Miller, C., Reuman, D., & Yee, D. (1989). Self-concepts, domain values, and self-esteem: Relations and changes at early adolescence. *Journal of Personality, 57*, 283–310.

Eccles, J. S., Wigfield, A., Harold, R., & Blumenfeld, P. B. (1993). Age and gender differences in children's self- and task perceptions during elementary school. *Child Development, 64*, 830–847.

Eccles, J. S., Wigfield, A., & Schiefele, U. (1998). Motivation to succeed. In N. Eisenberg (Vol. Ed.) & W. Damon (Series Ed.), *Handbook of child psychology* (5th ed., Vol. 3, pp. 1017–1095). New York: Wiley.

Eisenberg, N., Martin, C. L., & Fabes, R. A. (1996). Gender development and gender effects. In D. C. Berliner & R. C. Calfee (Eds.), *Handbook of educational psychology* (pp. 358–396). New York: Macmillan.

Erikson, E. H. (1963). *Childhood and society.* New York: Norton.

Etaugh, C., & Liss, M. B. (1992). Home, school, and playroom: Training grounds for adult gender roles. *Sex Roles, 18*, 129–147.

Feather, N. T. (1982). Expectancy-value approaches: Present status and future directions. In N. T. Feather (Ed.), *Expectations and actions: Expectancy-value models in psychology* (pp. 395–420). Hillsdale, NJ: Erlbaum.

Feather, N. T. (1988). Values, valences, and course enrollment: Testing the role of personal values within an expectancy-value framework. *Journal of Educational Psychology, 80*, 381–391.

Feather, N. T. (1992). Values, valences, expectations, and actions. *Journal of Social Issues, 48*, 109–124.

Felner, R. D., Ginter, M., & Primavera, J. (1982). Primary prevention during school transitions: Social support and environmental structure. *American Journal of Community Psychology, 10*, 277–290.

Felner, R. D., Primavera, J., & Cauce, A. M. (1981). The impact of school transitions: A focus for preventive efforts. *American Journal of Community Psychology, 9*, 449–459.

Finn, J. D. (1989). Withdrawing from school. *Review of Educational Research, 59*, 117–142.

Gardner, P. L. (1998). The development of males' and females' interests in science and technology. In L. Hoffmann, A. Krapp, K. A. Renninger, & J. Baumert (Eds.), *Interest and learning* (pp. 41–57). Kiel, Germany: Institute for Science Education, University of Kiel.

Hall, G. S. (1904). *Adolescence: Its psychology and its relations to anthropology, sex, crime, religion, and education.* New York: Appleton.

Harter, S. (1978). Effectance motivation reconsidered: Toward a developmental model. *Human Development, 21,* 34–64.

Harter, S. (1982). The Perceived Competence Scale for Children. *Child Development, 53,* 87–97.

Harter, S. (1990). Causes, correlates and the functional role of global self-worth: A life-span perspective. In J. Kolligian & R. Sternberg (Eds.), *Perceptions of competence and incompetence across the life-span* (pp. 67–98). New Haven, CT: Yale University Press.

Hill, J. P., & Lynch, M. E. (1983). The intensification of gender-related role expectations during early adolescence. In J. Brooks-Gunn & A. C. Petersen (Eds.), *Girls at puberty* (pp. 201–228). New York: Plenum Press.

Huston, A. (1983). Sex-typing. In P. H. Mussen (Ed.), *Handbook of child psychology* (Vol. 4, pp. 387–467). New York: Wiley.

Isakson, K., & Jarvis, P. (1999). The adjustment of adolescents during the transition into high school: A short term longitudinal study. *Journal of Youth and Adolescence, 28,* 1–26.

Jacobs, J. E., Lanza, S., Osgood, D. W., Eccles, J. S., & Wigfield, A. (2002). Changes in children's self-competence and values: Gender and domain differences across grades one through twelve. *Child Development.*

Keating, D. P. (1990). Adolescent thinking. In S. S. Feldman & G. R. Elliott (Eds.), *At the threshold: The developing adolescent* (pp. 54–89). Cambridge, MA: Harvard University Press.

Lerner, R., M., Entwisle, D. R., & Hauser, S. T. (1994). The crisis among contemporary American adolescents: A call for the integration of research, policies, and programs. *Journal of Research on Adolescence, 4,* 1–4.

Lipsitz, J., Mizell, M. H., Jackson, A. W., & Austin, L. M. (1997). Speaking with one voice: A manifesto for middle-grades reform. *Phi Delta Kappan,* 533–540.

Mac Iver, D. J., & Epstein, J. L. (1993). Middle grades research: Not yet mature, but no longer a child. *Elementary School Journal, 93,* 519–533.

Mac Iver, D. J., & Plank, J. B. (1997). Improving urban schools: Developing the talents of students placed at risk. In J. L. Irvin (Ed.), *What current research says to the middle level practitioner* (pp. 243–256). Columbus, OH: National Middle School Association.

Mac Iver, D. J., Young, E. M., & Washburn, B. (2002). Instructional practices and motivation during middle school (with special attention to science). In A. Wigfield & J. S. Eccles (Eds.), *The development of achievement motivation.* San Diego, CA: Academic Press.

Maehr, M. L., & Midgley, C. (1996). *Transforming school cultures.* Boulder, CO: Westview Press.

Marsh, H. W. (1989). Age and sex effects in multiple dimensions of self-concept: Preadolescence to early adulthood. *Journal of Educational Psychology, 81,* 417–430.

Marsh, H. W., Craven, R. G., & Debus, R. (1991). Self-concepts of young children 5 to 8 years of age: Measurement and multidimensional structure. *Journal of Educational Psychology, 83,* 377–392.

Marsh, H. W., Craven, R. G., & Debus, R. (1998). Structure, stability, and development of young children's self-concepts: A multicohort-multioccasion study. *Child Development, 69*, 1030–1053.

Meece, J. L., Wigfield, A., & Eccles, J. S. (1990). Predictors of math anxiety and its consequences for young adolescents' course enrollment intentions and performances in mathematics. *Journal of Educational Psychology, 82*, 60–70.

Midgley, C., & Edelin, K. C. (1998). Middle school reform and early adolescent well-being: The good news and the bad. *Educational Psychologist, 33*, 195–206.

Moshman, D. (1999). *Adolescent psychological developmental: Rationality, morality, and identity.* Mahwah, NJ: Erlbaum.

Murdock, T. B., Anderman, L. H., & Hog, S. A. (2000). Middle-grade predictors of students' motivation and behavior in high school. *Journal of Adolescent Research, 15*, 327–351.

Newman, B. M., Lehman, B. J., Newman, P. R., Myers, M. C., & Smith, V. L. (2000). Experiences of urban youth navigating the transition to ninth grade. *Youth and Society, 31*, 387–416.

Nicholls, J. G. (1979). Development of perception of own attainment and causal attributions for success and failure in reading. *Journal of Educational Psychology, 71*, 94–99.

Nicholls, J. G. (1984). Achievement motivation: Conceptions of ability, subjective experience, task choice, and performance. *Psychological Review, 91*, 328–346.

Pajares, F. (1996). Self-efficacy beliefs in academic settings. *Review of Educational Research, 66*, 543–578.

Parsons, J. E., & Goff, S. B. (1980). Achievement motivation and values: An alternative perspective. In L. J. Fans (Ed.), *Achievement motivation* (pp. 349–373). New York: Plenum Press.

Parsons, J. E., & Ruble, D. N. (1977). The development of achievement-related expectancies. *Child Development, 48*, 1075–1079.

Rohan, M. J. (2000). A rose by any name? The values construct. *Personality and Social Psychology Review, 4*, 255–277.

Rokeach, M. (1973). *The nature of human values.* New York: Free Press.

Rokeach, M. (1979). From individual to institutional values with special reference to the values of science. In M. Rokeach (Ed.), *Understanding human values* (pp. 47–70). New York: Free Press.

Ruble, D. (1983). The development of social comparison processes and their role in achievement-related self-socialization. In E. T. Higgins, D. N. Ruble, & W. W. Hartup (Eds.), *Social cognition and social development: A sociocultural perspective* (pp. 134–157). New York: Cambridge University Press.

Ruble, D. N., & Martin, C. L. (1998). Gender development. In W. Damon (Series Ed.) & N. Eisenberg (Vol. Ed.), *Handbook of child psychology* (5th ed., Vol. 3, pp. 933–1016). New York: Wiley.

Rumberger, R. W. (1987). High school dropouts: A review of issues and evidence. *Review of Educational Research, 57*, 101–122.

Ryan, R. M., & Deci, E. L. (2000). Intrinsic and extrinsic motivators: Classic definitions and new directions. *Contemporary Educational Psychology, 25*, 54–67.

Scheier, C. S., & Carver, M. F. (2000). On the structure of behavioral self-regulation. In M. Boekaerts, P. R. Pintrich, & M. Zeidner (Eds.), *Handbook of self-regulation* (pp. 41–84). San Diego, CA: Academic Press.

Schiller, K. S. (1999). Effects of feeder patterns on students' transition to high school. *Sociology of Education, 72,* 216–233.

Schunk, D. H., & Ertmer, P. A. (2000). Self-regulation and academic learning: Self-efficacy enhancing interventions. In M. Boekaerts, P. R. Pintrich, & M. Zeidner (Eds.), *Handbook of self-regulation* (pp. 631–649). San Diego, CA: Academic Press.

Schunk, D. H., & Lilly, M. V. (1982, April). *Attributional and expectancy change in gifted adolescents.* Paper presented at the Annual Meeting of the American Educational Research Association. New York.

Schwartz, S. H. (1992). Universals in the content and structure of values: Theoretical advances in empirical tests in 20 countries. In M. P. Zanna (Ed.), *Advances in experimental social psychology* (Vol. 24, pp. 1–65). San Diego, CA: Academic Press.

Seidman, E., Aber, J. L., Allen, L., & French, S. E. (1996). The impact of the transition to high school on the self-esteem and perceived social context of poor urban youth. *American Journal of Community Psychology, 24,* 489–515.

Shaklee, H., & Tucker, D. (1979). Cognitive bases of development in inferences of ability. *Child Development, 50,* 904–907.

Skinner, E. A., Zimmer-Gembeck, M. J., & Connell, J. P. (1998). Individual differences and the development of perceived control. *Monographs of the Society for Research in Child Development (63,* Serial No. 254).

Smith, J. B. (1997). Effects of eighth-grade transition programs on high school retention and experiences. *Journal of Educational Research, 90,* 144–152.

Stipek, D. J. (1984). The development of achievement motivation. In R. Ames & C. Ames (Eds.), *Research on motivation in education* (Vol. 1, pp. 145–174). New York: Academic Press.

Stipek, D. J., & Mac Iver, D. (1989). Developmental change in children's assessment of intellectual competence. *Child Development, 60,* 521–538.

Vallerand, R. J., Fortier, M. S., & Guay, F. (1997). Self-determination and persistence in a real-life setting: Toward a motivational model of high school dropout. *Journal of Personality and Social Psychology, 72,* 1161–1176.

Weiner, B. (1979). A theory of motivation for some classroom experiences. *Journal of Educational Psychology, 71,* 3–25.

Weiner, B., (1985). An attributional theory of achievement motivation and emotion. *Psychological Review, 92,* 548–573.

Wigfield, A. (1994a). Expectancy-value theory of achievement motivation: A developmental perspective. *Educational Psychology Review, 6,* 49–78.

Wigfield, A. (1994b). The role of children's achievement values in the self-regulation of their learning outcomes. In D. H Schunk & B. Zimmerman (Eds.), *Self-regulation of learning and performance: Issues and educational applications* (pp. 101–124). Hillsdale, NJ: Erlbaum.

Wigfield, A., Battle, A., Keller, L., & Eccles, J. S. (2002). Sex differences in motivation, self-concept, career aspirations, and career choice: Implications for cognitive development. In A. McGillicuddy-De Lisi & R. De Lisi (Eds.), *Biology, society, and behavior: The development of sex differences in cognition* (pp. 93–124) Westport, CT: Ablex Publishing.

Wigfield, A., & Eccles, J. S. (1992). The development of achievement task values: A theoretical analysis. *Developmental Review, 12,* 265–310.

Wigfield, A., & Eccles, J. S. (2000). Expectancy-value theory of motivation. *Contemporary Educational Psychology, 25,* 68–81.

Wigfield, A., & Eccles, J. S. (2002a). Children's motivation during the middle school years. In J. Aronson (Ed.), *Improving academic achievement: Contributions of social psychology.* San Diego, CA: Academic Press.

Wigfield, A., & Eccles, J. S. (2002b). The development of competence beliefs, expectancies for success, and achievement value from childhood through adolescence. In A. Wigfield & J. S. Eccles (Eds.), *The development of achievement motivation.* San Diego, CA: Academic Press.

Wigfield, A., Eccles, J., Mac Iver, D., Reuman, D., & Midgley, C. (1991). Transitions at early adolescence: Changes in children's domain-specific self-perceptions and general self-esteem across the transition to junior high school. *Developmental Psychology, 27,* 552–565.

Wigfield, A., Eccles, J. S., & Pintrich, P. R. (1996). Development between the ages of eleven and twenty-five. In D. C.. Berliner & R.C. Calfee (Eds.), *Handbook of educational psychology.* New York: MacMillan.

Wigfield, A., Eccles, J. S., Yoon, K. S., Harold, R. D., Arbreton, A., Freedman-Doan, C., & Blumenfeld, P. C. (1997). Changes in children's competence beliefs and subjective task values across the elementary school years: A three-year study. *Journal of Educational Psychology, 89,* 451–469.

Zimmerman, B. J. (2000). Attaining self-regulation: A social cognitive perspective. In M. Boekaerts, P. R. Pintrich, & M. Zeidner (Eds.), *Handbook of self-regulation* (pp. 13–39). San Diego, CA: Academic Press.

CHAPTER 4

THE PIVOTAL ROLE OF FRAMES OF REFERENCE IN ACADEMIC SELF-CONCEPT FORMATION: THE "BIG FISH–LITTLE POND" EFFECT

Herbert W. Marsh and Rhonda G. Craven
Self-Concept Enhancement and Learning Facilitation (SELF)
Research Centre, University of Western Sydney, Australia

The overarching aim of our research program is to address important societal issues by developing and promoting strategies to optimize self-concept as a valuable outcome and as a means to facilitate the attainment of other valued outcomes, along with a greater awareness of the worth of self in different social and cultural contexts. A positive self-concept is fundamental to all human endeavors, but is particularly relevant for adolescents in educational settings that are so pivotal in determining subsequent life directions and accomplishments. Self-concept in educational settings cannot be adequately understood if the role of frames of reference is ignored. Although academic self-concept is positively influenced by one's own academic accomplishments, the ability levels of others in the immediate context negatively influence it. This social comparison frame of reference has been identified in recent studies evaluating the big fish–little pond effect (BFLPE). The purpose of this chapter is to provide an overview of some exciting new research directions that extend theoretical predictions based on the BFLPE and elaborate the important implications of this research for policy and practice.

First, we evaluate the effects of placement in specialized education settings for gifted students and educationally disadvantaged students. The results of these studies provide support for BFLPE theoretical predictions that (a) educationally disadvantaged students have higher academic self-concepts in special education classes than in regular mixed-ability (mainstreamed) classes, whereas (b) academically gifted students have higher academic self-concepts in regular, mixed-ability classes than specialized education settings for gifted students. These recent results have important educational implications that counter the presumed benefits of current educational policy and practice for special education students being enacted throughout the world.

Second, we demonstrate the generalizabiltiy of the BFLPE by replicating this effect in two large-scale cross-cultural studies to provide further support for the external validity of the BFLPE. In the first study we compare East and West German students' self-concepts at the start of the reunification of the German school system following the fall of the Berlin Wall. East and West German systems prior to reunification differed in that West German students attended schools largely based on their academic ability, whereas East German schools were based on mixed ability groupings, and the East German education system's ethos emphasized more competitive educational processes compared to the West German system. The results support the BFLPE theoretical predictions that the BFLPE is initially larger for the West Germans at the start of the first year after the reunification, and the self-concepts of former East German students were lower overall than those of the former West German students.

Finally, we examine Hong Kong students' self-concepts to test the effects of attending academically selective schools in the context of an Eastern collectivist culture. In Hong Kong, schools are more highly segregated in relation to ability than most countries in the world, but collectivist cultural values prevail that are posited to counter social comparison processes (compared to more individualistic values in most Western countries). We empirically demonstrate that attending academically selective schools simultaneously results in a large negative contrast effect (more demanding standards of social comparison lead to lower academic self-concepts) and a smaller positive assimilation effect (pride in being selected to participate in a high ability school leads to higher academic self-concepts).

SIGNIFICANCE OF SELF-CONCEPT

Nathaniel Branden (1994), an eminent philosopher and psychologist, attests to the significance of the self-concept/self-esteem construct and outcomes that are mediated by it, stating that:

I cannot think of a single psychological problem—from anxiety to depression, to under-achievement at school or at work, to fear of intimacy, happiness or success, to alcohol or drug abuse, to spouse battering or child molestation, to co-dependency and sexual disorders, to passivity and chronic aimlessness, to suicide and crimes of violence—that is not traceable, at least in part, to the problem of deficient self-esteem. (p. xv)

As dramatically illustrated by Branden, self-concept research is highly relevant to important individual and societal problems that stem from low self-concept. At the heart of our research program is this universal importance and multidisciplinary appeal of self-concept as one of the most important constructs in the social sciences. This importance of self-concept and related constructs is highlighted by the regularity/consistency with which self-concept enhancement is identified as a major focus of concern in diverse settings, including education, child development, mental and physical health, social services, industry, and sports/exercise. Educational policy statements throughout the world list self-concept enhancement as a central goal of education. For example, in their model of effective schools, Brookover and Lezotte (1979) emphasized that maximizing academic self-concept, self-reliance, and academic achievement should be major outcome goals of schooling. Self-concept is also an important mediating factor that facilitates the attainment of other desirable psychological and behavioral outcomes. The need to think and feel positively about oneself, and the likely benefits of these positive cognitions on choice, planning, and subsequent accomplishments, transcend traditional disciplinary barriers and are central to goals in many social policy areas.

Self-concept is also one of the oldest, most important, most controversial, and most widely studied constructs in the social sciences. Despite this long history, advances in theory, research, and measurement of self-concept were slow, particularly during the heyday of behaviorism. It is only in the last three decades that there has been a resurgence in self-concept research. Even now, although many thousands of studies have examined self-concept, few researchers have published a significant number of studies or have conducted self-concept research over an extended period. In many studies, the major focus is on some other construct (e.g., academic achievement, school persistence, bullying, drug problems) and a measure of self-concept is included because of its assumed relevance. Reviews of this early research (e.g., Burns, 1979; Byrne, 1984; Shavelson, Hubner, & Stanton, 1976; Wells & Marwell, 1976; Wylie, 1974, 1979) emphasized weak theoretical bases, poor quality of measurement instruments, methodological shortcomings, and a lack of consistent findings. Similar observations led Hattie (1992) to describe this period as one of "dustbowl empiricism" in which the predominant research design in self-concept studies was to "throw it in and see what happens."

In contrast, studies since the 1980s made important advances in theory, measurement, and research. Particularly in educational psychology, but in other disciplines as well, much of this progress is due to an exciting new interplay between theory, research, measurement, and practice. Building on the work of Shavelson and colleagues, Marsh, Shavelson, and colleagues developed and refined this important theoretical model of self-concept (Marsh, Byrne, & Shavelson, 1988; Marsh & Shavelson, 1985; Shavelson et al., 1976; Shavelson & Marsh, 1986; see also Marsh & Hattie, 1996) and developed a construct validity approach (see Marsh, 1990c, 1993). They argued that the determination of theoretically consistent and distinguishable domains of self-concept should be prerequisite to the study of how self-concept is related to other variables. Theory building and instrument construction are inexorably intertwined, such that each will suffer if the two are separated. Using the Shavelson and colleagues model as a "blueprint," Marsh developed the set of Self Description Questionnaire (SDQ) instruments for preadolescents (SDQI), adolescents (SDQII), and late adolescents and young adults (SDQIII). Subsequent reviews of this early research (Byrne, 1984; Hattie, 1992; Marsh, 1990c, 1993; Marsh & Shavelson, 1985) supported the multifaceted structure of self-concept and demonstrated that self-concept cannot be adequately understood if its multidimensionality is ignored.

Much of our early applied research was in educational settings (see Marsh, 1990c, 1993; Marsh & Craven, 1997), where our emphasis on the multidimensionality of self-concept was critically important. Whereas academic achievement, coursework selection, and persistence were systematically related to academic self-concept (e.g., Marsh, 1993; Marsh & Yeung, 1997a, 1997b), they were nearly uncorrelated (or even negatively related) to nonacademic (social and physical) self-concept responses. Hence, this research demonstrated the importance of considering the mulitidimensionality of self-concept and the critical relationship between academic self-concept and desirable educational outcomes. This research demonstrated that self-concept has an important influence on students—how they feel about themselves, their accomplishments, persistence, and educational decisions.

FRAME-OF-REFERENCE EFFECTS IN THE FORMATION OF ACADEMIC SELF-CONCEPT: THE BFLPE

Self-concept cannot be adequately understood if the role of frames of reference is ignored. The same objective characteristics and accomplishments can lead to disparate self-concepts, depending on the frame of reference or standards of comparison that individuals use to evaluate themselves. Social comparison theory (Festinger, 1954) is one approach for studying frame-of-reference effects that has a long history in social psychology and provides the theoretical underpinning for this chapter. In an educational context, Marsh (1984a, 1984b; Marsh & Parker, 1984) proposed a frame of reference model called the big fish–little pond effect (BFLPE) to encapsulate frame-of-reference effects posited in social comparison theory. In the BFLPE, we propose that academic self-concept is influenced substantially by the ability levels of other students in the immediate context in addition to one's own ability and academic accomplishments. The purpose of this chapter is to review this research and summarize the results of recent research that expand the implications of the BFLPE.

In the theoretical model underlying the BFLPE (Marsh, 1984b), it is hypothesized that students compare their own academic ability with the academic abilities of their peers and use this social comparison impression as one basis for forming their own academic self-concept. A negative BFLPE occurs when equally able students have lower academic self-concepts when they compare themselves to more able students, and higher academic self-concepts when they compare themselves with less able students. For example, if average ability students attend a high-ability school (i.e., a school where the average ability level of other students is high) so that their academic abilities are below the average of other students in the school, it is predicted that this educational context will foster social comparison processes that will lead to academic self-concepts that are below average. Conversely, if these students attend a low-ability school, then their abilities would be above average in relation to other students in the school and social comparison processes will result in academic self-concepts that are above average. Thus, academic self-concepts depend not only on one's academic accomplishments but also on the accomplishments of those in the school that a student attends. According to this model, academic self-concept will be correlated positively with individual achievement (higher achieving children will have higher academic self-concepts). However, academic self-concept should be negatively related to school-average achievement (equally able students will have lower academic self-concepts in a school where the average ability is high and higher academic self-concepts in a school where the average ability is low).

The BFLPE is an example of external frame-of-reference effects that may impact upon students attending selective schools. Consider a capable student who has been evaluated as a top student throughout primary school. If the student is accepted into a selective high school, the student may be average or below average relative to other students in this school rather than at the top of the class. This can have detrimental effects on the student's self-concept as the student is no longer a big fish in a small pond (top of the class) but is in a large pond full of even larger fish (average or below average in a high-ability school). Anecdotal support for these contentions comes from in-service programs conducted by the authors for teachers from selective schools. Teachers in these programs often report that new students in Year 7 (the first year of high school) experience emotional, motivational, and academic difficulties in adjusting to the high-ability environment of selective schools. School-initiated research also offers further support for the BFLPE. For example, a school counselor from a selective school, after hearing information such as presented in this chapter, conducted a simple survey in which students in Years 7 to 12 were asked to indicate how bright they were relative to other students in the state. He reported that, on average, students' self-perceptions of their academic ability declined about five percentage ranks for each year they had been in the selective high school.

Case study evidence also supports the underlying processes of the BFLPE (Marsh, 1991). A student named Jane was attending an academically selective Australian high school, but she was doing poorly and not attending school regularly. A change in employment forced her parents to move and Jane changed to a new high school that was not a selective school. Due to her poor progress at the last school, Jane was initially placed in a class with the least able students in the new school. It quickly became evident, however, that she was a very able student and she soon worked her way into the most advanced classes in the new school. Her parents found that she was taking school more seriously and spending more time on her homework. Jane indicated that at the old (selective) school, she had to work really hard to get just average marks, which was not worth the effort. However, if she worked hard in her new school, she could be one of the best, which was apparently worth the effort.

The historical, theoretical underpinnings of this research (see Marsh, 1974, 1984b, 1991, 1993; Marsh & Parker, 1984) derive from research in psychophysical judgment (e.g., Helson, 1964; Marsh, 1974; Parducci, 1995), social judgment (e.g., Morse & Gergen, 1970; Sherif & Sherif, 1969; Upshaw, 1969), sociology (Alwin & Otto, 1977; Hyman, 1942; Meyer, 1970), social comparison theory (e.g., Festinger, 1954; Suls, 1977), and the theory of relative deprivation (Davis, 1966; Stouffer, Suchman, DeVinney, Star, & Williams, 1949). Coming from a psychophysical tradition, we use the term "contrast" when the judgment of a target stimulus shifts away from the background or context, whereas we use the term "assimilation" when the judgment shifts toward the context (Marsh, 1974). In the BFLPE, contrast occurs when higher school-average achievement levels (the context) lead to lower individual student academic self-concepts (target judgment), whereas assimilation occurs when higher school-average achievement leads to higher academic self-concepts (Marsh, 1984b). These terms are purely descriptive, but more "meaningful" terms are sometimes used to describe assimilation (e.g. reflected glory, labeling, and identification) and contrast (e.g., negative social comparison or negative BFLPE). This proliferation of terms creates some ambiguity in that social comparison processes can result in either contrast or assimilation, but the term "social comparison effects" is sometimes used to refer to only contrast effects. For purposes of this chapter, we treat BFLPE and social comparison as generic processes that can result in either (or both) contrast (negative social comparison) effects or assimilation (positive social comparison, reflected glory) effects.

Assimilation and Contrast Effects

Self-concept may be enhanced by membership in groups that are positively valued by an individual (Diener & Fujita, 1997; Tessor, 1988) through basking in the reflected glory of accomplishments or good qualities of other group members. Marsh (1984b, 1987, 1991, 1993; see also Felson, 1984) argued that it would be reasonable for students in academically selective classes to have improved academic self-concepts by virtue of being chosen to be in a highly selective educational program—an assimilation, reflected glory, or labeling effect (e.g., "If I am good enough to be selected to participate in this prestigious program with all these other very smart students, then I must be very smart"). Alternatively, if students use the other students in their academically selective class as a basis of comparison, then participation in academically selective classes should result in lowered academic self-concepts—a contrast or negative BFLPE effect (e.g., there are a lot of students better than I am so I must not be as good as I thought). Similarly, academically disadvantaged children in special classes with other academically disadvantaged students may have a lower academic self-concept than they would if they were in regular classes because they know that they are in a special class (labeling or assimilation effect). Alternatively, their academic self-concepts might be higher because they compare themselves with other students with similar academic accomplishments rather than students in regular classes who have higher academic accomplishments (contrast or negative BFLPE). Observed BFLPEs are likely to represent the counterbalancing, net effects of these two opposing processes. This implies that an assimilation (labeling, reflected glory) effect may be operating even though its effects are not so large as the contrast (negative BFLPE) effects, but little research has attempted to disentangle the two effects in BFLPE studies.

McFarland and Buehler (1995) specifically looked at the juxtaposition of the negative BFLPE and the positive reflected glory effects as a paradox, noting that there was surprisingly little work relating individuals' self-appraisals and perceptions of their groups. In a series of laboratory studies using feedback manipulations about individual and group performance, they found that people who feel more strongly about their group membership experience more positive affect when their group does well and more negative affect when their group does poorly. Following from cross-cultural research distinguishing between collectivist and individualist cultures that differ in the way they value social groups, McFarland and Buehler classified multicultural North American university students as coming from collectivist or individualist societies. They found that students from collectivist societies experienced significantly smaller negative BFLPEs than students from individualistic countries. They also noted an asymmetry such that individuals who value group membership can focus on their individual performances when they do well or on the performance of their group when they do poorly, thus allowing them to protect their self-concept. Based on their findings, they proposed a revision to the BFLPE metaphor: "Although everyone feels good about being a big fish in a little pond, not everyone feels bad about being a little fish in a big pond" (p. 1068).

Domain Specificity

Consistent with the growing recognition of the multidimensionality of self-concept and the need to distinguish between academic and nonacademic components of self-concept (Marsh et al., 1988; Marsh & Hattie, 1996), the BFLPE is very specific to academic self-concept. Marsh and Parker (1984; Marsh, 1987) showed that there were large negative BFLPEs for academic self-concept, but little or no BFLPEs on general self-concept or self-esteem. Marsh, Chessor, Craven, and Roche (1995) reported two studies of the effects of participation in gifted and talented programs on different components of self-concept over time and in relation to a matched comparison group. There was clear evidence for negative BFLPEs in that academic self-concept in the gifted and talented programs declined over time and in relation to the comparison group. These BFLPEs were consistently large for math, verbal, and academic self-concepts, but were small and largely nonsignificant for four nonacademic self-concepts and for general esteem. This domain specificity is illustrated even more dramatically in two studies (Marsh, 1990b, 1994) of the differential effects of school-average verbal and math achievement on math and verbal self-concepts.

DIFFERENTIAL EFFECTS OF SCHOOL-AVERAGE VERBAL AND MATH ACHIEVEMENTS: DOMAIN SPECIFICITY OF THE BFLPE

Marsh (1990c, 1994) tested the BFLPE model based on separate measures of math and verbal constructs. He began with separate analyses of the BFLPE for math self-concept (based on math achievement, school-average math achievement, and math self-concept) and corresponding model of verbal self-concept based on verbal constructs. When math constructs were considered, the effect of math achievement on math self-concept was substantial and positive (.46), whereas the effect of school-average mathematics ability was smaller and negative (–.14). Being mathematically able led to a higher math self-concept, but attending a high school where the other students are more mathematically able led to lower math self-concepts. A similar pattern of results was evident for the verbal self-concept model based on the effects of prior reading achievement and school-average reading achievement.

Marsh (1990c, 1994) then combined all the math and verbal constructs into a single BFLPE model. This model combined tests of the BFLPE considered separately for math and English self-concepts, but also provided a test of the internal/external (I/E) frame-of-reference model (see Marsh, 1986; Marsh et al., 1988). According to the I/E model, students use their relative accomplishments in their different school subjects as a basis for forming academic self-concepts in each school subject. Thus, for example, a student who is particularly good at mathematics will have a better math self-concept but a lower verbal self-concept. According to the I/E model, any variable that has a positive effect on math self-concept is likely to have a smaller, negative effect on verbal self-concept and vice versa.

Consistent with the BFLPE, the effects of school-average mathematics achievement on math self-concept were negative. A similar pattern of results is observed for English self-concept. What is new in this model was the content specificity of the BFLPE. School-average mathematics achievement had a negative effect on mathematics self-concept, but a smaller, positive effect on English self-concept. Conversely, school-average English achievement had a negative effect on English self-concept but a slight, positive effect on math self-concept. These results are certainly consistent with the content specificity of academic self-concepts that is an overarching principle of these studies.

It is interesting to note that school-average mathematics, despite its negative effect on math self-concept, had a slightly positive effect on English self-concept. That is, "If I attend a high school where the other students are mathematical geniuses, then my math self-concept will suffer but my verbal self-concept might be a little higher." The converse set of effects was observed for school-average verbal achievement. This finding is consistent with the general observation that a variable that positively affects mathematics self-concept tends to have a negative effect on verbal self-concept, and vice versa. This pattern of counterbalancing effects apparently reflects the internal comparison (ipsative) process embodied in the I/E model.

It should be noted that in the actual analyses, school-average achievements in verbal and mathematics were correlated highly. Because the school contexts in relation to these two subject areas were correlated highly, the amount of variance that could be explained by these differences was limited. For this reason, the results of this analysis might have greater theoretical significance than practical implications. This similarity in the mathematics and verbal contexts represents the natural state of affairs and it would be difficult to find schools where school-average mathematics achievement was high and school-average verbal achievement was low. If, however, this natural state of affairs was altered by specifically selecting students who were gifted mathematically without regard to their verbal abilities, for example, then the effects demonstrated here would have considerable practical significance. This is relevant, because selective high schools are increasingly specializing in particular areas of accomplishment (e.g., English, mathematics, science, performing arts).

EMPIRICAL SUPPORT FOR THE BFLPE

Empirical support for the BFLPE comes from numerous studies (e.g., Marsh, 1984a, 1984b, 1987, 1994; Marsh & Craven, 1994, 1997; Marsh & Parker, 1984) based on a variety of different experimental/analytical approaches. Marsh and Parker (1984) sampled sixth-grade classes from high and low SES areas in the same geographical area. The two samples differed substantially in terms of reading achievement and IQ scores. In path models of the relations among achievement, school-average ability and responses to the Self-Description Questionnaire—I (SDQI; Marsh, 1990d), the direct effect of school-average ability on academic self-concept was negative in models that controlled for individual achievement. In contrast, the effects of individual and school-average achievement were not statistically significant for nonacademic self-concept. Hence, the results provided an early demonstration of the BFLPE and its specificity to academic components of self-concept.

In an American study based on 87 high schools, Marsh (1987; see also Bachman & O'Malley, 1986) found that the effects of school-average ability on academic self-concept were negative, whereas the effects of school-average SES on academic self-concept were negligible. He also found that African American students, particularly those in segregated schools, did not differ substantially from Caucasian students in terms of academic self-concept even though there were substantial differences in terms of standardized achievement test scores. Whereas this pattern might suggest that the academic self-concept responses were "culturally biased," this is exactly the pattern predicted to occur in the BFLPE. African Americans had academic ability test scores that were below average, but—particularly in the segregated schools—compared themselves to classmates who also had below-average test scores. Thus, while their academic self-concepts were somewhat below average (due perhaps to self-perceptions that were independent of the immediate school context), they were not nearly as low as standardized achievement test scores would suggest.

The results of Marsh's (1987) analysis also clarified the distinction between academic ability and grade-point average (GPA), their respective influences on self-concept, and how this influenced the BFLPE. The 87 schools in the study differed substantially in terms of school-average academic ability, but not school-average GPA. Schools "graded on a curve" so that grade distributions were similar from one school to the next even though academic ability levels differed substantially. Hence, equally able students have lower GPAs in high-ability schools than in low-ability schools. Marsh demonstrated that this frame-of-reference effect influencing GPA was separate from, but contributed to, the BFLPE on academic self-concept. In further analysis of this same data, Marsh and Rowe (1996) replicated the finding using a multilevel modeling approach and demonstrated that the BFLPE generalized across all levels of initial ability level, including the very brightest students.

Sociologists studying school-context effects have found that school-average ability and particularly school-average SES are related to educational and occupational aspirations or attainments. In a review of this largely American literature, Alwin and Otto (1977) reported that school-average ability was negatively related to aspirations, whereas school-average SES tended to be positively associated with aspirations.

Rogers, Smith, and Coleman (1978) ranked a group of children in terms of academic achievement relative to their own classroom and academic achievement across the sample. They found that the within-classroom rankings were correlated more highly with self-concept than scores normed in relation to the entire sample.

Schwarzer, Jerusalem, and Lange (1983; see also Jerusalem, 1984) examined the self-concepts of West German students who moved from nonselective, heterogeneous primary schools to secondary schools that were streamed on the basis of academic achievement. At the transition point, students selected to enter the high-ability schools had substantially higher academic self-concepts than those entering the low-ability schools. However, by the end of the first year in the new schools, no differences in academic self-concepts for the two groups were present. Path analyses indicated that the direct influence of school type on academic self-concept was negative. The most able students in the low-ability schools were less able but had much higher academic self-concepts than the least able children in the high-ability schools.

Most research into the BFLPE has examined between-school grouping practices in which students attend mixed-ability schools or academically segregated schools. An interesting extension of this research is to look at within-school ability grouping practices. In a meta-analysis of the effect of ability grouping on self-concept, Kulik (1985; see also Kulik & Kulik, 1982; Marsh, 1984a) compared children in streamed and unstreamed classes. Kulik and Kulik (1982) initially reported that self-concepts did not differ on average in schools with and without ability groupings. Marsh (1984a) countered that whereas the average self-concept (average across all the different ability groupings) might not differ as a function of streaming practices, he predicted ability streaming would result in lower self-concept for students in high-ability streams (compared to equally able students in unstreamed classes) and higher self-concepts for students in low-ability streams. In a followup analysis of the initial 1982 meta-analysis, Kulik (1985) confirmed Marsh's predictions based on the BFLPE, in that high-ability students tended to have lower self-concepts, and low-ability students higher self-concepts when placed in streamed classes.

Brookover (1989) examined frame-of-reference effects on academic self-concept from the perspective of the extent to which students in different schools were streamed according to ability. In schools with ability streaming, low-ability students tended to be placed in classes with other low-ability students and high-ability students tended to be placed in classes with other high-ability students. To the extent that students use other students within their class as a frame of reference, low-ability students in streamed classes should have higher academic self-concepts (because they compare themselves primarily to other low-ability students) than low-ability students in unstreamed classes. High-ability students in streamed classes, however, should have lower academic self-concepts (because they compare themselves primarily to other high-ability students) than high-ability students in unstreamed classes. Thus, streaming should tend to increase the academic self-concepts of low-ability students and decrease the academic self-concepts of high-ability students. Consistent with these predictions, Brookover found that the academic self-concepts were much less variable in schools that streamed their classes.

Ireson, Hallam, and Plewis (2001) pursued a somewhat different study of within-school grouping practices that provided a more direct extension of BFLPE predictions based on between-school grouping practices. They evaluated the effects of within-school streaming for English, mathematics, and science for Year 9 students (age 13–14) from 45 comprehensive high schools. For English self-concept, the results were consistent with the BFLPE. The most able students in English had lower English self-concepts in schools with greater amounts of streaming, whereas the least able students in English had higher English self-concepts in schools with greater amounts of streaming. This follows in that the best English students in highly streamed schools attended classes with other students who were also very able in English. Hence, they tended to compare themselves with other students who were also very good English students, which resulted in a lower English self-concept. In contrast, the best English students in schools with no streaming attended classes with students who had a mixture of English abilities. Hence, they were more likely to be one of the top students in their (mixed-ability) English classes, which resulted in a higher English self-concept. Interestingly, the results of streaming in mathematics and science were not statistically significant. However, their results also indicated that variation in streaming practices was greater in English classes than science and particularly mathematics. For example, only 5 of 45 schools had mixed-ability mathematics classes in Year 9, whereas 20 or 45 schools had mixed-ability English classes. Because there was limited variation in streaming practices in mathematics, it is not surprising that this relatively weak streaming intervention had little effect. Hence, support for the BFLPE was strongest in the school subject (English) in which the streaming intervention was strongest.

Consistent with the BFLPE, Reuman (1989) found that within-school (between-class) ability grouping produced lower academic self-concepts for high-ability children and higher academic self-concepts for low-ability children. Reuman asked students if they would compare their test scores with those of a classmate and whether the selected classmate was perceived to be more or less able than they were. Consistent with the social comparison process, between-class ability grouping was associated with systematic differences in the perceived ability of the comparison classmate; high-ability children were more likely to select classmates with higher abilities than their own and low-ability children were more likely to select classmates with lower abilities than their own. These results support the role of social comparison processes in mediating the effects of ability grouping.

Zeidner and Schleyer (1999) tested the BFLPE in a large-scale study based on a nationally representative sample ($N = 1020$) of Israeli gifted students participating in either special homogenous classes for the gifted or mixed-ability classes. Path analyses indicated that gifted students in mixed-ability classes evidenced markedly higher academic self-concepts, lower anxiety, and higher school grades than gifted students in specialized classes.

Davis (1966) suggested a model similar to the BFLPE in a study of career decisions of American college students. Davis sought support for a theoretical explanation of why the academic quality of a college had so little effect on career choice. Expanding the educational policy implications of his research, Davis concluded: "Counselors and parents might well consider the drawbacks as well as the advantages of sending a boy to a 'fine' college, if, when doing so, it is fairly certain that he will end up in the bottom ranks of his graduating class. The aphorism 'It is better to be a big frog in a small pond than a small frog in a big pond' is not perfect advice but it is not trivial" (p. 31). Such advice may also be relevant for evaluating the likely impact of attending academically selective high schools.

SO WHAT IF STUDENTS HAVE LOWER SELF-CONCEPT IN ACADEMICALLY SELECTIVE SCHOOLS?

The results of the BFLPE are very important for understanding the formation of academic self-concept and testing frame-of-reference models. However, classroom teachers, policymakers, and particularly parents might be prompted to ask, "So what?" What are the consequences of attending high-ability schools on other academic outcomes and how are these related to academic self-concept? In order to address these issues, Marsh (1991) considered the influence of school-average ability on a much wider array of outcomes and the role of academic self-concept and educational aspirations formed early in high school as mediators of the effects of school-average ability on subsequent outcomes. The High School and Beyond data were ideal for this purpose because the database is very large (1,000 randomly selected high schools and approximately 30 randomly selected students from each school), is nationally representative of the United States, and contains longitudinal data, consisting of responses by the same high school students when they were sophomores (T1), seniors (T2), and two years after normal graduation from high school (T3). The major components of the path analysis in this research were (a) individual-level and school-average measures of academic ability (a battery of standardized tests) and SES; (b) self-concept (academic and general), academic choice behavior (taking advanced coursework), academic effort (time spent on homework and class preparation), school grades (GPA), educational aspirations, and occupational aspirations measured at T1 and T2; and (c) college attendance, educational aspirations, and occupational aspirations at T3.

Although the path model including all these outcome variables was complicated, the results were easy to summarize. The effects of school-average ability were negative for almost all of the T1, T2, and T3 outcomes; 15 of the 17 relations were significantly negative and 2 were not statistically significant. Even though it might be argued that most of the important outcome variables in educational research were considered in this study, the effect of school-average ability was not positive for a single outcome.

School-average ability most negatively affected academic self-concept as in the BFLPE studies and educational aspirations as in the school-context studies. School-average ability also negatively affected general self-concept, coursework selection, school grades, standardized test scores, occupational aspirations, and subsequent college attendance.

Marsh (1991) also evaluated process variables that might mediate the subsequent negative effects of school-average ability. Controlling T1 academic self-concept and T1 educational aspirations substantially reduced the negative effects of school-average ability at T2 and T3. This supported their proposed role as mediating variables. Even after controlling all T1 outcomes, however, school-average ability negatively affected 7 of 11 outcomes at T2 and T3. This demonstrated that school-average ability continued to affect negatively T2 and T3 outcomes beyond its already substantial negative effects at T1. The largest of these negative effects was for T2 academic self-concept. When T2 academic self-concept was also controlled, the remaining school-average ability effects were less negative. This study demonstrated the importance of academic self-concept as both a proximal outcome and a mediating variable that facilitated the attainment of more distal outcomes.

In summary, equally able students attending higher-ability high schools were likely to select less-demanding coursework and to have lower academic self-concepts, lower GPAs, lower educational aspirations, and lower occupational aspirations in both their sophomore and senior years of high school. Attending higher-ability schools also negatively affected standardized test scores in the senior year of high school and subsequent college attendance, although these effects were smaller. For many senior year and post-secondary outcomes, there were statistically significant negative effects of school-average ability beyond those that could be explained in terms of sophomore outcomes. This implies that there were new, additional negative effects of school-average ability during the last two years of high school beyond the already substantial negative effects found early in high school. These results were consistent with previous research but were more compelling because of the High School and Beyond's large sample size, diversity of academic outcomes, and longitudinal nature.

It was important to evaluate the effect of school-average ability after controlling SES and academic ability. Whereas a disproportionate number of high-achieving students come from higher-ability schools, it was also apparent that a substantial proportion of students attending such schools were not achieving academic outcomes commensurate with their initial academic ability. Using an input–output analogy, the value added by higher-ability schools was negative compared to that of the lower-ability schools. Thus, the academic outcomes produced by higher-ability schools were not as good overall as would be expected on the basis of the quality of students who attend these schools. It is also important, however, to emphasize that the sizes of these negative effects of school-average ability were typically small and represented an average across 1,000 high schools and many thousands of students. Hence, there will be some higher-ability schools that produce academic outcomes commensurate with the quality of their higher-ability students and some students who will be advantaged by attending such higher-ability schools. Nevertheless, it is unjustified to assume that higher-ability schools necessarily will advantage students. Attending higher-ability schools apparently disadvantages many students.

UNRAVELING EDUCATION ENIGMAS: NEW APPLICATIONS OF THE BFLPE FOR SPECIAL POPULATIONS OF ACADEMICALLY GIFTED AND DISADVANTAGED STUDENTS

Recent research expanding the scope and application of BFLPE theoretical predictions has begun to unravel some important, enduring issues in educational contexts. We now summarize some new developments of BFLPE research that greatly expands the scope of theoretical and practical implications. BFLPE studies have focused on the negative effects on academic self-concept of attending schools where the school-average ability level is high based on de facto segregation (e.g., the neighborhood where a student lives). In the theoretical basis underpinning the BFLPE, we emphasized that the observed effects are the net effects of two counterbalancing effects: contrast effects (negative social comparison effects or negative BFLPEs) and assimilation effects (labeling or reflected glory effects). However, BFLPE studies have not actually attempted to separate these two effects. This separation has important educational implications because critical policy decisions have been based on the assumption that labeling effects generated by specialized educational settings have important educational implications for students at both extremes of the special education spectrum. Based in part on a labeling theory rationale, special educators working in the gifted and talented (G&T) area (e.g., Gross, 1993) argue that very bright students will have higher self-concepts if they participate in full-time G&T classes. Labeling theory has had even more profound implications for academically disadvantaged students. Much of the theoretical rationale for the worldwide phenomena of mainstreaming these low-achieving students is that they will be forever labeled as slow learners if they are placed in special classes with other slow learners. However, both these claims imply that the net BFLPE is a positive assimilation effect rather than the negative contrast effects observed in earlier research. Such claims also run counter to a growing body of research evidence based on the theoretical underpinnings of the BFLPE described earlier.

Special Programs for Gifted and Talented (G&T) Students: The Big Fish Strikes Again

A major concern facing G&T researchers, policymakers, and practitioners is how best to educate G&T students. Debate has focused on whether full-time special programs best meet the needs of G&T students with educators supporting contradictory positions largely based on philosophical perspectives rather than theory and sound empirical research. Some educators advocate that special G&T programs best meet the needs of these students and therefore foster their full potential. These educators claim that grouping and segregating G&T students ensures academic achievement is maximized by an enriched intellectual environment and curriculum. Others are convinced that individualized instruction in the context of the regular classroom best meets the needs of G&T students.

In recent years Australia has experienced a substantial growth in the numbers of both G&T primary classes and secondary selective schools. This growth reflects strong parental interest in, and political support for, special educational settings for academically able students. Several early studies were undertaken by the NSW government to evaluate support for special educational provisions for G&T students. Sampson (1969) matched students in regular classes (who had declined offers to participate in specialized G&T classes) with students who participated in G&T classes in Years 5 and 6 (the last two years of primary school), on the basis of information collected in Year 4. He found that the two groups did not differ significantly in subsequent Commonwealth Secondary Scholarship Examinations scores, Higher School Certificate scores, or school persistence. However, regular-class students performed significantly better than G&T class students on the aggregate School Certificate in Year 10, although this difference occurred primarily with boys. In subsequent research, Sampson (1977) compared a random sample of 240 students from eight selective high schools and a comparison group of comprehensive high school students matched on the basis of gender, age, socio-economic status, IQ, and prior achievement. He found that there were no statistically significant differences between selective and comprehensive high school students on subsequent school certificate scores, higher school certificate scores, or school retention rates. This result was consistent across initial ability levels and for boys and girls. This research contributed to a ministerial report recommending that selective schools should be phased out, but this recommendation was not enacted, due in part to parental pressure to maintain these schools. In both studies, Sampson emphasized that he was unable to consider affective variables (e.g., self-concept) that he suggested might be enhanced by attending selective schools.

Despite this early research providing no support for selective schooling in Australia, references to well-established research findings are often absent from education policy rationales. The Commonwealth Schools Commission (1981, p. 47) seminar on the education of G&T students found that "the paucity of Australian research and the absence of any real attempt to harness and interpret overseas research . . . means that hypotheses are being stated and programmes are being developed within a data base vacuum." In part this was due to the dearth of educational research in Australia and elsewhere that systematically evaluates the different approaches to the education of G&T students, a problem identified a decade ago (e.g. Fox & Washington, 1985) and, more recently (e.g., Craven, Marsh, & Print, 2000; Goldring, 1990; Hoge & Renzulli, 1993; Marsh et al., 1995; Marsh & Craven, 1994, 1997), is still unresolved. Selective education settings are often assumed to enhance G&T students' self-concepts, yet research has typically not evaluated the impact of selective schools on psychological variables. Despite these weaknesses in current G&T research, "conventional wisdom" and some researchers assume that grouping G&T children together will enrich their education more fully than the regular classroom setting.

Gross (1992; see also Gross, 1993), in a study of profoundly gifted children, argued that "It might be anticipated that exceptionally gifted children who have been radically accelerated would score high on the index of academic self-esteem. By contrast, they display positive but modest scores, between the mean for their age groups and .7 of a standard deviation above . . . interestingly, it is the children who have not been radically accelerated whose academic self-esteem is unusually inflated" (p. 97). Although Gross argued that students in nonaccelerated settings have "inflated" academic self-concepts, her results support the BFLPE. Despite being 4 *SDs* above the mean IQ, radically accelerated children have "radically deflated" academic self-concepts that are only slightly above average because they compare their academic skills with those of their older, more able classmates. In contrast, the nonaccelerated children have realistically high academic self-concepts because they compare their abilities with those students from a normal range of abilities. Thus, radical acceleration is likely to produce substantial declines in academic self-concept that are consistent with the BFLPE. The implication of Gross's argument is that it is somehow bad for gifted children to have academic self-concepts commensurate with their high levels of academic achievement and good for them to experience a substantial decline in academic self-concept, but she provided no evidence in support of this implication.

In contrast to proponents of G&T classes and selective high schools, social comparison and BFLPE research (e.g., Coleman & Fults, 1985; Craven & Marsh, 1997; Hoge & Renzulli, 1993; Marsh, 1987, 1991, 1993; Marsh & Parker, 1984; Reuman, 1989; Rogers, 1979; Zeidner & Schleyer, 1999) supports predictions that participation in high ability selective classes or schools leads to declines in academic self-concept. In order to pursue this issue more fully, Marsh and colleagues (1995; see also Craven, Marsh, & Print, 2000) designed two studies to test BFLPE predictions about the effects of participation in full-time G&T primary school classes over time and in relation to matched students attending mixed-ability classes. A major emphasis of their research was on the differential effects on academic and nonacademic self-concepts, and also on the effects of initial ability levels. In both studies, G&T students attending a G&T class were matched to students of equal ability who attended mixed-ability classes. In both Study 1 and Study 2, students in the G&T program experienced significant declines in three domains of academic self-concept over time and in relation to matched comparison students. In both studies this general pattern of results was reasonably consistent across gender, age, and initial ability. A critical feature of these studies was a multidimensional perspective of self-concept. Consistent with a priori predictions based on theory and previous research, participation in G&T programs had a negative effect on academic self-concept and no effect on nonacademic self-concept. This result is important, because most previous G&T research has been based on a unidimensional perspective of self-concept and relied on a single self-concept score that confounded differences between academic and nonacademic self-concept.

In Study 2, measures were collected from only two occasions. Whereas there was a decline in the academic self-concepts of the G&T students across these two occasions, there was no way to determine when the decline occurred. In Study 1, however, measures were collected on three occasions. Here the results showed that there were declines between the first two occasions, but there were new, additional declines between the last two occasions. Hence, the BFLPE was not a short-term adjustment effect but continued to grow larger over the first year in the G&T setting.

Taken together, the results above suggest that specialized educational settings for G&T students have an adverse impact on academic self-concept. This is problematic in that the attainment of a positive academic self-concept has been demonstrated in longitudinal panel studies (Marsh, 1990a; Marsh, Byrne, & Yeung, 1999) to have a causal impact on coursework selection, educational aspirations, and subsequent academic achievement. Marsh and Craven (1997), on the basis of a review of aspects of this research, noted that "short-term gains in achievement are unlikely to be maintained unless there are corresponding gains in academic self-concept" and concluded that "enhancing a child's academic self-concept is not only a desirable goal but is likely to result in improved academic achievement as well" (p. 155). These findings have important implications for educational policy in that placing G&T students in specialized educational settings may be counterproductive if the goal of the educational program is to maximize academic self-concept and achievement.

Implications for Learning-Disabled (LD) and Mildly Intellectually Disabled (IM) Students.

The movement toward the inclusion of academically disadvantaged students in regular classrooms is also a contentious educational issue, which has generated much debate. Few topics in the field of special education elicit such a broad range of emotions and opinions. Labeling theory suggests that placing academically disadvantaged students in special classes with other low-achieving students will lead to lower self-concept and create a long-lasting stigmatization. On the basis of this theoretical argument, there has been widespread support for the practice of integrating academically disadvantaged students into regular classrooms (i.e., "mainstreaming"). In contrast, predictions based on BFLPE research contradict labeling theory in that academically disadvantaged students will have higher self-concepts when grouped with other academically disadvantaged students (compared to similarly disadvantaged students in regular classroom settings). In a review of relevant research, Marsh and Johnston (1993) reported that moving academically disadvantaged students from special classes into regular, mixed-ability classes was likely to result in lower academic self-concepts for academically disadvantaged students. This result is consistent with social comparison theory and the negative BFLPE in that the average ability level of students in the mixed-ability classes is higher than in special classes for academically disadvantaged students. Thus, academically disadvantaged students are likely to feel less academically able in comparison with nondisadvantaged students in regular classrooms than with other academically disadvantaged students in special classes. Burns's (1982) review of this literature also led him to conclude that placement of academically disadvantaged students in special schools resulted in an improvement in self-concept and that self-concept was positively related to the length of time academically disadvantaged students spent in special schools. He interpreted these results as favoring social comparison theory, but also noted that part of the problem may be that special schools do not prepare students for integration into mainstream society.

In a study of academically disadvantaged children, Strang, Smith, and Rogers (1978) tested the self-concepts of children who attended some classes with other disadvantaged children and other classes with nondisadvantaged children. Academically disadvantaged children were assigned randomly to experimental and control groups. Students in the experimental group were given a treatment to enhance the saliency of their membership in the regular classrooms. This led to lower self-concepts for students in the experimental group than those in the randomly assigned control group.

Chapman (1988) conducted a meta-analysis of studies of learning-disabled (LD) children's self-concepts. Of particular relevance to this chapter was his comparison of LD students who were (a) completely segregated in special classes, (b) partially segregated for some work and partially integrated in regular classes with non-LD students, and (c) "unplaced" in completely integrated settings (i.e., LD students in regular classes who were not receiving LD remedial assistance). The inclusion of the unplaced classification is particularly important in that labeling theory predicts that these are the least likely to be stigmatized and, therefore, have the highest self-concepts. In contrast, BFLPE predicts that these children should have the lowest self-concepts. Whereas LD children in all three settings had poorer self-concepts than did non-LD children, the setting did make a difference, for general self-concept students in fully segregated and partially segregated settings did not differ from each other but had better self-concepts than did unplaced LD students in regular classrooms. For academic self-concept, fully segregated children had higher self-concepts than partially segregated students and both groups had substantially better self-concepts than unplaced LD students. The decrement associated with being an unplaced LD student in regular classrooms was substantially larger for academic self-concept than for general self-concept. These results support social comparison theory, but are complicated by the potential confounding between the type of setting and the amount of special assistance LD students received in the different settings. LD students apparently have substantially lower self-concepts than do non-LD students, and these deficits were particularly large for academic self-concept. These deficits, however, were substantially reduced if LD students were placed in fully segregated classes with other LD students. There was clear evidence that this strategy increased the academic self-concepts of LD students and there was no evidence to suggest that this strategy had any systematic effect on academic achievement. These results are important because they support social comparison theory and contradict predictions from labeling theory that has been used to argue against segregated classes.

Recent research by Tracey and Marsh (2000) involving children with mild intellectual disabilities (IM) is particularly relevant. They began with a measurement perspective. Historically, they argued, special educators have tended to treat self-concept as a unidimensional, global construct represented by a single score. Although much recent research argues against this perspective in normal populations, research in the special education area has not clearly supported the multidimensionality of self-concept for students with learning disabilities. For example, in her review of self-concept instruments, Byrne (1996b; see also Byrne, 1996a) emphasized that "a search of the literature revealed such instrumentation to be disappointingly sparse and serves to highlight this critical void in the availability of self-concept measures for special populations" (p. 221). Tracey and Marsh, however, argued that this apparent failure to support the multidimensionality of self-concept in responses by academically disadvantaged children probably reflected a failure to develop appropriate multidimensional instruments and apply appropriate measurement procedures. In support of this contention, they cited research based on the individualized administration form of the Self Description Questionnaire—I (SDQI-IA; Marsh & Craven, 1997; Marsh, Craven, & Debus, 1998), which provides clear support for the multidimensionality of self-concept responses by children as young as 5 years of age.

Tracey and Marsh (2000) evaluated the individualized administration approach with the SDQI for a sample of 211 IM students enrolled in Grades 2–6. These students had previously been identified as having a mild intellectual disability (i.e., an IQ of 56 to 75 based on an individually administered test of intelligence and impairment in adaptive functioning). Confirmatory factor analysis clearly identified all eight factors that the SDQI was designed to measure and resulted in a good fit to the data. Reliability estimates for the eight factors were generally adequate (mean alpha of .85) for the total sample and for separate analyses of responses by younger and by older students. Importantly, this study was apparently the first to find support for reliable, multidimensional self-concept responses for this special population of students.

On the basis of the students' current educational placement, Tracey and Marsh (2000) compared two groups of IM students: Group 1 comprised 98 students who were enrolled full time in regular classes; Group 2 comprised 113 students who were enrolled full time in an IM support unit. Labeling theory predicts that students in regular classroom placements will have higher self-concepts. In contrast, social comparison theory and the BFLPE predicts that students in IM support units will have higher self-concepts and that these differences will be limited primarily to the three academic scales (math, verbal, and school self-concepts) of the SDQI. The results demonstrated that students in the two placement settings differed significantly on several dimensions of self-concept. Consistent with BFLPE predictions, students in special IM classes had significantly higher self-concepts for all three academic scales (reading, math, school). In addition, however, these IM students had significantly higher peer self-concepts and significantly higher general self-concepts. The two groups did not differ significantly for the remaining three nonacademic self-concepts (parents, physical ability, physical appearance). The results are clearly inconsistent with predictions based on labeling theory. The results for the academic self-concept scales and, perhaps, the general self-concept scales are consistent with predictions based on BFLPE. The negative effects of inclusion on peer self-concept, although not predicted a priori on the basis of BFLPE research, are understandable. Despite the rhetoric of inclusion, it is apparent that IM children who were in regular classrooms not only suffered lower academic self-concepts but they also apparently felt excluded socially.

It should be noted that Tracey and Marsh's (2000) results are based upon a cross-sectional design in which two intact groups are directly compared. Although potential counterexplanations based on nonequivalent groups are always worrisome, the direction of such a bias is likely to run counter to predictions of social comparison theory. Hence, to the extent that there were preexisting differences between the two groups, IM students in regular classes were likely to be more academically competent than those in the IM support units. From this perspective, these results are likely to be conservative and underestimate the negative effects associated with placing IM students in regular classes.

In summary, current research supports the BFLPE and social comparison theory and contradicts the labeling theory upon which current special education philosophy is currently based. These results challenge special education policymakers and practitioners to recognize that inclusion of IM students in regular classrooms is likely to result in lower academic self-concepts. Hence, appropriate strategies are needed to counter this negative effect of inclusion rather than accepting the largely unsupported inference from labeling theory that the effects of inclusion on self-concept are positive.

CROSS-CULTURAL AND CROSS-NATIONAL COMPARISONS: TESTING THE GENERALIZABILITY OF THE BFLPE AND EXTENDING THE THEORY

Sue (1999), along with many others, argues that psychological research has not taken sufficient advantage of cross-cultural comparisons that allow researchers to test the external validity of their interpretations, as well as to gain insights about the applicability of their theories and models. Tests of the cross-cultural support for predictions from a theoretical model developed in one culture to another culture provide an important basis for testing this generalizability. Theoretical models posit the cognitive basis that students use to determine appropriate frames of reference in the formation of their academic self-concepts. Because such frame-of-reference effects might be specific to particular cultural settings, it is useful to test the generalizability of predictions based on one culture to different cultures.

Importantly, previous tests of the BFLPE have been conducted primarily in Western countries and, typically, in those where the native language is English. In this respect, the results of two recent investigations—based on large, representative samples of East and West German students (Marsh, Koeller, & Baumart, in press) and Hong Kong students (Marsh, Kong, & Hau, 2000)—represents an important test of the cross-cultural generalizability of predictions based on the BFLPE.

REUNIFICATION OF EAST AND WEST GERMAN SCHOOL SYSTEMS: A UNIQUE TEST OF THE BIG FISH–LITTLE POND EFFECT

In 1991 East and West German students experienced a remarkable social experiment in which the very different school systems of the former East Germany and West Germany were reunified. The Marsh, Koeller, and Baumart (in press) study is part of a large longitudinal project conducted by the Max Planck Institute for Human Development designed to evaluate the implications of the reunification of the two school systems. The former East German system differed from the former West German system and the newly reunified system in two ways that were particularly important to social comparison processes in the formation of academic self-concept.

First, the former East German students had explicitly not been grouped into schools or classes according to their achievement levels, whereas the former West German students had attended schools based largely on their achievement levels for the two years prior to the reunification. Hence, it was predicted that the BFLPE should be initially larger for the West Germans at the start of the first year after the reunification. This difference in the size of the BFLPE was also predicted to be much smaller by the end of the first school year following reunification.

Second, the former East German system placed considerably more emphasis on highly competitive, social comparison processes that are likely to undermine academic self-concept. Hence, the self-concepts of former East German students were predicted to be lower overall than those of the former West German students.

Description of the Study

The sample consisted of large representative samples of students (2,778 students, 161 classrooms) from the former East and West German education systems who completed surveys on three occasions in the first year after the reunification of the German school system following the fall of the Berlin Wall. Three waves of math self-concept responses were collected at the start of 7th grade (T1, the first month of the newly reunified school system), at the middle of 7th grade (T2), and at the end of 7th grade (T3). A math achievement test derived from prior research was administered at T1. Statistical analyses consisted of multilevel models relating individual and classroom variables to self-concept. The researchers began by evaluating the effects of the major substantive constructs (individual student achievement, class-average achievement, and region (East versus West Germany) to academic self-concept separately at each occasion. Then they evaluated the effect of these variables on T2 self-concept controlling for T1 self-concept, and on T3 self-concept controlling for T1 and T2 self-concept, in order to evaluate how change in self-concept over time was related to the substantive constructs.

Results

The most basic test of the BFLPE consisted of an evaluation of the combined effects of individual achievement and class-average achievement on T1 math self-concept. Social comparison theory predicts that the effect of class-average achievement should be negative (i.e., the negative BFLPE). Individual student achievement based on the standardized mathematics test had a positive effect on math self-concept (standardized path coefficient of .34), whereas class-average math achievement had a negative effect on math self-concept (–.17).

Region (East versus West Germany) was a central variable in terms of evaluating the effects of this critical social experiment—the reunification of the two former school systems—on the formation of self-concept. Consistent with predictions based on school policies emphasizing social comparison and a unitary system in the former East German school system, East German T1 math self-concepts were significantly lower than those of West German students (–.11). Furthermore, also consistent with a priori predictions, there was a statistically significant interaction between region and class-average achievement; the BFLPE at the start of the first year after the reunification was more negative for West German students (who had already been tracked according to achievement in the previous two years) than for East German students (who were attending academically differentiated schools for the first time). Hence, there were both main and interaction effects associated with region. Overall, initial levels of self-concept were lower in East Germany (the main effect). However, the negative effect of class-average achievement on self-concept was smaller for East German students (the interaction effect). The BFLPE was also smaller for East German students at T1.

There was a substantively important change over time in the pattern of statistically significant effects. At T1 and, to a slightly lesser extent at T2, the negative effect of class-average achievement was more negative for West German than East German students. This is consistent with a priori predictions, because East Germans came from a system in which there was a strong policy against segregating students according to achievement levels, whereas for the previous two years the West Germans in this sample had attended schools that differed substantially in terms of school-average ability. In contrast to T1 and T2 but still consistent with a priori predictions, the region x class-average achievement interaction was not statistically significant at T3. By the end of the school year the frame of reference effects associated with the newly reunified school system overshadowed those associated with the former East German system, at least in terms of the BFLPE.

Discussion and Implications

History may view the reunification of East and West Germany as one of the most important social interventions in the 20th century, and these effects were particularly profound for the German education system. Based on these cultural differences in the two school systems, the authors predicted what differences in the formation of academic self-concept would exist at the onset of the intervention and how these differences would change over the first year of the reunification into a single system based primarily on the West German model. The results of this Marsh and colleagues (in press) study replicate a growing body of BFLPE research, conducted primarily in English-speaking countries, showing that academically selective educational programs have negative effects on academic self-concept. The results are also important in (a) providing strong support for the external validity of the BFLPE in a country where English is not the first language; (b) extending BFLPE research by showing how theoretical predictions vary consistently and logically in two groups (East and West German students) in a large-scale, quasi-experimental study; and (c) demonstrating how educational policy differences at the system level can impact on the academic self-concepts of individual students.

COUNTERBALANCING CONTRAST AND REFLECTED GLORY EFFECTS IN HONG KONG HIGH SCHOOLS: EXTENDING THE THEORETICAL PREDICTIONS OF THE BFLPE

Whereas previous BFLPE research has focused on negative contrast effects, as discussed previously, the BFLPE is hypothesized to be the net effect of two counterbalancing processes: (1) negative contrast effects that have been emphasized and (2) positive, reflected-glory, assimilation effects. Because the BFLPE is consistently negative, the negative contrast effect is apparently much stronger than the positive assimilation effect. Although reflected-glory assimilation effects have a clear theoretical basis, these effects have been implicit and have not been adequately operationalized in BFLPE studies.

To address this issue Marsh, Kong, and Hau (2000) conducted a four-year longitudinal study to evaluate the juxtaposition between assimilation and contrast effects for a large cohort of high schools in Hong Kong. On the one hand, this is the most highly achievement-segregated high school system in the world, which might be expected to lead to more negative contrast effects (i.e., the contextual differences are larger). On the other hand, because the Chinese culture is low on individualism and high on collectivism, Chinese students should be less susceptible to the negative contrast effects due to social comparison processes and should have a greater tendency to value their social group than those in individualistic settings. Consistent with this perspective, face—one's reputation—is of great concern in the Chinese culture and admission to a prestigious high school is highly valued in Hong Kong. Hence, the gain in status and face for oneself and one's family due to attending a prestigious high school (reflected glory, assimilation effect) may possibly overshadow the loss in academic self-concept due to negative contrast resulting from comparisons with high-achieving classmates. Also consistent with this potential deemphasis of social comparison processes, Hong Kong students attribute their examination results more to effort than to ability and concentrate more on their own improvement over time than on comparison with other students as determinants of perceived academic achievement. If Chinese students do value being members of academically selective schools (stronger assimilation effects) and their collective orientation reduces attention to social comparison processes (weaker contrast effects), the net BFLPE may be substantially less negative or close to zero.

Marsh et al. (2000) also incorporated several advantages over most previous BFLPE research in that it (a) specifically included a new measure of perceived school status to infer reflected glory; (b) used particularly good measures of pretest achievement collected prior to the start of high school that were not confounded with true school effects; and (c) employed multilevel modeling that more appropriately disentangled effects due to individual students and schools than inappropriate multiple regression analyses used in most previous research.

Description of the Study

In Hong Kong, at the end of Grade 6, secondary school places for Grade 7 are allocated according to parental choice in the order of merit of students' internal school examination results moderated by public examination performance. Students are largely free to apply to any high school in Hong Kong. The large sample (7,997 students from 44 high schools) was broadly representative of Hong Kong schools. Measures considered in this study were pretest (T0Ach) achievement, standardized achievement tests administered at T1, T2, and T3 (T1Ach, T2Ach, T3Ach), academic self-concept collected at T2 and T3 (T2ASC, T3ASC), and a measure of perceived school status. The survey instrument administered at T2 and T3 (in Grades 8 and 9) included a Chinese translation of the SDQ-II, but for purposes of this investigation, only responses to the academic self-concept scale were considered. The survey materials also contained a School Status scale (e.g., "My school has a good reputation"; "The academic standard of my school is high, many students want to get in"). Statistical analysis consisted of multilevel modeling.

Results: Negative Effects of School-Average Achievement: The BFLPE

Prior to presentation of the multilevel analyses, Marsh et al. (2000) presented some preliminary results to explicate the BFLPE. Academic self-concept was positively correlated with achievement. When both individual and school-average (pretest) achievement were regressed on academic self-concept, the effect of individual achievement was positive (β = .34 for Grade 8, .39 for Grade 9), whereas the effect of school-average achievement was negative (β = –.20 for Grade 8, –.22 for Grade 9). Although comparisons of beta-weights from different studies should be made cautiously, the sizes of these negative effects were comparable to those found in nationally representative samples of U.S. students (e.g., –.21, Marsh, 1987; –.23, Marsh, 1991).

Marsh and colleagues (2000) then conducted a series of multilevel regression analyses in which different predictor variables were related to different outcome variables. The main findings were the juxtaposition of the negative (contrast) effects of school-average ability on academic self-concept and the positive (assimilation, reflected glory) effects of school status on academic self-concept. The negative contrast effect was reflected in the negative effect of school average pretest achievement on academic self-concept after controlling at least individual pretest achievement (T0Ach). In the first set of models, the negative effect of school-average achievement on T2 academic self-concept varied from −.22 (when only T0Ach was controlled) to −.24 (when T0Ach, T1Ach, and T2Ach were controlled). This replicates the negative (contrast) effect found in many other BFLPE studies. Because academic self-concept was measured on two occasions, it was possible to evaluate the additional negative effects of school-average achievement at T3 beyond the negative effects at T2. These were models of self-concept change because the effects of T2 self-concept were partialled out of T3 self-concept. Not surprisingly, the largest effect on T3 self-concept was T2 academic self-concept, although individual academic achievement continued to have a positive effect. Of critical importance, the negative (contrast) effect of school-average achievement on T3 academic self-concept was still significantly negative even after controlling the negative effect of school-average achievement mediated by T2 self-concept. Hence, there were new, additional negative effects of school-average achievement on T3 academic self-concept beyond the negative effects at T2. In summary, the Marsh and colleagues findings provided clear support for the negative BFLPE in Hong Kong high schools. Not only were there negative BFLPEs for T2 and T3 academic self-concept considered separately, but the negative BFLPEs for T3 academic self-concept were larger than those that could be explained by the negative BFLPE already experienced at T2.

Results: Positive Effects of Perceived School Status— Reflected Glory, Assimilation Effects

In subsequent analyses, Marsh et al. (2000) modeled perceived school status as a function of prior achievement, academic self-concept, and school-average achievement. School-average achievement had very large, positive effects (.56 to .60). Perceived status was substantially a function of the school-average ability levels of students attending the school. Interestingly, the researchers found that individual student achievement had a negative effect on perceived school status; better students perceived the status of their school to be lower than did poorer students. Furthermore, the negative effect of student achievement on school status was more negative when school-average achievement was low. This pattern of results is logical and consistent with the researchers' interpretation of reflected glory effects.

Very high performing students performed better than most of the other students in their school—particularly if school-average achievement was low—so they did not experience as much "reflected glory" as did students not doing as well who could "look up to" the best students. Consistent with Buunk and Ybema's (1997) identification-contrast model, when students perceived themselves as being more able than their classmates, there was little benefit in identifying with them. A more effective strategy, at least in terms of maximizing academic self-concept, was to contrast their relatively superior skills with the weaker skills of their classmates. However, when students perceived their academic skills to be weaker than those of their classmates, it was a more effective strategy to identify with the high-perceived status of the school rather than to contrast their poorer skills with the superior skills of their classmates.

Marsh et al. (2000) also added students' perceived status of their school to models of T3 academic self-concept. The critical features of these models were the juxtaposition of the effects of school-average achievement in models that included school status with those in corresponding models that did not include school status. The effect of perceived school status on T3 academic self-concept was positive (.17) and continued to be positive even after controlling for T2 self-concept. In marked contrast, the effects of school-average achievement on T3 academic self-concept were substantially negative (−.33 and −.31). These negative effects of school-average achievement were substantially more negative than in corresponding models that did not include school status. Thus, for example, in corresponding models that differed only in the inclusion of school status, the negative effect of school-average achievement was −.33 when school status was included but only −.23 when school status was excluded. The negative effect of school-average ability was consistently more negative when school status was included in each of the different models that were considered.

In summary, the juxtaposition of the positive reflected glory assimilation effects of school status and the negative contrast effects of school-average achievement supported a priori predictions. Also consistent with a priori predictions, the inclusion of school status into models of academic self-concept resulted in the negative effects of school-average achievement becoming more negative. These suppression effects were consistent with theoretical predictions that the BFLPE is a net effect of the positive assimilation and negative contrast effects. Hence, when the positive assimilation effects are controlled by the inclusion of school status, the negative effect of school-average achievement becomes a more pure measure of the negative contrast effects and school-average achievement effects become more negative.

Discussion

Hong Kong is an ideal setting for testing the generalizability of the BFLPE and extending this research to more fully evaluate the juxtaposition between negative contrast and positive assimilation effects. The contextual differences are larger—because Hong Kong is one of the most highly achievement segregated high school systems in the world—and so the contrast effects should be more negative than in most Western settings. On the other hand, due to collectivist values in this Chinese setting and the value placed on attending a prestigious high school, the typical social comparison processes underlying the negative BFLPE should be weaker, whereas the reflected glory processes may be stronger. Apparently reflecting these counterbalancing predictions, the size of the negative contrast effects in the Marsh et al. (2000) study are comparable to those found in nationally representative U.S. samples (e.g., Marsh, 1987, 1991).

As predicted, the inclusion of perceived school status into the BFLPE model resulted in a positive effect of school status on academic self-concept (the reflected-glory assimilation effect) and an even more negative effect of school-average achievement on academic self-concept (the social comparison contrast effect). More specifically, (a) there was a strong negative contrast effect of school-average achievement on academic self-concept when both individual and school-average pretest achievement (but not perceived school status) were included in the model; (b) the negative effect of school-average achievement became more negative when school status was included in the model, whereas the effect of school status was positive; and (c) even in models of self-concept change there was evidence of new, additional contrast effects on T3 self-concept beyond the substantial negative effects on T2 self-concept, and these additional negative effects also became more negative with the inclusion of perceived school status.

The results of this study imply that attending a school where school-average achievement is high simultaneously results in a more demanding basis of comparison for students within the school to compare their own accomplishments (the negative contrast effects) and a source of pride for students within the school (the positive reflected glory, assimilation effects). By including a separate measure of perceived school status, Marsh et al. (2000) partialled out some of the reflected glory effects associated with school-average achievement so that school-average achievement became a better (less confounded) basis for inferring social comparison contrast effects, leading to a more negative BFLPE. These results also imply that previous research may have underestimated the size of the negative contrast effects.

More clearly than any previous BFLPE research, the Marsh et al. (2000) results differentiated between negative social comparison contrast effects and positive reflected glory assimilation effects that comprise the BFLPE. Whereas this finding is consistent with theoretical predictions and is implicit in previous explanations of the BFLPE, previous research has not operationalized the reflected glory effect. A major focus of BFLPE research has been on the substantively important and surprising implications of this research, undermining the assumed advantages of attending academically selective schools. Although obviously supportive of these well-established concerns, the present investigation provides stronger links between BFLPE and broader areas of social comparison theory.

SUMMARY, CONCLUSIONS, AND IMPLICATIONS

BFLPE research reviewed in this chapter provides an alternative, contradictory perspective to educational policy on the placement of students in special education settings that is being enacted throughout the world. Remarkably, despite the very different issues, this clash between our research and much existing policy exists at both ends of the achievement continuum in that:

1. In gifted education research and policy, there is an increasing trend toward the provision of highly segregated educational settings—special G&T classes and academically selective schools for very bright students. This policy direction is based in part on a labeling theory perspective, suggesting that bright students will have higher self-concepts and experience other psychological benefits from being educated in the company of other academically gifted students. Yet, our BFLPE and empirical evaluation of the effects of academically selective settings show exactly the opposite effects. Placement of gifted students in academically selective settings results in lower academic self-concepts, not higher academic self-concepts.

2. In recent research and policy for academically disadvantaged students, there is a worldwide inclusion movement to integrate these students into regular, mainstream classroom settings. Although economic rationalist perspectives appear to be the underlying motive for such decisions, the espoused rhetoric is based on a direct application of labeling theory. According to labeling theory, academically disadvantaged children are likely to be stigmatized and suffer lower self-concepts as a consequence of being placed in special classes with other academically disadvantaged students. Yet, theory underpinning our BFLPE and empirical evaluation of the effects of including academically disadvantaged students in regular, mainstream classrooms show exactly the opposite effects. Placement of academically

disadvantaged children into regular classrooms results in lower academic self-concepts, not higher academic self-concepts. Furthermore, the negative effects of inclusion on peer self-concept, reported by Tracey and Marsh (2000), makes it apparent that academically disadvantaged children in regular classrooms actually feel socially excluded, not included.

Based on our review of previous and new research, we recommend that research evaluating the potential effects of special settings (for academically disadvantaged students and for G&T students) in comparison to regular classroom settings needs to (a) include measures of self-concept and perhaps other psychological variables; (b) utilize multidimensional self-concept instruments with demonstrated reliability and validity to fully explore the impact of different settings on multiple facets of self-concept; (c) gather data on students' academic achievement, self-concepts, and other psychological variables prior to selection into the special programs and at different points of time thereafter; (d) more fully explore teaching and learning activities in the classroom to assess the effects of different classroom environments and types of curriculum on educational outcomes; (e) employ more sophisticated research designs and stronger statistical tools to more critically evaluate conclusions; and (f) use appropriate qualitative research procedures in combination with quantitative research procedures like those emphasized here to more fully explicate the nature of the effects. As noted by Marsh and colleagues (1995), previous research has focused on the definition and identification problems, but more emphasis is needed on identifying students who will benefit most from particular settings. Although special education researchers and policymakers give lip service to the adage that different programs must be tailored to the needs of particular students, there is a paucity of good research supporting this contention and pursuing its implications. More research is needed on how to optimally match special education programs and students with special needs rather than assuming that one type of setting is optimal for all students. In particular, special education programs need to be designed to ensure that curriculum activities include strategies to maintain and enhance students' self-concepts.

Important limitations may be inherent in studies seeking to evaluate the effects of special education settings for students at either end of the achievement continuum. Goldring (1990) noted that "researchers of gifted education programs can rarely assign students randomly to groups" (pp. 314–315). A stronger research design might consist of actually matching G&T students in selective settings with G&T students from other settings (e.g., Marsh et al., 1995). Marsh (1998), however, demonstrated that even this matching design is inherently biased in favor of students in selective settings under a variety of different matching strategies. He argued that alternative quasi-experimental designs such as the regression-discontinuity design should be considered. Although there seems to have been less critical evaluation of recent trends to include academically disadvantaged students in regular classroom settings, many of these concerns seem relevant here as well. Whereas true random assignment is a desirable design strategy, it is very rare that it can be implemented in special education research. Hence, it is likely that researchers evaluating the effects of placement at both ends of the achievement continuum will continue to struggle with interpretation complications that are inherent in quasi-experimental research designs with nonequivalent groups.

International interest in the BFLPE and its relevance to educational settings throughout the world provide exciting new opportunities to evaluate the cross-national and cross-cultural generalizability of our theory and empirical findings. As illustrated in the German and Hong Kong studies reviewed in this chapter, these opportunities provide a basis for expanding existing research and theory—not just replicating the results of previous "Western" research. The German (Marsh, Koeller, & Baumart, in press) study provided a unique opportunity to evaluate theoretical predictions based on social comparison theory relevant to the reunification of the East and West German school systems after the fall of the Berlin Wall. There were important cultural differences in the two systems prior to the reunification: East German students had only experience mixed-ability classes, whereas West German students had been taught in ability-segregated classes for the previous two years. In the reunification, the ability-segregated model of West Germany was adopted across Germany. Consistent with a priori predictions based on these cultural differences, the BFLPE at the very start of the reunification was stronger in West German schools than in East German schools. By the middle of the first post-reunification school year, the BFLPE was only slightly stronger in West German schools. By the end of this first year, however, there was no difference in the BFLPEs in East and West regions of the reunified Germany. The evolvement of the BFLPE in the East and West German settings provided strong support for the social comparison processes posited to underlie the BFLPE. In the Hong Kong study, Marsh and colleagues (2000) evaluated the generalizability of theory and research based on Western school settings that emphasize an individualist orientation in an Eastern setting with a collectivist orientation. The clear replication of results from Western research provided strong support for the generalizability of the BFLPE to different school settings. In addition, this study provided an important breakthrough in BFLPE research by successfully operationalizing the juxtaposition between assimilation and contrast effects that had been largely implicit in prior BFLPE research.

As demonstrated in the chapter, the juxtaposition between assimilation (reflected glory, labeling) effects and contrast (negative social comparison, BFLPE) effects has critical theoretical and substantive implications. On the one hand, assumed benefits associated with special settings for gifted students and with mainstreaming academically disadvantaged students are based in part on assimilation effects predicted by labeling theory. On the other hand, BFLPE research has demonstrated that contrast effects predicted by social comparison theory predominate. Although these two effects work in the opposite direction, it is important to emphasize that they are not mutually exclusive. Quite the contrary, as emphasized in this chapter, the BFLPE is the net effect of counterbalancing assimilation and contrast effects. Although this theoretical distinction has been emphasized in BFLPE research, it has not been operatationalized and most emphasis has been placed on the negative contrast effects. Given this importance, it is surprising that BFLPE studies and evaluations of assigning extremely bright and very disadvantaged students to special settings have not more fully evaluated these processes. Hence, the inclusion of perceived school status as an indicator of reflected glory, labeling effects is a unique feature of the Marsh et al. (2000) study. In addition to the face validity of the items in their perceived school status scale, there was empirical support for the construct validity of the perceived status responses. In particular, these responses were highly related to school-average achievement—hypothesized as a primary determinant of perceived school status—and contributed positively to the prediction of academic self-concept. Consistent with theoretical predictions, controlling the positive school status component in school-average achievement resulted in a more negative effect of school-average achievement on academic self-concept. More clearly than any previous BFLPE research and, perhaps, any other studies using the imposed social comparison paradigm, the Marsh et al. results unmistakably differentiated between negative social comparison contrast effects and positive reflected glory assimilation effects that comprise the BFLPE. For these reasons, perceived school status or other measures operationalizing labeling effects need to be incorporated into future BFLPE studies.

Diener and Fujita (1997, p. 350) related BFLPE research to the broader social comparison literature. They emphasized that Marsh's BFLPE provided the clearest support for predictions based on social comparison theory predictions in an imposed social comparison paradigm. They emphasized that the frame of reference, based on classmates within the same school, is more clearly defined than in most other research settings. Clearly, the importance of the school setting and the relevance of the social comparisons in school settings are much more ecologically valid than manipulations in the typical social psychology experiment conducted with university students. Indeed, except for opting out altogether, it is difficult for students to avoid the relevance of achievement as a reference point within a school setting or the social comparisons provided by the academic accomplishments of their classmates. A major focus of BFLPE research has been on the substantively important and surprising implications of this research, undermining the assumed advantages of attending academically selective schools and mainstreaming academically disadvantaged students. Although obviously supportive of these well-established concerns, research reviewed in this chapter also provides stronger links between BFLPE and broader areas of social comparison theory (e.g., Buunk & Ybema, 1997; Diener & Fujita, 1997; Lazarus & Folkman, 1984; McFarland & Buehler, 1995; Taylor & Lobel, 1989; Tessor, 1988; Wills, 1981).

ACKNOWLEDGMENTS

We would like to thank and acknowledge financial assistance for this research from the Australian Research Council. Correspondence in relation to this study should be sent to Professor Herbert W. Marsh, SELF Research Centre, University of Western Sydney, Bankstown Campus PENRITH SOUTH DC NSW 1797 Australia, or via e-mail: *h.marsh@uws.edu.au.* An earlier version of this chapter was presented at the Inaugural Self-Concept Enhancement and Learning Facilitation (SELF) Research Centre International Conference, Sydney, October 5–6, 2000 (see Web site: edweb .uws.edu.au/SELF).

REFERENCES

Alwin, D. F., & Otto, L. B. (1977). High school context effects on aspirations. *Sociology of Education, 50,* 259–273.

Bachman, J. G., & O'Malley, P. M. (1986). Self-concepts, self-esteem, and educational experiences: The frogpond revisited (again). *Journal of Personality and Social Psychology, 50,* 33–46.

Branden, N. (1994). *Six pillars of self-esteem.* New York: Bantam.

Brookover, W. B. (1989). *Self-Concept of Ability Scale—A review and further analysis.* Paper presented at the Annual Meeting of the American Educational Research Association.

Burns, R. B. (1979). *The self-concept: Theory, measurement, development and behaviour.* London: Longman.

Burns, R. B. (1982). *Self-concept development and education.* London: Holt, Rinehart, and Winston.

Buunk, B. P., & Ybema, J. F. (1997). Social comparisons and occupational stress: The identification-contrast model in P. P. Buunk & F. X. Gibbons (Eds.).

Health, coping, and well-being: Perspectives from social comparison theory (pp. 359–388). Mahwah, NJ: Erlbaum.

Byrne, B. M. (1984). The general/academic self-concept nomological network: A review of construct validation research. *Review of Educational Research, 54,* 427–456.

Byrne, B. M. (1996a). Academic self-concept: Its structure, measurement, and relation to academic achievement. In B. A. Bracken (Ed.), *Handbook of self-concept* (pp. 287–316). New York: Wiley.

Byrne, B. M. (1996b). *Measuring self-concept across the lifespan: Issues and instrumentation.* Washington, DC: American Psychological Association.

Chapman, J. W. (1988). Learning disabled children's self-concepts. *Review of Educational Research, 58,* 347–371.

Coleman, J. M., & Fults, B. A. (1985). Special class placement, level of intelligence, and the self-concept of gifted children: A social comparison perspective. *Remedial and Special Education, 6,* 7–11.

Commonwealth Schools Commission. (1981). *Proceedings of the National Seminar on the Education of Gifted and Talented Children.* Canberra, Australia: Author.

Craven, R G., Marsh, H. W., & Print, M. (2000). Selective, streamed and mixed-ability programs for gifted students: Impact on self-concept, motivation, and achievement. *Australian Journal of Education, 44,* 51–75.

Davis, J. A. (1966). The campus as a frog pond: An application of theory of relative deprivation to career decisions for college men. *American Journal of Sociology, 72,* 17–31.

Diener, E., & Fujita, F. (1997). Social comparison and subjective well-being. In B. P. Buunk & F. X. Gibbons (Eds.), *Health, coping, and well-being: Perspectives from social comparison theory* (pp. 329–358). Mahwah, NJ: Erlbaum.

Felson, R. B. (1984). The effect of self-appraisals on ability of academic performance. *Journal of Personality and Social Psychology, 47,* 944–952.

Festinger, L. (1954). A theory of social comparison processes. *Human Relations, 7,* 117–140.

Fox, L. H., & Washington, J. (1985). Settings for the gifted and talented: Past, present, and future. In F. D. Horowitz & M. O'Brien (Eds.), *The gifted and talented: Developmental perspectives* (pp. 223–250). Washington, DC: American Psychological Association.

Goldring, E. B. (1990). Assessing the status of information on classroom organizational frameworks for gifted students. *Journal of Educational Research, 83,* 313–326.

Gross, M. (1992). The use of radical acceleration in cases of extreme intellectual precocity. *Gifted Child Quarterly, 36,* 91–99.

Gross, M. (1993). *Exceptionally gifted children.* London: Routledge.

Hattie, J. (1992). *Self-concept.* Hillsdale, NJ: Erlbaum.

Helson, H. (1964). *Adaptation-level theory.* New York: Harper & Row.

Hoge, R. D., & Renzulli, J. S. (1993). Exploring the link between giftedness and self-concept. *Review of Educational Research, 63,* 449–465.

Hyman, H. (1942). The psychology of subjective status. *Psychological Bulletin, 39,* 473–474.

Ireson, J., Hallam, S., & Plewis, I. (2001). Ability grouping in secondary schools: Effects on pupils' self-concepts. *British Journal of Educational Psychology, 71,* 315–326.

Jerusalem, M. (1984). Reference group, learning environment and self-evaluations: A dynamic multi-level analysis with latent variables. In R. Schwarzer (Ed.), *The self in anxiety, stress and depression* (pp. 61–73). Amsterdam: Elsevier Science.

Kulik, C. L. (1985, August). *Effects of inter-class ability grouping on achievement and self-esteem.* Paper presented at the 1985 Annual Meeting of the American Psychological Association, Los Angeles.

Kulik, C. L., & Kulik, J. A. (1982). Effects of ability grouping on secondary school students: A meta-analysis of evaluation findings. *American Educational Research Journal, 21,* 799–806.

Lazarus, R. S., & Folkman, S. (1984). *Stress, appraisal and coping.* New York: Springer-Verlag.

Marsh, H. W. (1974). *Judgmental anchoring: Stimulus and response variables.* Unpublished doctoral dissertation, University of California, Los Angeles.

Marsh, H. W. (1984a). Self-concept, social comparison and ability grouping: A reply to Kulik and Kulik. *American Educational Research Journal, 21,* 799–806.

Marsh, H. W. (1984b). Self-concept: The application of a frame of reference model to explain paradoxical results. *Australian Journal of Education, 28,* 165–181.

Marsh, H. W. (1986). Verbal and math self-concepts: An internal/external frame of reference model. *American Educational Research Journal, 23,* 129–149.

Marsh, H. W. (1987). The big-fish–little-pond effect on academic self-concept. *Journal of Educational Psychology, 79,* 280–295.

Marsh, H. W. (1990a). The causal ordering of academic self-concept and academic achievement: A multiwave, longitudinal path analysis. *Journal of Educational Psychology, 82,* 646–656.

Marsh, H. W. (1990b). The influence of internal and external frames of reference on the formation of math and English self-concepts. *Journal of Educational Psychology, 82,* 107–116.

Marsh, H. W. (1990c). A multidimensional, hierarchical self-concept: Theoretical and empirical justification. *Educational Psychology Review, 2,* 77–172.

Marsh, H. W. (1990d). *The Self Description Questionnaire—I: Manual.* Sydney, Australia: University of Western Sydney.

Marsh, H. W. (1991). The failure of high ability high schools to deliver academic benefits: The importance of academic self-concept and educational aspirations. *American Educational Research Journal, 28,* 445–480.

Marsh, H. W. (1993). Academic self-concept: Theory, measurement and research. In J. Suls (Ed.), *Psychological perspectives on the self* (Vol. 4, pp. 59–98). Hillsdale, NJ: Erlbaum.

Marsh, H. W. (1994). Using the National Educational Longitudinal Study of 1988 to evaluate theoretical models of self-concept: The Self-Description Questionnaire. *Journal of Educational Psychology, 86,* 439–456.

Marsh, H. W. (1998). Simulation study of nonequivalent group-matching and regression discontinuity designs: Evaluations of gifted and talented programs. *Journal of Experimental Education, 66,* 163–192.

Marsh, H. W., Byrne, B. M., & Shavelson, R. (1988). A multifaceted academic self-concept: Its hierarchical structure and its relation to academic achievement. *Journal of Educational Psychology, 80,* 366–380.

Marsh, H. W., Byrne, B. M., & Yeung, A. S. (1999). Causal ordering of academic self-concept and achievement: Reanalysis of a pioneering study and revised recommendations. *Educational Psychologist, 34,* 155–167.

Marsh, H. W., Chessor, D., Craven, R. G., & Roche, L. (1995). The effects of gifted and talented programs on academic self-concept: The big fish strikes again. *American Educational Research Journal, 32,* 285–319.

Marsh, H. W., & Craven, R. G., (1994). Who benefits from selective schools? The role of academic self-concept and a call for further research. *Forum of Education, 49,* 3–13.

Marsh, H. W., & Craven, R. G. (1997). Academic self-concept: Beyond the dustbowl. In G. Phye (Ed.), *Handbook of classroom assessment: Learning, achievement, and adjustment* (pp. 131–198). Orlando, FL: Academic Press.

Marsh, H. W., Craven, R. G., & Debus, R. (1998). Structure, stability, and development of young children's self-concepts: A multicohort-multioccasion study. *Child Development, 69,* 1030–1053.

Marsh, H. W., & Hattie, J. (1996). Theoretical perspectives on the structure of self-concept. In B. A. Bracken (Ed.), *Handbook of self-concept* (pp. 38–90). New York: Wiley.

Marsh, H. W., & Johnston, C. F. (1993). Multidimensional self-concepts and frames of reference: Relevance to the exceptional learner. In F. E. Obiakor & S. Stile (Eds.), *Self-concept of exceptional learners: Current perspectives for educators.* Dubuque, IA: Kendall/Hunt.

Marsh, H. W., Koeller, O., & Baumart, J. (in press). Reunification of East and West German school systems: Longitudinal multilevel modeling study of the big fish little pond effect on academic self-concept. *American Educational Research Journal.*

Marsh, H. W., Kong, C. K., & Hau, K. T. (2000). Longitudinal multilevel modeling of the Big Fish Little Pond Effect on academic self-concept: Counterbalancing social comparison and reflected glory effects in Hong Kong high schools. *Journal of Personality and Social Psychology, 78,* 337–349.

Marsh, H. W., & Parker, J. (1984). Determinants of student self-concept: Is it better to be a relatively large fish in a small pond even if you don't learn to swim as well? *Journal of Personality and Social Psychology, 47,* 213–231.

Marsh, H. W., & Rowe, K. J. (1996). The negative effects of school-average ability on academic self-concept—an application of multilevel modeling. *Australian Journal of Education, 40*(1), 65–87.

Marsh, H. W., & Shavelson, R. J. (1985). Self-concept: Its multifaceted, hierarchical structure. *Educational Psychologist, 20,* 107–125.

Marsh, H. W., & Yeung, A. S. (1997a). The causal effects of academic self-concept on academic achievement: Structural equation models of longitudinal data. *Journal of Educational Psychology, 89,* 41–54.

Marsh, H. W., & Yeung, A. S. (1997b). Coursework selection: The effects of academic self-concept and achievement. *American Educational Research Journal, 34,* 691–720.

McFarland, C., & Buehler, R. (1995). Collective self-esteem as a moderator of the frog–pond effect in reactions to performance feedback. *Journal of Personality and Social Psychology, 68,* 1055–1070.

Meyer, J. W. (1970). High school effects on college intentions. *American Journal of Sociology, 76,* 59–70.

Morse, S., & Gergen, K. J. (1970). Social comparison, self-consistency, and the concept of self. *Journal of Personality and Social Psychology, 16,* 148–156.

Parducci, A. (1995). *Happiness, pleasure, and judgment: The contextual theory and its applications.* Mahwah, NJ: Erlbaum.

Reuman, D. A. (1989). How social comparison mediates the relation between ability-grouping practices and students' achievement expectancies in mathematics. *Journal of Educational Psychology, 81,* 178–189.

Rogers, B. S. (1979). *Effects of an enrichment setting screening process on self-concept and others-concept of gifted elementary children.* Unpublished doctoral dissertation, University of Cincinnati.

Rogers, C. M., Smith, M.D., & Coleman, J. M. (1978). Social comparison in the classroom: The relationship between academic achievement and self-concept. *Journal of Educational Psychology, 70,* 50–57.

Sampson, J. F. (1969). *The high school examination achievements of opportunity "C" class pupils* (Report No. 373.127 SAMP 1, NSW Department of Education Library). Sydney, Australia: New South Wales Department of Education.

Sampson, J. F. (1977). The secondary school performance of pupils in selective and comprehensive schools. In New South Wales Department of Education, *The education of the talented child* (pp. 111–131). Sydney, Australia: New South Wales Department of Education.

Schwarzer, R., Jerusalem, J., & Lange, B. (1983, April). *The change of self-concept with respect to reference groups in school.* Paper presented at the Annual Meeting of the American Educational Research Association, Montreal.

Shavelson, R. J., & Marsh, H. W. (1986). On the structure of self-concept. In R. Schwazer (Ed.), *Anxiety and cognitions.* Hillsdale, NJ: Erlbaum.

Shavelson, R. J., Hubner, J. J., & Stanton, G. C. (1976). Self-concept: Validation of construct interpretations. *Review of Educational Research, 46,* 407–441.

Sherif, M., & Sherif, C. W. (1969). *Social psychology.* New York: Harper & Row.

Stouffer, S. A., Suchman, E. A., DeVinney, L. C., Star, S. A., & Williams, R. M. (1949). *The American soldier: Adjustments during army life* (Vol. 1). Princeton, NJ: Princeton University Press.

Strang, L., Smith, M. D., & Rogers, C. M. (1978). Social comparison, multiple reference groups and the self-concepts of academically handicapped children before and after mainstreaming. *Journal of Educational Psychology, 70,* 487–479.

Sue, S. (1999). Science, ethnicity and bias: Where have we gone wrong? *American Psychologist, 54,* 1070–1077.

Suls, J. M. (1977). Social comparison theory and research: An overview from 1954. In J. M. Suls & R. L. Miller (Eds.), *Social comparison processes: Theoretical and empirical perspectives* (pp. 1–20). Washington, DC: Hemisphere.

Taylor, S. E., & Lobel, M. (1989). Social comparison activity under threat: Downward evaluation and upward contacts. *Psychological Review, 96,* 569–575.

Tessor, A. (1988). Toward a self-evaluation maintenance model of social behavior. In L. Berkowitz (Ed.), *Advances in experimental social psychology* (Vol. 21, pp. 181–227). San Diego, CA: Academic Press.

Tracey, D., & Marsh, H. W. (2000). Self-concepts of primary students with mild intellectual disabilities: Issues of measurement and educational placement. In *Conference Proceedings of the 2000 Self Research Centre Conference.* Sydney, Australia: SELF Centre, University of Western Sydney.

Upshaw, H. S. (1969). The personal reference scale: An approach to social judgment. *Advances in Experimental Social Psychology, 4,* 315–370.

Wills, T. A. (1981). Downward comparison principals in social psychology. *Psychological Bulletin, 90,* 245–271.

Zeidner M., & Schleyer, E. J. (1999). The big-fish–little-pond effect for academic self-concept, test anxiety and school grades in gifted children. *Contemporary Educational Psychology, 24,* 305–329.

CHAPTER 5

ADOLESCENTS' ACHIEVEMENT GOALS

Situating Motivation in Sociocultural Contexts

Avi Kaplan
Ben Gurion University of the Negev, Israel
Martin L. Maehr
University of Michigan

Achievement, especially *school* achievement of adolescents, is a major concern of parents, educators, indeed of society as a whole—and, sometimes, also the concern of adolescents themselves. Doing well in school involves taking responsibility for action and outcome, something that often is not automatic or inevitable. In most cases, it involves a decision to do what has to be done and persist at it. In other words, to a large degree, achievement depends on motivation. The study of motivation and its relation to achievement begins with and is anchored in the observation of variation in actions that involve making choices, exerting effort, and persisting. In turn, motivation theory is designed to explain and predict this variation, and ultimately also to provide insights to those who attempt to motivate others. An important test of motivation theories, therefore, is their usefulness to inform teachers, parents, coaches, youth leaders, counselors, and therapists, indeed all those who make their business to empower and encourage people to "do what needs to be done."

In this chapter we summarize developments in the study of motivation of the last two decades, particularly focusing on the emergence of a theory that has become one of the influential theories of achievement motivation in education: achievement goal theory. Our chapter begins with the origin of achievement goal theory and with a brief review of research findings of the last two decades. We continue with a review of recent theoretical developments that have challenged the original formulation of the theory. We then present a model that situates students' motivational orientations in the sociocultural context of their schools and discuss its implications to theory, research, and educational practice. We conclude the chapter with the implications of the model to understanding motivation in adolescence.

ACHIEVEMENT GOALS:
THE SITUATED MEANING OF ACTION

Two decades or so ago, a decided shift occurred in the study of motivation, especially achievement motivation. Up to and through the 1960s and 1970s, motivation was viewed in "dynamic" terms (McClelland, 1961). That in general meant that a hydraulic machine was the metaphor of choice and the preferred causal constructs were needs and drives. Motivation was largely construed as an unconscious process residing in the deepest recesses of the autonomic system and only barely cerebral. Cognitions associated with motivation were, in a phrase, "afterthoughts," not primary causes. Furthermore, the focus was on developmental origins, mostly during the first years of life. With that, there was a special concern with individual differences and little concern with contexts. It was a period of emphasis on "trait" rather than "state" (Maehr, 1974), with particular attention being given to individual differences with "personality" designated as the primary source of motivated behavior. There were other voices, of course (e.g., Festinger, 1942; Lewin, Dembo, Festinger, & Sears, 1944). Nevertheless, any brief characterization of the period would have to recognize a predominant focus on individual differences and on largely unconscious dynamics.

However, the insights of those looking beyond personality began to take hold; increasingly, attention was given to cognitive processes. One of the most important theoretical developments to emerge as a result was the adoption of attributional reinterpretation of achievement motivation put forward by Weiner and others (see Weiner, 1985, 1986). And alongside attributions, the importance of cognition in motivation was notably promoted by a return to the consideration of concepts of self as a source of motivation (cf. Bandura, 1986; Wylie, 1968; see also Baumeister, 1998). The case could be made that in the early phases of the "cognitive revolution," the motivational construct of choice revolved around the concept of self: one's general sense of competence, perceived efficacy or expectations of success and failure in a specific case, and internal or external attributions associated with success and failure.

In noting how achievement attributions varied with gender and culture, there emerged a parallel concern with values and ultimately purposes, intentions, and goals (e.g., Maehr & Nicholls, 1980). As it turned out, the concern with goals became more than an incidental part of the picture. In fact, research on achievement motivation has shifted significantly toward a focus on the purposes that individuals hold as a major if not the predominant causal factor (Ames & Ames, 1984; Maehr & Pintrich, 1991; Pervin, 1989). The prominence of the term goal and issue of purposiveness in general emerged in a variety of different forms (see Austin & Vancouver, 1996). Elliot and Sheldon (1997) have recently portrayed the motivational landscape traversed by goals, identifying "four basic variants, or levels, of goal representation." They define these as follows:

> (a) *task-specific* guidelines for performance, such as "Make this free-throw" (Bandura, 1986; Harackiewicz & Sansone, 1991; Locke & Latham, 1990); (b) *situation specific* orientations that represent the purpose of achievement activity, such as "Demonstrate my competence relative to others in this situation" (Ames, 1992; Dweck, 1991; Nicholls, 1989); (c) *personal* goals that represent idiographic, personalized achievement pursuits that often transcend particular situations, such as "Get good grades" (Cantor & Kihlstrom, 1987; Emmons, 1989; Klinger, 1977; Little, Lecci, & Watkinson, 1992); (d) *self-standards* and *images of the self in the future*, such as "Someday I will be a college graduate" (Higgins, Strauman, & Klein, 1986; Markus, Cross & Wurf, 1990... Cantor & Zirkel, 1990; Dweck, 1992; Harackiewicz & Sansone, 1991). (p. 171)

Each of the four goal concepts identified by Elliot and Sheldon provides insights into the processes that contribute to individuals choosing to act in a certain way. They differ in their level of specificity and in the roles that they assign to the characteristics of the person and of the situation. As such, each concept contributed to a literature concerned with somewhat different theoretical processes—literatures that in many ways complement each other. In this chapter we focus on the perspective most closely identified with that defined in (b) above, which defines goals as situated orientations that represent the meaning of achievement and the purpose of action in situations. This perspective on goals proved very useful in guiding theoretical and empirical investigations into the processes that lead students to act in ways that contribute to achievement. The large and diverse literature that emerged from this perspective was labeled "achievement goal theory" (Ames, 1992a; Dweck, 1986; Maehr, 1984; Nicholls, 1984).

Achievement goal theory emphasizes the meaning that students construct *vis-à-vis* the achievement situation. Of particular significance is the aspect of meaning that concerns the purpose in acting: Why should one do it? Is the activity worth doing in its own right, or is it primarily instrumental to achieving a reward or recompense? Is the task "intrinsically interesting" or is it done in anticipation of social recognition or approval? Research in achievement goal theory investigated how such different purposes for task engagement make a difference in the thinking, feeling, and action exhibited. Thus, in addition to considering the question, "Are students motivated?," achievement goal theorists have asked "*Why* are students motivated?" They have found enough empirical evidence to indicate that purpose may be especially important for the quality of action, feeling, and thought.

Mastery and Performance Goals

Early on, two purposes for engaging in schoolwork were identified that became central in framing research and theory to the present. One was variably labeled mastery goals, task goals, or learning goals, and the other variably labeled performance goals, ego goals, or ability goals (Ames, 1992a; Anderman & Maehr, 1994; Dweck, 1986; Nicholls, 1984). Ames (1992a) emphasized the convergence among the various constructs and in this chapter we adopt her terminology for these goal orientations—mastery and performance goals.

Generally, mastery goals refer to a focus on developing competence, making progress, and achieving mastery of the material and of the task. Success in the case of mastery goals is defined in relation to the task—that is, making progress on, or completing, a task successfully through investment of effort, understanding, and use of skills. Progress is measured in self-referential terms—that is, by evaluating improvement over previous performance (Ames, 1992a; Nicholls, 1984). In a learning situation, pursuing mastery goals takes the form of learning for the sake of learning (Ames, 1992a). Students exhibit mastery goals, for example, when they are working diligently on an interesting task and are experiencing the excitement of learning a new skill or acquiring new knowledge.

Research has shown consistent findings with regard to the positive consequences of being mastery oriented. The pattern of behavior associated with mastery goals is, therefore, considered adaptive and is often referred to as a "mastery pattern" of coping (e.g., Ames, 1992a; Dweck & Leggett, 1988). Results from studies using multiple methods (survey, experimental, qualitative) in various contexts (laboratory, school, sports, sales) and with various age samples indicate that mastery goals are associated with positive outcomes such as self-efficacy; preference for challenging tasks; persistence in the face of difficulties; use of adaptive cognitive, metacognitive, and motivational strategies for learning and self-regulation; adaptive help-seeking behavior; attributions of success to effort, interest, and strategy use; and positive attitude and affect in relation to self, context, and task (see Ames, 1992a; Covington, 2000; Dweck & Leggett, 1988; Elliot, 1999; Kaplan, Middleton, Urdan, & Midgley, 2002; Pintrich, 2000a, 2000b; Urdan, 1997, for reviews).

In the case of performance goals, the focus is especially on demonstrating competence (Ames, 1992a; Dweck, 1986; Nicholls, 1984). Since already at childhood, students understand that level of ability depends on normative performance (Nicholls, 1990), in many cases performance goals involve an orientation toward social comparison, and the demonstration of competence is done relative to that of others. In this regard, the understanding that effort and ability are inversely related directs attention to comparison not only on level of achievement but also on investment of effort (Nicholls, 1984). Thus, success in performance goal terms can be defined as achieving or surpassing normative standards, as in demonstrating that one is "smarter," or not less smart, than others, or as succeeding with little effort (Ames, 1992a). A central aspect of performance goals is, therefore, a concern with the *impression* that the person is making on others with regard to normative competence (Nicholls, 1989). These goals are evident, for example, in students' focus on grading and on comparing grades—a focus that is apart from the inherent purpose of schooling: learning.

Early in the development of goal orientation theory, theorists noted that the pursuit of performance goals does not result in similar behavior for all individuals. Nicholls (1984) and Dweck (1986) differentiated between performance-oriented individuals who have high perceived ability and those who have low perceived ability. While the former were predicted to be primarily oriented toward demonstrating their high ability, the latter were predicted to be primarily oriented toward *avoiding* demonstrating their *lack* of ability. This difference in focus manifested in a "mastery" pattern of behavior for the individuals with high perceived ability (similar to mastery-oriented individuals) and a "helpless" pattern of behavior for those with low perceived ability (Dweck & Leggett, 1988). Nevertheless, most theory and research have treated performance-oriented students with high and low perceived ability as having the same motivational orientation "in which individuals seek to maintain positive judgments of their ability *and* avoid negative judgments" (Elliott & Dweck, 1988, p. 5, emphasis added).

Generally speaking, research findings in the case of performance goals have been less consistent than those found in the case of mastery goals. More often than not, performance goals have been associated with a less adaptive pattern of cognition, affect, and behavior than have mastery goals. Several studies found endorsement of performance goals to be associated with such outcomes as avoidance of challenging tasks, academic self-consciousness (e.g., being afraid to make mistakes publicly), test anxiety, negative emotions following failure, avoidance of help seeking, and use of ineffective learning strategies; and to be negatively associated with self-efficacy and use of effective learning strategies. Other studies, however, found no association, weak, or even moderate associations between performance goals and positive outcomes such as self-efficacy, effective learning strategies, adaptive help-seeking behavior, and positive attitudes and affect (see Ames, 1992a; Dweck & Leggett, 1988; Nicholls, 1989; Urdan, 1997, for reviews).

Cross-Cultural Generalizability of Mastery and Performance Goals

In recent years, as goal orientation theory was found to be a useful explanatory framework for achievement behavior among white, middle-class North American students, researchers from other cultures explored its applicability to their own societies. Initially, the structure and associations were replicated among other "European-oriented" societies such as England and France (Biddle et al., 1995), Norway (Skaalvik, 1997), Jews in Israel (Butler, 1993), and European Australia (Archer, 1994; McInerney, 1995). Soon after, however, replications were conducted with increasingly diverse cultural groups such as African American students (Kaplan & Maehr, 1999; Midgley, Arunkumar, & Urdan, 1996); Japanese workers (Shwalb, Shwalb, Harnisch, Maehr, & Akabane, 1992); Greek students (Papaioannou, 1994); Aboriginal-Australian, Navajo, and Montagnais Betsiamite Indian students (McInerney, Roche, McInerney, & Marsh, 1997); Chinese students and athletes (Maehr, Shi, Kaplan, & Wang, 1999; Xiang, Lee, & Solmon, 1997); and United Arab Emirate students (Albaili, 1998).

Most studies conducted with students of different cultures confirm the meaningfulness of mastery and performance goals among the different cultural groups, and also support the relations between these goal orientations and correlates such as cognitive strategies and achievement. Of course, it is important to note that the general emphasis of cross-cultural research conducted until now has been on the similarities rather than the differences in achievement goal profiles and correlates across cultural groups. Furthermore, as with most studies on achievement goals, much of cross-cultural research investigating the generalizability of these orientations used survey methodology. Such research tends to look for the similarities among groups and disregards indications of possible uniqueness of the meaning of goals (e.g., McInerney et al., 1997). Nevertheless, some of this research did find indication of different processes associated with achievement goals in different ethnic and cultural groups. McInerney and colleagues (1997), for example, found that as a group, Navajo students had a higher tendency towards mastery goals than students of other groups participating in the study, whereas Anglo Australian students were less performance oriented than the others. McInerney, Hinkley, Dowson, and Van Etten (1998) found that, whereas the structure of achievement goals appeared to be very similar among Aboriginal, Anglo, and immigrant Australian high school students, there were some indications of differences in levels of endorsement of the different orientations between the Aboriginal students and students of the two other groups. Furthermore, there were some differences among students in the three groups in responses to questions that asked them to think about the achievement goals that would contribute to the success of other students in school.

Looking at the mediating processes between achievement goals and outcomes, Kaplan and Maehr (1999) found some indication of different patterns of relationships between achievement goals and self-efficacy among European American and African American students. Such findings of differences suggest that there is still much to be learned about the generalizable and unique aspects of achievement goals within different cultural groups. Indeed, as one of the fundamental processes that is underlying achievement goals concerns the meaning of action in context, it is likely that cultural factors would play an important role in influencing, for example, the prevalence of a certain achievement goal within a cultural group, or the emotional associations with achievement goals (e.g., the competitive-oriented performance goals; see Maehr & Nicholls, 1980). Indeed, some recent research that employed qualitative methods to investigate the meaning of motivational beliefs in different sociocultural contexts (e.g., Bempechat & Boulay, 2000) raised some challenges to the original framework of achievement goal theory. We elaborate on this and other developments later in the chapter.

Antecedents of Mastery and Performance Goals

Both mastery and performance goals are variously viewed as state and/or trait variables. As a trait variable, these goals are viewed as relatively enduring thoughts or orientations toward action that distinguish individuals and determine their action across a wide variety of achievement domains and contexts (Duda & Nicholls, 1992). As such, one might surmise that achievement goals could be traced to early socialization experiences influenced, for example, by childrearing practices or the nature of kindergarten and school settings (e.g., Heyman, Dweck, & Cain, 1992). In fact, however, little research has been specifically directed to this issue.

Conceptualized as dispositions, mastery and performance goals have been thought to be the purposes associated with different theories of intelligence (Dweck, 1999) or of success in education (Nicholls, 1992). When students understand intelligence to be an innate and fixed trait ("entity theorists"), they are more likely to adopt goals of demonstrating that they have much of this trait or engage in avoiding demonstrating their lack of it—performance goals. In contrast, when students understand intelligence to be a malleable quality that can be enhanced with effort, they are more likely to adopt goals of increasing and developing it—mastery goals (Dweck, 1999). Alternatively, mastery goals are perceived to be an integral aspect of students' theory of education that involves the beliefs that success in school involves being interested, investing effort, collaborating with others, and mastering knowledge. Performance goals are associated with the beliefs that success in school is achieved through being smart and attempting to outdo others (Nicholls, 1992).

However, when viewing mastery or performance goals as a state variable, the origins are as often as not attributed to immediately experienced situations (e.g., what is stressed in the school attended), though the role of individual differences in dispositions to achievement goals is not precluded (see Nicholls, 1992). Mastery and performance goals have been manipulated in the laboratory by focusing students on the possibility of gaining understanding and skills in the task versus on the evaluation of their performance relative to others, respectively. More broadly, various characteristics of the learning environment have been pointed to as facilitating the adoption of mastery or performance goals (Ames, 1992a, 1992b). For example, providing students with a choice among tasks, providing feedback on effort and improvement, and emphasizing collaboration is thought to facilitate mastery goals; whereas emphasizing speed of performance rather than deep processing, providing public recognition and evaluation of such performance, and encouraging competition among students for grades is thought to facilitate performance goals (Ames, 1990, 1992b; Maehr & Midgley, 1991, 1996).

Theorists tend to vary in the degree to which they focus on or emphasize trait or state characteristics of achievement goals. To date, researchers have provided multiple models of the origins of achievement goals, yet not a clear and generally convergent picture (see Kaplan & Maehr, 2002).

Assessment and Research Methods

Along with the dual trait/state usage, mastery and performance goals have been treated primarily in two ways in reported studies. First, they have been treated as a state or situated variable that can be created or primed by certain experimental manipulations. These manipulations essentially consist of statements that describe the purpose of the task as learning, making progress, and as individual and personal growth focused in the mastery condition; or as an opportunity for demonstrating ability, and as an evaluative situation in the performance condition.

Second, it is currently especially common to assess the existence of mastery and performance orientations with inventories using Likert-type scales. Researchers have experienced considerable success in developing reliable measures of achievement goals and in predicting a wide range of (self-reported) behavior from the type of orientations reported. These two research procedures seem to imply different views on the nature of goal orientations, including differences in the stability and situated nature of goal orientations—an issue that to date has gone largely unaddressed in the literature but will be specifically attended to later in this chapter. Thus, the origin of mastery and performance goals and their measurement still present open domains of inquiry. Particularly, the roles of context, social processes, and individual traits have yet to be effectively combined in a theoretical framework that incorporates and untangles conflicting findings from different research paradigms (see Kaplan & Maehr, 2002).

Applying Achievement Goal Theory to Motivational Change in Education

The parsimonious powerful framework of achievement goal theory led researchers to use it as a guide for educational change that aims at facilitating students' adaptive motivation. The convergent research findings of two decades that strongly suggested that mastery goals are adaptive, whereas performance goals may be sometimes maladaptive, have focused such interventions on changing characteristics of the learning environment in ways that increased emphasis on mastery goals and de-emphasized performance goals (e.g., Ames, 1990; Maehr & Midgley, 1991, 1996). Generally, these programs involve a collaborative effort by researchers and educators that focuses on the evaluation of the meaning that educational practices in the school setting seem to send to students. Then, decisions are made to replace practices that suggest that school is about performance rather than about learning, mastery, and making progress. A few of these interventions employed Epstein's (1989) structural analysis of the classroom as a useful framework for pointing to contextual domains that influence achievement goals (Ames, 1992b; Maehr & Midgley, 1991). The dimensions, for which Epstein used the acronym TARGET, include the academic *Task*, the distribution of *Authority* in the classroom, the *Recognition* system, *Grouping* practices, the system of *Evaluation*, and the way *Time* is managed. Ames (1992a, 1992b) points to environmental strategies concerning each of these domains that teachers can use to increase students' mastery goals. The experience of these interventions clearly suggests, however, that it is desired that change of practices would be comprehensive—that is, in all of the TARGET domains—and involve a strong commitment of the management and teachers to make such a change of their school culture (see Maehr & Midgley, 1996; Urdan, Midgley, & Wood, 1995).

RECENT DEVELOPMENTS IN ACHIEVEMENT GOAL THEORY

The two-goal framework that positions mastery and performance goals in comparison to each other has been a fruitful and parsimonious framework for understanding students' motivation and its relation to contextual characteristics (see Midgley, 2002). However, as research into the nature and correlates of goals has continued, there has been increasing criticism of this dichotomous conceptualization—criticism that raises questions with regard to the educational implications that researchers have derived from achievement goal theory. The criticism seems to emerge from several lines of theory and research, prominent among which have been the identification of additional goal orientations, the introduction of approach–avoidance motivations into achievement goal theory, the consideration of multiple achievement goals, the emergence of complex person x situation interactions, and the emphasis on grounded theory in exploring the characteristics of students' motivation in school. All of these have important implications for the understanding of students' motivation in school and for the practice of facilitating adaptive engagement in schoolwork.

Additional Goal Orientations

One of the earlier conceptualizations of achievement goal theory suggested that engagement in achievement tasks could be motivated by purposes other than those that concern competence (Maehr, 1984). Specifically, findings from research that investigated the meaning of achievement to individuals (see Maehr & Nicholls, 1980; Maehr & Braskamp, 1986) suggested that tangible extrinsic rewards (e.g., money or privileges) and social gains, such as approval from significant others or a desired social interaction, are important motivations in achievement contexts. Either of these desirable results can be conceptualized as a reason for engaging in and performing on an achievement task. Whereas these goals, which are not associated with competence per se, were frequently mentioned, they were mostly overshadowed by mastery and performance goals, and have been mostly neglected in the research on achievement goals in the past two decades. The reasons for this neglect are not so clear. Perhaps these noncompetence goals did not fit with the other programs of research that contributed to achievement goal theory. However, particularly in the case of social goals, research employing qualitative methods has suggested that these orientations are often associated with achievement. Since both social and extrinsic goals are perceived to involve criteria for success (or failure) external to level of task performance, some researchers have chosen to incorporate them into the performance goals category (e.g., Nicholls, Patashnick, & Nolen, 1985; Pintrich, Smith, Garcia, & McKeachie, 1993). Recently, however, several researchers called for the recognition of these goal orientations as important purposes for students' behavior in school (e.g., Dweck, 1996; Urdan & Maehr, 1995). Indeed, Dowson and McInerney (2001) went as far as to suggest that "social goals may actually be more salient and predictive of students' global motivation and achievement than either mastery or performance goals" and that "it is possible that researchers have got it wrong in putting the emphasis on mastery and performance goals" (p. 40). This may be particularly important to consider in adolescence, a period in which social relations with peers take on an increased significance (e.g., Kegan, 1982).

The renewed interest in extrinsic and social goals resulted with attempts at defining them as distinct from mastery and performance goals (e.g., Midgley et al., 1998; Urdan & Maehr, 1995) and at exploring in more depth the various subgoals that may provide reasons for engagement, particularly in the social goal category. Thus, for example, Urdan and Maehr (1995) suggested the following social reasons as possible achievement goals when engaging (or avoiding engaging) in a task: gaining approval from others, complying with group values and norms, establishing social solidarity, and pursuing issues of social concern (see also Dowson & McInerney, 2001). Other goals that have been suggested include social responsibility, such as to be dependable and a good citizen, social status, and intimacy[1] (e.g., L. Anderman, 1999; Wentzel, 1992).

The goals mentioned above are in accord with the original conceptualization of an achievement goal—that is, they can provide a general purpose for pursuing success in a specific achievement activity. However, in achievement contexts such as classrooms, certain individuals are not interested in pursuing success or even in avoiding demonstrating poor ability;

they simply want to be left alone. To capture this orientation, researchers formulated another goal—one that is an apparent opposite of an "achievement goal orientation"—that was variously labeled "work avoidance" and "academic alienation" (Archer, 1994; Meece, Blumenfeld, & Hoyle, 1988; Nicholls et al., 1985; Nolen, 1988). The purpose associated with this goal is completing the work with as little expenditure of effort as possible or outsmarting the system and not doing the work. The behavioral patterns associated with work-avoidance goals seem similar to that of performance-oriented individuals with low perceived ability and mostly involve a negative pattern of cognition, affect, and behavior (Archer, 1994; Meece et al., 1988; Nicholls et al., 1985; Nolen, 1988; Skaalvik, 1997). However, the similar behavior of individuals pursuing work-avoidance goals and performance goals stems from different underlying meaning systems of the achievement situation. As Archer (1994) notes, "For alienated students, their interests and source of self-esteem lie in areas other than the classroom and so a proclaimed lack of effort is not a hedge to conceal lack of ability" (p. 432). This assumption is supported by low correlations between performance goals and a work-avoidance orientation (Skaalvik, 1997).

The inclusion of noncompetence goals in achievement goal theory opens the framework for the conceptualization of other goals that have been identified as motives for behavior (e.g., Ford, 1992). Thus, for example, it is possible to consider motives such as gaining control over others, exploring and establishing one's uniqueness and individuality, or pursuing equity and social justice as possible reasons for engagement in tasks in achievement settings. Whereas some of these goals may be more or less prevalent in academic settings, it is the identification of additional achievement goals that has raised the concern that mastery and performance goals may not be able to account for the richness and complexity of students' motivational processes. Clearly, this line of research favors a more comprehensive understanding of the complex processes that affect behavior in achievement settings over parsimony. Particularly in young adolescence, the issue of different types of social goals as reasons for coming to school (cf. Urdan & Hicks, 1995) and as orientations when doing schoolwork (Urdan & Maehr, 1995) and their antecedents and consequences requires extensive investigation.

Approach and Avoidance Motivations

In a recent development within achievement goal theory, Elliot (1997) argued for the integration of the classic framework of achievement needs into goal theory. In this theoretical integration, Elliot noted the distinction between approach and avoidance motivations (e.g., Atkinson, 1957) and suggested that the inconclusive research findings concerning performance goals are the result of confounding the approach and avoidance aspects of performance goals (Elliot & Harackiewicz, 1996). He suggested that performance goals should be differentiated to two distinct motivational orientations: performance-approach goals and performance-avoidance goals. When pursuing performance-approach goals, the person is oriented toward the desired possibility of demonstrating high ability and engages in the task with that purpose. When pursuing performance-avoidance goals, the person is oriented toward the undesired possibility of demonstrating low ability and engages in the task with the purpose of avoiding such a demonstration (Elliot, 1997, 1999; see also Elliot & Harackiewicz, 1996; Middleton & Midgley, 1997; Skaalvik, 1997; Vandewalle, 1997).

In recent studies that employed the distinction between performance-approach and performance-avoidance goals, performance-avoidance goals were found to be consistently related to negative outcomes such as test anxiety, self-handicapping strategies, avoidance of help seeking, and low achievement. In contrast, performance-approach goals were mostly found to be related to positive outcomes such as task-engagement, positive attitude toward challenge, positive self-concept, self-efficacy, performance on tests, and even intrinsic motivation (Elliot & Church, 1997; Elliot & Harackiewicz, 1996; Skaalvik, 1997). Some studies, however, found performance-approach goals to have no relations with either positive or negative outcomes (e.g., Middleton & Midgley, 1997). And one recent study suggested that performance-approach goals may lead to adoption of performance-avoidance goals among some students when conditions in the educational environment change (Middleton, Kaplan, & Midgley, 2002; for reviews, see Elliot, 1999; Midgley, Kaplan, & Middleton, 2001). Several researchers noted that these findings seem to imply that whether performance-approach goals would be associated with more or less adaptive outcomes among students might depend on the age of students and on the contexts in which they learn (Pintrich, 2000c). More specifically, research suggests that performance-approach goals may be more beneficial for late adolescents than for early adolescents (Bouffard, Vezeau, & Bordeleau, 1998). Presently, more research is needed about this issue (Midgley, Kaplan & Middleton, 2001).

Elliot (1999) and Pintrich (2000a) suggested recently that the approach-avoidance distinction could also be applied to mastery goals. Elliot (1999) suggested, for example, that mastery-avoidance—a concern with failure in mastery goals terms (e.g., being concerned with not being able to understand or with forgetting information)—could be common among the elderly, but may also be prevalent among perfectionists and professionals at the peak of their careers (Elliot & McGregor, 2001). It might also be possible to conceptualize mastery-avoidance among students, for example, when they realize that they might not be able to learn the material in the time allotted. At present, there is too little research on mastery-avoidance goals to indicate its prevalence among students or its usefulness for educators. In one of the few studies to examine mastery-avoidance goals to date, Elliot and McGregor (2001) found that, among college students, these goals were positively related to both mastery-approach goals and performance-avoidance goals. Mastery-avoidance goals were unrelated to either deep processing learning strategies or surface processing and also to exam performance. However, they were found to be related to disorganization in learning and to test anxiety, worry, and negative emotionality concerning doing well on a test.

Other goals can also be conceptualized as involving approach and avoidance components. Extrinsic goals, for example, could be conceptualized as extrinsic-approach—engagement with the desire to gain material goods—and as extrinsic-avoidance—engagement with the purpose of avoiding punishment. Social-approach goals could be conceptualized in such terms as establishing intimacy or a desired social belonging, whereas social-avoidance goals could be conceptualized as avoiding isolation and low social status. Similarly, individuality-approach goals could be thought of as pursuing a sense of oneself as unique and different, whereas individuality-avoidance would be engagement with the purpose of avoiding being perceived as similar to others or as conforming (see Ford, 1992). We can hypothesize that in each of these purposes for action there would be meaningful differences in the quality of engagement between students who focus on success and pursue the approach form of the purpose and students who focus on the possibility of failure and pursue the avoidance form of the purpose (cf. Carver & Scheier, 1998). Research that points to the importance of the distinction between approach and avoidance performance goals is accumulating (Elliot, 1999). Again, however, parsimony is lost in favor of a better description of the possible venues or pathways by which students can construe the meaning of achievement situations and the purposes that they can adopt for engagement and success in achievement tasks.

Multiple Goals

Another development in achievement goal theory emerged from research that suggested that mastery and performance goals are not mutually exclusive, but rather that students are able to and do pursue multiple goals. Whereas experimental studies typically manipulated participants to adopt one goal *or* the other, survey studies indicate that students often endorse items of different goal orientations to varying degrees (Ames & Archer, 1988; Harter, 1992; Meece & Holt, 1993; Nicholls, Patashnick, Cheung,

Thorkildsen, & Lauer, 1989; Pintrich & Garcia, 1991; Urdan, 1996). Indeed, in correlational research, individuals' endorsement of mastery goals is very often weakly positively related or unrelated to their endorsement of performance goals (Midgley et al., 1998; Nicholls et al., 1985; see discussion in Button, Mathieu, & Zajac, 1996; Nicholls, Cheung, Lauer, & Patashnick, 1989), implying multiple configurations of different levels in the simultaneous pursuit of these two goal orientations. The few qualitative studies assessing students' achievement goals support the hypothesis that individuals endorse multiple achievement goal orientations (e.g., Dowson & McInerney, 1997; Lee & Anderson, 1993; Levy, Kaplan, & Patrick, 2000).

The notion that students pursue multiple goals raised questions concerning the adaptive outcomes that are associated with the pursuit of various configurations of mastery and performance goals. In particular, researchers have been interested in the value of a combined mastery and performance orientation. Several studies attempted to delineate the behavioral patterns that are associated with endorsement of various configurations of goal orientations. The general finding is that pursuit of mastery goals, whether in combination with performance goals or not, is associated with an adaptive pattern of outcomes. The pursuit of performance goals as a single dominating orientation is associated with a more adaptive pattern of behavior than not pursuing any achievement goals; however, it is thought to be less adaptive than pursuit of any of the configurations involving mastery goals (see Bouffard, Boisvert, Vezeau, & Larouche, 1995; Duda, 1988; Harackiewicz, Barron, Carter, Lehto, & Elliot, 1997; Hofmann & Strickland, 1995; Meece & Holt, 1993; Pintrich, 2000c; Pintrich & Garcia, 1991; Seifert, 1995; Urdan, 1996).

The claim that performance goals—more particularly, performance-approach goals—may be adaptive in some contexts (Harackiewicz, Barron, & Elliot, 1998) raised questions concerning the relative benefits of adopting a dominant mastery goals orientation in comparison to an orientation that combines high mastery and high performance-approach goals. Harackiewicz and her colleagues (1998; Barron & Harackiewicz, 2000; see also Elliot & Church, 1997) suggest, for example, that in a competitive context, performance-approach goals (pursued simultaneously with mastery goals or alone) would contribute to achievement and would not interfere with intrinsic motivation. Some findings even suggest that mastery and performance-approach goals may be contributing to different outcomes: mastery goals to the positive effect associated with learning and to deep processing of information and performance-approach goals to the achievement of standards (e.g., Barron & Harackiewicz, 2000; Elliot & Church, 1997; Elliot & McGregor, 1999; Elliot, McGregor, & Gable, 1999).[2]

However, so far, no explication has been suggested as to the psychological processes that are involved in adopting and pursuing multiple goal orientations simultaneously (Pintrich, 2000a). Are persons switching back and forth between goal orientations in a situation, using mastery and performance goals intermittently? How does the notion of multiple goals relate to the definition of achievement goals as an integrated pattern of cognition, emotion, and behavior (cf. Ames, 1992a; Elliott & Dweck, 1988) or a comprehensive meaning in a situation (cf. Maehr, 1984; Molden & Dweck, 2000)? Are students constructing a meaning that combines aspects of several goal orientations? There is also much to be learned about the consequences of pursuing different configurations of goal orientations, and how this may differ among students from different cultures and groups, with different individual characteristics, and in different situations. Indeed, more recent research suggests that these relations may be quite complex, providing a further challenge to the parsimonious framework of achievement goal theory.

Complex Person x Situation Interactions

Recent research seems to imply that mastery and performance goals may not operate similarly for all individuals in all situations. Rather, findings seem to suggest that the relationships between goal orientations and cognition, affect, and behavior are moderated by personal characteristics such as dispositions to achievement motivation and age, situational characteristics such as the contextual emphasis on mastery and performance goals, and by the interaction between these two types of characteristics. For example, in a series of studies conducted with college students and involving the task of playing pinball, Harackiewicz and her colleagues (Elliot & Harackiewicz, 1994; Harackiewicz & Elliot, 1993, 1998) found that whether achievement goals were related to interest and enjoyment of the task depended on participants' dispositional achievement motivation or alternatively on the congruence between the specific standards that they were asked to achieve (framed as mastery goals or performance goals standards) and the experimental condition: mastery or performance goals. Generally, the findings suggested that individuals with high achievement motivation enjoy engaging in the task under a performance goals condition more than under a mastery goals condition, whereas this was reversed among individuals with low achievement motivation. The findings also suggest that individuals enjoy the activity more when there is congruence between the specific standards that individuals are asked to achieve and the achievement goal that was emphasized in the experimental condition as framing the task—and this was found regardless of whether the achievement goal emphasized is mastery or performance. Barron and Harackiewicz (2000) replicated these findings in an experiment with college students that involved a mathematics task. In this study, an additional condition in which both achievement goals were emphasized produced moderate levels of interest among students high and low in achievement motivation.

Another recent study suggests that age may play a moderating role in the relations between achievement goals and outcomes. Findings by Bouffard and colleagues (1998) suggest that pursuit of both mastery and performance goals was associated with lower reports of cognitive and meta-cognitive strategies and with motivation in comparison to pursuit of only mastery goals among young students but not among older students. Barron and Harackiewicz (2000) suggest that with age and with increased experience in performance-oriented environments, students will develop the ability to integrate pursuit of both mastery and performance goals in an adaptive way. This suggestion seems also to highlight the role of the context in moderating the relations between different configurations of achievement goals and outcomes.

Similarly, research suggests that other individual differences, such as gender and ethnicity, may moderate the relations between achievement goals and outcomes. For example, Midgley and colleagues (1996) found that whereas performance goals were related to self-handicapping strategies among African American students, they were not related to these maladaptive behaviors among European American students. The work of Claude Steele and others (Steele, 1997; Steele & Aronson, 1995; Croizet & Claire, 1998) suggests that minority students and females who are aware of a negative stereotype of their group are likely to experience a "stereotype threat" under evaluative (performance-oriented) situations. This may make these students prone to ruminative worry that is detrimental to performance. Students who are not members of negatively stereotyped groups do not experience these detrimental drawbacks in the same achievement situations. Indeed, the findings from cross-cultural research reviewed above seem to suggest that achievement goals may have somewhat different meanings among students of different ethnic and cultural background (e.g., Kaplan & Maehr, 1999; McInerney et al., 1998).

This literature suggests that individual and group differences among students may interact with different contextual conditions to play important moderating roles on the relations between the emphasis on achievement goals in the learning environment, students' achievement goals, and cognitive, emotional, and behavioral processes. Linnenbrink and Pintrich (2000) note that research that attends to these possible interactions leads to "a more complex but perhaps more realistic and ecologically valid view of the role of different goal orientations in learning and achievement" (p. 222). The very complex picture that emerges from the various research programs presented above seems to suggest that the interrelationships of mastery, performance, others' achievement goals, and their various configurations with adaptive and maladaptive educational outcomes should be investigated in particular populations of students, within specific learning environments. This understanding has led several researchers to call for the abandonment of the prevalent research methods in goal theory in favor of qualitative methods and a grounded theory perspective that allow the exploration of these unique motivational processes.

Grounded Theory

Recently, several researchers criticized the dominant research methods used in achievement goal theory that gave rise to the dichotomous conceptualization of mastery and performance goals. These researchers (e.g., Bempechat & Boulay, 2000; Dowson & McInerney, 2001) argue that experimental and survey methods do not reveal the complexity of students' motivational orientations and the meaning that students construe for achievement situations. For example, building on ideas from psychological anthropology and cultural psychology, and noting the responsibility of motivational researchers for informing practice in specific settings, Bempechat and Boulay (2000) critique theories that emphasize categories of motivational orientations and emphasize the need to investigate motivational processes through qualitative methods that reveal the unique meaning making of particular students in specific sociocultural contexts.

Similarly, Dowson and McInerney (2001) argue that research that assumes *a priori* categories of students' goals "may (a) artificially limit the range of goals investigated by researchers and (b) artificially limit descriptions of the content of these goals" (p. 35). In their research they assume a phenomenological approach that emphasizes the use of "the actual words of students" (p. 36) in order to explore students' motivational orientations. Using multimethods that involved open-ended conversations, semi-structured and structured interviews, and observations with 86 adolescents of different ages and from different schools, Dowson and McInerney found that goals, such as work avoidance goals, "had many 'faces' that varied according to specific classroom features" (p. 40), and that students see social goals in a complex way in which these goals often contribute but might also hinder engagement and achievement.

Other researchers using qualitative work also point to the complex meanings that achievement goals may have for students. For example, Mac-Callum (2000), who interviewed 10 students in the last year of primary school (Grade 7) and again in the first year of secondary school (Grade 8), identified "subtle differences in the focus of students' concerns" (p. 69) within goal categories. For example, in the ego (performance) goal category, students expressed concerns for performing well and impressing others; however, they differed with regard to the level of standard of performance (e.g., being on top, performing well, performing at a reasonable standard, performing at a high standard, being recognized as smart informally, being recognized as smart formally, not appearing dumb) and their target of impression management concerns (e.g., peers, teachers, parents). In the task (mastery) goal category, students expressed concerns such as having interest in new tasks; having interest in new and different ideas; employing strategies to improve; concentrating and working hard; seeking help if needed; and exerting effort to understand and improve. In the work avoidant category, students expressed an orientation toward limiting effort; however, some students indicated that they do work if they like the subject or if the work is relevant, while others indicated that they limit their effort in all schoolwork. In the social goals category, students expressed such concerns as impressing teachers; impressing a wide audience; pleasing parents; getting support from parents, teachers, and peers; having anxiety about lack of support from peers; disliking support from peers; wanting status as a high achiever; wanting status as "different"; and accepting the responsibility of being a high achiever.

Clearly, qualitative work that emphasizes the meaning construction of individual students and of students in different sociocultural contexts suggests that there may be an infinite number of unique motivational orientations, that these orientations could interact in complex and idiosyncratic ways, and that what may seem as similar goal orientations may operate differently in different contexts. These findings seem to suggest that the focus on mastery and performance goals is limiting and misleading in trying to understand students' complex motivational processes. In regard to researchers' understanding of students' achievement goals and the way they affect cognition, emotion, and behavior, as well as the practical advice that can be given to practitioners for facilitating adaptive engagement, this line of research suggests that findings may be limited to the specific context in which a study was conducted.

An Interpretative Summary

In the past two decades, achievement goal theory has focused on two primary purposes for engagement in achievement tasks: mastery goals and performance goals. This parsimonious framework integrated much of the research findings concerning students' motivation at the time (see Dweck, 1986; Dweck & Legget, 1988; Maehr, 1989; Nicholls, 1984) and provided relatively clear guidelines for educational interventions that attempted to facilitate adaptive motivation (see Ames, 1990, 1992b; Maehr & Midgley, 1991, 1996). However, in the last five years or so, research suggested that the focus on these two goals is insufficient to explain the complex processes that lead students to engage in achievement tasks adaptively or maladaptively. The accumulating research that has examined the number and types of purposes that students can pursue in school settings and the moderating roles of various individual differences and contextual characteristics seems to highlight the idiosyncratic nature of motivational processes.

Achievement goal theory originated from an attempt to meaningfully reduce the meanings that students construe for achievement situations into a parsimonious framework that will allow the identification of processes leading to adaptive and maladaptive engagement. At this point, the research indicates that mastery and performance goals do not provide such broadly applicable meaningful categories, at least in any simple, consistent, and direct manner. Yet it could also be argued that the recent directions of research that criticize the original formulation of goal theory seem to divert somewhat from what arguably was the original conception of goal orientations. Whereas the original notion of achievement goals suggested that what is of concern is a comprehensive yet situated meaning of the action in the achievement situation (e.g., Ames, 1992a; Elliott & Dweck, 1988; Maehr, 1984; see also Molden & Dweck, 2000; Nicholls, 1992), at least some recent research seems to employ a somewhat narrower definition in its operationalization of achievement goals. For example, a focus on different combinations of the environmental emphasis on achievement goals and the self-set achievement goals of students (cf. Barron & Harackiewicz, 2000) conceptualizes students' motivational orientations as *contributing* to the meaning of the situation (e.g., as manifested in a sense of a mismatch between personal and environment values) rather than as being *derived* from or as *an aspect of* this meaning. Similarly, attempting to explore the relations between achievement goals and social goals and how they interact to relate to adaptive and maladaptive behavior also implies that students' (various) goal orientations combine to form a certain meaning of the situation (e.g., a sense of coherence, or of a conflict, between the desire to do well in school and to be accepted by peers) rather than that the goal orientation *is* the cognitions, emotions, and behavior that emerge from and are an integral part of the meaning construed (cf. Maehr, 1984).

This view of achievement goals could be said to be more in line with perspectives on goals that emphasize goal content and define goals as "cognitive representations of what we hope to accomplish" (Barron & Harackiewicz, 2000, p. 231), or "*what* it is that an individual is trying to achieve in a given situation" (Wentzel & Wigfield, 1998, pp. 160–161). This perspective on goals is a worthy one and has provided the basis for comprehensive theories of human behavior (e.g., Ford, 1992; Murray, 1938), yet it is also limited in its ability to predict adaptive behavior by the need to specify all the goals that people may be pursuing in a certain context, and the possible effects of different configurations of goals and the interaction of these various configurations with personal characteristics and contextual conditions. Indeed, it leads to the inevitable conclusion that motivational processes are unique to individuals who have particular individual characteristics and who learn in particular sociocultural environments.

Whereas a thorough qualitative investigation of the motivational processes, in particular educational environments, that results with insights concerning the interventions that could facilitate adaptive motivation in those settings is worthy and indeed desired, it seems that motivation theory should be able also to provide a more parsimonious framework that could guide researchers and practitioners in understanding the processes that lead students to engage meaningfully and deeply. Indeed, we believe that it is the responsibility of motivation researchers to seek such a framework. In the next section, we would like to propose a conceptualization that, while emphasizing the situated nature of motivational processes in sociocultural settings, attempts to integrate these understandings into a relatively parsimonious framework that could guide research as well as educational practice.

CONSTRUCTING ACHIEVEMENT GOALS IN THE CLASSROOM

The conceptualization that we present begins with the concept of achievement goal as the purpose for the activity that emerges from the situated meaning that the student construes. There are different theoretical approaches to the process of construction of a situated meaning. Some emphasize the role of the individual in this process, whereas others emphasize the role of the context. Some emphasize the importance of enduring characteristics (either of the individual or of the context), whereas others turn the light on the situated and transitory. In recent years, there have been different attempts at integrating these approaches to form a more complete picture of situated meaning making (e.g., Cobb, 1994; Martin & Sugarman, 1999; Moshman, 1982). The approach we espouse in this chapter suggests that the construction of meaning of action in a certain achievement situation employs individual as well as contextual processes. Each of these two components, however, has enduring as well as situated characteristics. Whereas they all play a role in the situated process of meaning construction, at different times, *depending on the situation* (e.g., whether it is a very familiar situation or not, or whether it involves content that touches on very important domains to the person or not), different aspects would assume a more significant role in affecting the meaning construed. In any event, however, the meaning and purpose of action construed is situated—

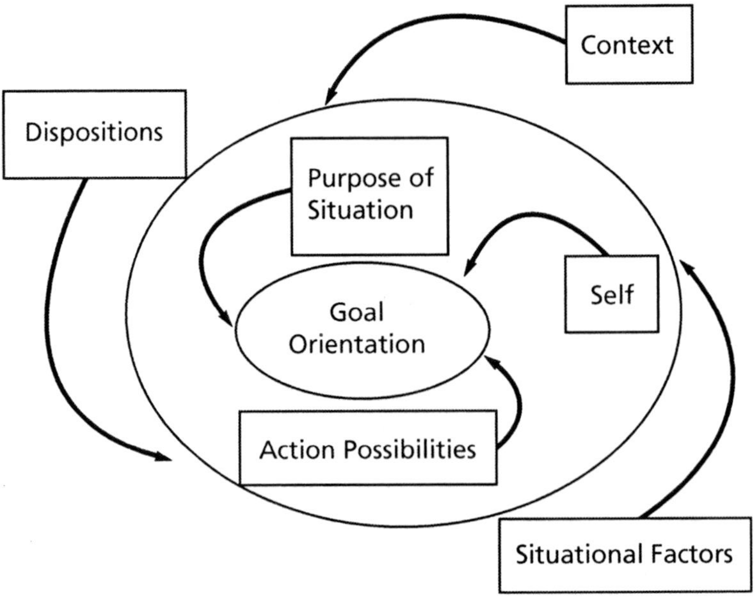

Figure 5.1. The processes contributing to the situated achievement goal orientation.

that is, it is recreated—in the situation. Such a perspective highlights the important role of educators in arranging situations that facilitate the construction of certain types of achievement goals over others.

Our model points to three major components that combine in the process of meaning construction to create the personal achievement goal: perceived purpose of action in a situation, self-processes, and perceived action possibilities (see Maehr, 1984). In the following sections we elaborate on the nature of each of the components and on the processes that contribute to their construction. Whereas the three components are presented serially, our perspective emphasizes the dynamic relations among them, as depicted in Figure 5.1. We understand the three components to operate and affect each other simultaneously in a process of which phenomenological aspect is that of adopting a personal purpose for action in an achievement situation.

Perceived Purpose in the Situation

The idea that people's achievement goals for action in a situation depend on what they understand the situation to be is logical. It is also supported by research (e.g., Kaplan & Maehr, 1999; Roeser, Midgley, & Urdan, 1996). A question arises with regard to the way such perceptions of purpose in situations are formed. Research suggests that people have schemas of proto-typical situations that are activated when a situation that is similar is encountered. These schemas involve, for example, goals of action and the appropriateness of certain behavior in the situation (e.g., Thorkildsen, 1989, 1991). They thus affect the way by which the purpose of behavior in the situation is interpreted (Cantor, Mischel, & Schwartz, 1982). There likely are individual differences in such schemas that are based on person-ality dispositions (McClelland, 1961). However, it is also clear that proto-typical schemas of situations are construed through social interactions within sociocultural contexts (D'Andrade, 1990). The meaning of achieve-ment situations, for example, is affected by the meaning of achievement in the cultural group (Maehr & Nicholls, 1980). Different discourse and prac-tices socialize students to construe achievement situations as having differ-ent purposes and different goals for action (cf. Rogoff, 1994) and to have different emotions associated with such purposes (cf. Kitayama & Masuda, 1995; Markus & Kitayama, 1991). Moreover, the effect of discourse on the purpose of achievement situations can be more localized than the context of an entire cultural group. Wertsch (1991), for example, characterizes the type of discourse that, together with the artifacts in the classroom, guides students' construction of the meaning of school, classroom, subject matter, and different situations. Wertsch notes that schools, perhaps more than other cultural institutions, have the goal of socializing students to use a particular discourse and to think in certain ways about what the purpose of being in school is all about. In asking questions such as "How many tens and how many ones are there in the top number?" (p. 112), teachers con-vey the message that the purpose of the situation is not gaining or obtain-ing information, but rather to get the student "to participate in formulating the problem in the 'right way'" (p. 112). When the discourse implies that the teacher knows the "right" answer, activities and learning assume purposes that are different from purposes of activities in which answers are not predetermined. In addition, the purpose of situations is construed through social negotiation. In school, this negotiation can occur between teacher and students, as when the teacher defines a new situation as having a certain meaning and the students ask questions and comment on the definition, and it can occur among students themselves, as when students explain to each other or debate the meaning of situations (e.g., Nicholls & Hazzard, 1993; Thorkildsen & Nicholls, 1991).

Thus, through sociocultural processes that guide them in appropriating cultural values, symbols, and tools, and through social constructivist pro-cesses that range from direct transmission to social negotiation, students construct understanding of the purpose of tests, contests, and multiple learning situations (e.g., silent reading, choice time, worksheet, group work, drawing). Students also construct prototypical understandings of the purpose of learning a particular subject matter, under a certain teacher, and in school in general. Perceptions of purpose of typical classroom situations can be viewed from an achievement goal perspective as varying on dimensions such as emphasizing social comparison and relative ability (e.g., tests and contests), social collaboration and responsibility (e.g., collaborative group work), and exploring material and learning for its own sake (e.g., personal reading time).

However, in addition to the prototype, the situated aspect of perceptions of purpose also incorporates various characteristics of the particular situation, the social negotiation that takes place, and the situated emotions of students. Together these result in a comprehensive phenomenological experience of a purpose for a specific activity at a particular moment (cf. Hicks, 1994). Newman, Griffin, and Cole (1989) go as far as to suggest that activities do not have a stable purpose: "Not only do the 'conditions for achieving the goal' change from situation to situation and over time in the same situation, but the goals also appear, disappear, and change. As children's actions are appropriated, the children's role in, and understanding of, the activity are modified" (p. 135).

Thus, prototypes of academic situations that are the result of cultural and contextual socialization can be "activated" to influence perceptions of purpose in a particular situation. However, situational and personal factors will vary the significance of a prototype to the situated meaning, and situated interaction can drastically change the meaning of an activity. In very ambiguous situations, when information cues, discourse, tools, and social interaction suggest that the purpose differs from that of a prototypical situation, students might construe a new purpose. In situations that are less ambiguous, situational features may still modify the prototypical purpose. The features of the situation and the purpose that is attached to it are an integral component of the continuous construction process of purpose of academic situations. Educators have much responsibility in designing environments and situations that send students messages concerning desired purposes of action—or what schooling should be about. The interventions already conducted (Ames, 1990; Maehr & Midgley, 1996) provide some guide in such practice. However, interventions that focus on the perceived purpose of the situation need to take account of other processes that combine to affect the personal achievement goals that students end up adopting. Perhaps the central one is self-processes.

Self-Processes

The second component in the dynamic process of the construction of purpose for action is the student's perceptions and sense of self. The self is a general term that refers to a cognitive-affective dynamic structure that includes a vast amount of knowledge and evaluations that people have of themselves (Markus & Wurf, 1987). This dynamic system provides an interpretive frame for most significant events and behaviors of the person. The self has enduring characteristics that are affected by individual attributes such as innate dispositions (e.g., temperament), normative processes such as those related to developmental stage (Harter, 1983), as well as by enduring environmental effects (e.g., childrearing, cultural values) (Markus & Kitayama, 1991; Triandis, 1989). However, the self is also reconstructed again and again in each situation, with different situations highlighting and activating different aspects of the self, which combine with the present experiences to create new self-understandings and self-evaluations (Gergen, 1991; Shotter, 1997). The aspects of the self that relate to the purpose of action in learning environments range from students' self-efficacy beliefs for performing the particular task (Pajares, 1996) to their social and cultural identity (Tajfel & Turner, 1986) and the implications of engaging in the activity to their acceptance by their cultural group and peers (see, e.g., Ogbu, 1992).

Cultures socialize students into constructing different enduring aspects of self (Markus & Kitayama, 1991; Triandis, 1989). Among members of collectivist cultures, collective aspects of self are likely to have higher levels of accessibility, and therefore to guide behavior in more situations. Among members of individualistic cultures, private aspects of self would be more accessible. Differential cultural treatments of individuals of different gender, ethnicity, SES, and other characteristics would result in different subcultural identities. Thus, students from different cultures and groups may be inclined to adopt different purposes that they perceive in the situation as personal achievement goals.

However, while cultures may facilitate chronic accessibility of certain aspects of self across many situations, characteristics of the situation have a critical role in the self-schemata that would be activated. The task structure (e.g., competition versus individualized work), content, social composition of the group, importance of the subject matter to the student, and social roles and norms would influence the dimension of self that is activated, the self-presentation that students will engage in, and the achievement goals that they will adopt (cf. Garcia & Pintrich, 1994; Markus & Nurius, 1986; Markus & Wurf, 1987). The norms and values of the situated group (e.g., of parents, same-gender peers, mixed-gender peers, able and competitive peers) would result in a differential activation of private and public self-aspects. The distinctiveness of a certain attribute in the situation (e.g., gender, ethnicity, academic ability) may direct students' attention to different self-schemata. Depending on the construction of the self-aspect that is activated (e.g., a girl's gender identity that involves uneasiness with academic success), the student may construe a personal purpose for the activity that adopts or rejects the perceived purpose of the situation. Furthermore, impression management will differ according to the values of the situated group, and thus prompt students to adopt different norms, some that might be in conflict with those of the main culture or with learning. In particular situations, therefore, students from collectivist cultures may still adopt achievement goals, such as performance goals, which are generally less valued in collectivist cultures than in individualistic cultures. Once a self-aspect has been activated, it is prone to be reconstructed through social processes such as social interaction and social comparison, and through individual processes such as self-observation. The construction also depends on individual differences such as personal dispositions, developmental stage, familiarity with the task, and prior knowledge in the domain. Educators should be aware of the self-related issues that are significant for their students. This is particularly important during adolescence, when self-understanding and self-exploration are becoming central in students' lives (Erikson, 1968). Such awareness by educators can facilitate the design of activities that would concern students' self-relevant issues and contribute to adoption of purposes for action that concern self-development and exploration. We elaborate on this issue later on.

Garcia and Pintrich (1994) contend that the self-schema is the mental structure that integrates motivational beliefs with behavioral strategies that result in learning. The activation of certain self-aspects is directly related to the norms that would be activated, and thus affect behavior. For example, when a gender identity becomes salient in a situation, cultural norms that are attached to this identity also become salient. These norms could be critical in guiding the orientation and the behavior of the student. The repertoire of behavioral strategies that students have available and are willing to perform is the third critical component in the adoption of a purpose as a personal achievement goal.

Action Possibilities

Action possibilities are "the behavioral alternatives or options that a person perceives to be available to him or her in any given situation" (Maehr, 1984, p. 124). When thinking about the behaviors that students can engage in so as to accomplish the various goals that they pursue in school, this category needs to be highly inclusive (cf. Garcia & Pintrich, 1994). Three assumptions have to be met for a student to perceive a behavior as a possible action. One is that the behavior has to be available—the student needs to have it in his or her repertoire. Another is that the behavior has to become an option in a given situation. Finally, the student has to adopt the behavior as suitable for him or her in a given situation.

Maehr (1984; Maehr & Braskamp, 1986) contends that "opportunity"—experiencing environments (e.g., culture, family, school) that provide exposure to multiple domains and that support individual reflection on and transfer of strategies—is the necessary but not sufficient foundation for the development of availability, awareness, and enactment of behavior. However, in addition to providing exposure and support for exploration, cultural and social environments could be active and directive in the socialization of behavior. Through participation in cultural practices, students appropriate norms and strategies, build a repertoire, and acquire guides for culturally appropriate usage (Rogoff & Lave, 1984). In addition, discrimination of people from different genders and ethnic groups may facilitate perceptions of options as limited. Indeed, prevalent power relations in societies manifest in organizational practices that limit opportunities for individuals from certain groups and influence these individuals' outcome expectations and motivational orientations (Delpit, 1988; Foucault, 1980; Goodnow, 1990; cf. Schunk, 1989).

The adoption of a certain behavior or strategy (e.g., to relate the material to previously learned knowledge, or to seek help when it is needed) is a fundamental element in students' achievement goals. A critical characteristic of this adoption is the level of internalization—or, in other words, the perceived origin—of the behavior (cf. Ryan & Grolnick, 1986). Strategies can be perceived as originating in the self (i.e., "I want to do this"), in an internal reference group (i.e., "I should be doing this"), or in an external reference group (e.g., "They force me to do this"). Garcia and Pintrich (1994) note that socialization of the self and its differentiation to multiple distinct self-schemata also involves socialization of distinct strategies that concern becoming, maintaining, and avoiding becoming particular selves. Thus, the motivational force aroused by an activation of a certain aspect of self (e.g., the desire to become "a good student in math") would be manifested in the use of particular strategies (e.g., math learning strategies, math class norms of behavior, math teacher pleasing behavior). The self-perspective taken (e.g., an internal reference group or a public-self) when a certain self-schema is activated would affect the norms and strategies that this self-schema is associated with, and thus affect the achievement goal adopted.

Schools are major agents in this enculturation. Through the control of the opportunities that children have to view and explore different behavior, cultures—and schools within cultures—allow the construction of a repertoire in which various possible strategies are available but others are not. Students appropriate strategies that they receive from the teacher, that they see peers perform, and that they construct collaboratively as they solve problems in groups. Individual differences that range from demographic characteristics such as gender and ethnicity to motivational dispositions and level of ability would influence these interactions and result in modified construction of strategies. The individual construction of strategies will also be influenced by personal characteristics such as previous knowledge, level of ability, and affect.

The construction and mastering of behavior and strategies would provide the student the necessary but not sufficient conditions for engaging deeply in the academic task. Situational characteristics that would influence the goal of the activity and the activation of certain self-aspects that might be conducive or disruptive to academic engagement would interact with availability and awareness of strategies to determine the purpose that the student will adopt in the activity and the manner by which she will pursue the purpose.

Implications for Theory, Research, and Practice

Understanding motivation as a dynamic process by which enduring and situated characteristics of the context and the individual combine to affect the meaning of the situation that the person construes—a meaning of which the central component is the purpose of action—emphasizes the dependence of motivational processes on the particular nature of the individuals and of the sociocultural contexts and situations in which they act. This model also suggests that investigation of motivational processes should involve a significant exploratory element that enables the unique meanings of situations and purposes of action that are specific to each sociocultural context to emerge. However, unlike the perspective that calls for abandoning generalizations and focusing on grounded theory, this model also offers a coherent conceptual tool for understanding motivational processes across sociocultural contexts. It highlights meaning-construction processes that operate among any group of people in any setting and thus it provides anchors for focused investigations as well as for targeted interventions.

So what does all that say about motivating students to "do what needs to be done"? One important implication is the understanding that students' "doing" or "acting" is inseparable from the purpose for action that they construe in the situation. Moreover, this purpose depends on the way the learning environment defines achievement and success and on the way students' identity—those self-processes that are highlighted in the situation—relates to these environmental definitions. The process of facilitating adaptive motivation should be conceived of as a complex transaction between the environment and the students. Therefore, in the process of searching for ways to motivate students, practitioners should first engage in exploring and defining what they believe achievement and success should be in their setting and which behaviors should contribute to this success—a process that is difficult but essential (Maehr & Midgley, 1996; Urdan, Midgley, & Wood, 1995). They then should figure whether their learning environments indeed emphasize these definitions to their students and whether their students would adopt them as purposes for action. Finally, educators should change the meanings that are sent to students by transforming the school culture (Kaplan & Maehr, 1997; Maehr & Midgley, 1996) so that it emphasizes and socializes students to adopt those desired purposes.

Clearly, success in such an endeavor requires good familiarity with the specific content of each of the three components that are involved in the construction of students' achievement goals. This means that educators should develop an understanding of the ways by which specific groups of students perceive different academic situations. They should also be familiar with the self-related issues that these students are concerned with and that would become salient in academic situations. Finally, educators should realize the repertoire of behaviors that students who belong to different subgroups perceive as available and legitimate in different contexts. It seems almost inevitable that a process that requires such familiarity of the psychological life of students would necessitate getting input from the students themselves, and perhaps even involve students in the process of designing the educational environments that would encourage them to adopt purposes that contribute to success. This too is not an easy process and should be conducted with the characteristics of the particular educational setting and of the students in mind. Perhaps in no other stage in students' lives is this task more difficult and yet crucial than in adolescence.

FACILITATING ADAPTIVE ACHIEVEMENT GOALS AMONG ADOLESCENTS

Our model suggests that investigations and interventions that concern the purposes of action that students construe should focus on the transaction between the characteristics of students and those of the context. It is important, therefore, that efforts that aim to change adolescents' perceptions and adoption of purpose in school take into consideration the characteristics of this developmental stage and the unique ways by which these characteristics manifest in specific sociocultural groups. A familiarity with the characteristics of adolescence provides an important starting point for the exploration of these transactional processes, which take place in educational environments that serve students of this age group.

Adolescence is characterized by an increase in cognitive capacities (Piaget & Inhelder, 1958) as well as an enhanced focus on self-processes and identity issues (Adams, Gullota, & Montemayor, 1992). Research conducted in the United States also highlights the increased need of American adolescents as compared to children for self-management and autonomous expression and for establishing relationships with adults that are not parents (Eccles & Midgley, 1989; Eccles et al., 1993).[3] This research suggests that the common drop in academic motivation and well-being among early adolescents as they make the transition from elementary school to middle school (or junior high) can be related to a mismatch between the characteristics of the junior high school learning environments and those needs and abilities of early adolescents. The typical junior high environment provides less challenging activities, puts more emphasis on social comparison, allows fewer opportunities to self-manage, and facilitates more impersonal teacher–student relationships than elementary schools do (Eccles & Midgley, 1989; Eccles et al., 1993). Of particular interest is that studies suggest that such changes in the characteristics of the learning environment are associated with a decrease in students' perceptions of emphasis on mastery goals (Anderman & Midgley, 1997; Midgley, Anderman, & Hicks, 1995). These changes are also associated with downward shifts in early adolescents' self-perceptions of ability and self-esteem (Eccles et al., 1993). Early adolescents who made the transition to middle-level schools that were facilitative of their needs did not experience the declines in self-perceptions of ability, self-esteem, and liking of schoolwork. These students' liking of school actually increased (Midgley, Feldlaufer, & Eccles, 1989a, 1989b). More recent research suggests that similar processes operate in the transition from middle-level school to high school, although findings also highlight some change from early to middle adolescence in the transaction between the educational environment and the developmental characteristics of students (see Middleton, Midgley, Gheen, & Kumar, 2002). Clearly, in order to facilitate a positive attitude, receptiveness, and responsiveness to the messages emphasized in the environment among adolescents, educators should first and foremost create contexts that provide support for their developmental needs.

Perhaps the important characteristic of adolescence that distinguishes it as unique from other age groups with regard to the processes described in our model is the changes in self-structure and processes and in attention to self and identity. Researchers suggest that the self-construct changes from a structure that is hierarchically organized during childhood and early adolescence, to an unstable and less integrated structure composed of unrelated components during middle adolescence, to a multifaceted, differentiated but not hierarchical structure in late adolescence (Wigfield, Eccles, & Pintrich, 1996). The instability of the self-structure, which is accompanied by a heightened self-focus, is a manifestation of the main developmental task associated with adolescence—exploring and constructing an identity (Erikson, 1968). The focus on self-processes and heightened self-awareness make adolescents prone to be especially sensitive to the implications of behaviors for their sense of self and for the way they are perceived by others (Elkind & Bowen, 1979; Nicholls, 1984). Therefore, interventions that aim at encouraging adolescents to adopt certain purposes for action and employ certain behaviors toward certain goals should involve consideration of the implications of these purposes and the associated behaviors for adolescents' concerns about self-perception and impression management (cf. Covington, 1992). Thus, for example, if the goal is to encourage adolescents to perceive the learning environment as emphasizing meaningful learning and to adopt this purpose as their achievement goal, it is crucial that educators make an effort to create contexts in which investing, exploring, helping, making mistakes, and taking on challenges have positive rather than negative implications in students' eyes.

The characteristics of the environment that would facilitate positive attitudes among students toward the purposes emphasized in the context depend on the particular issues and processes in the identity formation of adolescents. However, the processes of exploring the self and constructing an identity take different forms among adolescents of different ages, genders, cultures, and historical times (see Adams et al., 1992). For example, Kegan (1982) notes that among early adolescents, social relationships provide a fundamental defining characteristic of the self and play an organizing, formative role in the interpretation of situations; whereas among older adolescents, social relationships become an aspect of a more general and complex self-definition (see also Urdan & Hicks, 1995). As another example, Schiedel and Marcia (1985) suggest that in the process of constructing an identity, the issue of intimacy is related differently to the self among men and women. Whereas among men, identity and intimacy are organized in a step-like order, among women, these issues are merged. In addition to these differences in content, adolescents of different genders and cultures and of different dispositions go about the process of exploring and establishing their identity differently, employing different strategies of self-exploration (e.g., Berzonsky, 1992; Flum, 1994; Josselson, 1987).

As the foregoing review suggests, in addition to individual differences, the issues and processes involved in self-exploration and identity construction would also be very much dependent on the specific social environment and the unique social identities that are formed in the particular setting (cf. Tajfel & Turner, 1986). Particular contexts and situations that highlight such characteristics as majority and minority, social status, ethnicity, and immigrant status are all potentially influential in the self-processes that become salient for students and in the meaning of these self-processes to engagement in action. Being familiar with the issues and the processes that adolescents engage in as they explore self and identity could highlight for educators the content and structure of tasks that would encourage these particular adolescents to perceive and adopt the achievement goal that is emphasized. Such familiarity, for example, could highlight for educators the orientation of particular groups of students to interpret situations along certain dimensions (e.g., certain types of social issues such as discrimination) and the boundaries that adolescents perceive with regard to employing publicly certain behaviors (e.g., individual seat-work, collaboration across social status groups).

In summary, attention to the self-relevant processes and issues of adolescents is critical for understanding when and why they might adopt or reject the pursuit of achievement in school. It is also important for the design of environments that could facilitate the construction of adaptive purposes for learning. Clearly, such a process may result with different definitions of achievement and of success in different sociocultural contexts and in different educational institutions. Indeed, it is this malleability of the three goal components that allows this meaning construction and its dynamic and continuous revision as the situation changes.

CONCLUSION

Not surprisingly, the extensive interest in the topics covered in this chapter have created a complex picture of motivation. The initial studies that gave rise to achievement goal theory were largely simple in design and more often than not straightforward in results—and most researchers were all too willing to generalize findings across multiple contexts and persons. Findings of recent research have humbled us and also have stimulated some to search in new directions and hazard new interpretations and hypotheses. For our part, we have stumbled to the conclusion that research must refocus on the situation in which motivation arises. That was once said for practical reasons: Motivation theory is of little value to practitioners unless it speaks to motivation change over which they have some control. Increasingly, it also makes good theoretical sense, as we consider the situated nature of cognition and keep in mind that our most theoretically as well as practically useful constructs regarding motivation remain those that have to do with meaning: thoughts and emotions about purpose, self, and action alternatives. In order to explore those situated meanings, we emphasized the inseparability of the students from their environment. And for the facilitation of adaptive motivation, it is the inseparability of the environment from the students that needs to be emphasized. It is particularly with adolescents that such a conceptualization of motivational processes provides tools for the understanding of the situated transaction between people and environment. The concurrent occurrence of changes associated with puberty, increase in cognitive abilities, heightened focus on self and identity, and environmental transitions from elementary school to middle-level schools, to high schools, and then to college or the workforce leaves the adolescent particularly vulnerable to academic and socioemotional difficulties that have lasting implications for adult life (Wigfield et al., 1996). However, research accumulates that suggests that when educational environments are facilitative of adolescents needs, school can become a place where adolescents are motivated to learn. Moreover, the research also points to the strong positive links between adolescents' motivation in school and their well-being (Roeser, Eccles, & Sameroff, 2000). Thus, facilitating adaptive motivation among adolescents assumes a significance that is beyond their school achievement. Our model suggests that this task is quite difficult, but whoever said that understanding and intervening with human nature should be easy? We conclude with the hope that this chapter raised an idea or two that might generate further investigation regarding the nature of human motivation.

NOTES

1. Some of the goals were defined slightly differently from the way achievement goals have been defined. Rather than asking "why" are students trying to achieve on the academic task, these goals were conceptualized by their content and as representations of end states, that is, as "what" students are trying to achieve in school (see Wentzel, 1992).
2. Theorists focusing on goal content suggested that in addition to the simultaneous pursuit of mastery and performance goals, other goals, such as social goals, would also be pursued (Wentzel, 1992).
3. Recent research suggests that some of these characteristics also appear among adolescents in non-Western societies that are experiencing cultural change (e.g., Choo & Tan, 2000).

REFERENCES

Adams, G. R., Gullotta, T. P., & Montemayor, R. (1992). *Adolescent identity formation* (Vol. 4). Newbury Park, CA: Sage Publications.

Albaili, M. A. (1998). Goal orientations, cognitive strategies and academic achievement among United Arab Emirates college students. *Educational Psychology, 18,* 19–20.

Ames, C. (1990, April). *The relationship of achievement goals to student motivation in classroom settings.* Paper presented at the Annual Meeting of the American Educational Research Association, Boston.

Ames, C. (1992a). Classrooms: Goals, structures, and student motivation. *Journal of Educational Psychology, 84,* 261–271.

Ames, C. (1992b). Achievement goals and the classroom motivational climate. In D. Schunk & J. Meece (Eds.), *Student perceptions in the classroom* (Ch.15, pp. 327–348). Hillsdale, NJ: Lawrence Erlbaum.

Ames, C., & Ames, R. (1984). *Research on motivation in education* (Vol. 1). New York: Academic Press.

Ames, C., & Archer, J. (1988). Achievement goals in the classroom: Student learning strategies and motivation processes. *Journal of Educational Psychology, 80,* 260–267.

Anderman, L. (1999). Classroom goal orientation, school belonging, and social goals as predictors of students' positive and negative affect following the transition to middle school. *Journal of Research and Development in Education, 32,* 89–103.

Anderman, E. M., & Maehr, M. L. (1994). Motivation and schooling in the middle grades. *Review of Educational Research, 64,* 287–309.

Anderman, E. M., & Midgley, C. (1997). Changes in personal achievement goals and the perceived classroom goal structures across the transition to middle level schools. *Contemporary Educational Psychology, 22,* 269–298.

Archer, J. (1994). Achievement goals as a measure of motivation in university students. *Contemporary Educational Psychology, 19,* 430–446.

Atkinson, J. W. (1957). Motivational determinants of risk-taking behavior. *Psychological Review, 64,* 359–372.

Austin, J. T., & Vancouver, J. B. (1996). Goal constructs in psychology: Structure, process, and content. *Psychological Bulletin, 120,* 338–375.

Bandura, A. (1986). *Social foundations of thought and action: A social cognitive theory.* Englewood Cliffs, NJ: Prentice-Hall.

Barron, K. E., & Harackiewicz, J. M. (2000). Achievement goals and optimal motivation: A multiple goals approach. In C. Sansone & J. M. Harackiewicz (Eds.), *Intrinsic and extrinsic motivation: The search for optimal motivation and performance* (pp. 229–254). New York: Academic Press.

Baumeister, R. F. (1998). *The handbook of social psychology.* New York: McGraw-Hill.

Bempechat, J., & Boulay, B. A. (2000). Beyond dichotomous characterizations of student learning: New directions in achievement motivation research. In D. M. McInerney & S. Van Ettern (Eds.), *Research on sociocultural influences on motivation and learning* (Vol. 1, pp. 15–36). Greenwich, CT: Information Age.

Berzonsky, M. D. (1992). A process perspective on identity and stress management. In G. R. Adams, & T. P. Gullotta & R. Montemayor (Eds.), *Adolescent identity formation* (Vol. 4, pp. 193–215). Newbury Park, CA: Sage.

Biddle, S., Cury, F., Goudas, M., Sarrazin, P., Famose, J. P., & Durand, M. (1995). Development of scales to measure perceived physical education class climate: A cross-national project. *British Journal of Educational Psychology, 65,* 341–358.

Bouffard, T., Boisvert, J., Vezeau, C., & Larouche, C. (1995). The impact of goal orientation on self-regulation and performance among college students. *British Journal of Educational Psychology, 65,* 317–329.

Bouffard, T., Vezeau, C., & Bordeleau, L. (1998). A developmental study of the relation between combined learning and performance goals and students' self-regulated learning. *British Journal of Educational Psychology, 68,* 309–319.

Butler, R. (1993). Effects of task- and ego-achievement goals on information seeking during task engagement. *Journal of Personality and Social Psychology, 65,* 18–31.

Button, S. B., Mathieu, J. E., & Zajac, D. M. (1996). Goal Orientation in organizational research: A conceptual and empirical foundation. *Organizational Behavior and Human Decision Processes, 67,* 26–48.

Cantor, N., Mischel, W., & Schwartz, J. C. (1982). A prototype analysis of psychological situations. *Cognitive Psychology, 14,* 45–77.

Carver, C. S., & Scheier, M. F. (1998). *On the self-regulation of behavior.* New York: Cambridge University Press.

Choo, O. A., & Tan, E. (2000). Fathers' role in the school success of adolescents: A Singapore study. In D. M. McInerney & S. Van Ettern (Eds.), *Research on sociocultural influences on motivation and learning* (Vol. 1, pp. 183–203). Greenwich, CT: Information Age.

Cobb, P. (1994). Where is the mind? Constructivist and sociocultural perspectives on mathematical development. *Educational Researcher, 23,* 13–20.

Covington, M. V. (1992). *Making the grade: A self-worth perspective on motivation and school reform.* New York: Cambridge University Press.

Covington, M. V. (2000). Goal theory, motivation, and school achievement: An integrative review. *Annual Review of Psychology, 51,* 171–200

Croizet, J. C., & Claire, T. (1998). Extending the concept of stereotype threat to social class: The intellectual underperformance of students from low socioeconomic backgrounds. *Personality and Social Psychology Bulletin, 24,* 588–594.

D'Andrade, R. (1990). Some propositions about the relations between culture and human cognition. In J. Stigler, R. Shweder, & G. Herdt (Eds.), *Cultural psychology: Essays on comparative human development* (pp. 65–129). New York: Cambridge University Press.

Delpit, L. D. (1988). The silenced dialogue: Power and pedagogy in educating other people's children. *Harvard Educational Review, 58,* 280–298.

Dowson, M., & McInerney, D. M. (1997, March). *Psychological parameters of students' social and academic goals: A qualitative investigation.* Paper presented at the Annual Meeting of the American Educational Research Association, Chicago.

Dowson, M., & McInerney, D. M. (2001). Psychological parameters of students' social and work avoidance goals: A qualitative investigation. *Journal of Educational Psychology, 93,* 35–42.

Duda, J. L. (1988). The relationship between goal perspectives and persistence and intensity among recreational sport participants. *Leisure Sciences, 10,* 95–106.

Duda, J. L., & Nicholls, J. G. (1992). Dimensions of achievement motivation in schoolwork and sport. *Journal of Educational Psychology, 84,* 290–299.

Dweck, C. S. (1986). Motivational processes affecting learning. *American Psychologist, 41,* 1040–1048.

Dweck, C. S. (1996). Social motivation: Goals and social-cognitive processes. In J. Juvonen & K. Wentzel (Eds.), *Social motivation* (pp. 181–195). New York: Cambridge University Press.

Dweck, C. S. (1999). *Self-theories: Their role in motivation, personality, and development.* Philadelphia: Psychology Press.

Dweck, C. S., & Leggett, E. L. (1988). A social-cognitive approach to motivation and personality. *Psychological Review, 95,* 256–273.

Eccles, J., S., & Midgley, C. (1989). Stage-environment fit: Developmentally appropriate classrooms for young adolescents. In C. Ames & R. Ames (Eds.), *Research on motivation in education* (Vol. 3, pp. 139–188). San Diego, CA: Academic Press.

Eccles, J., S., Midgley, C., Wigfield, A., Buchanan, C., Reuman, D., Flanagan, C., & Mac Iver, D. (1993). Development during adolescence: The impact of stage-environment fit on young adolescents' experiences in schools and in families. *American Psychologist, 48,* 90–101.

Elkind, D., & Bowen, R. (1979). Imaginary audience behavior in children and adolescents. *Developmental Psychology, 15,* 38–44.

Elliot, A. J. (1997). Integrating the "classic" and "contemporary" approaches to achievement motivation: A hierarchical model of approach and avoidance achievement motivation. In M. L. Maehr & P. R. Pintrich (Eds.), *Advances in motivation and achievement* (Vol. 10, pp. 143–179). Greenwich, CT : JAI Press.

Elliot, A. J. (1999). Approach and avoidance motivation and achievement goals. *Educational Psychologist, 34,* 169–189.

Elliot, A. J., & Church, M. A. (1997). A hierarchical model of approach and avoidance achievement motivation. *Journal of Personality and Social Psychology, 72,* 218–232.

Elliot, A. J., & Harackiewicz, J. M. (1994). Goal setting, achievement orientation, and intrinsic motivation: A mediational analysis. *Journal of Personality and Social Psychology, 66,* 968–980.

Elliot, A. J., & Harackiewicz, J. M. (1996). Approach and avoidance achievement goals and intrinsic motivation: A mediational analysis. *Journal of Personality and Social Psychology, 70,* 461–475.

Elliot, A. J., & McGregor, H. A. (1999). Test anxiety and the hierarchical model of approach and avoidance achievement motivation. *Journal of Personality and Social Psychology, 76,* 628–644.

Elliot, A. J., & McGregor, H. A. (2001). A 2 × 2 achievement goal framework. *Journal of Personality and Social Psychology, 80,* 501–519.

Elliot, A. J., McGregor, H. A., & Gable, S. (1999). Achievement goals, study strategies, and exam performance: A mediational analysis. *Journal of Educational Psychology, 91,* 549–563.

Elliot, A. J., & Sheldon, K. M. (1997). Avoidance achievement motivation: A personal goals analysis. *Journal of Personality and Social Psychology, 73,* 171–185.

Elliott, E. S., & Dweck, C. S. (1988). Goals: An approach to motivation and achievement. *Journal of Personality and Social Psychology, 54,* 5–12.

Epstein, J. L. (1989). Family structures and student motivation: A developmental perspective. In C. Ames & R. Ames (Eds.), *Research on motivation in education* (Vol. 3, pp. 259–295). New York: Academic Press.

Erikson, E. (1968). *Identity: Youth and crisis.* New York: Norton.

Festinger, L. (1942). A theoretical interpretation of shifts in level of aspiration. *Psychological Review, 49,* 235–250.

Flum, H. (1994). The evolutive style of identity formation. *Journal of Youth and Adolescence, 23,* 489–498.

Ford, M. E. (1992). *Motivating humans: Goals, emotions and personal agency beliefs.* Newbury Park, CA: Sage.

Foucault, M. (1980). *Power/knowledge: Selected interviews and other writings 1972–1977.* New York: Pantheon.

Garcia, T., & Pintrich, P. R. (1994). Regulating motivation and cognition in the classroom: The role of self-schemas and self-regulatory strategies. In D. Schunk & B. Zimmerman (Eds.), *Self-regulation of learning and performance: Issues and educational applications* (pp. 127–153). Hillsdale, NJ: Erlbaum.

Gergen, K. J. (1991). *The saturated self: Dilemmas of identity in contemporary life.* New York: Basic Books.

Goodnow, J. J. (1990). The socialization of cognition: What's involved? In J. Stigler, R. Shweder, & G. Herdt (Eds.), *Cultural psychology: Essays on comparative human development* (pp. 259–286). Cambridge, UK: Cambridge University Press.

Harackiewicz, J. M., Barron, K. E., & Elliot, A. J. (1998). Rethinking achievement goals: When are they adaptive for college students and why? *Educational Psychologist, 33,* 1–21.

Harackiewicz, J. M., Barron, K. E., Carter, S. M., Lehto, A. R., & Elliot, A. J. (1997). Predoctors and consequences of achievement goals in the college classroom: Maintaining interest and making the grade. *Journal of Personality and Social Psychology, 73,* 1284–1295.

Harackiewicz, J. M., & Elliot, A. J. (1993). Achievement goals and intrinsic motivation. *Journal of Personality and Social Psychology, 65,* 904–915.

Harackiewicz, J. M., & Elliot, A. J. (1998). The joint effects of target and purpose goals on intrinsic motivation: A mediational analysis. *Personality and Social Psychology Bulletin, 24,* 675–689.

Harter, S. (1983). Developmental perspectives on the self system. In P. H. Mussen (Ed.), *Handbook of child psychology, Vol. 4: Socialization, personality, and social development* (pp. 275–385). New York: Wiley.

Harter, S. (1992). The relationship between perceived competence, affect, and motivational orientation within the classroom: Processes and patterns of change. In A. K. Boggiano & T. S. Pittman (Eds.) *Achievement and motivation: A social-developmental perspective.* Cambridge, UK: Cambridge University Press.

Heyman, G. D., Dweck, C. S., & Cain, K. M. (1992). Young children's vulnerability to self-blame and helplessness: Relationship to beliefs about goodness. *Child Development, 63,* 401–415

Hicks, D. A. (1994). Individual and social meanings in the classroom: Narrative discourse as a boundary phenomenon. *Journal of Narrative and Life History, 4,* 215–240.

Hofmann, D. A., & Strickland, O. J. (1995). Task performance and satisfaction: Evidence for a task- by ego-orientation interaction. *Journal of Applied Social Psychology, 25,* 495–511.

Josselson, R. (1987). *Finding herself: Pathways to identity development in women.* San Francisco: Jossey-Bass.

Kaplan, A., & Maehr, M. L. (1997). School cultures. In H. Walberg & G. Haertel (Eds.), *Psychology and educational practice* (pp. 342–355). Berkeley, CA: McCutchan.

Kaplan, A., & Maehr, M. L. (1999). Achievement goals and student well-being. *Contemporary Educational Psychology, 24,* 330–358.

Kaplan, A., & Maehr, M. L. (2002). *The contributions and prospects of a goal orientation theory perspective on achievement motivation.* Manuscript submitted for publication.

Kaplan, A., Middleton, M., Urdan, T., & Midgley, C. (2002). Achievement goals and goal structures. In C. Midgley (Ed.), *Goals, goal structures and patterns of adaptive learning* (pp. 21–53). Hillsdale, NJ: Erlbaum.

Kegan, R. (1982). *The evolving self: Problem and process in human development.* Cambridge, MA: Harvard University Press.

Kitayama, S., & Masuda, T. (1995). Reappraising cognitive appraisal from a cultural perspective. *Psychological Inquiry, 6,* 217–223.

Lee, O., & Anderson, C. W. (1993). Task engagement and conceptual change in middle school science classrooms. *American Educational Research Journal, 30,* 585–610.

Levy, I., Kaplan, A., & Patrick, H. (2000, April). *Achievement goals, intergroup processes, and attitudes towards collaboration.* Poster presented at the Annual Meeting of the American Educational Research Association, New Orleans, USA.

Lewin, K., Dembo, T., Festinger, L., & Sears, P. (1944). Level of aspiration. In J. McV. Hunt (Ed.), *Personality and the behavioral disorders* (Vol. 1, pp. 333–378). New York: Ronald.

Linnenbrink, E. A., & Pintrich, P. R. (2000). Multiple pathways to learning and achievement: The role of goal orientation in fostering adaptive motivation, affect, and cognition. In C. Sansone & J. M. Harackiewicz (Eds.), *Intrinsic and extrinsic motivation: The search for optimal motivation and performance* (pp. 195–227). San Diego, CA: Academic Press.

MacCallum, J. (2000). The contexts of individual motivational change. In D. M. McInerney & S. Van Ettern (Eds.), *Research on sociocultural influences on motivation and learning* (Vol. 1, pp. 61–97). Greenwich, CT: Information Age.

Maehr, M. L. (1974). Culture and achievement motivation. *American Psychologist,* 887–896.

Maehr, M. L. (1984). Meaning and motivation: Toward a theory of personal investment. In C. Ames & R. Ames (Eds.), *Research on motivation in education* (Vol. 1, pp. 115–144). New York: Academic Press.

Maehr, M. L. (1989). Thoughts about motivation. In C. Ames & R. Ames (Eds.), *Research on motivation in education: Goals and cognitions* (Vol. 3, pp. 299–315). New York: Academic Press.

Maehr, M. L., & Braskamp, L. A. (1986). *The motivation factor: A theory of personal investment.* Lexington, MA: Lexington Books.

Maehr, M. L., & Midgley, C. (1991). Enhancing student motivation: A schoolwide approach. *Educational Psychologist, 26,* 399–427.

Maehr, M. L., & Midgley, C. (1996). *Transforming school cultures.* Boulder, CO: Westview Press.

Maehr, M. L., & Nicholls, J. G. (1980). Culture and achievement motivation: A second look. In N. Warren (Ed.), *Studies on cross-cultural psychology* (Vol. 2, pp. 221–267). New York: Academic Press.

Maehr, M. L., & Pintrich, P. R. (1991). *Advances in motivation and achievement* (Vol. 7). Greenwich, CT: JAI Press.

Maehr, M. L., Shi, K., Kaplan, A., & Wang, P. (1999). Culture, motivation and achievement: Toward meeting the new challenge. *Asian Pacific Journal of Education, 19,* 15–29.

Markus, H. J., & Nurius, P. (1986). Possible selves. *American Psychologist, 41,* 954–969.

Markus, H. R., & Kitayama, S. (1991). Culture and the self: Implications for cognition, emotion, and motivation. *Psychological Review, 98,* 224–253.

Markus, H. R., & Wurf, E. (1987). The dynamic self-concept: A social psychological perspective. *Annual Review of Psychology, 38,* 299–337.

Martin, J., & Sugarman, J. (1999). *The psychology of human possibility and constraint.* Albany: State University of New York.

McClelland, D. C. (1961). *The achieving society.* New York: Free Press.

McInerney, D. M. (1995). Goal theory and indigenous minority school motivation: Relevance and application. In M. L. Maehr & P. R. Pintrich (Eds.), *Advances in motivation and achievement* (Vol. 10, pp. 153–181). Greenwich, CT: JAI Press.

McInerney, D. M., Hindley, J., Dowson, M., & Van Etten, S. (1998). Aboriginal, Anglo, and immigrant Australian students' motivational beliefs about personal academic success: Are there cultural differences? *Journal of Educational Psychology, 90,* 621–629.

McInerney, D. M., Roche, L. A., McInerney, V., & Marsh, H. W. (1997). Cultural perspectives on school motivation: The relevance and application of goal theory. *American Educational Research Journal, 34,* 207–236.

Meece, J. L., Blumenfeld, P. C., & Hoyle, R. H. (1988). Students' goal orientations and cognitive engagement in classroom activities. *Journal of Educational Psychology, 80,* 514–523.

Meece, J. L., & Holt, K. (1993). A pattern analysis of students' achievement goals. *Journal of Educational Psychology, 85,* 582–590.

Middleton, M. J., Kaplan, A., & Midgley, C. (2002). *The relations among middle school students' achievement goals in math over time.* Manuscript submitted for publication.

Middleton, M. J., & Midgley, C. (1997). Avoiding the demonstration of lack of ability: An under-explored aspect of goal theory. *Journal of Educational Psychology, 89,* 710–718.

Midgley, C. (Ed.). (2002). *Goals, goal structures and patterns of adaptive learning.* Mahwah, NJ: Erlbaum.

Midgley, C., Anderman, E., & Hicks, L. (1995). Differences between elementary and middle school teachers and students: A goal theory approach. *Journal of Early Adolescence, 15,* 90–113.

Midgley, C., Arunkumar, R., & Urdan, T. (1996). "If I don't do well tomorrow, there's a reason:" Predictors of adolescents' use of academic self-handicapping strategies. *Journal of Educational Psychology, 88,* 423–434.

Midgley, C., Feldlaufer, H., & Eccles, J., S. (1989a). Change in teacher efficacy and student self- and task-related beliefs during the transition to junior high school. *Journal of Educational Psychology, 81,* 247–258.

Midgley, C., Feldlaufer, H., & Eccles, J., S. (1989b). Student/teacher relations and attitudes toward mathematics before and after the transition to junior high school. *Child Development, 60,* 375–395.

Midgley, C., Kaplan, A., & Middleton, M. J. (2001). Performance-approach goals: Good for what, for whom, under what circumstances, and at what cost? *Journal of Educational Psychology, 93,* 77–86.

Midgley, C., Kaplan, A., Middleton, M., Maehr, M. L., Urdan, T., Anderman, L. H., Anderman, E., & Roeser, R. (1998). The development and validation of scales assessing students' achievement goal orientations. *Contemporary Educational Psychology, 23,* 113–131.

Midgley, C., Middleton, M. J., Gheen, M. H., & Kumar, R. (2002). Stage-environment fit revisited: A goal theory approach to examining school transitions. In C. Midgley (Ed.), *Goals, goal structures and patterns of adaptive learning* (pp. 109–142). Mahwah, NJ: Erlbaum.

Molden, D. C., & Dweck, C. S. (2000). Meaning and motivation. In C. Sansone & J. Harackiewicz (Eds.), *Intrinsic and extrinsic motivation: The search for optimal motivation and performance* (pp. 131–159). New York: Academic Press.

Moshman, D. (1982). Exogenous, endogenous, and dialectical constructivism. *Developmental Review, 2,* 371–384.

Murray, H. A. (1938). *Explorations in personality.* New York: Oxford University Press.

Newman, D., Griffin, P., & Cole, M. (1989). *The construction zone: Working for cognitive change in school.* New York: Cambridge University Press.

Nicholls, J. G. (1984). Achievement motivation: Conceptions of ability, subjective experience, task choice, and performance. *Psychological Review, 91,* 328–346.

Nicholls, J. G. (1989). *The competitive ethos and democratic education.* Cambridge, MA: Harvard University Press.

Nicholls, J. G. (1990). What is ability and why are we mindful of it? A developmental perspective. In R. Sternberg & J. Kolligian (Eds.), *Competence considered* (pp. 11–40). New Haven, CT: Yale University Press.

Nicholls, J. G. (1992). Students as educational theorists. In D. Schunk & J. Meece (Eds.), *Student perceptions in the classroom* (pp. 267–286). Hillsdale, NJ: Erlbaum.

Nicholls, J. G., & Hazzard, S. P. (1993). *Education as adventure: Lessons from the second grade.* New York: Teachers College Press.

Nicholls, J. G., Cheung, P. C., Lauer, J., & Patashnick, M. (1989). Individual differences in academic motivation: Perceived ability, goals, beliefs, and values. *Learning and Individual Differences, 1,* 63–84.

Nicholls, J. G., Patashnick, M., & Nolen, S. B. (1985). Adolescents' theories of education. *Journal of Educational Psychology, 77,* 683–692.

Nicholls, J. G., Patashnick, M., Cheung, P. C., Thorkildsen, T. A., & Lauer, J. M. (1989). Can achievement motivation theory succeed with only one conception of success? In F. Halisch & J. van der Bercken (Eds.), *International perspectives on achievement and task motivation.* Amsterdam: Swets & Zoitlinger.

Nolen, S. B. (1988). Reasons for studying: Motivational orientations and study strategies. *Cognition and Instruction, 5,* 269–287.

Ogbu, J. U. (1992). Understanding cultural diversity and learning. *Educational Researcher, 21,* 5–14.

Pajares, F. (1996). Self-efficacy beliefs in academic settings. *Review of Educational Research, 66,* 543–578.

Papaioannou, A. (1994). Development of a questionnaire to measure achievement orientations in physical education. *Research Quarterly for Exercise and Sport, 65,* 11–20.

Pervin, L. A. (1989). (Ed.). *Goal concepts in personality and social psychology.* Hillsdale, NJ: Lawrence Erlbaum.

Piaget, J., & Inhelder, B. (1958). *The growth of logical thinking from childhood to adolescence.* New York: Basic Books.

Pintrich, P. R. (2000a). The role of goal orientation in self-regulated learning. In M. Boekaerts, P. Pintrich, & M. Zeidner (Eds.), *Handbook of self-regulation: Theory, research and applications.* San Diego, CA: Academic Press.

Pintrich, P. R. (2000b). An achievement goal theory perspective on issues in motivation terminology, theory, and research. *Contemporary Educational Psychology, 25,* 92–104.

Pintrich, P. R. (2000c). Multiple goals, multiple pathways: The role of goal orientation in learning and achievement. *Journal of Educational Psychology, 92,* 544–555.

Pintrich, P. R., & Garcia, T. (1991). Student goal orientation and self-regulation in the college classroom. In M. L. Maehr & P. R. Pintrich (Eds.), *Advances in motivation and achievement* (Vol. 7, pp. 371–402). Greenwich, CT: JAI Press.

Pintrich, P. R., Smith, D. A. F., Garcia, T., & McKeachie, W. J. (1993). Reliability and predictive validity of the Motivated Strategies for Learning Questionnaire (MSLQ). *Educational and Psychological Measurement, 53,* 801–813.

Roeser, R. W., Eccles, J., S., & Sameroff, A. J. (2000). School as a context of early adolescents' academic and social-emotional development: A summary of research findings. *The Elementary School Journal, 100,* 443–471.

Roeser, R. W., Midgley, C., & Urdan, T. C. (1996). Perceptions of the school psychological environment and early adolescents' psychological and behavioral functioning in school: The mediating role of goals and belonging. *Journal of Educational Psychology, 88,* 408–422.

Rogoff, B. (1994). Developing understanding of the idea of communities of learners. *Mind, Culture, and Activity, 1,* 209–229.

Rogoff, B., & Lave, J. (Eds.). (1984). *Everyday cognition: Its development in social context.* Cambridge, MA: Harvard University Press.

Ryan, R. M., & Grolnick, W. S. (1986). Origins and pawns in the classroom: Self-report and projective assessments of individual differences in children's perceptions. *Journal of Personality and Social Psychology, 50,* 550–558.

Schiedel, D. G., & Marcia, J. E. (1985). Ego identity, intimacy, sex role orientations, and gender. *Developmental Psychology, 18,* 149–160.

Schunk, D. H. (1989). Self-efficacy and cognitive skill learning. In C. Ames & R. Ames (Eds.), *Research on motivation in education* (Vol. 3, pp. 13–44). San Diego, CA: Academic Press.

Seifert, T. (1995). Academic goals and emotions: A test of two models. *Journal of Psychology, 129,* 543–552.

Shotter, J. (1997). The social construction of our inner selves. *Journal of Constructivist Psychology, 10,* 7–24.

Shwalb, D. W., Shwalb, B. J., Harnisch, D. L., Maehr, M. L., & Akabane, K. (1992). Personal investment in Japan and the U.S.A.: A study of worker motivation. *International Journal of Intercultural Relations, 16,* 107–124.

Skaalvik, E. M. (1997). Self-enhancing and self-defeating ego orientation: Relations with task and avoidance orientation, achievement, self-perceptions, and anxiety. *Journal of Educational Psychology, 89,* 71–81.

Steele, C. M. (1997). A threat in the air: How stereotypes shape the intellectual identities and performance of women and African Americans. *American Psychologist, 52,* 613–629.

Steele, C. M., & Aronson, J. (1995). Stereotype threat and the intellectual test performance of African Americans. *Journal of Personality and Social Psychology, 69,* 797–811.

Tajfel, H., & Turner, J. C. (1986). The social identity theory of intergroup behavior. In S. Worchel & W. Austin (Eds.), *Psychology of intergroup relations* (pp. 7–24). New York: Nelson-Hall.

Thorkildsen, T. A. (1989). Justice in the classroom: The student's view. *Child Development, 60,* 323–334.

Thorkildsen, T. A. (1991). Defining social goods and distributing them fairly: The development of conceptions of fair testing practices. *Child Development, 62,* 852–862.

Thorkildsen, T. A., & Nicholls, J. G. (1991). Students' critiques as motivation. *Educational Psychologist, 26,* 347–368.

Triandis, H. C. (1989). The self and social behavior in differing cultural contexts. *Psychological Review, 96,* 506–520.

Urdan, T. (1996, April). *Examining students' multiple goals profiles.* Poster presented at the Annual Meeting of the American Educational Research Association, New York.

Urdan, T. (1997). Achievement goal theory: Past results, future directions. In M. L. Maehr & P. R. Pintrich (Eds.), *Advances in motivation and achievement* (Vol. 10, pp. 99–141). Greenwich, CT: JAI Press.

Urdan, T., & Hicks, L. (1995, April). *What adolescent students say about the interface of peer relationships and motivation in school.* Paper presented at the Annual Meeting of the American Educational Research Association, San Francisco.

Urdan, T. C., & Maehr, M. L. (1995). Beyond a two-goal theory of motivation and achievement: A case for social goals. *Review of Educational Research, 65,* 213–243.

Urdan, T., Midgley, C., & Anderman, E. (1998). The role of classroom goal structure in students' use of self-handicapping strategies. *American Educational Research Journal, 35,* 101–122.

Urdan, T., Midgley, C., & Wood, S. (1995). Special issues in reforming middle level schools. *Journal of Early Adolescence, 15,* 9–37.

Vandewalle, D. (1997). Development and validation of a work domain goal orientation instrument. *Educational and Psychological Measurement, 57,* 995–1015.

Weiner, B. (1985). An attributional theory of achievement motivation and emotion. *Psychological Review, 92,* 548–573.

Weiner, B. (1986). *An attribution theory of motivation and emotion.* New York: Springer-Verlag.

Wentzel, K. R. (1992). Motivation and achievement in adolescence: A multiple goals perspective. In D. H. Schunk & J. Meece (Eds.), *Student perceptions in the classroom* (pp. 287–306), Hillsdale, NJ: Erlbaum.

Wentzel, K. R., & Wigfield, A. (1998). Academic and social motivational influences on students' academic performance. *Educational Psychology Review, 10,* 155–175.

Wertsch, J. V. (1991). *Voices of the mind: A sociocultural approach to mediated action.* Cambridge, MA: Harvard University Press.

Wigfield, A., Eccles, J. S., & Pintrich, P. R. (1996). Development between the ages of 11 and 25. In D. C. Berliner & R. C. Calfee (Eds.), *Handbook of educational psychology* (pp. 148–185). New York: Simon & Schuster Macmillan.

Wylie, R. C. (1968). The present status of self theory. In E. Borgatta & W. Lambert (Eds.), *Handbook of personality theory and research*. Chicago: Rand McNally.

Xiang, P., Lee, A. M., & Solmon, M. A. (1997). Achievement goals and their correlates among American and Chinese students in physical education: A cross-cultural analysis. *Journal of Cross Cultural Psychology, 28,* 645–660.

CHAPTER 6

REWARDS AND INTRINSIC MOTIVATION

A Needs-Based, Developmental Perspective

Martin V. Covington
University of California at Berkeley

Consider the following parable of an old gentleman (probably a retired psychology professor) who was bothered by the noisy play of boys in his neighborhood (Casady, 1974, as reported in Covington & Beery, 1976):

> How could he get the boys to stop? The old man called the boys together, told them he was quite deaf, and asked that they shout louder so that he might enjoy their fun. In return, he was willing to pay each of them a quarter. Needless to say, the boys were delighted to combine business with pleasure, and on that first day the old man got more than his money's worth. On the second day he told the boys that owing to his small pension, he could afford to pay only twenty cents. As the pay rate dwindled day by day, the boys became angry and finally told the old man they would not return. The sly old gentleman had turned play into work and then paid so little that making noise for five cents was not worth the effort. (pp. 24–25)

The point of this fable, a warning of sorts, is that paying people for what they might otherwise do freely can transform play into drudgery, and further that work that is undercompensated is likely not worth the effort. This parable appears to have stood the test of time. It has been so widely accepted for so long that the principle it espouses has attained the status of an "illuminated" truth. Indeed, this author has often drawn on this fable to bolster the proposition that tangible rewards adversely affect intrinsic interest and subject-matter appreciation (e.g., Covington, 1992). Other observers have also been quick to accept this negative verdict regarding the effects of tangible rewards on intrinsic engagement, a principle commonly referred to in a matter-of-fact way in many introductory psychology text-books (for a commentary, see Pittenger, 1996).

Explanations for the allegedly negative influence of tangible rewards take several forms. One view focuses on the extrinsic nature of many rewards as the culprit—extrinsic because such payoffs as social recognition and monetary prizes are typically unrelated to the act of learning itself, and thus are likely to draw attention away from the inherent benefits of learning. As a result it is feared that learning may merely become a way to get rewards, and when these rewards are no longer available, the willingness to continue learning will decline (Condry & Chambers, 1978).

Another view proposed by Edward Deci and Richard Ryan (1985) focuses on the subjective meaning of extrinsic rewards regarding the individual's feelings of self-determination. This self-determination theory suggests that being offered rewards for one's actions may create the experience of being controlled by others, thereby diminishing feelings of freedom, autonomy, and competency, which, in turn, it is thought, lead to a reduction in task interest and creativity.

Yet a third perspective, self-perception theory (Bem, 1970), suggests that receiving extraneous, unnecessary rewards for performing an already personally satisfying activity may cause individuals to discount the value of their actions, reasoning that "if I have to be paid to do this, then it must not be worthwhile doing for its own sake alone." The parable of the deaf professor speaks most directly to this interpretation.

Although some researchers continue to search for the mechanisms responsible for this deterioration in task engagement, others have questioned, more fundamentally, first, whether there is, in fact, any deterioration at all; and second, assuming that there is, if the deterioration is the result of other processes unrelated to the nature of rewards. As many readers are well aware, this debate has generated a heated controversy in recent years. But, whatever the final verdict, it seems clear that using tangible rewards as a motivational tool is an uncertain, even risky, business. The potential dangers take a number of forms. For example, the offering of tangible rewards as inducements to achievement produces students who are less persistent in their studies (Fincham & Cain, 1986), less adaptive in their problem-solving efforts (Amabile, 1982), and more likely to choose easier assignments. Moreover, students who are compensated with tangible payoffs are less likely to remember what they learned (Grolnick & Ryan,

1986) and appear less willing to redouble their problem-solving efforts once rewards are removed.

The larger, decidedly ominous significance of these findings taken as a whole implies a potential threat aimed at the very heart of the educational mission, that is, the encouragement of a love of learning among our youth now and for a lifetime. A vast array of tangible rewards and incentives dominate classroom life in part because of the uncritical acceptance by educators and the lay public alike of the notion that the offering and with-holding of rewards produce good results—better, in fact, than any other teaching strategy, including punishing students for not trying, reasoning with students, or just simply not interfering. Underlying this assumption regarding the motivational benefits of rewards is the notion that the greater the reward, the more eagerly students will compete. These beliefs are often accompanied by the further expectation that exposing students to the rigors of competition by means of scarce rewards prepares them for future economic survival in later life as well as the building of character via adversity (for a critique, see Covington, 1992, 1998; Kohn, 1993).

Many observers have despaired of the prospects of encouraging intrinsic values in a world controlled by such an overweening network of tangible, extrinsic rewards. Indeed, given these circumstances, one may ask what is to become of the value of learning for its own sake? Is caring about learn-ing marginalized?

The purpose of this chapter is to revisit the long-standing question of whether intrinsic objectives such as subject-matter appreciation and intrin-sic involvement can coexist, let alone thrive, in the face of massive, unre-lenting extrinsic payoffs—praise, gold stars, and grades, whose main function is seen by educators as an enabling factor—to provide the right rewards and enough of them, or threaten sufficient penalties by withhold-ing them, to arouse (drive) students to higher levels of achievement.

I will argue that the debate over the potentially adverse effects of extrin-sic payoffs is largely misplaced, owing to a narrow, almost exclusive focus on the *tangible* attributes of rewards as the culprit. Actually, I believe the issues surrounding the offering of rewards and the motives and actions they arouse are far broader than this. For example, as I will propose, the proper concern regarding the effects of rewards is less their tangible nature and more their *meaning* as a measure of self-definition; and less the offering of rewards per se, and more a matter of their being withdrawn or withheld as a means of control. To anticipate this latter point, the withhold-ing from students of otherwise well-deserved rewards simply because of their competitive scarcity amounts to a punishment, psychologically speak-ing (Kohn, 1993). The feelings of self-loathing, anger, and the fears of incompetence that follow such punishments can be devastating to the will to learn, far more so, it can be argued, than whether or not the rewards in question are merely tangible and thereby extrinsic to the process of learning. The debate over rewards needs to be reconsidered in light of the broader perspectives suggested by these examples.

What, then, is my approach? First, I believe we need to adopt a developmental view of the relationship between rewards and intrinsic motivation—a perspective essentially absent from the debate thus far, because the processes involved in this relationship mature and change over the life course. More specifically, I will maintain that the disposition for being intrinsically motivated evolves out of the progressive satisfaction of various positive psychological needs, which themselves have a developmental history of growth and expression. As only one example, we can cite the need to establish and maintain feelings of personal competence (Deci & Ryan, 1985). Likewise, certain negative forces arrayed against the expression of intrinsic engagement, especially self-defeating dynamics linked to competitive reward structures, also chart a developmental course—in this instance, unfortunately, increasing in strength and vitality as children move through the educational system (Harari & Covington, 1981).

I believe that it is at the confluence of these collective, developmentally conditioned factors—some negative and others positive—that the debate over the effects of rewards needs to be situated. In order to promote this developmental perspective, I will draw on the accounts of college students regarding their personal recollections of those forces that influenced their willingness to learn for its own sake as they moved from one level of schooling to another. In this particular study (Covington & Dray, 2002), the recollections of some 400 Berkeley undergraduates were prompted by an extensive set of Likert-type self-report scales. One series of scales reflected the degree to which the basic developmental needs featured in self-determination theory were thought to be satisfied: *relatedness* needs, both those associated with teachers (e.g., "How much did you feel you could turn to teachers for help?") and with other students (e.g., "How much did you feel left out by your classmates?"); *autonomy* needs (e.g., "How much did teachers trust you to make decisions on your own?"); and feelings of *competency* (e.g., "How much did you worry that you were not smart enough to keep up?"). As part of this self-report protocol, students also rated the degree of competitive pressure they experienced as well as judged the saliency of several different motives (or reasons) for learning, including striving in order to avoid failure, to stay out of trouble, and to prove one's worth. The dependent variables of interest were self-ratings of various intrinsic aspects of the process of knowledge acquisition (e.g., "How much did you enjoy learning, apart from any grade?"). Our informants rated this panel of some 200 questions four separate times, initially regarding their memories of the elementary years, next reminiscing about the middle school years, then the high school years, and finally regarding their experiences during the first year of college. Following the completion of these ratings, participants were randomly assigned to smaller subgroups to explain their ratings on each of several individual items in the form of brief essays.

Let me add one important point regarding the appropriateness of this highly selected college sample to our inquiry. The very fact of the extraordinary scholastic and school achievements of these individuals—a near-majority were, for instance, either high school valedictorians or class officers—would appear to put them uniquely at risk regarding the issues under consideration here, and therefore especially valuable to our analyses. Specifically, I wondered if any value these youngsters had originally placed on learning for its own sake had become so compromised by the extrinsic trappings of their accumulated successes that their capacity for intrinsic enjoyment had long ago been compromised.

Interestingly enough, this was not the case. To anticipate briefly, our data told a far different and more complex story. First, rather than a progressive deterioration in the valuing of learning, our informants indicated that much of what they had learned over the years was inspired by personal interest and curiosity, and was not simply a by-product of the pursuit of grades for the sake of self-aggrandizement. Second, this positive valuing grew incrementally, as far as memory served, from the earliest years of schooling to a maximum in the high school years, with only a temporary dip during the middle school years. At the same time, however, as our students entered college, they recorded a precipitous drop in the frequency with which they experienced feelings of intrinsic task engagement. Overall, this was a sufficiently curious pattern to prompt a closer look.

What, then, permitted these youngsters to experience progressive increases in their enjoyment of learning during their formative years, despite an increasing presence of tangible payoffs, notariety, and recognition? It appeared that there might be "life beyond grades" after all. But what of the decline in levels of intrinsic involvement upon their entry into college? Had the potentially negative features of tangible rewards, most notably grades, become exacerbated due to some unique characteristics of the college experience? Whatever the answers, given these tantalizing findings, it seems reasonable to consider the possibility that the potential undermining effects of tangible rewards on intrinsic task engagement are neither universal nor inevitable and might under some circumstances even be positive.

To put this observation in the allegorical context with which we began, I question whether the fable of the deaf professor is the only, or even the best, way to frame the issues concerning the relationship between extrinsic rewards and intrinsic motivation. One problem is that this fable is not provocative of potentially positive uses of rewards when it comes to encouraging the enjoyment of learning. For example, what if the old man's purpose had been to encourage the boys to enjoy their game play? How would he have used his limited financial resources to this end? I gave this challenge to a number of my Berkeley undergraduates. The outpouring of suggestions was variously funny, sometimes outright hilarious, typically impish yet sometimes stimulating of serious thought. Although there are few operating counterparts of these ingenious ideas in the real world of schooling today, some of them are provocative of experimentation. I consider the implications of these proposals in closing.

THE CONTROVERSY

Before proceeding, it is important to place the current controversy in perspective, the disputed proposition being that the offering of tangible rewards and incentives undercuts intrinsic task engagement. What more precisely are the issues at hand, and equally important, what are *not* the issues? To begin, the issue is not that offering tangible rewards will necessarily interfere with learning. Sometimes rewards clearly do interfere, as amply demonstrated by the evidence cited earlier. Other times, however, the offering of rewards are known to increase student learning, particularly when the tasks are boring, repetitive, or of little personal interest (e.g., DeCharms, 1957; Shaw, 1958). Nor is the issue that rewards necessarily inhibit the generation of creative ideas. To the contrary, it has long been known that if individuals are instructed in how to produce creative ideas as contrasted to mundane ones, and are then rewarded tangibly for doing so, they will readily increase the quality of their ideational output (Maltzman, 1960). Quite apart from the matter of encouraging the production of unusual ideas on demand, however, the nub of the question before us is whether or not tangible, extrinsic rewards create negative, counterproductive reasons for performing so that the act of learning is robbed of any inherent value to the individual.

A Brief History

One of the earliest studies to implicate the offering of extrinsic rewards as detrimental to the enjoyment of an activity was conducted by Lepper, Greene, and Nisbett (1973). Preschool children were asked by these investigators to draw pictures. Some of the youngsters were promised a reward, a good citizen award, for complying, while a second group received the same award but only unexpectedly at the end of the drawing session. A third control group received no rewards for their drawings. During a subsequent free-play session, children in the unexpected reward and control conditions spontaneously devoted more time to drawing pictures than they had spent doing so in the initial session, while those students in the expected reward condition spent less time drawing during free play than they had previously. These results were interpreted as evidence favoring an overjustification hypothesis, that is, performing a creative action initially justified in its own right, presumably because drawing is fun, was subsequently inhibited because of the addition of unnecessary inducements, hence overjustified.

A number of other studies inspired by self-determination theory soon followed (see Ryan & Deci, 2000, for a recent review). However, rather than invoking attributional arguments underlying the overjustification hypothesis, this body of research focused on capturing the meaning of offering rewards regarding feelings of self-determination, especially feelings of competency and autonomy. For example, Deci and his colleagues argued that rewards would interfere with creative expression to the extent that they were perceived by subjects as controlling, and conversely, to the extent that rewards provided competency information, they would encourage intrinsic task engagement. Such differential predictions regarding various reward contingencies added considerably to the sophistication with which the research proceeded. Moreover, in general, the evidence from a number of these studies favored self-determination predictions. When rewards were perceived by subjects as more controlling than empowering, various indices of task engagement plummeted, including the free-time activities of subjects as well as subjective self-reports of task enjoyment. Conversely, when the positive informational aspects of rewards predominated, their offering proved to be either neutral toward or supportive of intrinsic task engagement. These basic findings have been replicated and extended in various ways.

During these years of intense research, other investigators largely representing a behavioral tradition raised doubts about the interpretation of many of these findings, and in some cases questioned if a detrimental phenomenon associated with tangible rewards existed at all, and failing that possibility, whether decreases in joyful engagement were simply an artifact of the experimental design or the procedures employed. For example, some critics have argued that any undermining is likely only transitory, akin to temporary satiation (see Eisenberger & Cameron, 1996). In rebuttal, Deci, Koestner, and Ryan (1999) point to the results of several studies that employed delayed assessments, some of which occurred up to a week after the initial experimental manipulation. As a group, these studies tend to support the view that undermining effects on intrinsic motivation are more than transitory. However, as was readily acknowledged, these studies are few in number and are based primarily on children using only a free-choice assessment procedure. Behaviorists have also been sharply critical of the fact that many of the studies employed only single sessions, whereas in real-world contexts, multiple sessions with the administration of successive rewards over time is the norm. Although it is true that appropriately designed multisession studies show little or no evidence of undermining, they are too few in number and focus on only a handful of subjects, thus rendering any generalizations premature. These two examples of critique and rebuttal illustrate how one's efforts to reach definitive conclusions in this area can be easily frustrated despite a volume of research that now approaches 150 studies.

Researchers have also sought to resolve the issue of the potential undermining effects of tangible rewards by aggregating the results of a number of studies. To date, five meta-analyses have been published (Cameron & Pierce, 1994; Deci, Koestner, & Ryan, 1999; Rummel & Feinberg, 1988; Tang & Hall, 1995; Wiersma, 1992) as well as a sixth, forthcoming analysis (Cameron, Banko, & Pierce, 2002). It is beyond the scope of this chapter to review these accumulated findings in detail. For our purposes, it is sufficient to say that the conclusions reached by successive investigators have not been consistent, and that far more than mere shades of interpretation linger. For example, based on a review of the previous literature, Cameron (2001) concludes that there is "no inherent negative property of reward. Rewards can be used to produce positive, negative, or no effects on measures of intrinsic motivation" (p. 41). By contrast, based on the most comprehensive published analysis to date, Deci and colleagues (1999) conclude "that tangible rewards tend to have a substantially negative effect on intrinsic motivation, with the limiting conditions we have specified. Even when tangible rewards are offered as indicators of good performance, they typically decrease intrinsic motivation for interesting activities" (p. 659).

Steps Toward Reconciliation

It is here that the debate rests at least for the moment. Can we move forward beyond this point? The danger is that controversy may have eclipsed other perspectives that could place the issues at hand on a more certain, constructive footing. I propose an alternative way of couching the issues, which seems simplicity itself. Rather than continuing to ask solely if the offering of tangible rewards inhibits intrinsic task engagement—it certainly seems that the potential is there—would we not be better advised also to enquire if there are any situations in which tangible rewards might actually serve to benefit the will to learn, and if so, how? In part, this shift in thinking requires that we ask not only why, according to various theories, the tangible nature of rewards is potentially harmful, but what might be done to offset these negative factors? For instance, following the thrust of Deci's work, we might wonder in what ways tangible rewards could be offered to students without conveying the impression that they are being controlled or are under the surveillance of others.

Yet more is needed than merely reframing questions. We also need to shift the context in which we pursue these questions. Far too much current research is unhelpful, not merely by reason of being in dispute, but possibly being beside the point as well because it disregards the situated factors in which rewards and incentives operate in the real world of classrooms. In effect, there is reason to wonder if many of the findings inspired by laboratory-type paradigms, even if they had provoked no debate, could be generalized to actual classrooms. Although laboratory research has contributed immeasurably to our understanding of the issues discussed here, I believe we cannot truly understand how students come to appreciate and deeply hold the values of exploration and discovery unless the processes involved are also studied in the context of real-life schooling, where success and failure carry enormous public promise and penalties, respectively.

Much previous research has focused on only a narrow set of rewards and on tasks of questionable relevance. In the latter instance, all too often the tasks chosen for study are quite divorced from the practical realities of typical classroom assignments, rendering any results of suspect value when it comes to real-world applications. More on this point later. As to the matter of rewards, their selection for study has been spotty and uneven at best, the most significant consequence being that investigators have not sufficiently considered those rewards that are likely to benefit intrinsic task engagement, even after tangible support is withdrawn. One promising candidate is the use of *encouragement* whose message of guidance for the sake of improvement (e.g., "Here are some ways to do even better") is likely to enhance learner confidence as well as focus attention on the process of learning itself. Feedback regarding the quality of one's efforts and how to improve can act as a reward of sorts—an incentive to remain engaged and resilient in the face of any learning setbacks. And, interestingly, such feedback need not always be positive to be effective. For example, Butler and Nisan (1986) found that by providing feedback that described one aspect of a task that had been performed well and another aspect less well, students continued to express interest in the task and to improve their performance compared to other youngsters who received feedback simply to arouse effort level.

This observation suggests that the issues before us might best be resolved by situating our inquiries within the broader study of feedback mechanisms for which there is already a rich literature, rather than to continue focusing on oppositional distinctions such as extrinsic/intrinsic rewards, which may ultimately prove misleading and unhelpful (see Covington & Müeller, 2001).

While potentially positive sources of rewards beg for consideration, we have likewise neglected possibly the most corrosive and in any case certainly the most ubiquitous of all school incentives/rewards: grades. Yet if we are ever to understand fully the nature and nurturing of intrinsic task engagement, we need to explore what it is about grades and grading practices that present such an overarching threat to intrinsic task engagement. The work of Deci and his colleagues regarding feelings of being under surveillance and controlled by others as potentially negative components of rewards can clearly be applied profitably to the study of grades.

Adopting the naturalistic perspective of students and teachers not only authenticates the processes involved in the offering of rewards, but it also alerts us to the broader circle of threats to caring about learning of which the presence of tangible rewards is merely a part and, I would argue, of only marginal importance. As we will see, this latter perspective calls for a more fundamental reconsideration of the institutional aspects of schooling in America beyond simply questioning the wisdom of using extrinsic rewards to motivate students. Unless we consider a wider perspective than is presently being entertained, our efforts to discover fully satisfactory answers to the question of the impact of rewards on intrinsic task engagement are unlikely to be forthcoming.

RAPPROCHEMENT

The most encouraging note at present regarding the current controversy was sounded by Deci and colleagues (1999) when they concluded that focusing on need satisfaction offers important alternatives to extrinsic rewards and social control when it comes to encouraging intrinsic task engagement. I, too, believe that the facilitation of intrinsic motivation ultimately depends on the satisfaction of psychological needs. Indeed, this needs-satisfaction argument was largely the inspiration for our research on student memories of their prior school experiences. In this connection, the most important task facing us as investigators was to place these developmental recollections in a serviceable theoretical framework, which properly reflected the dynamics that produced these memories in the first place. In effect, the satisfaction of psychological needs must always be negotiated within a context of many competing forces, some supportive of need satisfaction, others detractive, and still others neutral regarding satisfaction, and yet forces that also change over time. How best to portray these dynamics and the conditions that influence them in a naturalistic context?

Our answer was based on two models of classroom achievement dynamics within whose real-world parameters need theory, on the one hand, and reward contingencies, on the other, could be properly situated. The first model adopted Doyle's (1983) notion of academic work. Doyle proposed a functional linkage between the offering of school incentives and the motives for learning that are reinforced by those rewards. A second interlocking perspective was provided by self-worth theory (Beery, 1975; Covington, 1992, 1998; Covington & Beery, 1976), which details the self-preservation dynamics set in motion by the reward contingencies described by Doyle.

Doyle (1983) argues that every classroom embodies some kind of reward structure, which conveys to students, either implicitly or explicitly, how their work will be judged, the activities they must perform, and how well they must perform them if they hope to succeed. This "playbook" amounts to a set of rules by which the academic game is conducted, and in essence, how the quality and amount of work to be undertaken translate into sought-after rewards—usually tangible in nature, including praise, grades, and privileges.

Self-worth theory extends the need-based achievement theory pioneered by John Atkinson (1957) and David McClelland (1965, 1980) in the 1950s and 1960s. From the perspective of self-worth theory, the concept of need translates into a struggle for self-acceptance. In our society individuals are widely considered to be only as worthy as their ability to achieve competitively. As a result, many individuals equate their personal worth with their accomplishments, and because they perceive ability as a primary ingredient for success, especially competitively defined success, and inability a major cause of failure, then ability becomes critical to one's self-definition. This self-worth perspective transforms Doyle's achievement game into an ability game. The rules of this competitive ability game dictate that an inadequate supply of rewards (e.g., top grades) be distributed unequally with the greatest number going to the best, the quickest, or the most able performers. This arrangement amounts to a zero-sum scoring system. When one student (player) wins (or makes points), then other students must lose points. Thus success depends on one's academic ability because rewards are more available to the most able. Because the supply of good grades is limited, the majority of students must struggle to avoid failure in the form of poor or mediocre grades rather than to approach success. And, if students are unsuccessful in achieving their grade goals, especially when they interpret any disappointment as falling short as a person, then the fear of being judged incompetent by others can be devastating. Ability-linked anxiety narrows one's attention to matters of self-preservation, especially the creation of self-serving excuses to deflect the causes of poor performance away from insufficient ability (Thompson, 1993, 1996; Urdan, Midgley, & Anderman, 1998). Such a self-serving, defensive agenda bodes ill for the acquisition of knowledge, let alone for the valuing of learning for its own sake.

Putting this argument in developmental terms, Atkinson's (1957) distinction between approach and avoidant tendencies and their relative balance within individuals helps explain many of the changes our students reported in their capacity for intrinsic engagement as they moved from the early years of schooling through late adolescence. To the extent that the opportunities for rewards become limited, their availability carries information about the relative competency of students, and, as rewards become scarce, the starker these ability distinctions also become. Based on these emerging competency judgments, then, students tend to adopt either approach or avoidant learning goals that eventually crystallize into trait-like behaviors. The progressive decrease in self-perceived competency ratings over the years among our students suggests that the process of negotiating these goals favors the disproportionate emergence of an avoidant mentality even among this highly selected, intellectually promising group. This approach/avoidant analysis also reveals something about the nature of grades as rewards. The benefits of being successful, grade-wise, differs from person to person, depending on their approach/avoidance disposition. The rewards enjoyed by approach-oriented individuals involve pride in a job well done, further confirmation of their ability to succeed in the future, and useful feedback regarding how to succeed in the future. By contrast, those avoidant-oriented students driven by the fear of failure are more likely to view their successes, when they occur, in terms of being lucky or having succeeded by chance, attributions that do nothing to bolster their self-confidence nor engender pride in their accomplishments. Rather, these emotional rewards are most likely couched in terms of relief, not pride—relief that failure has been avoided one more time. These timid, defensive, and pallid versions of success are a thin foundation on which to base the intrinsic pleasures of learning.

According to this self-worth perspective, then, it is unlikely that rewards *per se*, not even their tangible nor their extrinsic nature, are the cause of diminished task engagement. Rather, the causes more likely concern the high-stakes meaning of grades as conveyors of a sense of worth, combined with their relative scarcity. These realities need to be addressed in any proper discussion of the impact of rewards on caring about learning. Several important points emerge from this perspective when considered in light of our student retrospective data.

Scarcity of Rewards

Doyle's (1983) perspective alerts us to the possibility that it is the way in which rewards are distributed in school—the rules of engagement, so to speak—that causes their negative impact on task engagement, not necessarily the fact that most school incentives are tangible in nature. More specifically, it is the scarcity of valued rewards, due to competitive pressure and the resulting fear-induced scramble to attain them, that creates student dis-satisfaction, withdrawal, and face-saving efforts to deflect the implications for poor performance away from insufficient ability. By this reasoning, intrinsic values become imperiled, not principally because of the tangible, extrinsic features of rewards, but because all too often the individual's sense of worth becomes equated with high marks, which are rendered scarce by competitive rules.

Our college informants were quite emphatic in singling out competition as a major cause of intrinsic disengagement, and especially noteworthy was the fact that they recalled competitive pressures as progressively intensified as they moved through school. Another casualty of competitive pressure was feelings of competency. Regression analyses of our data indicated that feelings of competency, as judged by our informants, made a substantial contribution to variations in the degree to which they valued learning in the early and middle school years—in effect, feeling intellectually equal to a task is closely associated with being task engaged. Given the robustness of this competency/enjoyment linkage, it was troublesome to discover that feelings of competency were remembered as steadily declining from a max-imum in the elementary years to a low point in college.

But why should our students recall experiencing increased task engage-ment as they progressed through school in the face of such collateral dete-rioration? The answer proved to be simplicity itself: Diminishing feelings of competency and increasing judgments of competitive pressures did not operate alone to affect the propensity for task engagement. According to our informants, other positive, countervailing forces were at work simulta-neously. Chief among these were the abundant academic successes enjoyed by this highly selected group of students. Our students confirmed what is well known among both the lay public and the experts alike: Individuals enjoy pursuing those activities at which they do well (Renninger, Hidi, & Krapp, 1992). Conversely, doing poorly (or failing) diminishes one's valu-ing of an activity and, indeed, may even cause an outright rejection of its importance in an effort to distance oneself from the implications of failure (Birney, Burdick, & Teevan, 1969). Yet, despite the obviousness of these propositions, little, if any, prior research on task engagement has consid-ered the degree to which students were succeeding (or not) in learning the material they were expected to value or enjoy. But such research would seem a critical step for setting limits on the alledgedly negative effects of rewards, a point to be considered in more detail momentarily. Perhaps det-rimental effects are limited largely to situations in which students fail to achieve a given standard of performance or actually succeed reasonably well, but are precluded from receiving rewards due to competitive scarcity.

Other positive sources of influence on the growth of task engagement were also reported by our informants. These included progressive increases over the years in opportunities to exercise freedom of choice in their studies and permission from teachers to act autonomously in pursuit of their interests, opportunities that were recalled to have peaked in the high school years. Variations in these perceived opportunities contributed substantially to the explained variance in intrinsic motivation beyond that already accounted for by subjective feelings of success. These findings reinforce the importance accorded the satisfaction of a need for autonomy by Deci and his colleagues (Deci, Vallerand, Pelletier, & Ryan, 1991; Vallarand, Fortier, & Guay, 1997). Also, another source of need satisfaction featured in our self-report questionnaire and championed by Deci, that of *relatedness*, also proved to be a significant, positive contributor to variations in intrinsic motivation. More specifically, perceptions of peer support increased steadily through time, whereas perceptions of teacher support, although declining somewhat in the middle school years, rebounded to a maximum in high school.

Rewarding Reasons

Although success paves the way for task engagement, success alone does not ensure involvement. The reasons for being successful are critical as well. If one counts success merely in terms of extrinsic benefits, such as the public accolades that accompany success, then the very event of success itself may well compromise task valuing. For example, if we hope to ignite a student's interest in an unfamiliar task, especially in the early stages of learning, by offering tangible rewards for compliance, then compliance is likely all we will get unless additional, personally satisfying reasons for learning are also reinforced at the same time.

What might these payoffs be? In a separate, unpublished study, we ask our college informants to identify those personally meaningful payoffs that cause them to invest more time and energy in assignments beyond the minimum amount of work needed for a good grade. This request provoked a rich and provocative set of responses. They included a considerable representation of what could be called "process" payoffs, that is, satisfactions arising out of the discovery of unexpected yet intriguing subject-matter nuances, feelings of accomplishment for making progress toward a meaningful goal, and an increasing sense of mastery over the material.

Another distinctly different category of valued payoffs included, surprisingly, a number of patently extrinsic rewards, nominally unrelated to the inherent virtues of self-discovery, but which in the school context nonetheless provide potent support in the service of intrinsic valuing. These "social-support" goals included being able to share with others why the material being studied was meaningful to students. These sources of satisfaction imply provocative possibilities for aligning tangible classroom reward structures in ways that support intrinsic task engagement.

As part of this general inquiry regarding the nature of tangible yet meaningful payoffs and how they might operate to support intrinsic valuing, we ask another group of Berkeley undergraduates to recall a time when they were coaxed, bribed, or otherwise coerced into taking up some new activity that initially commanded little or no interest, but that in time became a great source of personal enjoyment. Every student had at least one such experience to relate. Learning to play the piano was a favorite extracurricular scenario, and foreign language acquisition dominated those scenarios drawn from school settings. Students were directed to describe the process of moving from "chore to joy" as bipolar anchor points along a timeline of their own creation. At five different points in their narratives, say, midway along the timeline, students were directed to rate, retrospectively, the importance of several reasons for their being motivated to continue learning, including among them, being tangibly rewarded by others, feeling a continuing sense of obligation, becoming increasingly skillful, and experiencing an increasing sense of personal control over events. Increasing skillfulness was consistently rated as the most important of these factors across all the narratives, from beginning to end, and irrespective of the nature of the activity undertaken. Incidentally, although the offering of tangible rewards such as promises of increased allowances or the privilege of borrowing the family car commanded a continuing presence over the course of the timelines, variations in the frequency of such incentives were unrelated to subjective judgments of increasing task enjoyment. This finding supports the contention that the offering of tangible incentives may serve a constructive purpose by keeping individuals task-focused until more personally satisfying reasons emerge for continuing. Dynamics such as these, which involve the scaffolding of intrinsically satisfying motives onto initially extrinsic reasons for learning, recall the stagewise progression of motive internalization proposed by Deci and Ryan (1985).

Interests

Finally, current research pays scant attention to the quality of task interest as an independent variable. In particular, much of the experimental research, especially that addressing the overjustification effect, has merely presumed, often without proper empirical verification, that those activities that serve as targets for extrinsic rewards are inherently interesting to all participants. These activities include, among others, pinball play and drawing. Most readers would likely agree that such activities are certainly novel and at a minimum at least superficially intriguing. However, those qualities of engagement of greatest motivational importance as sustainers of the will to learn joyfully and for prolonged periods are not necessarily captured by mere novelty and certainly not uniformly for all students by one activity. The qualities of engagement to which I refer are deeply held, sometimes idiosyncratic, individualized interests whose presence is powerful enough to overcome rebuff and failure. For all their recreational value, pinball playing and painting are insufficient surrogates for true interests. Moreover, they bear little resemblance to those classroom activities in which it is expected that students should take an interest. What, then, is the impact of rewarding abiding, deeply held interests, using even obviously extrinsic rewards such as praise, social recognition, and monetary prizes? Here, too, we have little systematic evidence to inform an answer.

In summary of these several arguments, I propose, in actuality, that the effects of offering or bestowing tangible rewards, most especially grades, on intrinsic task engagement depend on whether or not students feel successful in their studies; whether or not what they are studying is personally meaningful to them; and whether their prevailing reasons for achieving are task focused, not self-aggrandizing, nor self-protective in response to competitive pressures.

A THOUGHT EXPERIMENT

I conducted a modest thought experiment in order to test whether or not this set of propositions was sufficiently plausible to incorporate into one's thinking about actual curriculum design when intrinsic valuing is a priority goal (Covington, 1999). Some 400 Berkeley undergraduates were asked to imagine themselves starting work on the last assignment in a college course. This hypothetical achievement context was varied along two dimensions: first, whether the subject matter of the course was personally meaningful or not, and, second, whether students had done well or poorly, grade-wise, on all preceding assignments. These two conditions were crossed so that all students rated the degree to which they would likely enjoy and value what they were learning on this final assignment under each of the four possible combinations. Finally, a between-subjects factor was introduced by dividing our students into two groups: those whose dominant reasons for learning were task oriented (approach) and those whose reasons were largely self-protective (avoidant).

The results were revealing. Being previously successful, grade-wise, substantially increased the expectation among students that what they would learn next would be personally valuable compared to a decreased expectation in valuing associated with their being previously unsuccessful. Thus, far from diminishing valuing, our students believed that being rewarded, grade-wise, would actually increase the likelihood of task enjoyment. Our students' written explanations for this positive linkage between grade satisfaction and engagement were quite compelling. Based on numerous personal anecdotes, students argued, among other things, that being successful stimulates them to study more, and according to their logic, the more one learns, the more interesting the material is likely to become. Such anecdotes should stimulate further inquiries along new lines into the relationship between tangible payoffs and a commitment to learning.

As to the main effect for interest, students estimated that they would enjoy learning more when studying what was already interesting to them than studying what was not especially interesting, irrespective of being either satisfied or disappointed with their grade. Although this finding in itself is scarcely surprising, what was not so obvious was a significant interaction between the success/disappointment condition and interest level, indicating that the appreciation for learning would be far greater in a failed but task-interested cause than when students succeed, grade-wise, but on assignments that held little interest. Another aspect of this interaction effect was also intriguing in that it appeared to limit further the essential holdings of the overjustification argument. Rather than diminishing enthusiasm for an already established interest by being rewarded, even in extrinsic terms (grades), valuing actually increased beyond what would be expected from either being successful alone or being interested alone. Here, too, anecdotal student explanations for this winning combination of grade success/interest were compelling, including the argument that doing well reduces worry about failing so that students are freer to explore what is potentially most interesting to them.

Finally, what was the impact of different reasons for achieving on caring about learning as reflected in the student types? The most important point, pedagogically speaking, is that differences in the expression of subject-matter appreciation between the task-oriented and self-protective groups were modest. Moreover, the dynamics that controlled appreciation were essentially the same for both groups. For example, both groups responded positively to grade success, with task-oriented students only slightly more appreciative of the subject matter. Likewise, both groups were affected adversely by disappointing grades, and self-protective students more so, but again, the differences were only a matter of slight degree. This suggests that all students—at least when they are identified in terms of approach/avoidance dimensions, possess a capacity for intrinsic engagement, irrespective of the degree to which they have been driven by the fear of failure.

Perhaps the most intriguing implication of this study concerns the potential intrinsic benefits of being successful, grade-wise. Why should this be, given concerns over the potentially detrimental effects of such rewards?

Several interlocking explanations are worthy of consideration. For one thing, success conveys a message of competence. And, as we were reminded, individuals tend to like and enjoy doing things at which they excel. For another thing, as noted by our informants, success mediates a willingness to learn more, which in turn leads to further discoveries of personal value. Finally, as pointed out by Urdan (personal communication, 2002), feelings of success may become an inherent property of work itself, such that enjoyment becomes a measure of success (e.g., "I felt successful because I really enjoyed the activity"). Naturally, all these considerations need to be tempered by the larger motivational perspective. The degree of intrinsic valuing associated with being successful, grade-wise, ultimately depends on the reasons for learning so that, for example, those successes achieved as a means to avoid failure will do little to engender enjoyment in one's accomplishments.

TASK ENGAGEMENT IN DECLINE: THE COLLEGE YEARS

Now consider the precipitous drop in the frequency of intrinsically satisfying experiences reported by our informants upon their entry into college—precipitous in that these ratings slipped sharply and suddenly from their pinnacle in high school. The reactions of our informants to this unwelcome void were potentially destructive of the valuing of whatever might be learned in college. For some students, we detected a sense of resignation and defeat regarding the prospects of their ever appreciating what they would be learning in college. Other students alleged a cynicism on the part of the university, which, while officially honoring the pursuit of knowledge, in practice, they argued, encourages merely the pursuit of grades. And among yet other students, we detected a deliberate decision to postpone the pursuit of personal academic interests and intellectual enjoyment until after the joyless gauntlet of the college years has ended, a most unlikely possibility.

One explanation for this decline in intrinsic experiences followed from our need-based analysis. Simply put, intrinsic engagement as a value was whipsawed, on the one side, by the persistent and accelerated presence of factors that undercut task engagement, and, on the other side, by a decreasing presence of those positive, countervailing factors that had set intrinsic engagement on a sustained, upward course in earlier years. As to those constructive factors reported to be in eclipse, we found a decline in the frequency with which students felt they were achieving their grade goals compared to their recollections of virtually uninterrupted academic successes in high school. This sense of decline can be attributed largely to the fact that this intellectually accomplished group, which competed with disproportional success against other less well-prepared students from the general population in precollege years, must continue to compete, but now within an elite circle and for an even more limited supply of rewards. Correlatively, the presence of factors disruptive of the achievement cycle were reported to be on the rise, creating a progressive overbalancing of factors in a negative direction. Not surprisingly, students perceived their new achievement climate as far more competitive than they did in the high school years, and inevitably, doubtless in a cascading effect, they also rated their competence at the lowest ebb compared to any point in their precollege years. Moreover, at the very moment of considerable self-doubt, our students experienced an increasing need to prove themselves by trying to outperform others. This situation approaches the cruelest of ironies: Students believe themselves to possess to a decreasing degree the very quality of mind, ability, that becomes increasingly critical in their test of their self-worth, that is, doing better than others.

This analysis allows us, once again, to place in perspective the question of the potential impact of tangible rewards on intrinsic task engagement. The culprit is primarily a scarcity of rewards, not necessarily their extrinsic nature. It appears to us that scarcity drives a number of negative dynamics, including the disruption of satisfying the need for belonging: Competition creates contestants, not colleagues; moreover, scarcity exacerbates fears of incompetency at a time, ironically, when students are being increasingly offered potentially self-affirming opportunities for autonomous, independent exploration and discovery.

Despite this daunting confection of selective sorting in the college years, of the massive presence of coercive, extrinsic inducements and an overweening grade focus, our students continued to value learning. What was missing for them, as reflected by their declining ratings, was a lack of opportunity to savor the personal, social, and intellectual implications of what they were learning, not necessarily a lack of willingness to do so. Indeed, they expressed considerable regret at the choices they often felt forced to make in favor of focusing on what they believed would be tested in class versus attending to the personal meaning of what they were studying. I believe this observation is enormously important to our understanding of the true nature of the relationship between performing for the sake of grades and caring about learning. Although our students reported themselves in considerable conflict over these goals, the feelings evoked were not necessarily those associated with goal incompatibility—between achievement and caring—as much as with the need to prioritize these goals. From this perspective, our task as educators should be to help students redress these priorities in favor of caring about learning. Potentially, this task is made easier for the fact that the promotion of effective learning and its appreciation go hand-in-hand. A review of our student essays makes clear that they see successful achievement, with its material benefits such as being the gateway to prestigious occupations, and valuing what is being learned as two sides of the same coin. Recall, for example, the observations of many of our students that being successful prompted them to study more, and the more they learned, the more likely they were to discover things of interest. And additionally, being successful reduces worries about failing so that, according to our informants, they are freer to explore what is of potential interest. Nonetheless, despite such anecdotal reassurances, the task of modifying priorities is no simple proposition.

CONCLUSION

Based on the reasoning thus far, I have concluded that the threat to intrinsic task engagement posed by the offering of rewards, especially in the form of grades, has less to do with the extrinsic nature of such rewards than the fact that many students tie their sense of worth to their ability to compete successfully for a limited number of payoffs so that these rewards become sought after for self-defeating, defensive reasons, which undercut the love of learning. Assuming that this argument properly assesses the real issues associated with the potentially undermining effects of school-based rewards, we can rephrase the questions with which we began in a more proactive form by asking under what conditions might the offering of rewards—even blatantly tangible rewards, like grades—benefit creative expression and in the very competitive context in which grades often carry the burden of self-definition. The previous reasoning offers a starting point for these deliberations. I believe that we will not satisfactorily resolve the issue of using rewards as a motivational tool until the research community takes into account more fully (a) the psychological meaning that rewards convey, (b) the reasons that students seek out these rewards in the first place, and (c) the developmental needs that rewards can potentially satisfy. Consider the negative side of this proposition: When classroom reward structures encourage self-defeating, defensive reasons for learning, as in the case of outperforming others, then the basic psychological needs associated with the will to learn identified by Deci and his colleagues will be stifled. Self-confidence will falter needlessly when perfectly competent performances are undervalued due to competitive pressure; relatedness needs will be undercut when competition turns colleagues into competitors; and needs for personal control, autonomy, and freedom of expression will be overwhelmed by the fear of failure. By contrast, on the optimistic side of the ledger, I suggest that all students, even those who are self-protective by inclination, can behave with considerable enthusiasm despite a competitive, grade-focused context if (a) rewards are potentially plentiful, that is, available to anyone as long as their performances live up to the quantity and quality of workmanship required by an instructor; (b) a number of different kinds of rewards are available in addition to those associated with performance outcomes, especially payoffs that reinforce students in the pursuit of their own goals and unique interests; and (c) rewards encourage autonomy of expression and independence of thought in a cooperative context.

But how can practitioners incorporate these principles into school learning? Here we can take inspiration from the retelling by my students of the story of the old deaf professor in ways that make positive use of rewards in the service of task enjoyment. An important point made by these storytellers was to maintain a distinction between rewards for performance versus rewards for the process by which achievements occur. Many students argued, in effect, that the old man's money should be offered to enhance greater enjoyment in game play, not just to establish winners and losers. Their suggestions included the purchase of athletic equipment so that higher skill levels could be attained than otherwise, and rewarding compliance with rules of play that fully engaged all the children, with none left out. Such payoffs are reminiscent of those uniquely personal, idiosyncratic rewards mentioned earlier, which are potentially plentiful, and are also supportive of autonomous or collective action. Indeed, perhaps one reason that rewards have received such bad press is that the target behaviors typically are performance outcomes whose quality is often defined in reward-scarce, competitive terms. What if, by contrast, payoffs encourage the personal discoveries, insights, and challenges inherent in the process of achievement, processes that are open to all students?

One potential problem with this proposal is obvious. There is the possibility that process rewards may lose their motivational value simply because they *are* plentiful. In effect, who wants to play if everyone can win? Fortunately, we have some reassurances on this point. Another sample of our students identified at least one measure of excellence that, by their reckoning, maintains its motivational value while reflecting a dimension along which anyone can excel: self-improvement. Nonetheless, paying students to arrange their learning in ways that promote personal meaning is a risky proposition—what if, in the process of also satisfying student grade aspirations, we undercut the very essence of our higher objectives?

We have addressed this question empirically in an introductory psychology course, that I teach yearly with a typical enrollment of some 400 students. Over the past several years, I have allocated a small percentage of the total points students can earn toward their final grade to the seeking of personal relevance in their assignments. This involves, for instance, encouraging students to modify otherwise uninteresting tasks in order to increase their attractiveness for challenge and exploration; to seek out deeper connections that might link assignments not only in my course, but across courses; and to reflect on their own thought processes as they work, remaining alert to serendipity, chance, and the opportunity for expanded exploration. Students are uniformly positive about this feature of the course, not simply because it presents a novel yet virtually foolproof way to enhance their grades, but—and this is the important point—also because the process-related experiences brought to light are precisely the kinds of intangibles that students feel are typically missing when instructors calculate grades. These rewards take on a disproportionate importance, far beyond their modest contribution to the final grade tally, by elevating intrinsic task engagement to a favored instructional priority.

It appears that attending to the intrinsic aspects of learning via a grade inducement holds considerable promise. On the one hand, our informants conceded that without this tangible payoff, little attention would have been given to the rich personal satisfactions associated with their learning. Yet on the other hand, once our students became engaged, the fact of their having been paid initially was generally discounted as being a distraction.

These findings stimulate further inquiries. For instance, we may still wonder how genuine are such self-induced revelations, and if robust and enduring, are they sustained merely by material success or correspondingly diminished by disappointing grades? In short, just how much do expressions of task engagement remain the creatures of extrinsically controlled rewards, once they are induced? It is by pursuing questions such as these that presume a potentially positive motivational role for tangible rewards that will most likely settle the issues raised here in constructive ways.

REFERENCES

Amabile, T. M. (1982). Children's artistic creativity: Detrimental effects of competition in a field setting. *Personality and Social Psychology Bulletin, 8,* 573–587.

Atkinson, J.W. (1957). Motivational determinants of risk-taking behavior. *Psychological Review, 64,* 359–372.

Beery, R. G. (1975). Fear of failure in the student experience. *Personnel Guidance Journal, 54,* 190–203.

Bem, D. J. (1970). *Beliefs, attitudes, and human affairs.* Belmont, CA: Brooks/Cole.

Birney, R. C., Burdick, H., & Teevan, R. C. (1969). *Fear of failure.* New York: Van Nostrand.

Butler, R., & Nisan, M. (1986). Effects of no feedback, task-related comments, and grade on intrinsic instruction and performance. *Journal of Educational Psychology, 78,* 210–216.

Cameron, J. (2001). Negative effects of reward on intrinsic motivation—A limited phenomenon: Comment on Deci, Koestner, and Ryan (2001). *Review of Educational Research, 71*(1), 29–42.

Cameron, J., Banko, K. M., & Pierce, W. D. (2002). Pervasive negative effects of rewards on intrinsic motivation: The myth continues. *The Behavior Analyst, 24,* 1–44.

Cameron, J., & Pierce, W. D. (1994). Reinforcement, reward, and intrinsic motivation: A meta-analysis. *Review of Educational Research, 64,* 363–423.

Condry, J. D., & Chambers, J. (1978). Intrinsic motivation and the process of learning. In M. R. Lepper & D. Greene (Eds.), *The hidden costs of reward: New perspectives on the psychology of human motivation.* Hillsdale, NJ: Lawrence Erlbaum Associates, Inc.

Covington, M. V. (1992). *Making the grade: A self-worth perspective on motivation and school reform.* New York: Cambridge University Press.

Covington, M. V. (1998). *The will to learn: A guide for motivating young people.* New York: Cambridge University Press.

Covington, M.V. (1999). Caring about learning: The nature and nurturing of subject-matter appreciation. *Educational Psychologist, 34,* 127–136.

Covington, M.V. & Beery, R. G. (1976). *Self-worth and school learning.* New York: holt, Rinehart & Winston.

Covington, M. V., & Dray, E. (2002). The developmental course of achievement motivation: A need-based approach. In A. Wigfield & J. S. Eccles (Eds.), *Development of achievement motivation* (pp. 33–56). New York: Academic Press.

Covington, M. V., & Müeller, K. J. (2001). Intrinsic versus extrinsic motivation: An approach/avoidance reformulation. *Educational Psychology Review, 13*(2), 111–129.

DeCharms, R. (1957). Affiliation motivation and productivity in small groups. *Journal of Abnormal and Social Psychology, 55,* 222–226.

Deci, E. L., Koestner, R., & Ryan, R. M. (1999). A meta-analytic review of experiments examining the effects of extrinsic rewards on intrinsic motivation. *Psychological Bulletin, 125,* 627–668.

Deci, E. L., & Ryan, R. M. (1985). *Intrinsic motivation and self-determination in human behavior.* New York: Plenum Press.

Deci, E. L., Vallerand, R. J., Pelletier, L. G., & Ryan, R. M. (1991). Motivation and education: The self-determination perspective. *Educational Psychologist, 26,* 325–346.

Doyle, W. (1983). Academic work. *Review of Educational Research, 53,* 159–199.

Eisenberger, R., & Cameron, J. (1996). Detrimental effects of reward: Reality or myth? *American Psychologist, 51,* 1153–1166.

Fincham, F. D., & Cain, K. M. (1986). Learned helplessness in humans: A developmental analysis. *Developmental Review, 6,* 301–333.

Grolnick, W. S., & Ryan, R. M. (1986). *Parent styles associated with children's school-related competence and adjustment.* Unpublished manuscript, University of Rochester.

Harari, O., & Covington, M. V. (1981). Reactions to achievement behavior from a teacher and student perspective: A developmental analysis. *American Educational Research Journal, 18,* 15–28.

Kohn, A. (1993). *Punished by rewards.* New York: Houghton Mifflin.

Lepper, M. R., Greene, D., & Nisbett, R. E. (1973). Undermining children's intrinsic interest with extrinsic rewards: A test of the "overjustification" hypothesis. *Journal of Personality and Social Psychology, 28*, 129–137.

Maltzman, I. (1960). On the training of originality. *Psychological Review, 67*, 229–242.

McClelland, D. C. (1965). Toward a theory of motive acquisition. *American Psychologist, 20*, 321–333.

McClelland, D. C. (1980). Motive dispositions: The merits of operant and respondent measures. In L. Wheeler (Ed.), *Review of personality and docial psychology* (Vol. 1, pp. 10–41). Beverly Hills, CA: Sage.

Pittenger, P. J. (1996). Reconsidering the overjustification effect: A guide to critical resources. *Teaching Psychology, 23*, 234–236.

Renninger, K. A., Hidi, S., & Krapp, A. (1992). *The role of interest in learning and development*. Hillsdale, NJ: Erlbaum.

Rummel, A., & Feinberg, R. (1988). Cognitive evaluation theory: A meta-analytic review of the literature. *Social Behavior and Personality, 16*, 147–164.

Ryan, R. M., & Deci, E. L. (2000). Self-determination theory and the facilitation of intrinsic motivation, social development, and well-being. *American Psychologist, 55*, 68–78.

Shaw, M. E. (1958). Some motivational factors in cooperation and competition. *Journal of Personality, 26*, 155–169.

Tang, S. H., & Hall, V. C. (1995). The overjustification effect: A meta-analysis. *Applied Cognitive Psychology, 9*, 365–404.

Thompson, T. (1993). Characteristics of self-worth protection in achievement behavior. *British Journal of Educational Psychology, 63*, 469–488.

Thompson, T. (1996). Self-worth protection in achievement behavior: A review and implications for counselling. *Australian Psychologist, 31*, 41–51.

Urdan, T., Midgley, C., & Anderman, E. M. (1998). The role of classroom goal structure in students' use of self-handicapping strategies. *American Educational Research Journal, 35*, 101–122.

Vallerand, R. J., Fortier, M. S., & Guay, F. (1997). Self-determination and persistence in a real life setting: Toward a motivational model of high school dropout. *Journal of Personality and Social Psychology, 72*, 1161–1176.

Wiersma, U. J. (1992). The effects of extrinsic rewards on intrinsic motivation: A meta-analysis. *Journal of Occupational and Organizational Psychology, 65*, 101–114.

CHAPTER 7

WHAT ADOLESCENTS NEED

A Self-Determination Theory Perspective on Development within Families, School, and Society

Jennifer G. La Guardia
University of Wisconsin–Madison
Richard M. Ryan
University of Rochester

Adolescence is characterized first and foremost by change. Arguably at no other time in development are so many factors in flux. Changes in physical, emotional, and intellectual capacities are manifold. Among the critical developmental and psychological challenges that adolescents face are relational tasks, such as transforming childlike ties in familial relationships into ones of adult mutuality, and forming enduring and satisfying extrafamilial relationships with partners and friends. Also, competency-relevant tasks, such as meeting the demands of school and work, and successfully choosing and developing vocational and avocational interests become more pressing (Csikszentmihalyi & Larson, 1984). Finally, internalizing specific norms and practices—shifting from mere compliance to self-regulated, willing adherence and endorsement of a coherent set of social values—is a central task toward identity formation and passage into adulthood.

The changes associated with puberty, physical maturation, and the transition from childhood to adult roles are clearly universal and inherent aspects of adolescence. However, the structure of modern society has both prolonged this developmental stage and exacerbated some of its tasks and challenges. Specifically, how adolescents engage developmental tasks and formulate an identity remains more "open" for most adolescents today, in contrast to most previous societies, in which their social roles, economic positions, marriages, and social support networks were automatically conferred or predetermined to a much greater extent (Ryan & Deci, in press). Adolescents today must "find their place"—exploring which values, lifestyles, friends, group identifications, and vocations to adopt. This process of self-definition takes place over an extended time period, and in many cases makes the tasks of adolescence last far past the teenage years.

Given such challenges, it is noteworthy that most adolescents successfully negotiate this period and mature in a relatively healthy manner (Collins & Laursen, 1992). Most remain closely connected with parents and siblings, carve out a reasonably satisfying identity, successfully develop new relationships, and internalize and integrate some abiding values. However, this majority stands alongside the still significant number of adolescents who find the challenges overwhelming, who experience great conflict, and who wind up alienated or compromised in their entry into the adult world.

This chapter focuses precisely on the issue of why some teens are able to successfully negotiate the "tasks" of adolescence, while others find themselves blocked or frustrated in their development. In particular, our interest is to define the *psychological needs* of adolescence, or the necessary nutriments that make optimal development possible. In line with this aim, we are also interested in identifying the types of social environments that meet the psychological needs of teens and thus facilitate their healthy development, versus those social contexts that do not meet needs and accordingly inhibit or derail optimal functioning and growth.

Specifically using the framework of self-determination theory (SDT) (Ryan & Deci, 2000), we examine the social-contextual factors in home and school environments that foster versus undermine adolescent well-being, self-motivation, and the internalization of important social values and practices. We also discuss the issue of identity formation in terms of not only finding a place, but finding the "right place." More specifically, we look at the degree to which identities are truly integrated into the self, and the implications of the relative integration of identity for adolescents' mental health and ongoing development.

SELF-DETERMINATION THEORY IN BRIEF

SDT is in many ways both a classical view of development, and a new way to analyze psychological and social issues. As a classical view, SDT is an organismic theory. In line with theorists such as Goldstein (1939), Rogers (1963), and White (1963), SDT assumes that people are active agents in the tasks of development. SDT holds that humans are liberally endowed with *intrinsic motivation*, a natural and spontaneous tendency to be curious and interested in exploring novelty and tackling new challenges. SDT also assumes that humans have an assimilative tendency to *internalize and integrate* social norms and practices. The specific forms of internalization are viewed as dependent on the kind of supports provided by the socializing environment. As such, SDT differentiates between relatively primitive or incomplete forms of internalization, mostly based on reward and punishment socialization contingencies, and some relatively sophisticated and well-synthesized forms of internalization that are related to more informational and relationally based forms of socialization (Ryan, 1993). With these assumptions in mind, SDT suggests that it is the degree to which individuals can both experience intrinsic motivation and integrate regulations of social behaviors into the self that predicts well-being and full functioning at every age and in every domain (Ryan & Deci, 2000).

Perhaps the most radical assumption of SDT is that in order to function optimally, the processes of intrinsic motivation, internalization, and integration require *basic psychological needs* to be supported (Deci & Ryan, 2000; Ryan, 1995). Just as the organic development of a plant depends on the nutriments of soil, sunlight, and water, healthy psychological development of the person requires, according to SDT, some basic nutriments in the form of social supports for psychological growth. Accordingly, SDT suggests that the most basic psychological nutriments are the needs for relatedness, competence, and autonomy.

Relatedness concerns feelings of connection and belongingness with others. The experience of belonging or being intimately connected with others provides the requisite emotional security to actively venture out into the world and explore (Baumeister & Leary, 1995; Deci & Ryan, 2000). Furthermore, relatedness needs provide a central motive for internalizing social regulations and adapting to interpersonal and cultural circumstances. *Competence* represents the need to feel effective in one's actions and capable of meeting the challenges of everyday life (White, 1963). Supports for competence include structure and guidance, as well as the provision of optimally challenging (rather than overwhelming) tasks and responsibilities. Finally, *autonomy* concerns the developmental need to self-regulate activity rather than to be heteronomously controlled (Deci & Ryan, 1987, 2000). Autonomy describes the full endorsement by, and participation of, the self in one's behavior, and is dependent on awareness of inner motives, emotions, and external demands. This stands in contrast to controlled or fragmented functioning, which is associated with behavior that is regulated by forces that are perceived to be alien or external to the self. Controlled functioning impedes the development of awareness of inner motives and emotions, and consequently the development of healthy self-regulation.

The dynamic interplay of these three basic needs and the opportunities afforded in the social environment for their satisfaction define the trajectories of motivation, growth, and integrity. Although the expression of autonomy, competence, and relatedness needs may vary at different points in development and may vary from culture to culture, a rich body of evidence has shown that satisfaction of these needs within varied contexts, domains, and relationships is salient to adolescents' "coming of age" in all cultures (Chirkov, Ryan, Kim, & Kaplan, 2001) and is related to optimal growth and development across the lifespan (Deci & Ryan, 2000; Ryan & Deci, 2001; Ryan & La Guardia, 2000). As we shall see as we explore home, school, and the greater social context, how needs are satisfied is perhaps the most critical factor in shaping adolescents' negotiation of developmental tasks and determining their resultant well-being.

AUTONOMY AND RELATEDNESS: THE ADOLESCENT IN THE FAMILY

The foundation of healthy adolescent development rests upon relationships with parents or caregivers. By providing supports for the psychological development of their growing child, parents foster the confidence and active motivation needed to meet developmental tasks, as well as the relational security and sense of self needed to promote resilience in the face of challenges. In childhood, parents support development by creating structured environments that provide a coherent, rational, and guided navigation of developmental tasks. Parents must devote significant time, energy, and attention to assisting the child as he or she takes on challenges, explores new skills, and stretches him- or herself in terms of self-expression. In adolescence, however, although the provision of structure and involvement of parents continues to be important, adolescents begin to develop the cognitive and emotional capacities to increasingly self-regulate their own behaviors. They also spend less time in the presence of their parents, developing much of their interests and forming their identities in the context of new relationships with peers and other adults (e.g., teachers). As such, the parent–adolescent relationship evolves significantly during this time and requires a deeper level of trust, more open communication, and support that is commensurate with the adolescents' developmental capacities. Parents remain involved through maintaining reasonable limits and providing optimal challenges for their adolescents—allowing them to exercise their agency and self-initiative, explore new challenges, and extend their relations to peers and other adults. Thus, parents who support their adolescents' needs by being involved and setting appropriate limits, while showing empathy, trust, and interest, lay the strongest foundation for adolescents' optimal development (Grolnick, Deci, & Ryan, 1997), while parents who fail to meet their adolescents' needs foster rebellion, reactance, or apathy.

Given the importance of parents, it is interesting that many Western psychological theorists have portrayed adolescence as a time that necessitates detaching from parents. For example, a quite popular view is that adolescents engage in a process of *individuation* that is characterized by "breaking" or weakening of familial bonds in the service of forging new, extrafamilial relationships, and an identity of "one's own" (Blos, 1979; Freud, 1958/1969; Steinberg & Silverberg, 1986). In such views, individuation requires separateness from parents, or a distancing from their love and influence, in order to forge one's own set of adult values, goals, and social relationships.

The SDT view of adolescent development is quite different from this traditional formulation. According to SDT, the process of individuation indeed concerns internalization of values, identity development, and extrafamilial relatedness. However, none of these developmental tasks is seen as necessitating separateness, independence, or "breaking away" from parents. In fact, such detachment is viewed as neither "natural" nor particularly healthy. Instead, separateness, rebellion, or breaking away are seen as *reactions* to familial and cultural conditions that frustrate psychological needs. Specifically, SDT predicts that teens detach mainly when parents are excessively controlling (thereby frustrating autonomy needs), cold or rejecting (thereby frustrating relatedness needs), or are unrealistically demanding (thereby frustrating competence needs). Thus, insofar as parents fail to support needs, adolescents will more likely need to break away or detach from them, a nonoptimal but all too common outcome.

Research has borne out this SDT contention. For example, based on the theories of Blos (1979), Steinberg and Silverberg (1986) argued that adolescents individuate by becoming "emotionally autonomous" from parents. Their construct of emotional autonomy (EA) reflects detaching or distancing oneself from parents, being less trusting of their guidance, and being more reluctant to follow their lead. Ryan and Lynch (1989) suggested that such EA from parents represents neither autonomy (defined as self-regulation or volition) nor healthy individuation. Instead, they argued that parents who are supportive of their adolescent's needs are more likely to have a teen who willingly relies on them, who is more likely to listen to their inputs, and who feels closer to them. Accordingly, Ryan and Lynch showed empirically that EA was (a) negatively related to parental support of their teenager's autonomy as well as the teenager's felt connectedness to the family, and (b) negatively related to adolescent well-being.

Subsequent research has shown that, among adolescents, those with higher EA have parents that are characterized as non-nurturing, too cold, or controlling (Lamborn & Steinberg, 1993; Turner, Irwin, & Millstein, 1991); are more commonly children of divorce; and are more commonly in high-risk families who have low cohesion (Ryan & Lynch, 1989) than those with lower EA. EA has also been negatively associated with authoritative and positively associated with authoritarian practices of parenting (McBride-Chang & Chang, 1998; Ryan & Lynch, 1989). In terms of adolescents' functioning, those higher in EA have shown lower self-esteem and greater susceptibility to negative peer pressure (Chen, 1999), lower school achievement (McBride-Chang & Chang, 1998), and lower overall well-being and higher risk behaviors such as drug use, alcohol use, smoking, and unprotected sex (Ryan & Lynch, 1989; Turner et al., 1991) than those lower in EA. In sum, these findings, which have been obtained in both Asian and North American samples, suggest that EA is negatively related to the development of true autonomy and well-being. Indeed, the only circumstance in which EA appears to be a favorable characteristic is when adolescents have extremely non-nurturing parents (Fuhrman & Holmbeck, 1995). Thus, only when parents fail to support psychological needs might such detachment or "emotional autonomy" convey advantages.

In contrast, adolescents' individuation, internalization of adult roles, and growth in self-regulation have been shown to proceed more optimally when parents and other adults (e.g., teachers) provide support for basic needs. When adults support needs, adolescents are more likely to rely on them, accept their guidance, and also experience more positive well-being in the context of their developmental transitions (Ryan, La Guardia, Butzel, Kim, & Chirkov, 2002). Additionally, when parents support psychological needs, their adolescent offspring remain more attached to them, show better school functioning, and are able to form more healthy extrafamilial relationships. In essence, adolescents utilize parental relationships as the supportive backdrop from which they can venture out to explore the world and define themselves.

For example, La Guardia, Ryan, Couchman, and Deci (2000) investigated the relations between security of attachment with close relationship partners, including parents, and perceived need supportiveness of these partners in a sample of late adolescents. As predicted, the relative security felt with social partners was strongly associated with the extent to which each supported autonomy, competence, and relatedness needs. Thus, consistent with the SDT formulation, when parents supported psychological needs, adolescents and young adults did not detach from them but instead were more securely attached. Leak and Cooney (2001) replicated this general model, showing both the positive relations between autonomy support and attachment.

In terms of school functioning, Avery and Ryan (1987) investigated pre-adolescents' mental health and classroom adjustment as a function of children's interview-based descriptions of their parents. Parents who were described as more nurturant were those who were shown to be more warmly involved with their children. Greater nurturance, in turn, predicted better social and academic functioning of the children within the classroom. Similarly, Ryan, Stiller, and Lynch (1994) found that among adolescents, greater relatedness to parents, as assessed by indicators of felt security, utilization, and emulation of parents, predicted stronger engagement in school, as well as higher self-esteem and well-being.

Parental autonomy support has also been shown to foster greater identification with and intrinsic motivation for school activities. As compared to children of more controlling parents, autonomy-supportive and warmly involved parents have children who report more self-motivation for school, who are rated by teachers as less behaviorally or academically troubled, and who actually achieve higher grades and standardized test outcomes (Grolnick & Ryan, 1989; Grolnick, Ryan, & Deci, 1991). Students also exhibit more inner resources for school—showing greater volition, confidence, and sense of control—when they experience parents as more autonomy supportive and involved (Grolnick, Ryan, & Deci, 1991). Such findings have also been supported cross-culturally. For example, Chirkov and Ryan (2001) examined perceptions of parental autonomy support in both Russian and U.S. high school students, and found that both overall mental health and identification with the importance of school were associated with greater autonomy support by parents in both nations, to equal degrees.

Finally, the importance of familial relations to the formation of nurturant relationships outside of the family has been demonstrated. For example, Ryan and colleagues (1994) found that the quality of relatedness to parents predicted quality of relatedness to teachers and peers, with greater support from parents associated with more supportive relations with teachers and peers. Also, Dresner and Grolnick (1996), examining the development of intimate relationships in young women, found that those women who successfully attained healthy intimate relationships with partners were those who experienced their parents as autonomy supportive and emotionally accepting. Thus, a supportive family environment can conduce toward greater support and relatedness in extrafamilial relationships as well.

In sum, the SDT viewpoint suggests that parental supports for basic psychological needs provide the foundation for teens to tackle the challenges of individuation, achievement-related tasks, and formation of new relationships. When homes are nurturant, teens not only experience greater well-being, but they also appear to be more likely to internalize constructive societal and school-related goals, and form more healthy extrafamilial relationships. Importantly, in such homes, there is less need to detach, suggesting that the development of autonomy and the maintenance of connectedness to family are not at all antithetical.

PSYCHOLOGICAL NEEDS IN THE CONTEXT OF SCHOOL

Outside of the family, school is the central domain for most teens to engage in tasks of development. In modern societies, schools serve as a place to forge adult self-concepts, and they function as a gateway into other identities and professions. Certainly, how well adolescents adjust to school and engage the tasks of development varies. According to SDT, much of that variance is determined by the extent to which psychological needs for autonomy, competence, and relatedness are able to be fulfilled or are largely frustrated within school. Thus, in part on the basis of school experiences, teens can learn to see themselves as able or incompetent, as belonging or outcast, as personally empowered or weak and without voice. SDT suggests that if teens can feel autonomy, competence, and belongingness in school, they will experience more intrinsic motivation to learn, they will more deeply value and engage school-relevant tasks, and they will experience greater well-being. We now review the influences of needs on the processes of intrinsic and extrinsic motivations to learn, and the impact on well-being.

Intrinsic and Extrinsic Motivation

Many theories of motivation suggest that motivation is a unitary phenomenon—one has more or less motivation. However, SDT suggests that the primary issue in motivation is not how much motivation a person has, but what kind. Accordingly, SDT distinguishes types or orientations of motivation. The first distinction is between intrinsic motivation (motivation based on the inherent satisfactions of activity) and extrinsic motivation (motivation based on instrumentalities). Further, extrinsic motivation is differentiated by one's level of relative autonomy. SDT does not embrace a simple intrinsic/extrinsic dichotomy, but rather suggests a differentiated family of motives that have both different antecedents and consequences and are associated with different subjective experiences.

Intrinsic motivation refers to the innate tendency to explore, take interest in novelty and challenges, and stretch one's capacities. When intrinsically motivated, people engage in activities for their inherent satisfactions, and they experience their activity as self-originated and organized, as well as effective (Deci, 1975). Thus, intrinsic motivation is characterized by experiences of autonomy and competence.

Intrinsic motivation plays a primary role in development (Elkind, 1971; Harter, 1978; Krapp, Renninger, & Hoffmann, 1998). Through spontaneous interest, playful engagement, and exploration of one's environment, one's capacities are stretched, new skills are acquired and mastered, and knowledge is expanded. As such, intrinsic motivation is an important process underlying cognitive, affective, and motor development, as well as the exploration of interests toward identity formation.

Research has clearly demonstrated the importance of intrinsic motivation to engagement with and success in school. Researchers have linked intrinsic motivation for schoolwork with more interest, curiosity, independence, and desire for challenge in the classroom (Boggiano & Katz, 1991; Harter, 1978), as well as with better cognitive performance at complex tasks (Benware & Deci, 1984; Grolnick & Ryan, 1987). For example, Ryan, Connell, and Plant (1990) asked students to read a passage and rate their interest and enjoyment of the material. Students' interest and enjoyment of the material was associated with both their self-reported comprehension and their actual recall of the material. Other studies have also shown that focusing on the interest in materials (fostering intrinsic motivation) is associated with higher learning. In a sample of college students, Benware and Deci (1984) showed that those who learned material with the intent of teaching it to others reported higher intrinsic motivation for learning the material than those who learned material in order to be tested on it. Greater intrinsic motivation was in turn associated with better conceptual learning of the material.

Despite numerous studies both in the Eastern and Western cultures that show that intrinsic motivation is clearly important during adolescence, intrinsic motivation for school often declines for many adolescents (e.g., Eccles, 1993; Gottfried, 1985). One possible reason for this decline is that changes in the school context during adolescence impacts satisfaction of autonomy and competence needs. Cognitive evaluation theory (CET) (Deci & Ryan, 1980), a component of SDT theory, explains how contextual conditions may support versus thwart intrinsic motivation, and thus why these declines in adolescent intrinsic motivation might result.

According to CET, when people perceive that their behavior is caused by forces external to the self (external perceived locus of causality), or when events/feedback decrease perceived competence, people experience diminished intrinsic motivation. By contrast, intrinsic motivation is

202 J.G. LA GUARDIA and R.M. RYAN

enhanced by events that facilitate an internal perceived locus of causality (autonomy) and promote perceived competence. Unlike social learning views (e.g., Bandura, 1983), which suggest that efficacy is the only necessary component for intrinsic motivation, SDT instead holds that unless a behavior is accompanied by a sense of autonomy, then perceived competence will not enhance intrinsic motivation. Thus, satisfaction of autonomy and competence needs are both necessarily implicated for intrinsic motivation to flourish.

Field studies have shown that teachers who are autonomy supportive catalyze greater intrinsic motivation, curiosity, and desire for challenge in students (Deci, Schwartz, Sheinman, & Ryan 1981; Flink, Boggiano, & Barrett, 1990; Ryan & Grolnick, 1986). For example, Ryan and Grolnick (1986), using both self-reports and projective stories to assess classroom climate, found that teachers high in autonomy support and warmth were those whose students reported greater intrinsic motivation and greater confidence regarding school. Similarly, Deci and colleagues (1981) found that when teachers advocated solutions that primarily considered the child's perspective (autonomy supportive), students showed greater mastery motivation, specifically more curiosity and more desire for challenge. In contrast, when teachers were more controlling (e.g., used contingencies, rewards and punishments, social comparisons, external praise, or pressure), students showed lower mastery motivation, lower confidence in their abilities, and lower self-worth. Furthermore, longitudinal data showed that teachers who were more controlling in their orientation before school even began had students who became less intrinsically motivated and who also decreased in their sense of competence and self-esteem over the early course of the school year.

Research has also shown that opportunities to express competence impacts intrinsic motivation. Activities that are either simple or overly challenging limit opportunities for competence, while activities that are optimally discrepant from people's skill levels tend to be more intrinsically motivating (Danner & Lonky, 1981). Also, contexts that provide structure, including a rationale for behavior and meaningful feedback to guide behavior, support the need for competence and allow greater opportunities for intrinsic interests to flourish (Koestner, Ryan, Bernieri, & Holt, 1984). Thus, importantly in the context of school, environments that pose optimal challenges for students and provide structure and guidance conduce to greater growth in terms of intrinsic motivation, and instead can be detrimental to growth if overstimulating or alternatively boring.

One prominent way that intrinsic motivation is thwarted is through the use of rewards as a means to motivate. When a person uses rewards to influence another's behavior (even when the rewards are desirable and positive), that person is conveying external control and is implicitly devaluing the task at hand. In essence, the message that is conveyed is that "I am responsible for motivating you" and that "You wouldn't do this unless rewarded." Indeed, the implied messages are antithetical to being intrinsically motivated, and specifically to feeling interest and autonomy.

Although some behaviorists continue to suggest that rewards do not negatively affect intrinsic motivation (e.g., Eisenberger & Cameron, 1996), overwhelming evidence suggests otherwise. That is, when people are contingently rewarded for doing an interesting task, they express less interest in the task than those people who are not given rewards, and they are subsequently less likely to persist at the task when given freedom to do so (Deci, Koestner, & Ryan, 1999). This undermining effect of rewards on intrinsic motivation has been demonstrated across a variety of reward contingencies and methods of reward (e.g., Ryan & Deci, 2000; Ryan, Mims, & Koestner, 1983). Additionally, threats of punishment (Deci & Cascio, 1972), external evaluations (Smith, 1974), imposed deadlines (Amabile, DeJong, & Lepper, 1976), imposed goals (Mossholder, 1980), and symbolic awards (Lepper, Greene, & Nisbett, 1973), all of which can diminish the experience of autonomy, have also been shown to undermine intrinsic motivation. Alternatively, providing choice (Zuckerman, Porac, Lathin, Smith, & Deci, 1978) and acknowledging feelings (Koestner et al., 1984), which conduce to fostering autonomy, have been associated with enhanced intrinsic motivation. Thus, intrinsic motivation is diminished under conditions of contingent reward and other external controls, and is enhanced instead by environments that are autonomy supportive.

Another prominent way in which others thwart autonomy and competence needs, and consequently undermine intrinsic motivation, is by the style and language with which they engage students and intervene in their behavior. Research suggests that perceived competence is strengthened and intrinsic motivation consequently enhanced when positive competence feedback is administered in an autonomy-supportive context, while feedback in the form of pressure-laden evaluation diminishes feelings of competence and intrinsic motivation (Fisher, 1978; Ryan, 1982; Vallerand & Reid, 1984). Kast and Conner (1988) have also found that controlling praise undermines intrinsic motivation, whereas praise that is not controlling, and instead is effectance relevant, enhances it. Similarly, Ryan and colleagues (1983) found that the application of performance-contingent rewards, when accompanied by language reflecting a controlling style ("you should" or "you have to" perform) undermined intrinsic motivation, while similar rewards administered with a more autonomy-supportive style (e.g., "Do as well as you can") were less likely to undermine intrinsic motivation.

Clearly, as these findings suggest, support for autonomy and competence needs in the classroom indeed has a tremendous impact on students' inner motivation and confidence about school. Classrooms that nurture autonomy tend to promote intrinsic motivation and perceived competence, whereas those that attempt to incite achievement through external regulations actually undermine intrinsic motivation in students and diminish their personal confidence toward learning.

As we have noted, the diminishment in intrinsic motivation is particularly evident in adolescence. Indeed, a prominent body of research has documented that the school context shifts considerably after elementary school in ways that significantly impinge on the fulfillment of autonomy and competence needs (Eccles, 1993).

First, in comparison to elementary schools, many middle schools and junior highs place greater emphasis on teacher control and discipline, and the use of rewards or other contingencies to control behavior (Eccles & Midgley, 1989). Midgley, Feldlaufer, and Eccles (1988) found that middle school teachers believed that their students needed more discipline and control, and were less trustworthy, than did teachers of sixth graders. Thomas (1980) also suggests that much of teacher verbiage at the end of primary grades is geared more toward behavior management than it is toward provision of information or instruction. Accompanying this emphasis on control are also fewer opportunities for students' inputs and choice. For example, Midgley and Feldlaufer (1987) found that despite students' desire for more input in decision making, students and teachers both reported that students have less opportunities for decision making when they enter middle school than they had previously. Indeed, these contextual shifts clearly impact adolescents' autonomy.

Another important shift occurring at the middle school and junior high levels is that there is an increased emphasis on grades as the primary means of feedback and greater public comparison of students, teachers, and schools as a means to "motivate" performance. For example, Midgley, Anderman, and Hicks (1995) found that middle school environments place a greater emphasis on performance goals (those aimed at achieving top grades and emphasizing social comparisons with other peers as measures of success) than on task goals (those that value self-improvement, effort, mastery, and understanding of materials), while elementary schools promote task-focused learning more than performance-focused learning. Importantly, research has shown that when students are task focused, they exert more effort, take on more challenging work, persist longer, and are more creative than when they are performance focused. When performance focused, students tend to engage in more surface-learning strategies, withdraw effort at the potential of failure, and lose interest in the tasks at hand (Kellaghan, Madaus, & Raczek, 1996).

A more recent development that also promotes a system-wide performance orientation is the use of "high stakes" standardized tests (Ryan & La Guardia, 1999). When standardized tests are used in a "high stakes" fashion, performance is translated into "reports cards" for students as well as teachers, schools, and districts. Teachers and schools are threatened with sanctions or promised rewards in accord with their performance, and students are "academically tracked" or "departmentalized" according to performances on these tests. The school climate created by "high stakes" testing emphasizes test-focused teaching (performance orientation) and crowds out alternative assessments of students' performance (e.g., portfolios, special demonstration projects) that allow optimal expression of their skills and talents (task orientation). Thus, the system often ignores students' unique talents and skills, and forces some into tracks that might not appropriately fit their development (e.g., pacing) or optimal style of learning. Importantly, these test-focused pressures to perform affect not only students who struggle with school but also high-achieving students by changing the focal point of learning, and consequently move all students even further away from intrinsically motivated behavior.

As this evidence would suggest, in line with SDT predictions, the declines evidenced in teens' intrinsic motivation suggest that the changing school climate may compromise needs via increased controls and pressures, as well as less choice and optimal challenges. Indeed, at an age when development of self-regulatory capacities is extremely salient and personal competencies are rapidly expanding, shifts in the organization and structure of schools may impinge on adolescents' needs and their natural tendencies to explore and learn, and thus result in lower intrinsic motivation and well-being.

Extrinsic Motivation and Internalization

Although the diminishment of intrinsic motivation during adolescence is an important issue, much, if not most, of what adolescents do in school is *extrinsically motivated*. That is, adolescents are engaging in activities that may not be inherently interesting, but are instead socially prescribed behaviors that may be instrumentally important. Indeed, one of the central tasks of adolescence is that of *internalization* of social values which underly and sustain such behaviors and the integration of these values into the self.

Behaviors that are extrinsically motivated may be valued or adopted to varying degrees. As previously noted, theories in the past have cast extrinsic behaviors as simply a single category of those activities that are instrumental to attaining outcomes. However, Ryan, Connell, and Deci (1985) suggested a more differentiated conceptualization of extrinsic motivation, outlining a continuum of extrinsic motivation based on the relative autonomy of behavior and specifying the contextual factors that affect internalization and integration of behavior. Under this formulation, regulation is categorized as external, introjected, identified, or integrated. The least autonomous of extrinsic behaviors are termed *externally regulated*, and are performed to avoid punishments or reap rewards from others. These behaviors are typically experienced as having an external perceived locus of causality (deCharms, 1968), and thus are relatively nonautonomous. *Introjected* behaviors are those done in order to appease the ego (e.g., out of pride) or to avoid guilt or anxiety. These behaviors are simply done to maintain or enhance a sense of self-worth, and are thus regulated by self-esteem contingencies (Deci & Ryan, 1995). Behaviors regulated through introjection are also experienced as somewhat external to the self but are, in contrast to externally regulated behaviors, driven by internal rather than purely external contingencies and pressures.

More autonomous forms of extrinsically motivated behavior include *identification* and *integration*. Both of these forms of regulation are perceived to be emanating from the self and are experienced as self-valued and directed. Identification refers to those behaviors that one values and finds personally important but have yet to be wholly integrated with other behavioral repertoires of the person. For instance, adolescents may embrace their newfound sexuality and fully endorse engaging in sexual activity. They may also endorse a religious affiliation that does not necessarily coalesce with that sexual side. Thus, although both are identifications that are valued as part of the self, they are not reconciled with each other. When behaviors are fully integrated with other valued behaviors, they are then referred to as integrated, the most autonomous of extrinsically motivated behavior.

Although there is evidence that regulatory styles tend to become more internalized (i.e., more autonomous) over time (Chandler & Connell, 1987), often with the increases in cognitive capacity and ego development (Loevinger & Blasi, 1991), the internalization continuum as described here is not a stage-oriented process or developmental trajectory across time. Instead, people can internalize behaviors to relative degrees along this continuum and utilize different regulatory styles across time, and these may differ with each experience, context, or interpersonal milieu. Thus, although adolescence is touted as a period of movement toward greater self-regulation, behaviors may continue to be more or less internalized.

Considerable research has demonstrated differential outcomes as a function of how internalized, or relatively autonomous, an adolescent's motivation is (see Deci & Ryan, 2000, and Ryan & Deci, 2000, for reviews). Especially relevant are studies on school motivation. Numerous studies have shown that the more autonomous students' extrinsic motivation, that

is, the more internalized the regulation of behavior, the better their performance (e.g., Miserandino, 1996), the greater their engagement (e.g., Connell & Wellborn, 1991), and the greater the quality of their learning (e.g.,
Grolnick & Ryan, 1987). Additionally, the more autonomously regulated
students are, the more enjoyment and positive coping strategies they have
for school (Grolnick & Ryan, 1989), and the more likely they are to stay in
school (Vallerand, Fortier, & Guay, 1997).

Researchers have also investigated how supports for autonomy and relatedness in the school environment affect the development of more internalized motivation, and consequently healthier functioning. For example,
Chirkov and Ryan (2001) have demonstrated in both Russian and U.S.
samples that teacher autonomy support (e.g., provision of choice, informational feedback) facilitates both intrinsic motivation and identification,
whereas controlling teaching styles (e.g., use of rewards and contingencies
to elicit performance) foster external regulation as a motivational orientation toward school. Chirkov and Ryan also showed that, in both nations,
teacher autonomy support fosters greater adjustment and well-being, such
as higher self-esteem and greater life satisfaction. Furthermore, Ryan and
colleagues (1994), investigating students in Grades 7 through 9, found that
students who had positive relationships with their teachers were more
likely to approach them for help, and were more self-motivated in school
than those who did not feel close to their teachers. Goodenow (1993) similarly suggested that greater acceptance and connection with teachers con-
duced toward more positive attitudes about school and higher
achievement. Together, these studies suggest that greater autonomy and
relatedness experienced with teachers promotes greater internalized, self-
endorsed school values, and greater adjustment and school achievement.

In sum, schools are an important place in which adolescents' needs are
influenced. Environmental supports for autonomy, competence, and relatedness help students flourish to their potentials—they promote intrinsic
motivation and help students internalize values for learning. When healthier in school functioning, adolescents can develop self-regulation toward
adult values, goals, pathways, and relationships. In contrast, insults to
needs leave adolescents ill-equipped to deal with the challenges of school,
and this may also affect how they negotiate further tasks of adulthood.

PSYCHOLOGICAL NEEDS IN SOCIETY: THE TASK OF
IDENTITY FORMATION

Perhaps the penultimate task of adolescence is that of identity formation.
Adolescents are thrust into a period of self-discovery in which their whole
self is on the line—who they are and what they want to be comes into ques-

tion at almost every turn. Identities are formed around their roles within the family, academic interests and affiliations, the activities they pursue, the peer groups with whom they socialize, the vocation they choose, the lifestyles they emulate, and the culture in which they are embedded. From an SDT perspective, what identities are adopted and how they are chosen can be understood in terms of psychological needs.

SDT suggests that identities are formed in the service of psychological needs. Primarily, people assume roles, beliefs, and practices in order to connect to their social groups. Thus, the adoption of a particular identity serves to foster relatedness with important others. Identities are also assumed to be in the service of competence or autonomy needs as well. Identities in which people can stretch their skills and knowledge through optimal challenges will extend their feelings of effectance or competence, while identities in which people can exercise their true interests and capacities allows autonomy to be expressed. Optimally, of course, each of these needs will be fulfilled within a given identity. However, there are many ways in which needs are thwarted or pitted against each other that serve to make the choices of identity paths quite complex.

Adolescents are often controlled or pressured toward assuming certain identities (undermining autonomy) rather than being afforded support for exploration and choice. For example, some teens experience tremendous pressure from parents, teachers, or peers to adopt certain career paths (e.g., "You will be a doctor"), belief systems (e.g., "You must go to church"), or lifestyles (e.g., "If you don't join our gang, you are nobody"). Pressures such as these can lead to less internalized or endorsed identities precisely because opportunities to experiment, or to more reflectively select values and lifestyles, are foreclosed. Often, pressures to conform to the wishes or expectations of a parent, teacher, or peer also carry the threat of loss of love, connectedness, or esteem if noncompliant, thereby pitting autonomy and relatedness needs against each other. Threats to relatedness further undermine establishment of a secure base from which to explore and extend the self. By having to rely on themselves instead, adolescents have less energy and internal resources (e.g., emotional regulatory capacities) available for their processes of exploration and discovery. Finally, competence needs may be undermined by discouraging feedback from others or the presentation of nonoptimal challenges in the identity formation process. Adolescents will not be likely to deeply explore or assume identities in which they cannot feel competent, and thus they may abandon an identity path as a result. Certainly, school is a central arena in which feelings of effectance may be critically affected, and thus serves to shape the identities pursued and consequently adopted. Clearly, the ways in which adolescents are supported in this process becomes extremely important to how identity develops.

SDT contends that adolescents are naturally oriented toward "trying on" identities, sampling and temporarily emulating various lifestyles, career goals, and group affinities. Kaplan, Assor, and Kanat-Maymon (2001) have indeed shown evidence that adolescents are autonomously oriented toward, and authentically engaged in, the exploration and formulation of a conscious sense of identity in terms of goals, values, and commitments, despite at times feelings confused and uncomfortable in the process.

The identities that are "tried on" can be a product of intrinsic interests (e.g., a penchant for music leads to playing an instrument), early environmental influences (e.g., following the profession of one's father, adopting the same political affiliation as one's family), as well as possibilities encountered in extrafamilial contexts (e.g., acquiring value for activism from school experiences). Thus, some identities may be intrinsically motivated and may serve as the source for a person's avocation, career, or lifestyle (Krapp, in press). Still other identities may be formed because they have instrumental value or importance. That is, many identities are not energized by intrinsic interests but are instead roles, responsibilities, and tasks that are modeled or taught to be important and valuable. Although some of these identities too may emerge from the interests of the individual and may serve to form the rudiments of a particular identity, many of the identities that are "tried on" are those that others (e.g., parents, teachers, peers, society) originally proffer. Thus, many identities are internalized from the social environment.

Regardless of how identities are acquired, each identity formed has associated goals, values, and beliefs (Archer & Waterman, 1990), and these identities as well as the associated components may vary with respect to roles (Donahue, Robins, Roberts, & John, 1993; Sheldon, Ryan, Rawsthorne, & Illardi, 1997), domains (Linville, 1987), and relationships (La Guardia, 2001). Thus, people will generally have multiple identities and multiple identity components (goals, beliefs, values, emotions, behaviors) that may be more or less conferred versus actively selected, and may differ in content to varying degrees.

Importantly, SDT suggests that the extent to which each component of identity is authentically held, or in line with one's "true self," is strongly tied to how others support or discourage the experiences and expressions of these identity components. For example, although a religious viewpoint may be espoused within one's family, and thus in some ways conferred early on to a child, the child may grow to fully embrace these values and hold an identity that converges with these beliefs. Alternatively, she could feel pressured to adopt the religious identity espoused by her family in order to remain in favor with her parents or the greater religious community, despite experiencing these values as alien or antithetical to the self. According to SDT, the degree to which identities are internalized, endorsed, and valued is a function of whether opportunities for need fulfillment are afforded. Accordingly, identities that are identified or integrated are those that are more autonomously regulated and endorsed and have been acquired in need-supportive contexts, while externally regulated or introjected identities are those identities that have been foreclosed or inadequately explored and emerge in contexts that are less need supportive.

Some recent research has borne out this proposition. For example, Sheldon and colleagues (Sheldon & Elliot, 1998; Sheldon & Kasser, 1998) have shown that self-concordant identities—those that fulfill basic needs for autonomy, competence, and relatedness—are experienced as authentic and are fully internalized within the self, while nonconcordant identities are introjected or externally regulated, and serve as compensatory ways of getting needs met. Also, Gagné, Ryan, and Barghman (2001), surveying a sample of aspiring young female gymnasts over the course of a season, found that gymnasts who perceived their coaches and parents to be more autonomy supportive reported more identified and intrinsic motivation for gymnastics and greater well-being, while those who perceived their coaches and parents to be more controlling reported more external regulation for gymnastics and lower well-being. Gymnasts who were identified and intrinsically motivated perceived parents and coaches to be more involved in terms of dedicated time, resources, and overall support than those who were externally regulated. Thus, perceptions of support were related to how deeply these girls internalized their identity as gymnasts.

As we reviewed earlier, the level of internalization of behaviors is also exquisitely tied to well-being. Accordingly, SDT suggests that the degree to which identities conduce toward self-realization or eudaimonia (Waterman, 1993) is a function of whether the identity formation is in line with psychological needs. That is, regardless of whether identities are conferred or actively selected, they must be authentically held and must allow needs to be actively fulfilled in order to truly contribute to well-being. Recent research has indeed shown that greater authenticity in adolescents' identities is indicated in relationships with greater support for autonomy, competence, and relatedness needs and is associated with fuller experiences of the self, greater openness to expression, and greater vitality within close relationships (La Guardia, 2001). Also, goal attainments that are self-concordant with one's identity (those in line with psychological needs) have been shown to conduce to greater well-being than nonconcordant goal attainments (Sheldon & Elliot, 1998), and goal progress on self-concordant goals has been shown to yield greater well-being benefits than progress on nonconcordant goals (Sheldon & Kasser, 1998).

Research has also shown how the lack of support for basic psychological needs can engender insecurity in adolescents and catalyze alternative values, goals, lifestyles, and compensatory activities that conduce to lower well-being. Ryan and Kuczkowski (1994) examined the effects of teenagers' felt security with parents on their development of autonomy and individuation. They showed that in earlier adolescence, self-consciousness, tendencies toward peer conformity, and fears of standing out or being different are normatively quite high, but that these waned as teenagers gained more sense of themselves, their values, and their identity. Importantly, however, older adolescents who experienced emotional insecurity with their parents remained more preoccupied with internal self-controls and appeared to be more susceptible to conformity and self-consciousness than those who felt secure with their parents.

Furthermore, Kasser, Ryan, Zax, and Sameroff (1995) surveyed late adolescents about their orientations toward intrinsic (e.g., value focused on relationships, community, personal growth) versus extrinsic (e.g., materialism, financial success) goals, and their maternal and social environments in which they grew up. They found that teens who valued extrinsic goals had mothers who, by both teen and mother self-report, were less supportive of autonomy and relatedness than those who were more focused on intrinsic goals. Kasser and colleagues suggested that failure of parents to support basic needs leads teens to feel greater insecurity, and as such adopt excessive materialistic values to bolster their own sense of self-worth. Similarly, Williams, Cox, Hedberg, and Deci (2000) showed that parents who were more controlling versus autonomy supportive had teens who were more focused on extrinsic goals, such as materialism and image, and who were more likely to engage in high-risk behaviors, such as illicit drug use and risky sexual practices.

Together these findings suggest that parents who foster insecurity, primarily through poor autonomy and relatedness support, inhibit their teenagers' development of self-regulation and can contribute to their adolescents' conformity and image-focused identities. Importantly, these studies also suggest that the relative authenticity by which adolescents come to adopt identities, as opposed to acquiring identities as compensatory means for satisfying needs, affects how healthy and vital they are in their everyday lives.

Although this research reviewed focused mainly on the impact of parents, indeed schools and peers become centrally influential in adolescents' adoption of identities. For example, teachers' interest in and attention to their students' unique skills, talents, and interests centrally affect students' pursuit of vocations, as well as their moral and emotional development. Some research has suggested that adolescents experience a decline in the quality of their relationships with their teachers after their transition to middle or junior high school (see Midgley & Edelin, 1998). With school becoming such an influential arena in adolescent development, the loss of relatedness in this arena becomes an even greater concern for adolescents' optimal development and well-being.

As an aside, we want to emphasize that we believe that providing a supportive backdrop for adolescents' optimal identity formation is not merely a task of families and schools but is a task of the greater global community as a whole. That is, increasingly as the task of identity formation involves teenagers internalizing and integrating a way of being that fits within society, we must pay attention to the varied societal influences that promulgate identities. As we noted earlier, the nature of modern societies is such that identities are increasingly not assigned or conferred, but instead are necessarily forged by each individual. The growth of the global economy and the expansion of the media have resulted in a proliferation of "possible selves" that adolescents can try on, much more so than any time in the past. There is a sense of what everyone else is doing and how everyone else is "being"— affording exciting new possibilities but also in turn making identity formation potentially a more daunting task.

Many of the messages in popular culture today suggest that the "good life" or "the best way to be" are defined by image, money, and hedonic pleasures. Thus, one must have the "right clothes," the "right car," the "right job," and "be attractive" in order to be somebody. Such images have a special attraction to those who are vulnerable to insecurities, as Kasser and colleagues (1995) have suggested, yet have little connection to the paths that are truly self-realizing or conducive to a healthy identity and way of being.

Again, we emphasize that some identities will be effective in yielding true need satisfactions, whereas others will be poor servants of needs. As the research we have reviewed has suggested, identities adopted as "compromise" formations represent attempts to satisfy needs through indirect, substitute, or reactive means, and conduce to lower well-being, while those that are authentically held and allow true expression of one's needs conduce to self-realization and growth. Clearly, with all of the possible potentialities, finding the identity fit that will conduce toward self-realization has seemingly become even more challenging, with optimal identity formation requiring adequate need support at a more global community level.

CONCLUSION: THE TASKS OF ADOLESCENCE REVISITED

The tasks of adolescence are formidable. Adolescents are faced with transforming familial relationships, forming extrafamilial relationships with partners and friends, meeting the demands of school and work, choosing and developing vocational and avocational interests, and internalizing and integrating a coherent set of social values. The modern societal landscape has afforded exciting new possibilities and avenues for exploration and experimentation of "possible selves." However, with this expansion of possibilities, there is also an increased risk that adolescents can get lost, confused, or pushed down the "wrong" paths.

In this chapter we have argued that support for psychological needs for autonomy, competence, and relatedness are essential to meeting the tasks and challenges of adolescent development in a healthy way. Using the framework of self-determination theory, we illustrated how social environments that meet these psychological needs facilitate healthy development, while those social contexts that do not meet needs accordingly inhibit or derail optimal functioning and growth. Specifically, we focused on how parental relationships can provide a secure foundation from which adolescents can tackle the challenges of their passage into adulthood. We also reviewed how need fulfillment in the school context plays a crucial role in the promotion of intrinsic motivation and the internalization of values. Finally, we identified how the concept of needs informs the acquisition of identities more generally in the social context.

The development of adolescents is a systemic issue—one that requires the collaborative energies of parents, schools, communities, legislators, and government leaders to identify and attend to the needs of adolescents and work toward providing supportive and nurturant environments for their growth and development. The more parental relationships, school environments, and the greater society promote adolescents' exploration and experimentation in a context of need support, the more adolescents will be able to engage the world with energy, authentically internalize and self-regulate their behaviors, and actualize their potentials. Conversely, the more environments serve to foreclose identity formations by limiting opportunities or forcing adherence to particular values, goals, or pathways, the more adolescents will likely lead a stunted and unsatisfying existence that is experienced as alien to the self, and lacks vitality and meaning. The choice and responsibility of how we promote development is collectively ours.

REFERENCES

Amabile, T. M., DeJong, W., & Lepper, M. (1976). Effects of externally imposed deadlines on subsequent intrinsic motivation. *Journal of Personality and Social Psychology, 34*, 92–98.

Archer, S. L., & Waterman, A. S. (1990). Varieties of identity diffusions and foreclosures: An exploration of subcategories of identity statuses. *Journal of Adolescent Research, 5*, 96–111.

Avery, R. R., & Ryan, R. M. (1987). Object relations and ego development: Comparison and correlates in middle childhood. *Journal of Personality, 56*, 547–569.

Bandura, A. (1983). Self-efficacy mechanisms of anticipated fears and calamities. *Journal of Personality and Social Psychology, 34,* 92–98.

Baumeister, R., & Leary, M. R. (1995). The need to belong: Desire for interpersonal attachments as a fundamental human motivation. *Psychological Bulletin, 117,* 497–529.

Benware, C., & Deci, E. L. (1984). Quality of learning with an active versus passive motivational set. *American Educational Research Journal, 21,* 755–765.

Blos, P. (1979). *The adolescent passage.* New York: International Universities Press.

Boggiano, A. K., & Katz, P. A. (1991). Mastery motivation in boys and girls: The role of intrinsic versus extrinsic motivation. *Sex Roles, 25,* 511–520.

Chandler, C. L., & Connell, J. P. (1987). Children's intrinsic, extrinsic and internalized motivation: A developmental study of children's reasons for liked and disliked behaviours. *British Journal of Developmental Psychology, 5,* 357–365.

Chen, Z. Y. (1999). Ethnic similarities and differences in the association of emotional autonomy and adolescent outcomes comparing Euro-American and Asian-American adolescents. *Psychological Reports, 84,* 501–516.

Chirkov, V. I., & Ryan, R. M. (2001). Parent and teacher autonomy-support in Russian and U.S. adolescents: Common effects on well-being and academic motivation. *Journal of Cross Cultural Psychology, 32,* 618–635.

Chirkov, V. I., Ryan, R. M., Kim, Y., & Kaplan, U. (2001). *Differentiating autonomy and individualism: A self-determination theory perspective on internalization of cultural orientations and well-being.* Manuscript submitted for publication.

Collins, W. A., & Laursen, B. (1992). Conflict and relationships during adolescence. In C. U. Shantz & W. W. Hartup (Eds.), *Conflict in child and adolescent development* (pp. 216–241). New York: Cambridge University Press.

Connell, J. P., & Wellborn, J. G. (1991). Competence, autonomy, and relatedness: A motivational analysis of self-system processes. *The Minnesota Symposia on Child Psychology* (Vol. 23, pp. 43–77). Hillsdale, NJ: Erlbaum.

Csikszentmihalyi, M., & Larsen, R. (1984). *Being adolescent: Conflict and growth in the teenage years.* New York: Basic Books.

Danner, F.W., & Lonky, E. (1981). A cognitive-developmental approach to the effects of rewards on intrinsic motivation. *Child Development, 52,* 1043–1052.

deCharms, R. (1968). *Personal causation.* New York: Academic Press.

Deci, E. L. (1975). *Intrinsic motivation.* New York: Plenum Press.

Deci, E. L., & Cascio, W. F. (1972, April). *Changes in intrinsic motivation as a function of negative feedback and threats.* Paper presented at the Eastern Psychological Association, Boston.

Deci, E. L., Koestner, R., & Ryan, R. M. (1999). A meta-analytic review of experiments examining the effects of extrinsic rewards on intrinsic motivation. *Psychological Bulletin, 125,* 627–668.

Deci, E. L., & Ryan. R. M. (1980). The empirical exploration of intrinsic motivational processes. In L. Berkowitz (Ed.), *Advances in experimental social psychology* (Vol. 13, pp. 39–80). New York: Academic Press

Deci, E. L., & Ryan. R. M. (1987). The support of autonomy and the control of behavior. *Journal of Personality and Social Psychology, 53,* 1024–1037.

Deci, E. L., & Ryan. R. M. (1995). Human autonomy: The basis for true self-esteem. In M. Kernis (Ed.), *Efficacy, agency, and self-esteem* (pp. 31–49). New York: Plenum Press.

Deci, E. L., & Ryan. R. M. (2000). The darker and brighter sides of human existence: Basic psychological needs as a unifying concept. *Psychological Inquiry, 11*, 319–338.

Deci, E. L., Schwartz, A. J., Sheinman, L., & Ryan, R. M. (1981). An instrument to assess adults' orientations toward control versus autonomy with children: Reflections on intrinsic motivation and perceived competence. *Journal of Educational Psychology, 73*, 642–650.

Donahue, E. M., Robins, R. W., Roberts, B. W., & John, O. P. (1993). The divided self: Concurrent and longitudinal effects of psychological adjustment and social roles on self concept differentiation. *Journal of Personality and Social Psychology, 64*, 834–846.

Dresner, R., & Grolnick, W. S. (1996). Constructions of early parenting, intimacy and autonomy in young women. *Journal of Social and Personal Relationships, 13*, 25–39.

Eccles, J. S. (1993). School and family effect on the ontogeny of children's interests, self-perceptions, and activity choices. In J. Jacobs (Ed.), *Nebraska Symposium on Motivation: Developmental perspectives on motivation* (Vol. 40, pp. 145–208). Lincoln: University of Nebraska Press.

Eccles, J. S., & Midgley, C. (1989). Stage-environment fit: Developmentally appropriate classrooms for early adolescents. In C. Ames & R. Ames (Eds.), *Research on motivation in education: Vol. 3. Goals and cognitions* (pp. 139–186). New York: Academic Press.

Eisenberger, R., & Cameron, J. (1996). Detrimental effects of reward: Reality or myth? *American Psychologist, 51*, 1153–1166.

Elkind, D. (1971). Cognitive growth cycles in mental development. *Nebraska Symposium on Motivation* (pp. 1–31). Lincoln: University of Nebraska Press.

Fisher, C. D. (1978). The effects of personal control, competence, and extrinsic reward systems on performance. *American Journal of Psychology, 94*, 387–398.

Flink, C., Boggiano, A. K., & Barrett, M. (1990). Controlling teaching strategies: Undermining children's self-determination and performance. *Journal of Personality and Social Psychology, 59*, 916–924.

Freud, A. (1958). Adolescence. In R. S. Eissler, et al. (Eds.), *Psychoanalytic study of the child* (Vol. 13, pp. 255–278). New York: International Universities Press.

Fuhrman, T., & Holmbeck, G. N. (1995). A contextual-moderator analysis of emotional autonomy and adjustment in adolescence. *Child Development, 66*, 793–811.

Gagné, M., Ryan, R. M., & Barghman, K. (2001). *The effects of parent and coach autonomy support on need satisfaction and well-being of gymnasts.* Unpublished manuscript, University of Rochester.

Goldstein, K. (1939). *The organism.* New York: American Book Company.

Goodenow, C. (1993). Classroom belonging among early adolescent students: Relationships to motivation and achievement. *Journal of Early Adolescence, 13*, 21–43.

Gottfried, A. E. (1985). Academic intrinsic motivation in elementary and junior high school students. *Journal of Educational Psychology, 20*, 205–215

Grolnick, W. S., Deci, E. L., & Ryan, R. M. (1997). Internalization within the family. In J. E. Gruseck & L. Kuczynski (Eds.), *Parenting and children's internalization of values: A handbook of contemporary theory* (pp. 135–161). New York: Wiley.

Grolnick, W. S., & Ryan, R. M. (1987). Autonomy in children's learning: An experimental and individual difference investigation. *Journal of Personality and Social Psychology, 52,* 890–898.

Grolnick, W. S., & Ryan, R. M. (1989). Parent styles associated with children's self-regulation and competence in school. *Journal of Educational Psychology, 81,* 143–154.

Grolnick, W. S., Ryan, R. M., & Deci, E. L. (1991). The inner resources for school achievement: Motivational mediators of children's perceptions of their parents. *Journal of Educational Psychology, 83,* 508–517.

Harter, S. (1978). Effectance motivation reconsidered: Toward a developmental model. *Human Development, 1,* 661–669.

Kaplan, H., Assor, A., & Kanat-Maymon, Y. (2001, August). *Self-exploratory regulation: The role of identity-formation processes in self-determined action.* Paper presented at the meeting of the European Association for Research on Learning and Instruction, Fribourg, Switzerland.

Kasser, T., Ryan, R. M., Zax, M., & Sameroff, A. J. (1995). The relations of maternal and social environments to late adolescents' materialistic and prosocial values. *Developmental Psychology, 31,* 907–914.

Kast, A., & Conner, K. (1988). Sex and age differences in response to informational and controlling feedback. *Personality and Social Psychology Bulletin, 14,* 514–523.

Kellaghan, T., Madaus, G. F., & Raczek, A. (1996). *The use of external examinations to improve student motivation.* Washington, DC: American Educational Research Association.

Koestner, R., Ryan, R. M., Bernieri, F., & Holt, K. (1984). Setting limits on children's behavior: The differential effects of controlling versus informational styles on intrinsic motivation and creativity. *Journal of Personality, 52,* 233–248.

Krapp, A. (in press). An educational-psychological theory of interest and its relation to SDT. In E. L. Deci & R. M. Ryan (Eds.), *Handbook of self-determination research.* Rochester, NY: University of Rochester Press.

Krapp, A., Renninger, K. A., & Hoffmann, L. (1998). Some thoughts about the development of a unifying framework for the study of individual interest. In L. Hoffmann, A. Krapp, K.A. Renninger, & J. Baumert (Eds.), *Interest and learning* (pp. 455–468). Germany: Institu fur die Padagogik der Naturwissenschaffen an der Universitat Kiel.

La Guardia, J. G. (2001). *Interpersonal compartmentalization: An examination of self-concept variation, need satisfaction, and psychological vitality.* Unpublished doctoral dissertation, University of Rochester.

La Guardia, J. G., Ryan, R. M., Couchman, C., & Deci, E. L. (2000). Within-person variation in security of attachment: A self-determination theory perspective on attachment, need fulfillment, and well-being. *Journal of Personality and Social Psychology, 79,* 367–384.

Lamborn, S. D., & Steinberg, L. (1993). Emotional autonomy redux: Revisiting Ryan and Lynch. *Child Development, 64,* 483–499.

Leak, G. K., & Cooney, R. R. (2001). Self-determination, attachment styles, and well-being in adult romantic relationships. *Representative Research in Social Psychology, 25*, 55–62.

Lepper, M. R., Greene, D., & Nisbett, R. E. (1973). Undermining children's intrinsic interest with extrinsic rewards: A test of the "overjustification" hypothesis. *Journal of Personality and Social Psychology, 28*, 129–137.

Linville, P. (1987). Self-complexity as a cognitive buffer against stress-related illness and depression. *Journal of Personality and Social Psychology, 52*, 663–676.

Loevinger, J., & Blasi, A. (1991). Development of the self as subject. In J. Strauss & G. R. Goethals (Eds.), *The self: Interdisciplinary approaches* (pp. 150–167). New York: Springer-Verlag.

McBride-Chang, C., & Chang, L. (1998). Adolescent–parent relations in Hong Kong: Parenting styles, emotional autonomy, and school achievement. *Journal of Genetic Psychology, 159*, 421–436.

Midgley, C., Anderman, E., & Hicks, L. (1995). Differences between elementary and middle school teachers and students: A goal theory approach. *Journal of Early Adolescence, 15*, 90–113.

Midgley, C., & Edelin, K.C. (1998). Middle school reform and early adolescent well-being: The good news and the bad. *Educational Psychologist, 33*, 195–206.

Midgley, C., & Feldlaufer, H. (1987). Students' and teachers' decision-making fit before and after the transition to junior high school. *Journal of Early Adolescence, 7*, 225–241.

Midgley, C., Feldlaufer, H., & Eccles, J. S. (1988). The transition to junior high school: Beliefs of pre and post-transition teachers. *Journal of Youth and Adolescence, 17*, 543–562.

Miserandino, M. (1996). Children who do well in school: Individual differences in perceived competence and autonomy in above average children. *Journal of Educational Psychology, 88*, 203–214.

Mossholder, K.W. (1980). Effects of externally mediated goal setting on intrinsic motivation: A laboratory experiment. *Journal of Applied Psychology, 65*, 202–210.

Rogers, C. (1963). The actualizing tendency in relation to "motives" and to consciousness. In M. R. Jones (Ed.), *Nebraska Symposium on Motivation, 1962* (pp. 1–24). Lincoln: University of Nebraska Press.

Ryan, R. M. (1982). Control and information in the interpersonal sphere: An extension of cognitive evaluation theory. *Journal of Personality and Social Psychology, 43*, 450–461.

Ryan, R. M. (1993). Agency and organization: Intrinsic motivation, autonomy and the self in psychological development. In J. Jacobs (Ed.), *Nebraska Symposium on Motivation: Developmental perspectives on motivation* (Vol. 40, pp. 1–56). Lincoln: University of Nebraska Press.

Ryan, R. M. (1995). Psychological needs and the facilitation of integrative processes. *Journal of Personality, 63*, 397–427.

Ryan, R. M., Connell, J. P., & Deci, E. L. (1985). A motivational analysis of self-determination and self-regulation in education. In C. Ames & R. E. Ames (Eds.), *Research on motivation in education: The classroom milieu* (pp. 13–51). New York: Academic Press.

Ryan, R. M., Connell, J. P., & Plant, R. W. (1990). Emotions in nondirected text learning. *Learning and Individual Differences, 2*, 1–17.

Ryan, R. M., & Deci, E. L. (2000). Self-determination theory and the facilitation of intrinsic motivation, social development, and well-being. *American Psychologist, 55*, 68–78.

Ryan, R. M., & Deci, E. L. (2001). To be happy or to be self-fulfilled: A review of research on hedonic and eudaimonic well-being. In S. Fiske (Ed.), *Annual review of psychology* (Vol. 52, pp. 141–166). Palo Alto, CA: Annual Reviews.

Ryan, R. M., & Deci, E. L. (in press). On assimilating identities to the self: A self-determination theory perspective on internalization and integrity within cultures. In M. R. Leary & J. P. Tangney (Eds.), *The handbook of self and identity.* New York: Guilford Press.

Ryan, R. M., & Grolnick, W. S. (1986). Origins and pawns in the classroom: Self-report and projective assessments of individual differences in children's perceptions. *Journal of Personality and Social Psychology, 50*, 550–558.

Ryan, R. M., & Kuczkowski, R. (1994). Egocentrism and heteronomy: A study of imaginary audience, self-consciousness, and public individuation in adolescence. *Journal of Personality, 62*, 219–238.

Ryan, R. M., & La Guardia, J. G. (1999). Achievement motivation within a pressured society: Intrinsic and extrinsic motivations to learn and the politics of school reform. In T. Urdan (Ed.), *Advances in motivation and achievement: Vol 11* (pp. 45–85). Greenwich, CT: JAI Press.

Ryan, R. M., & La Guardia, J. G. (2000). What is being optimized over development?: A self-determination theory perspective on basic psychological needs across the life span. In S. Qualls & R. Abeles (Eds.), *Dialogues on psychology and aging.* Washington, DC: APA Books.

Ryan, R. M., La Guardia, J. G., Butzel, J. S., Kim, Y., & Chirkov, V. (2002). *Emotional reliance across gender, relationships, and cultures: The self-determination of dependence.* Unpublished manuscript, University of Rochester.

Ryan, R. M., & Lynch, J. (1989). Emotional autonomy versus detachment: Revisiting the vicissitudes of adolescence and young adulthood. *Child Development, 60*, 340–356.

Ryan, R. M., Mims, V., & Koestner, R. (1983). Relation of reward contingency and interpersonal context to intrinsic motivation: A review and test using cognitive evaluation theory. *Journal of Personality and Social Psychology, 45*, 736–750.

Ryan, R. M., Stiller, J., & Lynch, J. H. (1994). Representations of relationships to parents, teachers, and friends as predictors of academic motivation and self-esteem. *Journal of Early Adolescence, 14*, 226–249.

Sheldon, K. M., & Elliot, A. J. (1998). Not all personal goals are personal: Comparing autonomous and controlled reasons for goals as predictors of effort and attainment. *Personality and Social Psychological Bulletin, 24*, 546–557.

Sheldon, K. M., & Kasser, T. (1998). Pursuit of personal goals: Skills enable progress, but not all progress is beneficial. *Personality and Social Psychological Bulletin, 24*, 1319–1331.

Sheldon, K. M., Ryan, R. M., Rawsthorne, L., & Ilardi, B. (1997). Trait self and true self: Cross-role variation in the Big Five traits and its relations with authenticity and subjective well-being. *Journal of Personality and Social Psychology, 73,* 1380–1393.

Smith, W. E. (1974). *The effects of social and monetary rewards on intrinsic motivation.* Unpublished doctoral dissertation, Cornell University.

Steinberg, L., & Silverberg, S. (1986). The vicissitudes of autonomy in adolescence. *Child Development, 57,* 841–851.

Thomas, J. W. (1980). Agency and achievement: Self-management and self-regard. *Review of Educational Research, 50,* 213–240.

Turner, R. A., Irwin, C. E., & Millstein, S. G. (1991). Family structure, family processes, and experimenting with substances during adolescence. *Journal of Research on Adolescence, 1,* 93–106.

Vallerand, R. J., Fortier, M. S., Guay, F. (1997). Self-determination and persistence in a real-life setting: Toward a motivational model of high school dropout. *Journal of Personality and Social Psychology, 72,* 1161–1176.

Vallerand, R. J., & Reid, G. (1984). On the causal effects of perceived competence on intrinsic motivation: A test of cognitive evaluation theory. *Journal of Sport Psychology, 6,* 94–102.

Waterman, A. S. (1993). Two conceptions of happiness: Contrasts of personal expressiveness (eudaimonia) and hedonic enjoyment. *Journal of Personality and Social Psychology, 64,* 678–691.

White, R.W. (1963). *Ego and reality in psychoanalytic theory.* New York: International Universities Press.

Williams, G. C., Cox, E. M., Hedberg, V. A., & Deci, E. L. (2000). Extrinsic life goals and health-risk behaviors in adolescents. *Journal of Applied Social Psychology, 30,* 1756–1771.

Zuckerman, M., Porac, J., Lathin, D., Smith, R., & Deci, E. L. (1978). On the importance of self-determination for intrinsically motivated behavior. *Personality and Social Psychology Bulletin, 4,* 443–446.

CHAPTER 8

FROM DUTY TO DESIRE

The Role of Students' Future Time Perspective and Instrumentality Perceptions for Study Motivation and Self-Regulation

Willy Lens, Joke Simons, Siegfried. Dewitte
University of Leuven, Belgium

Learning, performing, and achieving in school are intentional, goal-oriented activities. Students may have many and very different reasons for studying. For most (if not all) students, learning and studying are "multidetermined." The goals that are strived for and that determine student motivation can be situated on two dimensions: intrinsic versus extrinsic goals and immediate versus future goals.

Until recently, research on student motivation mostly discussed different types of intrinsic motivation (Ames, 1992; Ames & Ames, 1984; Covington, 2000; Dweck, 1986; Stipek, 1993). For example, Atkinson's theory of resultant achievement motivation (Atkinson & Feather, 1966) was developed as a within-subject decision theory, trying to explain people's preferences for achievement tasks with different levels of difficulty. The theory was, however, mostly used to explain interindividual differences in achievement motivation and in the level of performance in achievement tasks (e.g., GPA). It is a theory about the intrinsic motivation to strive for success and to avoid failure in the achievement task at hand. Pride in accomplishment when succeeding in a difficult task and shame when failing in a not-too-difficult task are the emotions that are inherently associated with the need for achievement and the fear of failure. Other types of intrinsic motivation are curiosity, interest, need for competence, and need for autonomy (see Pintrich & Schunk, 1996).

Motivational research in educational psychology stresses the importance of students being intrinsically motivated and neglects the role of extrinsic motivation. In organizational psychology, it is more or less the reverse. Theories of work motivation emphasize more the role of extrinsic motivation than of intrinsic motivation. In spite of these emphases, we argue not only that workers and their bosses can be intrinsically motivated for their job but that many students are also extrinsically motivated to do their best at school. The total motivation to learn (and to work) is a combination of intrinsic and extrinsic motivation. Students are intrinsically motivated when learning or performing is a goal in itself. They are extrinsically motivated to the extent that those activities are done for the sake of material or other rewards and contingencies that are not intrinsically related to school learning. Learning and doing well in tests and exams are then instrumental activities to earn rewards or to avoid punishment. The main topic of this chapter is to discuss one particular type of extrinsic motivation—we will call it *instrumental motivation*—and how it relates to intrinsic student motivation.

For many years, the total motivation to study or to work was assumed to be a function of the sum of intrinsic and extrinsic motivational components. Each intrinsic and extrinsic goal of an action can be conceived of as an additional source of motivation for that action. However, numerous experimental studies over the last 25 years show that intrinsic and extrinsic sources of motivation are not necessarily additive. Salient, promised extrinsic rewards that are exogenous to the nature of the learning or the achievement task may undermine the existing intrinsic motivation (Deci, 1975; Deci, Koestner, & Ryan, 1999; Deci & Ryan, 1985, 1992; Lepper & Greene, 1978; Luyten & Lens, 1981). Rewards and other controlling variables may cause a shift in the locus of causality from internal to external. Intrinsically motivated individuals see their own interest in the subject matter or the task as their sole reason for doing it. When they then repeatedly receive extrinsic rewards for doing the same activities, those rewards will gradually be perceived as the (external) reasons for learning or performing. After a while, the extrinsic rewards rather than the intrinsic interest come to control the activities. The perception of autonomy or self-determination and the intrinsic interest disappear. Lepper and Greene (1978) refer to this phenomenon as "the hidden costs of reward."

Not only announced rewards but also summative evaluation, surveillance, coercion, time, and pressure may cause a change in locus of causality from internal to external. These circumstances undermine the intrinsic motivation and very often lower the quality of performance. It is our opinion that the low level of intrinsic motivation among many high school pupils is partly due to this undermining effect of the many extrinsic rewards they receive for doing their best at school and for high marks.

Harter and Jackson (1992) found "a systematic, grade-related, shift from a predominantly intrinsic motivational orientation in third grade to a more extrinsic motivational orientation by ninth grade, the biggest shift occurred between the sixth grade elementary school students and the seventh grade junior high school students" (pp. 223–224).

More recent experimental and meta-analytical studies show, however, that the adverse effects of extrinsic rewards only occur under restricted conditions (Cameron, 2001; Deci, Koestner, & Ryan, 2001; Deci, Ryan, & Koestner, 2001; Eisenberger, Pierce, & Cameron, 1999; Eisenberger & Cameron, 1996; Eisenberger, Rhoades, & Cameron, 1999). Extrinsic rewards do not have this negative effect on intrinsic motivation when they are given in such a way that their controlling aspect is much less salient than their informative aspect. They can then enhance self-perceptions of competence and increase even intrinsic motivation itself (Deci & Ryan, 1985; Rigby, Deci, Patrick, & Ryan, 1992, p. 168).

A still ongoing discussion between Cameron and her collaborators on one hand and Deci and his collaborators on the other deals with how limited or how general the undermining effect of extrinsic rewards or contingencies seems to be in empirical research. We refer the interested reader to the publications by Cameron and Deci in *Review of Educational Research* (2001, Vol. 71, Number 1).

Finally, students (and employees) who are not intrinsically motivated at the start may develop an intrinsic interest in an activity. As long as they are purely extrinsically motivated, the action is a means to obtain the extrinsic rewards. But, as noted by James (1890), Woodworth (1918), Allport (1937), and Lewin (1938), means may become ends. Activities such as studying, carpentry, or jogging may originally be motivated by extrinsic goals such as rewards, making a living, or staying in good health. Nevertheless, after a while, the same activities can become intrinsically interesting for an individual. Allport (1937) wrote about "the functional autonomy of needs" and Woodworth (1918) referred to this process as "mechanisms become drives." Pupils who solve mathematical problems because the teacher or the parents promises them a reward for doing it may find out that they are good at it or that it is fun to find a solution for a challenging problem. Their feelings of competence will be strengthened and an intrinsic interest in math may develop.

Many good students are not only intrinsically motivated toward their studies, they also have future educational, professional, and even life goals that motivate them as students. "Do your best at school, it is so important for your future" is motivating advice that many parents and teachers use around the world. Schooling is future oriented. Many students are motivated to do their best and to do well because they want to follow a particular type of education in high school, college, or graduate school and to have a particular profession in adult life.

This component of motivation, which derives from future goals that are contingent on present schoolwork and school grades, is called *instrumental motivation*. Learning and earning good grades have a utility value (Eccles, 1984; Eccles, Barber, Updegraff, & Wigfield, 1997; Wigfield & Eccles, 1992) when they are perceived as instrumental for achieving other goals in the near or distant future. This implies that instrumental motivation requires that students have set goals for themselves in the near and distant future; that they have developed a future orientation or future time perspective.

In this chapter, we first discuss the concept of future time perspective as a cognitive-motivational personality characteristic. Future time perspective is motivationally relevant in the sense that it results from motivational goal setting. Moreover, it can have motivational consequences because it provides utility value or instrumental value to present activities. As a consequence, additional instrumental motivation will be added to the already present intrinsic and extrinsic motivation. We also discuss experimental and correlational research validating the notion of instrumental motivation and show how it relates to intrinsic motivation, task orientation, performance orientation, level of information processing, time spent studying, and academic grades.

MOTIVATIONAL GOAL SETTING AND FUTURE TIME PERSPECTIVE

Time perspective refers to the chronological past, present, and future insofar as they are part of an individual psychological life space. Future time perspective (FTP) is then the degree to which and the way in which the chronological future is integrated in the present life space of an individual (Lewin, 1942). The integration of the future in the present is analogous to the integration of more or less remote places in the present life space. Being aware of places and distances in space and of moments or intervals in time (the past and the future) is necessary but not sufficient to have much psychological effect. The psychological distance to a given place can differ strongly among people living in the same city. For many Belgian people, Paris is psychologically very far away. They will never consider any action that would require them to travel there. For others, Paris is almost in their backyard. Analogous to the psychological experience of the spatial world, there are large individual differences in the extension or depth of future time perspective. Some people have a short FTP—only the very near chronological future is part of the temporal world in which they live; they do not take into account what will come later. Others live with a long FTP; their present temporal life space extends into the very distant future. People with a long FTP have no problem considering and being motivated by, in the present, events or action outcomes expected to happen in the rather distant future.

We conceptualize future time perspective as an acquired personality characteristic that results from motivational goal setting and delay of gratification (Lens, 1986; Nuttin & Lens, 1985). On the covert level, people cognitively elaborate and concretize their needs, motives, and cravings into more specific motivational goals, means–end structures, or behavioral plans and projects. Students, for example, specify their need for achievement and/or their need for self-realization by planning to succeed in their exams, going to college, becoming a teacher or farmer. It is only after such specifications that needs and motives will affect overt behavior. Such motivational goals and behavioral plans can be analyzed for their content or the motivational domain to which they belong (e.g., hunger, thirst, sex, affiliation, curiosity, achievement, power) and by their spatiotemporal localization (where and when they will be achieved). By definition, presently anticipated positive and negative motivational goals are situated in the future. But the temporal distance to subgoals and final goals can vary from very short (e.g., going for a swim this afternoon) to very long (e.g., the student who prepares for an entrance examination for college because she intends to become a surgeon). They can even extend beyond the individual lifetime (e.g., saving money for one's funeral, going to heaven). Formulating distant motivational goals and developing long-range behavioral projects to achieve those goals creates a long or extended future time perspective. As such, FTP can be defined as the present anticipation of future goals. People with a rather short FTP set most of their realistic goals in the near future. People with a longer or deeper FTP set for themselves more goals that can only be achieved in the distant future. In comparison with people with a short FTP, people with a long FTP have relatively more long-term than short-term goals. Thus, "future time perspective evolves from motivational goal setting. It is formed by the more or less distant goal objects that are processed by an individual" (Nuttin & Lens, 1985, p. 22).

From adolescence, most youngsters start to develop realistic plans and projects regarding their education, profession, and life in general. This is one of their important developmental tasks (Nurmi, 1994; Verstraeten, 1980). Goal setting and developing such motivational and behavioral projects are motivating because they attach utility to a number of activities such as doing one's best in high school, going to high school, or keeping up physical training. Having important future goals also makes it easier to delay gratifications and to forsake immediate but less important and also attractive rewards and pleasures (Mischel, 1981).

This motivational conceptualization of FTP as resulting from goal setting and motivational planning has a long history in psychology, especially in Europe:

> The setting of goals is closely related to time perspective. The goal of the individual includes his expectations for the future. (Lewin, 1948, p. 113)

> Wie die Vergangenheit, so ist andererseits auch die Zukunft in der Gegenwart des Erlebens enthalten. Jede erlebte Gegenwart ist Vorgriff in die Zukunft. Das gilt im dem Masse, als jeder Augenblick des seelischen Lebens durchwirkt ist von der Thematik und Dynamik seelischer Strebungen, die auf die Verwirklichung eines noch nicht bestehenden Zustandes gehen. (Lersch, 1966, p. 47)

> For Fraisse (1963), "the future only unfolds in so far as we imagine a future which seems to be realizable.... There is no future without at the same time a desire for something else and awareness of the possibility of realizing it." (pp. 172, 174)

> For Nuttin (1964), "the psychological future is not just a learning effect of the past, it is essentially related to motivation ... the future is the time quality of the goal object; the future is our primary 'motivational space'"(p. 63) and "le phénomène primaire de la direction vers le futur, tel qu'il se produit grâce au besoin, n'est qu'une orientation générale; elle se limite à un futur très immédiat, comme c'est le cas chez l'animal.... C'est grâce au développement supérieur des fonctions cognitives et leur influence dans l'élaboration des besoins—notamment dans les processus de position de but...que, chez l'homme, l'anticipation va se détacher graduellement de la situation actuelle et que des "perspectives" profondes vont s'ouvrir. (Nuttin, 1980, p. 13)

> For Gjesme (1981), "an individual's future time orientation (FTO) develops gradually to become a relatively stable personality characteristic in terms of a general capacity to anticipate and enlighten the future, including a cognitive elaboration of plans and projects and reflecting the degree of concern, involvement and engagement in the future." (p. 125)

As we conceive it, future time perspective results from motivational goal setting and affects the strength of the motivation to strive for those goals and realize projects and plans. The motivational importance of individuals' perception of the future is also present in the concept of "possible selves," developed by Markus and her colleagues. For them "possible selves represent individuals' ideas of what they might become, what they would like to become, and what they are afraid of becoming . . . ; possible selves . . . as the cognitive manifestation of evolving goals, aspirations, motives, fears and threats . . ." (Markus & Nurius, 1986, p. 954; Markus & Wurf, 1987). Oyserman and Markus (1990a, 1990b) found that balanced possible selves—combining positive (hoped for) and negative (feared) possible selves within a given domain—are more adaptive than are unbalanced possible selves that consist of only positive or negative future selves.

We now discuss the process behind the motivational effects of individual differences in future time perspective. We first formulate a theoretical model that explains these motivational effects of individual differences in FTP (De Volder & Lens, 1982; Lens, 1986; Zaleski, 1987, 1994) and then apply it to student motivation. The underlying process is conceptualized in terms of the psychological distance toward future moments (Gjesme, 1982) and the expectancy x instrumentality x value models (VIE models) of human motivation (Eccles, 1984; Feather, 1982).

MOTIVATIONAL EFFECTS OF FUTURE TIME PERSPECTIVE

The top part of Figure 8.1 shows how the cognitive processing of motives or needs leads to individual differences in the extension of future time perspective we discussed earlier. The second part outlines how these individual differences have motivational consequences via the psychological distance toward the future, the perceived instrumental value of present actions for future goals, and the anticipated incentive value of those goals in the near or more distant future.

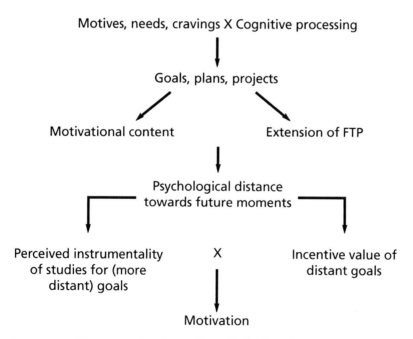

Figure 8.1.   The motivational meaning of individual differences in future time perspective.

Table 8.1.   Psychological distance (in cm.) of time intervals into the near future. (1 week & 1 month) and into the distant future (0.5, 1, and 5 years) as a function length of future time perspective (FTP)

FTP	N	Near Future	N	Distance
Very long	61	2.93	61	9.03
Long	61	3.69	61	9.48
Short	61	4.10	60	9.67
Very Short	62	4.54	62	10.38

People who live with a long FTP experience a given chronological time interval into the future as shorter than do people with a short FTP experience. This is especially true for intermediate intervals of time (further than tomorrow or next week, but not so far as 20 years or more). Individuals with a long FTP do indeed experience the intermediate future as more near than do individuals with a short FTP. To measure the psychological distance, Moreas and Lens (1991) used Cottle's line test (Cottle & Pleck, 1969) and asked high school students (Grade 9) to draw lines representing how far away 1 week, 1 month, 6 months, 1 year, and 5 years from now was for them. The maximum length permitted was 15 centimeters. The longer the experienced distance, the longer were the lines. The order of the chronological intervals was randomized. As shown in Table 8.1, Moreas and Lens found that students with a long future time perspective drew significantly shorter lines for the near future (1 week and 1 month) and for the distant future (0.5, 1, and 5 years) than did students with a short future time perspective. For the 5-year period, 149 of 244 participants (61%) used the maximum line of 15 centimeters. The psychological distance of 5 years for high school students may have been underestimated in this study, given the ceiling of 15 centimeters.

There is a curvilinear relationship between age and length of FTP. Young adolescents start to develop a realistic FTP that expands with increasing age until midlife. From then on, length of FTP decreases. That is of course highly correlated with the number of years one realistically can expect to live. Length of FTP is also correlated with socioeconomic status (SES). Individuals with lower SES generally have a shorter FTP than do those in the middle class (Lens & Gailly, 1980). For which chronological distance the difference in psychological distance between people with a long and a short FTP is largest depends on variables such as intelligence, age, and SES that are correlated with FTP extension. For example, 20 years from now will be very far for adolescents, whatever their FTP. For young adults with a long FTP it will be nearer than for those with a short FTP. But 50 years from now will be so far away psychologically for that age group that the length of their FTP does not make a difference any longer.

To explain the motivational effects of individual differences in FTP, De Volder and Lens (1982) made a distinction between a cognitive and a dynamic aspect in FTP. The *cognitive aspect* refers to the capacity to anticipate in the present not only the immediate but also the long-term consequences of a potential action. Students with a long FTP can more easily anticipate the implications of their present class activities for the more distant future and elaborate on the covert level longer behavioral means–end structures (plans or projects). As a consequence, the utility value, or the instrumentality of present actions (e.g., studying, getting good grades), increases. This will increase the instrumental motivation for their present learning and achievement tasks in school.

The *dynamic aspect* of FTP is conceived of as a disposition to ascribe a high valence to goals, even if these goals can only be reached in the more distant future. In general, the incentive value of a given reward decreases as a function of the length of its temporal delay (Ainslie, 1992; Hernnstein, 1970; Logue, 1988; Mischel, 1981; Rachlin, 1995). This decrease is less steep for individuals with a long FTP than for individuals with a short FTP. Because the psychological distance toward such delayed goals is shorter for individuals with a long FTP, the incentive value of chronologically distant goals will be higher the longer the FTP. As a consequence, the effect of individual differences in the extension of FTP on the incentive value will be smaller for goals in the very near or very distant goals than for goals in the intermediate future.

We know from empirical research validating the expectancy value—or VIE theories—in motivational psychology that people are more motivated when (a) they can expect that their behavior will result in the outcomes (instrumentality) in which they are interested and (b) the subjective value of the outcomes is higher.

De Volder and Lens (1982) found a positive correlation between students' motivation (Grade 11) and the length of their FTP. More motivated students attach significantly more value to goals in the distant future than do less motivated students. More motivated students also attach significantly more instrumental value to their schoolwork for reaching goals in the near and the distant future.

Analogous to De Volder and Lens (1982), Shell and Husman (2001) make a distinction between two aspects or components of future time perspective: *valence* and *perceived instrumentality/utility*. They call this second aspect "FTP connectedness." They found that, in a group of predominantly white, middle-class undergraduates, FTP connectedness (but not FTP value) correlated with GPA, study time, and study effort.

Lens and Decruyenaere (1991) measured the instrumental value of studying in general (in three different types of high school education) for success in later life (also in general). They found that high, medium, and low motivated subgroups of students significantly differed (in the predicted direction) in the instrumental value or utility of "doing your best in school" for success in life in general.

Van Calster, Lens, and Nuttin (1987) also found a significant main effect of perceived instrumentality on motivation. Students in Grades 11 and 12 (ages 17–19) who perceive their education as important for their future (high instrumentality) are significantly more motivated than are students who rate their high school education as less important (less instrumental). But the researchers also found a significant interaction effect of perceived instrumentality and affective attitude toward the individual future. Perceived instrumentality enhanced student motivation, but only for those students who had a positive attitude toward their individual future. Attaching high utility to school results had the opposite effect on the motivation to study for students with a negative outlook on their future. The combination of a high-perceived instrumentality (of doing your best in school for the personal future) and a positive attitude toward the personal future had a positive effect on motivation and school results. A very bleak outlook on the future seemed to be a demotivating variable.

Moreas and Lens (1991; see also Lens, 2001) provided further evidence for the positive correlations between FTP, perceived instrumentality, and student motivation. They asked ninth-grade students to rate the importance or value of 10 motivational goals in the rather near future (within two years, that is, during their high school years) and 10 goals in the more distant future. They also asked the students to indicate the instrumentality of "doing my best for my studies" for reaching each of those 20 goals. Students with a very long FTP were significantly more motivated than were students with a short or very short FTP. They also found a significant positive relationship between the length of FTP and the anticipated value of goals, the perceived instrumentality of study behavior to reach future goals, and, hence, between the length of FTP and the product of value and instrumentality. As expected, these relations were stronger for distant goals than for near goals.

Creten, Lens, and Simons (2001) studied the motivational role of perceived instrumentality or utility in vocational schools in Flanders, Belgium. Many of the students in those schools had serious motivational problems, especially for theoretical courses such as mathematics, languages, and history. Most had started in a much more demanding type of secondary education (e.g., humanities, math, and sciences) but failed. They (and especially their parents) were forced to change their educational aspirations during high school, first to a more technical education and then finally to the lower educational level of a mostly practical vocational training (in high school).

Even before they have to change to a vocational school, most students cease to be intrinsically motivated to study, especially for their more theoretical courses. If they are motivated at all, it is because of extrinsic reasons. They study because they are forced to or because they will receive material or financial rewards when they receive good grades (Lens & Decruyenaere, 1991).

Many vocational students also have a rather short future time perspective (Lens & Decruyenaere, 1991; Phalet & Lens, 1995). They do not look very far into the future; they prefer to live "here and now." As a consequence, they are not well aware of, or do not care much about, the instrumentality or utility of their present school career. This is even more so for theoretical courses than for more practical courses. Creten, Lens, and Simons (2001) were interested in whether or not the relation between FTP and motivation would also apply to this problem group, or, in other words, if those students in vocational education who perceived the future relevance of, for example, a second language, were more motivated for that course than were students who are not aware of the future importance of the same course. Is it possible to motivate these students by pointing to the future contingencies of their present schoolwork?

Table 8.2 provides mean scores for students' motivation and perceived importance or instrumentality of these courses for personal goals in the near and the distant future for two theoretical courses (PAV or "project general education" and French as a second language) and one practical course.

Table 8.2.   Mean motivation to study and instrumentality for two theoretical and one practical course

Courses	Student Motivation	Instrumentality for Near Goals	Instrumentality for Distant Goals
PAV (theoretical)	2.61	2.15	2.16
French language	2.56	2.49	2.62
Practical	3.21	2.53	2.89

Students were significantly more motivated for the practical course than for each of the two theoretical courses. For each of the three courses, Creten and colleagues (2001) measured the perceived instrumentality for near (within two years) and for more distant goals. As expected, the perceived instrumentality differed from course to course, for both near and distant goals. For the near future goals, the instrumentality of French was as high as for practical courses. For long-term goals, practical courses were perceived as most useful. Students also found French important for the future, whereas with regard to PAV, many students had problems seeing its utility either for the near or the distant future.

For the full sample of 733 students, there were significant correlations between instrumentality and student motivation (.14 for near goals and .19 for distant goals). Table 8.3 shows that, in general, students who perceived their studies as low instrumental for their goals in the near or the more distant future were less motivated. For the near goals, students with low perceived instrumentality were significantly less motivated (M = 2.61) than were students with medium (M = 2.90) or high-perceived instrumentality (M = 2.86); the same result was found for the distant goals.

Table 8.3.   Student motivation as a function of perceived instrumentality for near and distant goals

	Motivation	
Instrumentality	*Near Goals*	*Distant Goals*
Low	2.61	2.58
Medium	2.90	2.81
High	2.86	2.96

Students who ascribed more utility to their practical courses were more motivated for these courses than they were for French or PAV. The students were not more motivated for French than for their general theoretical course PAV, although they attached a higher utility value to French. It seems that perceived instrumentality or utility was an important but not sufficient condition for developing student motivation. For example, the students knew that in bilingual Belgium, French is important for their future professional career and for life in general, but they complained that the content of the course and the way in which it was taught was not motivating enough.

Zaleski (1987, 1994) found that self-reported, goal-oriented striving, effort, and persistence are higher for distant goals. Long-term goals require more work. Achieving long-term goals is facilitated by formulating a series of short-term subgoals, leading to the (provisional) final goal in the more distant future (Bandura & Schunk, 1981; Bandura & Simon, 1977). But Zaleski (1987) also found that "if proximal goals are intermediate, instrumental subgoals necessary for attainment of the final end states, then those who have distal goals work harder on the proximal ones" (p. 34).

However, one may wonder whether the motivational effect of distal goals (or FTP) is homogenous and merely relying on the temporal aspect. In the next section, we distinguish different types of instrumental relationships between present tasks or goals and goals in the more distant future. We also discuss how these different types of distant goals may affect present goal orientation and intrinsic motivation. Finally, we discuss the resultant motivation for a learning or achievement task for which the individual is intrinsically motivated (intrinsic proximal goal) but that also has important consequences for the future because of its utility (instrumentality) for different kinds of future goals.

INSTRUMENTAL MOTIVATION, INTRINSIC MOTIVATION, AND GOAL THEORY

To the extent that learning is motivated by future goals (instrumental motivation), it is not in itself rewarding. Adopting the traditional and broadly used definitions of intrinsic motivation and task orientation, instrumental motivation can only be extrinsic motivation. Eccles (1984) contrasted utility value, which she described as "the importance of [a] task for some future goal that might itself be somewhat unrelated to the process nature of the task at hand" (p. 90) with interest value, which she described as "the inherent, immediate enjoyment one gets from engaging in an activity" (p. 89). In line with the traditional definition of intrinsic motivation, Eccles also characterized utility value as a form of extrinsic motivation and interest value as a form of intrinsic motivation.

Raynor (1969, 1981; Raynor & Entin, 1982) elaborated Atkinson's theory of intrinsic achievement motivation to incorporate the concept of instrumentality, utility, or future time perspective in the research on achievement motivation. His theory provides a mathematically formalized model of how to combine intrinsic and instrumental motivation. Future orientation or future time perspective is "the impact on motivation for some present activity of perceiving its instrumental relationship, as a step in a longer path, to more distant future goals and threatening consequences" (Atkinson & Raynor, 1974, p. 5). But Raynor's theory only applies when the "present activity" is an achievement task, the "future goal" is success in another achievement task, and the "threatening consequences" are failures in those future achievement tasks. In other words, the present and the future goals are intrinsic achievement-related goals: achieving success and avoiding failure in an achievement task. The motivation to strive for success and to avoid failure in a forthcoming achievement task is for Raynor not only a function of the individual's motive to succeed and motive to avoid failure, as well as of the difficulty of that present task, but also of its utility or instrumentality for getting opportunities to strive for successes in future achievement tasks. In Raynor's theory, the immediate goals and the future goals, which affect the present motivation, belong to the same motivational category, the intrinsic achievement motivation. For Raynor, in contrast to certain "intrinsic theorists" (Deci, Koestner & Ryan, 1999, 2001; Lepper & Greene, 1978; Vallerand, 1997), motivation for the present task is not diminished if the person perceives the task as instrumental to future achievement goals. On the contrary, seeing tasks as instrumental increases the resultant achievement motivation.

If instrumental motivation is a form of extrinsic motivation, a first question is then to know if this also means that the utility value of learning and performing well in school will undermine the intrinsic task motivation in the same way as extrinsic rewards do under certain circumstances. Does instrumentality preclude being task oriented? Second, is future-oriented learning by definition externally controlled and hence not self-regulated? Based on empirical research, we answer these two questions for different types of instrumental student motivation.

To answer the first question about the motivational implications of perceived instrumentality or utility, four different types of instrumentality are distinguished (Lens, 2001; Lens & Rand, 1997; Simons, De Witte, & Lens, 2000, 2001). These types are defined by combining two dimensions. The first dimension refers to the kind of conditions that regulate behavior. Behavior can be externally or internally regulated (Deci & Ryan, 1985, 2000; Rigby et al., 1992). Behavior is considered as externally regulated when its underlying motives originate outside the person (e.g., the promise of a reward, an order, the threat of punishment). A behavior is internally regulated when its underlying motives are internal to the individual (e.g., intrinsic motivation, own development, life projects).

The second dimension refers to the kind of capacities needed now (during their training or as a student) and in the future (working as a professional). In other words, this dimension concerns the relation between a present task and a future task or goal. Tasks in the present are to some extent instrumental to some future outcomes. Different capacities are used when studying compulsory courses that are not related to future professional goals (for example, studying mathematics to become a nurse). The capacities or competencies used in the present task and the future task or goal achievement can also be the same (for example, studying anatomy so as to become a nurse). When the present task requires the same competencies or capacities as the future task, it has a higher utility or instrumentality than when it is unrelated to the capacities or competencies needed in the future.

The combination of these two dimensions (regulation and kind of capacities/utility value) results in four types of instrumentality (see Table 8.4). In the first type, the present task and the future task require different capacities (low utility value or low instrumentality) and the future task or goal externally regulates the present activities. In other words, the individual is mainly interested in obtaining future rewards that follow the behavior and that are external to the individual (externally regulated). For example, a student can study for a test to obtain good grades so as to show

Table 8.4.   Types of instrumentality

Kind of Capacities Needed	Reasons for Studying	
	Extrinsically Regulated	Intrinsically Regulated
Different at both moments	LU-E	LU-I
The same at both moments	HU-E	HU-I

off, or because his parents promised him a car when he succeeds at the test. This type will be referred to as LU-E (i.e., Low Utility value and Externally regulated). In the second type, there is also no direct relation between the present and the future task (they are different regarding the capacities they require), but the future task or goal internally regulates the present activities. For example, "I want to become a nurse. I am studying hard in this psychology class because this course contributes to greater personal development." In other words, the required capacities now and in the future are different but one acknowledges that the skills and knowledge that one is acquiring while studying may be personally relevant. In this case, the behavior originates within the person; there is no obligation to study. One engages in studying for the sake of one's own development. It will be referred to as LU-I (i.e., Low Utility and Internally regulated). In the third type, the same capacities are at stake now and in the future (high utility), but the future task externally regulates the present one. For example, one may be studying hard for anatomy so as to become chief nurse in the future and make a lot of money. This type of instrumentality will be referred to as HU-E (i.e., High Utility and Externally regulated). In the fourth type, the same capacities and knowledge are used at both moments (high utility) and the future task or goal internally regulates the present activities. For example, one may be studying hard for history to become a good history teacher. The skills and the knowledge that one is acquiring now are the same ones one will use later. This type of instrumentality will be referred to as HU-I (i.e., High Utility and Internally regulated).

The motivational correlates of these four types of instrumentality or utility were studied in a group of 293 students following their first year training as teachers (kindergarten teachers, primary school teachers, and junior high school teachers). This was the first year after graduating from high school. The mean age for all students was 19.5 years with SD = 1.7. All students voluntarily participated during regular class hours.

Students were administered a self-report questionnaire that measured different aspects of student motivation and cognition. The students' name, age, gender, and previous studies in secondary school were assessed at the beginning of the questionnaire. The remainder of the questionnaire included assessment of the subjects' motivation for the courses they had to take during their first year, the perceived instrumentality of the courses, the preferred learning strategies (surface and deep level learning strategies), perceived ability, students' orientation toward task goals and ego goals (task goals, positive and negative ego goals, their study habits (studying during the week, studying during the weekend, and neglecting the course), and their persistence when encountering some difficulties.

All students had to fill in all items for all courses. Administration took approximately 1 hour. Students also had to classify their 12 courses according to both instrumentality dimensions. First, they had to check whether the course was useful for their education only or also for their future job. Second, they had to indicate if the motives underlying their efforts were rather internally or externally regulating their behavior. The combination of both judgments for each course allowed us to assign every course for every participant to one of the four cells in Table 8.4. The highest variability across participants was observed for the course "social and cultural engagement" (see the N-values in Table 8.5). Therefore, we only use that course in the analyses.

Table 8.5.   Goal Orientation, Learning Strategies, Motivational Behaviors, Study Behavior, and Performance as a Function of Type of Instrumentality

	Type of Instrumentality				Significance	
	LU-E N = 78	LU-I N = 68	HU-E N = 67	HU-I N = 80	F-score	p-score
Task goal	2.02[d]	2.59[b]	2.38[c]	2.99[a]	42.13	0.0001
Positive ego goal	2.35[a]	1.82[c]	2.02[b]	1.64[d]	42.31	0.0001
Negative ego goal	2.23[a]	1.81[c]	2.04[b]	1.67[d]	39.95	0.0001
Surface level learning	2.22[a]	1.75[c]	2.03[b]	1.54[d]	38.52	0.0001
Deep level learning	2.32[d]	2.82[b]	2.61[c]	3.11[a]	34.07	0.0001
Motivation	2.00[d]	2.53[b]	2.26[c]	2.97[a]	36.92	0.0001
Interest	2.08[d]	2.59[b]	2.21[c]	2.98[a]	36.73	0.0001
Persistence	2.44[d]	3.01[b]	2.78[c]	3.33[a]	48.68	0.0001
Effort	2.36[d]	2.91[b]	2.64[c]	3.34[a]	48.98	0.0001
Studying during the week	2.03[d]	2.84[b]	2.45[c]	3.26[a]	57.12	0.0001
Studying during weekend	1.69[d]	2.39[b]	1.91[c]	2.74[a]	36.06	0.0001
Neglecting the course	2.80[a]	1.85[c]	2.22[b]	1.59[d]	47.97	0.0001
Perceived ability	2.65	2.67	2.64	2.69	1.23	ns
Performance (on 20)	10.25[d]	13.67[b]	11.42[c]	14.95[a]	55.15	0.0001

Note: Means with another superscript are significantly different (within a row).

To explore differences between the different types of instrumentality, we conducted univariate analyses of variance. The overall mean scores for each of the outcome measures as well as F and p values are presented in Table 8.5.

Do different types of instrumentality elicit different goal orientations? For task goals, the analysis yielded a significant overall effect of type of instrumentality ($F(3, 289) = 43.13$, $p < 0.0001$). Type HU-I led to most task orientation, whereas students characterizing a course as type LU-E were least task oriented. For positive and negative ego orientation, a significant overall effect of type of instrumentality was found (respectively $F(3, 289) = 42.31$, $p < 0.0001$; $F(3, 289) = 39.95$, $p < 0.0001$). When students characterized the course as an example of type LU-E or type HU-E, they were not only more positive ego oriented, but also more negative ego oriented than were students who characterized the course as type LU-I or type HU-I. At the same time, they wanted to avoid looking stupid and were worried about how others perceived them when asking questions or making mistakes.

Results indicated a significant overall effect of type of instrumentality on surface and on deep level learning strategies (respectively $F(3, 289) = 38.52$, $p < 0.001$; $F(3, 289) = 34.07$, $p < 0.001$). Students who classified the course as type LU-E or as type HU-E used fewer deep level strategies and more surface level strategies than did students who classified the course as an example of type LU-I or type HU-I.

The analyses also yielded a significant overall effect of type of instrumentality on motivation ($F(3, 289) = 36.92$, $p < 0.0001$), interest ($F(3, 289) = 36.73$, $p < 0.0001$), persistence ($F(3, 289) = 48.68$, $p < 0.001$), and effort ($F(3, 289) = 48.98$, $p < 0.0001$). Students who characterized the course as internally regulated (LU-I or HU-I) were more motivated and interested. They also persisted longer and spent more time trying to master the material. Perceiving the course as type LU-E was even more harmful than perceiving the course as an example of type HU-E.

Results indicated a main effect of type of instrumentality on studying regularly during the week and during the weekend (respectively $F(3, 289) = 57.12$, $p < 0.001$ and $F(3, 289) = 36.06$, $p < 0.001$) and on neglecting the course ($F(3, 289) = 47.97$, $p < 0.001$). In line with expectations, characterizing the course as an example of type LU-I or type HU-I encouraged positive study habits. These students studied more regularly and neglected their course less than did students who characterized the course as an example of type LU-E or as type HU-E. The analysis of type of instrumentality on perceived ability did not reveal a significant main effect ($F(3, 289) = 1.23$, n.s.).

Analysis of variance with instrumentality as the independent variable and students' marks as the dependent variable revealed a significant main effect of type of instrumentality on students' marks ($F(3, 289) = 55.15$, $p < 0.001$).

Students who characterized the course as an example of type HU-I received the highest marks, followed by students who characterized the course as an example of type LU-I and type HU-E. Students who characterized the course as an example of type LU-E received the poorest marks.

These findings provide evidence that the type of perceived instrumentality has a differential influence on motivation, learning strategies, goal orientation, study behaviors, and academic achievement. In particular, the most positive and adaptive pattern emerges when students value both intrinsic reasons and the utility/instrumentality of the course for their future job (type HU-I).

These findings also underline that it is time to abandon the overly prudent attitude toward extrinsic motivations. This attitude, which continues to be prominent in current goal theories (e.g., Ames, 1992, Covington, 2000), has dominated educational psychology since Deci's (1975; Deci & Ryan, 1985) and Lepper and Greene's (1978) influential work on the undermining effect of extrinsic goals on intrinsic motivation. The present study suggests that so-called extrinsic motivations (derived from intrinsically motivated future activities as well as from anticipated future activities that invoke the same skill as the present activity) may not only be harmless, but may even enhance optimal goal orientation and study motivation.

VOLITIONAL IMPLICATIONS OF FUTURE TIME PERSPECTIVE AND INSTRUMENTALITY PERCEPTIONS

Even when overall motivation is high, it is likely that students often face subtasks that they do not much enjoy. They may not feel like going to the library or completing homework. In other words, although intrinsic motivation may well be invaluable on the short term, students will need other things to meet all their responsibilities during an entire course or program. Therefore, it is worthwhile to explore the volitional implications of instrumentality perceptions and future time perspective.

We reviewed evidence that future time perspective in general, and instrumentality in particular, are positively related to motivation. However, the overview does not address the process that underlies this relation. At first sight, the theoretical analysis suggests that instrumentality directs volitional resources to the behavior that is considered instrumental to the distant goal. Students realize how important their studying behavior is for later success and therefore consider studying hard as their duty. However, we doubt that this is a realistic or durable strategy. In other words, we are skeptical about the power of extrinsic motivation that originates in instrumentality perceptions to *continually* provide the necessary motivation.

The main reason for this skepticism is that volitional resources that are typically relied on when one tries to convince oneself to engage in a certain activity are strongly limited and depletive (Baumeister, Bratslavsky, Muraven, & Tice, 1998; Muraven, Baumeister, & Tice, 1999). That is, people are very limited in their use of these resources. For instance, Baumeister and colleagues (1998) showed that people who were led to resist a tasty piece of cake did not persist as long on a difficult anagram. They replicated this with a host of other tasks. The paradoxical implication is that when one needs volitional resources to start a task that one does not fancy very much, one is more vulnerable to distracters for the minutes (or even hours?) to come. This is not a great forecast. Moreover, as Dewitte, Verguts, and Lens (2001) found, the nature of this mental resource might well be working memory capacity. Given that studying heavily relies on working memory and related mental resources, these data suggest that people may even be more vulnerable to distraction or temptation during studying than during other (less mental) activities. In sum, the extrinsic motivation provided by instrumentality perceptions is unlikely to provide the durable additional motivation needed to increase efforts and investments in less attractive behaviors. What other process could explain the relationship? The only other possibility is that the major avenue by which instrumentality works is by increasing intrinsic motivation, and not by increasing extrinsic motivation (in a durable way).

Indeed, as the data provided in Table 8.5 show, high utility and self-determined distant goals are not only related to more adaptive behavior (performance, persistence, effort, and studying time), but also to affective variables such as intrinsic motivation and even interest in the course. That is, the mere awareness that the activity in which one is engaged might be useful for later success enhances interest in the activity. We believe that increased interest, which is probably the main driving force or impetus for the enhanced behavior, has little to do with volition or self-control. Specifically, increasing interest is not related to a self-originating attempt to convince oneself to engage in an activity that may be dull. Rather, it is a highly reactive and affective change. Furthermore, relying on changed affect promises to be much more stable than relying on depletive willpower resources.

Nevertheless, as mentioned above, for most students, most courses will continue to have boring or less attractive aspects to them. It is in these circumstances that volitional processes come to the fore. At such times, students need to motivate themselves, relying on the depletive resources described earlier. Our findings suggest that higher instrumentality perceptions will substantially reduce the frequency of these occurrences. The implication is that the depletive resource may then not be overused so readily as they are by students who lack these instrumentality perceptions. However, instrumentality perceptions may yield an additional volitional asset. They may reduce the internal conflict, as they provide self-controlling students with a ready-made argument during their internal conflict. These students no longer have to motivate themselves by trying to find out reasons why they should start studying now. Instead, they quickly remember why studying makes sense to them.

To summarize, instrumentality perceptions (and probably also future time perspective, as it facilitates instrumentality perceptions) have two important volitional implications. First and probably most important, they reduce the need for volitional resources to be directed at studying. The main process behind this change is hypothesized to be increased interest and intrinsic motivation. Second, in those remaining episodes in which self-control is really needed, instrumentality perceptions may also favor the self-control options to the disadvantage of the temptation (e.g., not studying but watching television) because it reminds the students of the good cause.

CONCLUSION

Our primary goal was to show the positive effects of perceived instrumentality or utility for students' motivation and self-regulation. Adopting the traditional definition of intrinsic motivation and task orientation, instrumental motivation should be defined as a type of extrinsic motivation. Different types of instrumentality or utility value are distinguished. In contrast with other types of extrinsic motivation that are based on rewards, punishments, or orders, some types of instrumentality do not seem to have any negative effect on intrinsic motivation, task orientation, or intrinsic interest. One type of instrumentality that is characterized by the future relevance of a task and its internal regulation elicits the most adaptive motivational behavior. This implies that educational psychology should reconsider the role of future time perspective for students' motivation. Intrinsic motivation and task-orientation require a concentration on present learning and achievement tasks. Our data show, however, that motivation, task orientation, and self-regulation are enhanced when one is oriented toward future goals and tasks that are endogenously related to the present tasks and that are not perceived by students as external regulators of their behavior. These data corroborate the rather new trend in motivational psychology that gives less importance to the distinction between so-called intrinsic and extrinsic motivation (see Deci & Ryan, 2000, in press). Perceptions of internal regulation, autonomy, and self-determination, versus perceptions of external regulation, seem to hold greater relevance. Self-set future goals and tasks that are experienced as internal regulators of present behavior enhance students' motivation and interests, and hence persistence. Therefore, instrumentality perceptions are likely to diminish the need for costly volitional resources during studying. Rather than having to spoil these limited resources to enhance persistence, students can save them for learning how to master difficult problems. So, after all, parents and teachers are not necessarily wrong when they try to motivate their children or students by repeating again and again, "Do your best at school, it is so important for your future."

REFERENCES

Ainslie, G. (1992). *Picoeconomics: The strategic interaction of successive motivational states within the person.* Cambridge, UK: Cambridge University Press.

Allport, G. W. (1937). *Personality: A psychological approach.* New York: Holt.

Ames, C. (1992). Classrooms: Goals, structures, and student motivation. *Journal of Educational Psychology, 84*, 261–271.

Ames R. E., & Ames, C. (Eds.). (1984). *Research on motivation in education: Vol. 1. Student motivation.* Orlando, FL: Academic Press.

Atkinson, J. W., & Feather, N. T. (Eds.). (1966). *A theory of achievement motivation.* New York: Wiley.

Atkinson, J. W., & Raynor, J. O. (1974). Introduction and overview. In J. W. Atkinson & J. O. Raynor (Eds.), *Motivation and achievement* (pp. 3–11). Washington, DC: Winston & Sons.

Bandura, A., & Schunk, D. H. (1981). Cultivating competence, self-efficacy, and intrinsic interest through proximal self-motivation. *Journal of Personality and Social Psychology, 41*, 586–598.

Bandura, A., & Simon, K. M. (1977). The role of proximal intentions in self-regulation of refractory behavior. *Cognitive Therapy and Research, 1*, 177–193.

Baumeister, R. F., Bratslavsky, E., Muraven, M., & Tice, D. M. (1998). Ego depletion: Is the active self a limited resource? *Journal of Personality and Social Psychology, 74*, 1252–1265.

Cameron, J. (2001). Negative effects of reward on intrinsic motivation—A limited phenomenon: Comment on Deci, Koestner, and Ryan (2001). *Review of Educational Research, 71*, 29–42.

Cottle, J. T., & Pleck, J. H. (1969). Linear estimations of temporal extensions: The effect of age, sex, and social class. *Journal of Projective and Personality Assessment, 33*, 81–93.

Covington, M. (2000). Goal theory, motivation, and school achievement: An integrative review. *Annual Review of Psychology, 51*, 171–200.

Creten, H., Lens, W., & Simons, J. (2001). The role of perceived instrumentality in student motivation. In A. Anastasia, J. Kuhl, & R. M. Sorrentino (Eds.), *Trends and prospects in motivation research* (pp. 37–45) Dordrecht, Netherlands: Kluwer Academic.

Deci, E. L. (1975). *Intrinsic motivation.* New York: Plenum Press.

Deci, E. L., Koestner, R., & Ryan, R. M. (1999). A meta-analytic review of experiments examining the effects of extrinsic rewards on intrinsic motivation. *Psychological Bulletin, 125*, 512–598.

Deci, E. L., Koestner, R., & Ryan, R. M. (2001). Extrinsic rewards and intrinsic motivation in education: Reconsidered once again. *Review of Educational Research, 71*, 1–27.

Deci, E. L., & Ryan, R. M. (1985). *Intrinsic motivation and self determination in human behavior.* New York: Plenum Press.

Deci, E. L., & Ryan, R. M. (1992). The initiation and regulation of intrinsically motivated learning and achievement. In A. K. Boggiano & T. S. Pittman, (Eds.), *Achievement and motivation: A social-developmental perspective* (pp. 9–36). Cambridge, UK: Cambridge University Press.

Deci, E. L., & Ryan, R. M. (2000). The "what" and "why" of goal pursuits: Human needs and the self-determination of behavior. *Psychological Inquiry, 11*, 227–268.

Deci, E. L., Ryan, R. M, & Koestner, R. (2001). The pervasive effects of rewards on intrinsic motivation: Response to Cameron (2001). *Review of Educational Research, 71*, 43–51.

De Volder, M., & Lens, W. (1982). Academic achievement and future time perspective as a cognitive-motivational concept. *Journal of Personality and Social Psychology, 42*, 566–571.

Dewitte, S., Verguts, T., & Lens, W. (2001). *What is the ego in "egodepletion"?: The relation between working memory overuse and self-control.* Manuscript submitted for publication.

Dweck, C. S. (1986). Motivational processes affecting learning. *American Psychologist, 41*, 1040–1048.

Eccles, J. (1984). Sex differences in achievement patterns. *Nebraska Symposium on Motivation, 32*, 97–132.

Eccles, J., Barber, B., Updegraff, K., & Wigfield, A. (1997, March). *Expectancies and values as predictors of gender differences, course enrollment decisions, and occupational plans in math and science.* Paper presented at the annual meeting of the American Educational Research Association, Chicago.

Eisenberger, R., & Cameron, J. (1996). Detrimental effects of reward: Reality or myth? *American Psychologist, 51*, 1153–1166.

Eisenberger, R., Pierce, W. D., & Cameron, J. (1999). Effects of reward on intrinsic motivation: Negative, neutral, and positive: Comment on Deci, Koestner, and Ryan (1999). *Psychological Bulletin, 125*, 677–691.

Eisenberger, R., Rhoades, L., & Cameron, J. (1999). Does pay for performance increase or decrease perceived self-determination and intrinsic motivation? *Journal of Personality and Social Psychology, 77*, 1026–1040.

Feather, N. T. (1982). *Expectations and actions: Expectancy-value models in psychology.* Hillsdale, NJ: Erlbaum.

Fraisse, P. (1963). *The psychology of time.* Westport, CT: Greenwood.

Gjesme, T. (1981). Is there any future in achievement motivation? *Motivation and Emotion, 2*, 115–138.

Gjesme, T. (1982). Psychological goal distance: The lost dimension in achievement motivation research. In W. Hacker, W. Volpert, & M. von Cranach (Eds.), *Cognitive and motivational aspects of action* (pp. 86–98). Amsterdam: North-Holland.

Harter, S. (1981). A new self-report scale of intrinsic versus extrinsic orientation in the classroom: Motivational and informational components. *Developmental Psychology, 17*, 300–312.

Harter, S., & Jackson, B. K. (1992). Trait vs. nontrait conceptualizations of intrinsic/extrinsic motivational orientations. *Motivation and Emotion, 16*, 209–230.

Hernnstein, R. J. (1970). On the law of effect. *Journal of the Experimental Analysis of Behavior, 13*, 243–266.

James, W. (1890). *The principles of psychology.* New York: Holt.

Lens, W. (1986). Future time perspective: A cognitive-motivational concept. In D. R. Brown & J. Veroff (Eds.), *Frontiers of motivational psychology* (pp. 173–190). New York: Springer-Verlag.

Lens, W. (2001). How to combine intrinsic task-motivation with the motivational effects of the instrumentality of present tasks for future goals. In A. Anastasia, J. Kuhl, & R. M. Sorrentino (Eds.), *Trends and prospects in motivation research* (pp. 23–36). Dordrecht, Netherlands: Kluwer Academic.

Lens, W., & Decruyenaere, M. (1991). Motivation and demotivation in secondary education: Student characteristics. *Learning and Instruction, 1*, 145–159.

Lens, W., & Gailly, A. (1980). Extension of future time perspective in motivational goals of different age groups. *International Journal of Behavioral Development, 3*, 1–17.

Lens, W., & Moreas, M. A. (1994). Future time perspective: An individual and a societal approach. In Z. Zaleski (Ed.), *Psychology of future orientation* (pp. 23–38). Lublin, Poland: Towarzystwo Naukowe KUL.

Lens, W., & Rand, P. (1997). Combining intrinsic goal orientations with professional instrumentality/utility in student motivation. *Polish Psychological Bulletin, 28*, 103–123.

Lepper, M. R., & Cordova, D. I. (1992). A desire to be taught: Instructional consequences of intrinsic motivation. *Motivation and Emotion, 16*, 187–208.

Lepper M. R., & Greene, D. (1978). (Eds.). *The hidden costs of reward.* Hillsdale, NJ: Erlbaum.

Lersch, P. (1966). *Aufbau der Person.* München: Johann Ambrosius Barth.

Lewin, K. (1938). *The conceptual representation and the measurement of psychological forces.* Durham, NC: Duke University Press.

Lewin, K. (1942). Time perspective and morale. In G. Watson (Ed.), *Civilian morale.* Boston: Houghton Mifflin.

Lewin, K. (1948). *Resolving social conflicts: Selected papers on group dynamics* (G. W. Lewin, Ed.). New York: Harper & Brothers.

Logue, A. W. (1988). Research on self-control. An integrating framework. *Behavioral and Brain Sciences, 11*, 665–709.

Luyten, H., & Lens, W. (1981). The effect of earlier experience and reward contingencies on intrinsic motivation. *Motivation and Emotion, 5*, 25–36.

Malone, T. W., & Lepper M. R. (1987). Making learning fun: A taxonomy of intrinsic motivations for learning. In R. E. Snow & M. J. Farr (Eds.), *Aptitude, learn-*

ing, and instruction. Vol. 3. Conative and affective process analyses (pp. 223–253). Hillsdale, NJ: Erlbaum.

Markus, H., & Nurius, P. (1986). Possible selves. *American Psychologist, 41,* 954–969.

Markus, H., & Wurf, E. (1987). The dynamic self-concept: A social psychological perspective. *Annual Review of Psychology, 38,* 299–337.

Mischel, W. (1981). Objective and subjective rules for delay of gratification. In G. d'Ydewalle & W. Lens (Eds.), *Cognition in human motivation and learning* (pp. 33–58). Leuven, Belgium & Hillsdale, NJ: Leuven University Press & Erlbaum.

Moreas, M. A. & Lens, W. (1991). *De motivationele betekenis van het individueel toekomst-perspectief: Project OT/88/6* (Vols. 1–3) [The motivational significance of the individual future time perspective: An unpublished research report]. K. U. Leuven: Departement Psychologie, niet-gepubliceerd onderzoeksrapport.

Muraven, M., Baumeister, R. F., & Tice, D. M. (1999). Longitudinal improvement of self-regulation through practice: Building self-control strength through repeated exercise. *Journal of Social Psychology, 139,* 446–457.

Nurmi J. E. (1994). The development of future-orientation in a life-span context. In Z. Zaleski (Ed.), *Psychology of future orientation* (pp. 63–74). Lublin, Poland: Towarzystwo Naukowe KUL.

Nuttin, J. (1964). The future time perspective in human motivation and learning. In *Proceedings of the 17th International Congress of Psychology* (pp. 60–82). Amsterdam: North-Holland.

Nuttin, J. (1980). *Motivation et perspectives d'avenir.* Leuven, Belgium: Presses Universitaires de Louvain.

Nuttin, J., & Lens, W. (1985). *Future time perspective and motivation: Theory and research method.* Leuven, Belgium & Hillsdale, NJ: Leuven University Press & Erlbaum.

Oyserman, D., & Markus, H. (1990a). Possible selves and delinquency. *Journal of Personality and Social Psychology, 59,* 112–125.

Oyserman, D., & Markus, H. (1990b). Possible selves in balance: Implications for delinquency. *Journal of Social Issues, 46,* 141–157.

Phalet, K., & Lens, W. (1995). Achievement motivation and group loyalty among Turkish and Belgian youngsters. In M. L. Maehr & P. R. Pintrich (Eds.). *Advances in motivation and achievement. Vol. 9: Culture, motivation, and achievement* (pp. 32–72). Greenwich, CT: JAI Press.

Pintrich, P. R., & Schunk, D. (1996). *Motivation in education: Theory, research, and applications.* Columbus, OH: Merrill/Prentice-Hall.

Rachlin, H. (1995). Self-control: Beyond commitment. *Behavioral and Brain Sciences, 18,* 109–159.

Raynor, J. O. (1969). Future orientation and motivation of immediate activity: An elaboration of the theory of achievement motivation. *Psychological Review, 76,* 606–610.

Raynor, J. O. (1981). Future orientation and achievement motivation: Toward a theory of personality functioning and change. In G. d'Ydewalle & W. Lens (Eds.), *Cognition in human motivation and learning* (pp. 199–231). Leuven, Belgium & Hillsdale, NJ: Leuven University Press & Erlbaum.

Raynor, J. O., & Entin, E. E. (1982). *Motivation, career striving, and aging.* Washington, DC: Hemisphere.

Rigby, C. S., Deci, E. L., Patrick, B. C., & Ryan, R. M. (1992). Beyond the intrinsic-extrinsic dichotomy: Self-determination in motivation and learning. *Motivation and Emotion, 16*, 165–185.

Shell, D. F., & Husman, J. (2001). The multivariate dimensionality of personal control and future time perspective beliefs in achievement and self-regulation. *Contemporary Educational Psychology, 26*, 481–506.

Simons, J., Dewitte, S., & Lens, W. (2000). Wanting to have versus wanting to be: The effect of perceived instrumentality on goal orientation. *British Journal of Psychology, 91*, 335–351.

Simons, J., Dewitte, S., & Lens, W. (2001). *The effect of different types of instrumentality on motivational and cognitive variables.* Unpublished research paper, Department of Psychology, University of Leuven, Belgium.

Stipek, D. J. (1993). *Motivation to learn: From theory to practice* (2nd ed.). Boston: Allyn and Bacon.

Vallerand, R. J. (1997). Toward a hierarchical model of intrinsic and extrinsic motivation. In M. P. Zanna (Ed.), *Advances in experimental social psychology* (Vol. 29, pp. 271–360). San Diego, CA: Academic Press.

Van Calster, K., Lens, W., & Nuttin, J. (1987). Affective attitude toward the personal future: Impact on motivation in high school boys. *American Journal of Psychology, 100*, 1–13.

Verstraeten, D. (1980). Level of realism in adolescent future time perspective. *Human Development, 23*, 177–191.

Wigfield, A., & Eccles, J. S. (1992). The development of achievement task values: A theoretical analysis. *Developmental Review, 12*, 265–310.

Woodworth, R. S. (1918). *Dynamic psychology.* New York: Columbia University Press.

Zaleski, Z. (1987). Behavioral effects of self-set goals for different time ranges. *International Journal of Psychology, 22*, 17–38.

Zaleski, Z. (1994). (Ed.). *Psychology of future orientation.* Lublin, Poland: Towarzystwo Naukowe KUL.

CHAPTER 9

INTEREST AND ADOLESCENCE

Suzanne Hidi
Ontario Institute for Studies in Education
of the University of Toronto (OISE/UT)
Mary Ainley
University of Melbourne, Australia

Motivation has been defined in various ways by psychologists, educators, and laypersons. Recently, Wegge (2001) extended Kanfer's (1994) definition of motivation as the psychological mechanism determining the direction, intensity, and persistence of individuals' activity by suggesting that individuals' motivation also explains predecisional processes involved in goal selection, and the persistence and intensity of pursuing a selected goal. He further argued that while cognitive processes and representations that are the focus of various motivational theories (e.g., expectancy-value theory, self-efficacy beliefs, and goal theories) undoubtedly contribute to the regulation of human behavior, motivational phenomena cannot be reduced solely to the impact of these cognitive factors. Rather, emotional processes and physiological factors that contribute to the psychological state of the organism and to the energizing of behavior need to be included in the theories of motivation (Hidi, 1990; Krapp, 1999; Sorrentino, 1996). Interest is one motivational concept that incorporates affective and cognitive factors to explain how and why individuals choose to engage in certain activities (Hidi & Berndorff, 1998; Krapp, 2000). Interest may also have strong and yet not fully explained associations with the selection and pursuit of goals (Hidi & Harackiewicz, 2000; Krapp, 2002; Sansone &

Harackiewicz, 1996). In this chapter we focus on adolescents and consider the role of interest in learning.

As early as in 1806, German philosopher Herbart concluded that the cultivation of diversified interest was a prerequisite for learning and should be a primary goal of education. Dewey (1913) extended this view by pointing out that interest-based learning differed from learning that lacked interest. He further argued that interest was essential to maintain self-initiated, content-related activities that result in pleasure, satisfaction, and learning. In the last two decades with a renaissance of interest research, educators and psychologists specifically recognized that interest is central in determining how we select and persist in certain activities, such as processing certain types of information in preference to others (Hidi, 1990). As the literature indicates, interest facilitates learning (Krapp, 2000; Renninger, 2000; Renninger & Hidi, 2002). Schiefele (2001) and Schiefele and Krapp (1996) demonstrated that this facilitation occurs especially with respect to qualitative measures such as deeper level learning.

Unfortunately, research over this time period also indicated that as children get older, their interest and attitudes toward academic activities may decline (Anderman & Maehr, 1994; Haladyna & Thomas, 1979; Harter, 1981; Hidi & Harackiewicz, 2000; Krapp, 2002; Wigfield & Eccles, 1992). Such deterioration is especially characteristic of many adolescents' motivation, creating special difficulties for them. As Rudolph, Lambert, Clark, and Kurlakowsky (2001) argued, understanding adolescents' adjustment difficulties in this critical stage of individual development may be essential for improving long-term educational outcomes. To understand the special problems created by adolescents' declining interest in many academic subjects such as mathematics and physics (Eccles, Wigfield, & Schiefele, 1998; Epstein & McPartland, 1976; Hoffmann & Haussler, 1998; Wigfield & Eccles, 1992), one must recognize that when children reach adolescence they are subject to a wide and sometimes conflicting array of social expectations. Within the framework of their school subjects, they are expected to take charge of their learning. Increasingly, schools are expecting students to become independent learners and to develop self-regulation strategies, both of which require agency and purpose in learning (Walker, 2001; Zimmerman, 1989). Simultaneously, specific organizational and management structures that regulate students' lives in middle school often serve to diminish student autonomy rather than promoting learner self-regulation and responsibility. This has been demonstrated in the work of Eccles and colleagues (e.g., Eccles & Midgley, 1989; Maehr & Midgley, 1996). Therefore, at a time when many students' interest in academic areas is declining, they are being expected to show self-regulation and purpose in their learning while at the same time they need to conform to relatively restrictive and controlling school organizational structures.

As our subsequent discussion demonstrates, interest has been conceptualized in various ways and consideration of these differences offers new insights into the character of adolescents' responses to their educational experiences. The definition of interest as a psychological state and/or as an individual disposition underlies these various conceptualizations (Krapp, Hidi, & Renninger, 1992; Schiefele, 2001; Todt & Schreiber, 1998). Focused attention, persistence, increased cognitive functioning, and affective involvement characterize the psychological state of interest (Hidi, 2000). Although increased effort is usually required to maintain focused attention and cognitive functioning, when interest is high, the activities feel relatively effortless. In the educational literature, two types of interest, situational and individual, have been associated most frequently with experiencing the psychological state of interest.[1]

SITUATIONAL INTEREST

Particular conditions and/or objects in the environment generate the psychological state referred to as situational interest. This psychological state involves focused attention, persistence, and increased cognitive functioning. Situational interest appears to be associated with combinations of emotions that are not necessarily all positive (Hidi & Harackiewicz, 2000; Renninger & Hidi, 2002). As early as 1987, Iran-Nejad demonstrated that interest and liking are not identical concepts. He noted that some objects can be interesting even though they may elicit negative emotions (for example, animals such as snakes). Hidi and Harackiewicz (2000) used the example of medical students dissecting cadavers to demonstrate that interesting experiences can have negative as well as positive affective tones.

The ways in which tasks are organized and presented may influence students' situational interest (Ainley, Hidi, & Berndorff, in press), and it has also been pointed out that situational interest is not necessarily associated with high levels of content knowledge (Renninger, 2000). The attention and affective reactions associated with this type of interest are often transitory (Hidi, 1990; Murphy & Alexander, 2000), and this has led to the suggestion that there are two potential phases of situational interest, one in which interest is triggered and a subsequent phase in which the triggered interest is maintained (Harackiewicz, Barron, Tauer, Carter, & Elliot, 2000; Hidi & Baird, 1986; Mitchell, 1993). Further information on situational interest is provided by two recent reviews of the topic by Hidi and Berndorff (1998) and by Schraw and Lehman (in press).

INDIVIDUAL INTEREST

When through repeated engagements, individuals experience positive affects, increase their related knowledge, and come to value highly the object of their activity, they develop an individual interest (Alexander, Jetton, & Kulikowich, 1995; Renninger, 2000). In this sense, individual interest is a relatively enduring predisposition to attend to certain objects and events and to engage in certain activities (Krapp et al., 1992; Renninger, 1992, 2000; Schiefele, 1998). As the literature indicates, individual interest is associated with positive affect and persistence and tends to positively influence learning. Renninger (2000) presented a detailed description of various aspects of individual interest. She specifically reviewed evidence that individual interest develops in relation to activity, it holds attention, and it facilitates learning.

Ainley and colleagues (in press) pointed out that within the broader domain of schooling, students, rather than having just one individual interest, may have several individual interests, some closely related to the goals of classroom learning and others antithetical to such learning. Ainley and colleagues further argued that there are different levels of generality implicit in the various conceptualizations of individual interest. For example, individual interests can be defined in terms of special content of subject areas (literature, history, etc.) or activities in specific areas (music, physical education, etc.). Individual interest may also refer to a more general tendency of individuals to seek out more new information or to have a desire to find out about new ideas, objects, and events. Ainley (1998) characterized this general interest in learning as individuals' characteristic way of approaching novel and/or puzzling phenomena with a desire to understand events and phenomena and has shown that it is associated with a range of positive attitudes to schooling. A similar argument has been developed by Pintrich (2000) in relation to his conceptualization of achievement goal orientations. At the general level, students have broad life goals; at the most specific level, they have particular task goals. In between are achievement goal orientations, more general than task goals and less general than life goals.

Described in this way, it is clear that individual interest is one of a number of motivational concepts adding insight into student learning (see Murphy & Alexander, 2000). Achievement motivation and intrinsic motivation are two of the terms closely associated with discussion of interest as it has been investigated in relation to student learning. How interest and intrinsic motivation are related has recently been discussed by Hidi (2000) and by Hidi and Harackiewicz (2000). They have noted that intrinsic motivation has been typically defined as motivation to engage in activities for their own sake and independently of external influences. As interest has also been seen to be associated with similar characteristics, researchers have either considered intrinsic motivation and interest to be synonymous terms (Tobias, 1994) or have viewed interest as an implicit aspect of intrinsic motivation (Deci, 1992, 1998). Thus, it is not surprising that in many motivational studies, individuals' self-reported levels of interest served as a basic measure of intrinsic motivation.

However, using the two terms interchangeably overlooks important distinctions between these concepts. As others have pointed out (e.g., Bergin, 1999; Guthrie & Wigfield, 1999) intrinsic motivation is a more general concept than interest. More specifically, interest is only one of several motives that may result in intrinsically motivated behavior. Hidi (2000) proposed that needs and desires are some other forms of motivation that may result in intrinsically motivated behavior. In addition, the origins of interest and intrinsic motivation have been conceptualized differently. Whereas the origins of intrinsic motivation tend to be explained by individuals' need to achieve competence, to overcome challenges, and to exercise control of their environment (Deci, 1975; Hunt, 1965; Lepper & Henderlong, 2000), the origins of interest are not seen as the outcome of needs. Rather, interest results from specific interactions between a person and an object or aspect of his/her environment. Person–object interaction and object specificity are basic to the conceptualization of interest (Hidi & Baird, 1986; Krapp, 2000; Schiefele, Hausser, & Schneider, 1979). According to this view, interest is always in reference to a specific object or class of objects, which helps explain why individuals prefer to engage in certain activities over others (Schiefele, 1998).

THE RELATIONSHIP BETWEEN SITUATIONAL AND INDIVIDUAL INTEREST

As Renninger and Hidi (2002) noted, almost all students have individual interests and can also expect to find themselves having experiences that trigger situational interest. Both types of interest may operate simultaneously (Ainley et al., in press; Haussler & Hoffmann, 1998). In addition, situational interest once maintained, can contribute to the development of well-developed individual interest (Bergin, 1999; Follings-Albers & Hartinger, 1998; Hidi, 1990; Hidi & Anderson, 1992; Hidi & Harackiewicz, 2000; Hoffman & Haussler, 1998). More specifically, when situational interest continues over extended periods of time, it can lead to increased knowledge and value as well as to positive affect (Hidi, 2000).

For educators the potential of situational interest to contribute to the development of individual interest is critical. It suggests that through environmental influences, teachers and parents can contribute to situational interest that in turn may facilitate the development of school-related individual interests in students who are lacking such interest (Hidi & Berndorff, 1998; Mitchell, 1993; Schraw & Dennison, 1994).

INTEREST DEVELOPMENT

It has been argued that at the early stages of intellectual development, infants have only undifferentiated interest and this is manifested in their search for structure in the environment (Piaget, 1967; Schiefele, 2001; Travers, 1978). As children's experience of the environment becomes wider, interest becomes organized into more differentiated structures that vary among individuals. For example, some children may develop a strong interest in numbers, music, sports, and so on. Other children's interest can be focused on people or on animals.

Studies of young children indicate that they have identifiable individual interests (Krapp & Fink, 1992; Renninger, 1992). Schiefele (2001) noted that between 3 and 8 years of age, children's gender-specific interests develop. Based on Kohlberg's (1967) theory, Schiefele links the development of gender-specific interests to children's acquisition of gender identity. That is, children strive to be consistent with their self-concept and activities/objects that fit are likely to be evaluated positively. Consequently, boys become mainly interested in male toys such as cars and machines, and girls' interests focus on female toys such as dolls and their houses. Renninger and Wozniak's (1985) seminal research demonstrated that children as young as 3 years of age have relatively stable individual interests that are gender specific and that these interests influence their attention, memory, and activities.

Although gender-specific interests have been widely documented (see Gardner, 1998, for a review), there is no clear agreement over exactly how those interests develop. Maccoby (2000) cites a range of theories that have been offered to explain the development of gender identity, including socialization, cognitive, ethological, and psychobiological perspectives. What is clear from her analysis is that children do develop strong gender identity and that they generally "socialize themselves to conform to what they know to be stereotypical for children of their own sex" (p. 400). Further research into the way in which biological, cognitive, and social experience factors together influence the development of gender identity and associated gender-specific interests will also contribute to understanding the processes that underlie the development of individual interests that are compatible with and support adolescents' academic achievement.

According to Schiefele (2001), the next stage of interest development covers the ages between 9 and 13. Individual interests between these years reflect a combination of social affiliation and cognitive competence issues. As was true earlier in childhood, at puberty adolescents manifest interests that accord with their gender-role stereotypes (Bergin, 1999; Fivush, 1998; Hannover & Kessels, 2001; Krapp, 2002). The content of the gender-role stereotypes may have different foci to the gender-role stereotypes of childhood, but they are still an important influence on individual interests. Adolescents reevaluate existing interests and generally align themselves with those that accord with the dominant gender-role stereotypes. Krapp (2000) argued that boys and girls develop different academic and recreational interests during adolescence. He noted that Schiefele and Stocker (1990) found that, at the upper secondary level, boys tend to read about science and technology and girls more often read texts on history, society, and travel, suggesting that gender is a significant factor in interest development. Krapp further proposed that these results are in accordance with many other studies of subject-matter interests in secondary schools indicating that the developmental patterns of individual interest in the areas of mathematics, physics, and chemistry are gender specific, with girls' average interest in these areas declining strongly during this stage (Gardner, 1998; Hoffman & Haussler, 1998). It is noteworthy that there is a complex relationship between the actual content of school subjects such as physics and girls' interest in physics. It has been shown that the interest of girls in physics can be improved by designing physics topics in light of known differences in gender-specific interests. For example, Hoffmann and Haussler (1998) reported that explaining the functioning of pumps in terms of the human body (pumping blood during surgery) rather than pumping gas from the ground significantly increased girls' interest in the content of the physics lesson and improved their subsequent learning.

The decline of academic interests during adolescence has been interpreted by many as a proof of problems with schools (Krapp, 1999; Schiefele, 2001; Travers, 1978). Whereas schools, curricula, and teachers undoubtedly influence school-related motivation (Eccles, Barber, Updegraff, & O'Brien, 1998), it may be inappropriate to place the entire blame for academically unmotivated children on various aspects of the school systems. Hidi (2000, 2001) argued that whereas researchers have suggested that societal and cultural influences and/or pressures result in the reduction of academic motivation, there are other factors inherent in age-related changes that contribute to these decreases. She contrasted young children's intrinsic motivation and boundless energy to explore, their joy in learning new skills on their own, and their continuing efforts to satisfy their own curiosity with the perceptions of some older children who view learning as more of a chore than a challenging, exciting, and rewarding activity (Hidi & Harackiewicz, 2000; Lepper & Cordova, 1992).

As children advance in school, the content of their courses become more complex and more difficult to learn. At the same time, some children may be confronted with the fact that they do not learn as quickly as some of their peers. More information has to be processed, reviewed, and retained, and strategies must be developed to deal with tasks that are not necessarily interesting. Two examples of complex tasks that require hard work and may not be intrinsically motivating are acquisition of revision skills in writing (Zimmerman & Kitsantas, 1999) and learning to speak a second language. Hidi (2000) noted that, just as Zimmerman and Kitsantas (1999) argued, acquisition of these skills are long-term processes that require high levels of personal discipline, many hours of practice, and self-regulation. Learning a second language and acquiring revision skills are only two examples of the complex academic tasks adolescents encounter in schools. However, they illustrate the distance children have to travel from their joyful discovery of the world to the focused attention, serious effort, and long-term self-disciplined commitment complex academic tasks require. In other words, whereas strong interest is generally associated with effortless, focused attention, many academic tasks at this level require considerable effort to maintain the focused attention that is required for successful task performance.

Hidi (2000) further proposed changes in social relationships may also contribute to the undermining of adolescent's academic motivation. Whereas younger children's explorations, play activities, and acquiring new skills tend to subsume social relations, with increasing age, there is the potential for academic and social activities to diverge. For some adolescents, social activities become the focus of their interests, preferences, goals, and choices and so compete with academic activities. For other adolescents, social and academic goals are complementary (Urdan & Maehr, 1995). When students' academic interests decline as a direct response to increasing social interests, this becomes a serious problem for educators (Eccles & Midgley, 1990; Follings-Albers & Hartinger, 1998; Sansone & Smith, 2000; Shernoff, Schneider, & Csikszentmihalyi, 1999; Wigfield & Eccles, 1992).

INDIVIDUAL INTEREST AND ACHIEVEMENT

Renninger and Hidi (2002) argued that the relationship between individual interests and achievement may differ depending upon the type and strength of interest a student holds. More specifically, they proposed that individuals are the most successful with subject content for which they have a well-developed interest. Using their case study of an adolescent, Sam, they illustrated how this might occur. Sam's individual interests included reading, soccer, and friends. In situations that involve these interests, Sam demonstrated a sustained ability to work at and be challenged by the activities. He did not appear to need explicit target goals in these academic endeavors. Rather, Sam appeared to engage in a fluid process of generating and revising answers to the challenges he set for himself. Renninger and Hidi concluded that this process is like a flow of activity (Csikszentmihalyi, 1990). It resembles the behavior of expert problem solvers who can, when asked, specify their actions, but who would not consider breaking down their task into a sequence of limited goals in case the process hampers their problem solving (Chi, Glaser, & Farr, 1998). The authors noted that the effort that Sam put into activities related to his well-developed individual interests, such as reading, did not cause him to feel stressed. Rather, in spite of considerable time he invested into the tasks, he reported that these activities seemed to feel effortless.

In contrast, Sam's participation in a science project on the Indonesian Box Turtle that was unrelated to his well-developed interests was more tangible and was highly dependent on support from others (teachers, peers, and parents). Eventually the project triggered and maintained Sam's situational interest, and he developed a connection with the content that resulted in his committing considerable effort to the process. However, without outside support, Sam did not appear to generate questions he wanted to answer and was not thinking about how to fuel the potential for improved performance, although he manifested such activities in the case of subject content for which he had well-developed interest.

In addition to the above differences, Renninger and Hidi (2002) noted that Sam seemed to have different emotions depending on the strength of his interests. Whereas he experienced extremes of emotions such as elation and frustration when performing activities that were related to his well-developed interest, he did not appear to experience a similar range of emotions while working on the science project.

How students perceive their own learning experiences, and how others respond to their successes and failures, are likely to contribute to shaping subsequent learning experiences. If students' positive feelings and willingness to work with different content areas are supported, this may help develop a variety of school-related (academic) interests. Such interests may facilitate students' ability to work with their courses and complete their academic tasks. For example, during the science project, as Sam's situational interest increased, he began taking responsibility for completing his assignment more independently. In the early stages of the project, Sam not only required support to focus on his work and to suggest questions to answer, but he also had relied on goals set by the teacher to conduct a set of experiments. With the help of goals laid out for him in the rubric for the project and his situational interest maintained, Sam focused on completing the project and achieving a high evaluation and a good grade. The description of Sam's behavior when working on tasks unrelated to his well-developed interests suggests that experts and peers in Sam's life have a role in the emergence and maintenance of his developing interests.

Renninger and Hidi (2002) concluded that although the process of interest development may be dependent on students' cognitive development, as suggested by Eccles and colleagues (1998), it is also the product of their culture, a culture that supports, empowers, and constrains the development of some interests as opposed to others (Anderman & Maehr, 1994; Eccles & Midgley, 1990). By middle school, differences in individual interests begin to emerge (Krapp, 2000; Todt & Schrieber, 1998). Students begin to have a sense that in comparison to other students they are capable in some areas and not in others and that they are more interested in some educational topics and activities than in others. Based on Sam's case, it appears that the role of schools and school culture in shaping the emergence and maintenance of interest needs to be acknowledged and further investigated.

DEVELOPMENT OF THE SENSE OF SELF IN ADOLESCENCE

In terms of understanding the broader role of these interest processes within the framework of adolescent development, it is important to consider the role of interest in the development of the sense of self and specifically to focus attention on the development of competencies. As Steinberg and Morris (2001) pointed out, much of the contemporary research on adolescent development appears to start with the assumption that "healthy adolescent development is about avoidance of problems rather than the growth of competencies" (p. 85).

Contemporary perspectives on adolescent development typically refer to this period as a time for establishment of a sense of identity (Erikson, 1968), a time when young people are "preoccupied with the challenge of self-definition" (Harter, 1990). The social and cultural expectations within Western industrialized societies are that young persons arrive at the end of adolescence having a clear sense of who they are and what they want to be as adult members of society. The most common form of these expectations can be expressed by questions such as, "What are you going to do when you finish your studies?" or "What are you going to do when you leave school?" Other expectations can be probed through questioning adolescents' lifestyle plans that may reflect whether they have achieved an identity (or self-definition). The underlying assumptions are that adolescents are formulating some clear and consistent future plans and working toward achieving a sense of self. Although the time-frame for many of these issues to be translated into decision and commitment appears to have been extended beyond the teenage years (Steinberg & Morris, 2001), these decisions and commitments are still the important developmental tasks of adolescence.

Identity and self-concept represent two well-known models for exploring the development of the sense of self in adolescence. The identity concept developed by Erikson (1959, 1968) has been taken up and elaborated by psychosocial identity theorists (e.g., Adams & Marshall, 1996; Kroger, 2000a; Marcia, 1966). Self-concept perspectives have been elaborated both by Harter (1986, 1990) and Marsh (1989). Typically, theoretical frameworks for understanding identity formation and self-definition focus on functional aspects of self-development. The emphasis is on crisis and commitment in psychosocial identity theory (Erikson, 1968; Marcia, 1966) and on differentiation (Marsh, 1989) or on both differentiation and integration (Harter, 1990) in self-concept theory. However, to provide a more complete understanding of this developmental stage, a study of competencies within the contents of the self-system is necessary alongside the analysis of the changing structure of the self. It is with respect to the study of the contents of the developing self that investigations of individual interests have much to offer.

In a review of the status of research on identity formation, Blasi (1988) clearly articulated how both concrete contents and individuals' attitudes were essential aspects of the identity construct popularized by Erikson (1959, 1968).

> A full understanding of identity requires the study of two components: the set of concrete contents (perhaps a specific focus on religion, or on one's career, or on political ideology) and the set of attitudes (of choice and commitment, of integration, individuation, etc.) by which the concrete contents become the substance of one's subjective identity ... The attitudinal component, namely the experience of oneself as an individual whole, is what makes a certain psychological phenomenon to be identity ... the content component, instead, accounts for the fact that different people, all having arrived at a subjective sense of identity, dramatically differ from each other on the basis of their identities. (p. 234)

Blasi's (1988) main proposition is that the essence of identity is intentionality, an agentic stance implicit in the sense of self. Within this framework of understanding the self, individual interests are important contents. Interests by their very nature have an intentional or agentic character once they contribute to self-determination (e.g., deCharms, 1968; Deci & Ryan, 1985). To pursue an interest or to act on an interest is to have some measure of intention and control over the direction of behavior.

Individual Interests and the Contents
of Self-Concept Studies

A number of theoretical frameworks have informed the construction of measures to assess identity and self-concept. The most commonly used measures within the psychosocial perspective on identity development have been based on Marcia's (1966) identity status interview (Kroger, 2000b; Marcia, Waterman, Matteson, Archer, & Orlofsky, 1993). Marcia defined the contents as those domains that Erikson proposed were central to identity development in Western societies, and he included "occupation, religion, and politics." Identity status was determined by the occurrence of crisis (self-questioning, revaluation) and commitment (decision) processes within these three key life areas. Hopkins (1982) pointed out that there was an "outer space" or masculine bias in these designated identity contents and added a number of "inner space" or more feminine issues. Issues concerning aspects of interpersonal relationships and interpersonal lifestyle decisions, "premarital sex, life plan, and sex roles," were added to the more traditional occupation, religion, and politics questions. These interview measures were first used with college-age students but with their wider acceptance are increasingly being used with younger adolescents as researchers investigate the precursors of later identity status (e.g., Flum, 1994).

Another strong line of measurement of the sense of self can be seen in the development of self-concept measures. These measures specify a set of domains and measure self-concept in terms of individual variability across those domains. For example, Harter (1990) measured the major components of self-concept as scholastic competence, athletic competence, social acceptance, behavioral conduct, appearance, and global self-worth. Marsh's (1989) widely used Self Description Questionnaire (SDQ-II: secondary school level; SDQ-III: tertiary level) measures adolescent self-concept in terms of a number of specific domains: physical abilities, physical appearance, opposite-sex relationships, same-sex relationships, parent relationships, honesty/trustworthiness, spiritual values/religion (SDQ-III only), emotional stability, school (academic), verbal, math, problem solving (SDQ-III only), and general esteem. A number of these domains of the self are defined by Marsh in terms of "students' perceptions of their skills (abilities) and interest in ..." (p. 430). As is the case for the SDQ, interests are often explicitly stated to be a component of the specific contents of domains of self-concept. However, the broad domains used in these measures of self-concept do not do justice to the variety and complexity of individual interests whereby adolescents define themselves.

The importance of capturing some of the complexity and variability inherent in the ways individual interests define adolescents' self or identity

(Renninger & Hidi, 2002) can be appreciated from different perspectives on adolescents' development. The relationship between interests, self, and learning can be identified at the individual student level. Hannover and Kessels (2001) suggested that poor performances of German students in the international studies of mathematics and science achievement may be linked to students not liking these subjects. Looking deeper into what this means, they proposed that the students' images of the hard sciences were incompatible with their self-images or self-concept, and this incompatibility may have resulted in negative feelings and underachievement in the so-called hard sciences. Self-image is based on self perceptions and, according to Hannover and Kessels, during childhood and adolescence, self-image undergoes critical changes when different goals become salient. These changes can be due to biological, cognitive, and/or social conditions. Introduction of a new subject such as physics or a branch of mathematics places students in a psychological situation where they must evaluate the new topic in relation to themselves, their perception of their own abilities and interests, and compatibility with their social goals and commitments. Hannover and Kessels found that students were more likely to favor school subjects when there was a similarity between students' perceptions of the subject and their actual or desired self-concept. The developmental process implied in Hannover and Kessels's research is similar to the differentiation processes that Marsh (1989) proposed and to the differentiation and integration processes described by Harter (1990).

Another perspective on the complexity and variability inherent in the ways individual interests define adolescents' self or identity can be seen when attention is drawn to the changes in the social and cultural context, which form the backdrop for identity formation and self-definition. As many historical treatments of adolescent development have pointed out (e.g., Baumeister & Muraven, 1996), across the 20th century there were marked changes in the "locus and burden" of self-definition. Adolescents in the early part of the 20th century often had their adult identity determined for them by family and community. The family farm, the family business, or the family trade was passed on from one generation to the next. With the changing structure of social organization across the 20th century, more and more options for occupational, lifestyle, and personal identities have become available for adolescents. The range of contents has broadened dramatically and it is becoming far less common for succeeding generations within families to be continuing the specific life course set by parents and grandparents. Lifestyle choices are more likely to be made by young adults themselves rather than by their family or community. Hence, an understanding of the variety and patterning of the contents of identity and the sense of self requires more intensive analysis of the contents of identity, in particular individual goals, interests, and attitudes. One way this can be pursued is through examination of the relationship between individual interests and the occupational interests that define adolescents' future careers and lifestyles.

INDIVIDUAL INTERESTS AND OCCUPATIONAL INTERESTS

Studies of individual interests and studies of the development of occupational or vocational interests are two research literatures that have grown in relative isolation from each other. This is surprising considering that the central construct of interest is common to both. Again, an important barrier to a better integration between these literatures has been the level of generality implicit in the way each literature has defined its central construct. On the one hand, the study of individual interests has generally taken place within the educational research literature with a focus on elementary and secondary students. Specific individual interests, defined in terms of some combination of knowledge, value, and affective components, have generally been considered in terms of domains represented by school subjects (see Renninger, 2000; Schiefele, 1998). For example, Haussler, Langeheine, Rost, and Sievers (1998) have made intensive studies of students' individual interest in physics, while Baumert, Schnabel, and Lehrke (1998) and Kreitler and Nussbaum (1998) have reported on individual interest in mathematics. On the other hand, the study of vocational or occupational interests has been more likely to focus attention on senior secondary students, tertiary students, and young adults entering the workforce. The central interest construct in these investigations has been defined in terms of a set of broad areas of experience corresponding to types of people characteristically found in different work environments. Holland's (1985) Realistic, Investigative, Artistic, Social, Enterprising, and Conventional (RIASEC) model of the fit between an individual's vocational interests and specific workplace environments has been widely used in these investigations.

The meaning of "interests" is critical here. It is our contention that by establishing the interconnections between what has been studied as adolescents' individual interests in the educational domain and adolescents' occupational interest in vocational research, researchers could extend their understanding of the development of competencies that are related to successful educational outcomes.

INDIVIDUAL INTERESTS, BASIC INTERESTS, AND GENERIC INTERESTS

One problem in examining the interconnections between the interest terms is that the development of occupational interests from early childhood through adolescence into adulthood has not been well documented. Studies of occupational development are far more likely to take middle adolescence as their starting point. For example, Kroger's (2000a) recent volume on identity from a psychosocial perspective makes its first reference to vocational interests when describing the contents of identity in mid-adolescence. However, when researchers do make some reference to childhood and early adolescence, they generally refer to what has been described in this chapter as individual interests. Kelso (1986), for instance, concluded that

> the special heredity and experiences of the child lead to preferences for some activities, aversions to others. Later, these preferences emerge as well-defined interests. Interests, in turn, lead to the development of competencies, and the crystallization of associated values. All of these events are held to contribute to the creation of a person who is predisposed to exhibit a characteristic life style and personality traits. (pp. xviii–xix)

The developmental sequence as described by Kelso (1986) starts with "preferences for activities" and expands into a general self-structure in late adolescence and adulthood where what Holland (1985) refers to as RIASEC interests are the basic organizational units. This theme can be detected in a number of writings on occupational development and attests to the importance of the individual interests of childhood for the developed occupational interests of late adolescence and early adulthood.

There are a number of writers who have described in some detail the course of development contributing to vocational and occupational interests as measured in middle and late adolescence. Ginzberg (1972) proposed three stages of vocational development. The first stage was described as a childhood *fantasy* stage. In a child's imagination, the child becomes the hero, or cultural model. The 10-year-old who asserts that "When I grow up I want to be a pop star (a firefighter, a doctor, a farmer)" is at the fantasy stage. The second stage, corresponding to early and into middle adolescence, was identified as a *tentative* stage "where one's thoughts about a vocation begin to reflect one's own interests" (p. 172). This represents a movement from fantasy choices to choices reflecting that adolescents are incorporating some awareness of what they know about and what they value in their expressions of vocational intention. A 14-year-old boy may state that he wants to become a scientist "because he likes science classes where they do experiments and look through microscopes."

The final stage extends broadly from middle to late adolescence and was referred to by Ginzberg (1972) as a *realistic* stage. At this level the tentative choices are tested against opportunity, abilities, and interests. When asked about career intentions, the 16-year-olds are likely to include how well they do at school as well as what they enjoy and value. Ginzberg's description of vocational development is framed around two core personal attributes of adolescents, their abilities and interests. Labeling the stages as *fantasy, tentative,* and *realistic* puts centre stage developmental processes that involve increasing reliance on social comparison and feedback. In this way adolescents become more aware of their strengths and limitations with respect to abilities and interests. They become more aware of what are their personal competencies and whether they will be able to overcome any constraints or obstacles that might restrict realization of their specific work interests.

The extensive research into the nature of the self and allied theories of the development of self-concept, which have been developed since Ginzberg's (1972) description of this stage in the development of vocational interests, has drawn attention to a range of complex issues confronted by adolescents that are implicated at this *realistic* stage. For example, Markus and Nurius (1986) proposed that some of the contents of the self are a representation of what the person might become, both what they would like to become and what they might fear becoming. These self structures were referred to as "possible selves." Others such as Lens (see this volume; Husman & Lens, 1999) and Nuttin (e.g., Nuttin & Lens, 1984), link students' perceptions of themselves in time as an important dimension underpinning concrete intentions and plans. Future time perspective theorists propose that the setting of specific goals with their implicit sense of extension into the future are important motivational contents in the developing self. Hence, expressions of occupational interests by older adolescents are a complex construction of intentions that include components of liking, valuing, personal competencies, and also perceptions of opportunities and obstacles.

Consider the role of interest in this developmental model. At the *fantasy* stage, expression of future work is about wishes expressing desires to be part of something that is perceived to be good or heroic: the wish to be the policeman who catches criminals, the doctor who makes sick people better, or the firefighter who rescues people and puts out dangerous fires. The *tentative* stage is described in terms of interest rather than wishes or simple liking. By early and middle adolescence, the self-concept shows the marks of social comparison. The individual student has been and continues to be confronted by the abilities and competencies of friends and peers. Expressed future work intentions also bear this mark and represent a more complex approach tendency that includes some awareness of personal strengths and weaknesses. Expressing a desire to become a firefighter is more likely to involve recognition of having some of the qualities required for being a firefighter, for example, physical strength and tenacity when confronted with danger, as well as the thrill of being a hero. The occupational interest expressed is more complex than fantasy in that it involves some knowledge of what is required by that occupation, some knowledge of one's own abilities and value of the activity. The term *interest*, as used by Ginzberg (1972), implicates knowledge and value components in much the same way as Renninger (2000) has used both knowledge and value components to define what is meant by a well-developed personal or individual interest.

Finally, at the *realistic* stage, opportunity adds a further dimension to occupational interests. Expressions of "what I want to be" are tempered by contextual constraints and are more often expressed as "what I think I could be."

There are other models of the development of vocational interest (e.g., Super, 1980) that venture back into childhood, but these make up only a small part of the vocational and career development literature. However, the point to be made here is that when early aspects of career development are considered, authors generally give prominence to interest concepts that are analogous to what is referred to by researchers in the educational area as individual interests.

From the perspective of the occupational interest literature, the centrality of the interest construct in occupational preference and choice has also been documented. Naylor (1993) highlighted this in his overview of the historical roots of contemporary vocational preference measurement. Two of the earliest leaders in this field, Strong (1943) and Kuder (1948), both used interest as the central building blocks of their work. For Strong, interests defined what members of a specific occupation were like. Interests were key to matching how individuals described themselves in relation to membership of an occupational group. When assessment tools were designed to measure these interests, they enabled the matching of persons and workplaces to be "comprehensive, objectively based, and to have a high degree of predictive validity" (Naylor, 1993, p. 1). The most influential figure in this field has been John Holland (1985, 1996), whose theory of interest themes expanded perspectives on the connections between interest and work preferences. As Naylor (1993) concluded,

> Holland's six-fold typology is consistent with what has gone before, but is much more comprehensive in its theoretical scope, extending from interests to personality characteristics and competencies, and from persons to the characteristics of workplaces. Interests, therefore, are not logically or empirically limited to work. Indeed work might be argued to be a special case, or a limited manifestation, of much broader characteristics. (p. 3)

In all these writings there are different emphases in the meaning attributed to the term interest. Naylor's (1993) review suggested that interest was in some sense a fundamental aspect of personal definition. Ginzberg, Ginsburg, Axelrad, and Herma (1966) earlier had drawn attention to a number of critical distinctions that were important for the meaning of the term interest. Ginzberg and colleagues suggested that interest should be distinguished from preference or liking because it implies more commitment, and commitment is generally manifested in participation.

> We have used the term interests to mean an awareness on the part of the individual that through directed effort and activity in one direction he can gain more satisfaction than in another. The essential component in this definition is the factor of investment—the individual gains the satisfaction only as a result of effort and output. A person may prefer bow ties to other ties; he may like chocolate ice-cream sodas more than other sodas; but he does not just "like" to collect stamps or read books. If he actually devotes a considerable part of his time and efforts to such an activity, he is probably interested in it. Without this criterion, any stated preference must have the same value as any other... Interests imply more differentiation and complexity than preferences. (pp. 244–245)

From the career and occupational interest literature, Osipow (1983) suggested that different meanings of the word interest need to be recognized. He detailed three specific meanings, and, although they are related to each other, the three are not identical. He defined the first form of interest as *tested interest*, which is measured by testing knowledge that reflects involvement in an activity. The second is *inventoried interest*, which is measured in the traditional interest inventories when people are asked about the types of things they like to do. Osipow referred to the third type of interest as *manifest interest*, which is inferred by observing what people choose to do when they are in a situation in which they have some free choice.

What Osipow (1983) has referred to as manifest interest and Ginzberg's (1972) emphasis on the investment factor of time and effort when defining interest have much in common with the substance of individual interest as investigated within educational contexts (see Hidi & Harackiewicz, 2000; Renninger, 2000). Unfortunately, the why and how of the development of interests has not been extensively researched.

The boundaries between the research looking at individual interests, often specified in terms of school subject domains, and investigation of vocational interests have been joined recently in studies investigating the relationships between vocational interest themes and senior students' choices of school subjects. This research is consistently showing that students' choices of subjects in senior secondary school occur along dimensions that are congruent with the interest themes of the occupational groups elaborated by Holland (1985, 1996). Recently Elsworth, Harvey-Beavis, Ainley, and Fabris (1999) have reviewed a number of these studies from the Australian educational context and have modeled the factors associated with subject choice in senior secondary school using a large national sample. They reported a number of significant findings. There were strong and persistent associations between gender, socioeconomic status, and subject enrollments in senior secondary school. Nationally, school and system effects were weak. On the other hand, when the subjects that students took in their final years of secondary schooling were grouped into domains of specialization, each domain was positively associated with one, or at most two, of the RIASEC vocational interest scores. "Further there was a small number of very strong positive associations, suggesting that some subject areas represent a particular focal point for interest motivated choices" (p. 307). For example, participation in creative arts studies was strongly associated with ARTISTIC; computing, economics, and business studies with CONVENTIONAL; mathematics and the physical sciences with INVESTIGATIVE; and technology studies were associated with REALISTIC.

It has always been known that students choose their courses and subjects in line with career or occupational interests. However, the importance of this research lies in the demonstration that the relationship between occupational interests and subject choice remains when factors such as gender and socioeconomic status that clearly have strong influences on occupational interests (see Jodl, Michael, Malanchuk, Eccles, & Sameroff, 2001) have been controlled. These findings point to the fact that what have been referred to as vocational and occupational interests share common "thematic content" with educational choices and this common thematic content reflects core systems of personal organization of the self.

A CLOSER LOOK AT THE INTEREST CONSTRUCT

Elsworth and colleagues (1999) and Naylor (1993) have used the various findings concerning the relationships between occupational interest and choice of specific school subjects to distinguish three levels of meaning for the interest construct. At the most specific level, they refer to *situational interest* to indicate a state-like response to a specific event or contingency. At the next level, they identify *domain-specific interest* as a relatively enduring predisposition of the person to interact with a specific class of objects or events. Choice of a specific school subject, for example mathematics or history, represents a domain-specific interest. A cluster of subjects such as mathematics, physics, and chemistry represents a domain-specific interest in science. What is considered to be a domain varies, but domain-specific interests constitute an important part of the self-concept.

The third and critical level described in these studies is referred to as *generic interests*. Generic interests move the level of analysis to the broader personality level and denote "general predispositions of individuals to prefer engagement with a broad class of similar objects and/or activities" (Elsworth et al., 1999, p. 292). General or generic interests are presumed to involve considerable breadth and structure in the organization of an individual's predispositions and, in contrast to domain-specific interests, are viewed *independently* of the specific activities, content, and contexts from which they are inferred. In this sense, Elsworth and colleagues concluded that generic interest is analogous to a personality trait or general ability. This means that each student has a profile made up of his or her position with respect to the six modes of interacting with the environment: realistic, investigative, artistic, social, enterprising, and conventional. Holland's (1985) theory of fit between worker personality and work environment proposed that the interest profile that distinguishes effective workers within any specific occupation represents a particular organization of core components of the self. The successful scientist has a different profile to the successful mechanic or hospital orderly.

In addition, Elsworth and colleagues (1999) elaborated on what they refer to as an "implied causal model." They proposed that generic interests are a fundamental or core unit of personality organization and this has direct implications for questions concerning the development of both individual interests and occupational interests.

> The implied causal model is, thus, one from correlated contextual and "background characteristics" to a relatively stable psychological predisposition to a more specific response; from school and system, student gender and SES, to a generic interest and then to a domain-specific choice. (p. 300)

Hence, all of these distinctions between types of interest represent different foci on a dimension varying in the generality of the referents rather than mutually exclusive categories. Therefore, vocational interest themes give an insight into the broader structure of the personal organization whether defined in terms of the contents of identity or of self-concept. The insights from the individual interest literature and the vocational interest literatures considered together may provide some useful insights into the educational situation of particular groups of students. For example, much is written about students identified in various ways of being *at risk*, and many intervention programs have been designed to address the needs of these students. One source contributing to students' *at risk* status may be found in their patterns of individual interests and occupational interests. For example, Care,

Ainley and Dowsett (2002) found that a small group of 10th-grade girls identified by teachers as being *at risk* of dropping out of school had a flat profile
of occupational interests. The students completed an Australian vocational
interest inventory (AIM) (Care & Naylor, 1999) and, in comparison to other
students, *at risk* girls were found to express little interest in any of the major
six occupational interest areas. Further information is needed to establish
whether the very flat interest profile was also typical for their out-of-school
activities, or whether the problem really is one of mismatch between their
interests and what is offered by the school curriculum. Exploring young students' sense of themselves and their learning from other perspectives, for
example, their future time perspective, as developed by Lens (see this volume), may also provide further insight into how to motivate learning in
these *at risk* female students. In contrast, the group of boys considered *at risk*
were measured with very strong REALISTIC interests. For them the problem
appears to be not so much absence of interests but that their interests were
in an area not well represented within the learning areas offered in the main
school curriculum.

Clearly, educators should have some understanding of the extent to
which interest contributes to adolescents' developing sense of self. Both situational and individual interest perspectives impact on the responsiveness
of students to the educational experiences offered as part of their school
curriculum. Bringing to their schooling a well-developed set of interests
that match the domains represented by school subjects, some students find
schooling challenging and enjoyable. For many others this is not the case.
Where there are no compatible, well-developed interests the task for teachers is much more demanding. However, the fact that students can have
their interest triggered by events and activities that have personal meaning
and value or that deal with issues of universal significance can be used to
connect students with important learning (see Cordova & Lepper, 1996;
Hidi & Berndorff, 1998; Lepper & Cordova, 1992; Lepper & Henderlong,
2000; Mitchell, 1993). Looking specifically at students' lack of interest in
physics, a group of German researchers (Haussler et al., 1998) concluded
that in order to develop individual interest, first, situational interest should
be stimulated during physics lessons. They described three types of students and matched these with different emphases in the way physics could
be presented in order to trigger interest. Type A students were interested
in all areas of physics and were more likely than other types to be interested in physics as a scientific enterprise, to be interested in technical
objects and technical vocations, and to be interested in handling or building technical objects. Type B students were more likely to be mainly interested in physics that they used as a vehicle to understand how physics can
serve humankind and help explain natural phenomena. Finally, Type C
students showed their strongest interest in physics when it was concerned

with the impact of physics on society. These patterns were used to guide the development of curriculum. By taking into account the specific context or situation of the physics problems, programs of study were designed to trigger interest in physics lessons for the different types of students. The researchers reported some success with this program, especially where it was used to enhance the interest and performance of girls in physics classes (Hoffmann & Haussler, 1998). Situational interest associated with physics lessons increased as did achievement outcomes.

We have argued that individual interests have an important place as contents of the developing self during adolescence. Educators are continually devising new ways to trigger situational interest (see Hidi & Harackiewicz, 2000; Mitchell, 1993). As Hannover and Kessels (2001) have proposed, when triggered in domains such as physics, languages, history, mathematics, or music, interest is more likely to persist if individuals attach the new experience to themselves. This involves reorganizing their self-concept to incorporate "I am a person who likes physics" or "I am a person who likes learning languages."

NOTE

1.   As subsequent segments of our chapter demonstrate, several other conceptualizations of interest can be found in the wider literature of the topic.

ACKNOWLEDGMENTS

The preparation of this manuscript was partially supported by a grant from the Social Science and Humanities Research Council of Canada. Our thanks go to André Tremblay for his help and patience in the preparation of this manuscript.

REFERENCES

Adams, G. R., & Marshall, S. K. (1996). A developmental social psychology of identity: Understanding the person-in-context. *Journal of Adolescence, 19,* 429–442.

Ainley, M. D. (1998). Interest in learning in the disposition of curiosity in secondary students: Investigating process and context. In L. Hoffman, A. Krapp, K. Renninger, & J. Baumert (Eds.), *Interest and learning: Proceedings of the Seeon Conference on interest and gender* (pp. 257–266). Kiel, Germany: IPN.

Ainley, M., Hidi, S., & Berndorff, D. (in press). Interest, learning and the psychological processes that mediate their relationship. *Journal of Educational Psychology.*

Alexander, P. A., Jetton, T. L., & Kulikowich, J. M. (1995). Interrelationship of knowledge, interest, and recall: Assessing a model of domain learning. *Journal of Educational Psychology, 87,* 559–575.

Anderman, E. M., & Maehr, M. L. (1994). Motivation and schooling in the middle grades. *Review of Educational Research, 64,* 287–309.

Baumeister, R. F., & Mauraven, M. (1996). Identity as adaptation to social, cultural, and historical context. *Journal of Adolescence, 19,* 405–416.

Baumert, J., Schnabel, K., & Lehrke, M. (1998). Learning math in school: Does interest really matter? In L. Hoffmann, A. Krapp, & K. A. Renninger (Eds.), *Interest and learning: Proceedings of the Seeon Conference on interest and gender* (pp. 327–326). Kiel, Germany: IPN.

Bergin, D. A. (1999). Influences on classroom interest. *Educational Psychologist, 34,* 87–98.

Blasi, A. (1988). Identity and the development of the self. In K. D. Lapsley & F. C. Power (Eds.), *Self, ego and identity* (pp. 226–242). New York: Springer-Verlag.

Care, E., Ainley, M., & Dowsett, A. (2002). *Motivational characteristics of Year 10 students including those "at risk."* Manuscript in preparation.

Care, E. & Naylor, F. D. (1999). *AIM: Technical and applications guide.* Kew, Victoria, Australia: Career-Wise.

Chi, M. Glaser, R. & Farr, M. (Eds.). (1998). *The nature of expertise.* Hillsdale, NJ: Erlbaum.

Cordova, D. I., & Lepper, M. R. (1996). Intrinsic motivation and the process of learning: Beneficial effects of contextualization, personalization, and choice. *Journal of Educational Psychology, 88,* 715–730.

Csikszentmihaly, M. (1990). *Flow: The psychology of optimal experience.* New York: HarperCollins.

DeCharms, R. (1968). *Personal causation: The internal affective determinants of behavior.* New York: Academic Press.

Deci, E. L. (1975). *Intrinsic motivation.* New York: Plenum Press.

Deci, E. L. (1992). The relation of interest to the motivation of behavior: A self-determination of theory perspective. In K. A. Renninger, S. Hidi, & A. Krapp (Eds.), *The role of interest in learning and development* (pp. 43–70). Hillsdale, NJ: Erlbaum.

Deci, E. L. (1998). The relation of interest to motivation and human needs: The self-determination theory viewpoint. In L. Hoffman, A. Krapp, K. Renninger, & J. Baumert (Eds.), *Interest and learning: Proceedings of the Seeon Conference on interest and gender* (pp. 146–163). Kiel, Germany: IPN.

Deci, E. L., & Ryan, R. M. (1985). *Intrinsic motivation and self-determination in human behavior.* New York: Plenum Press.

Dewey, J. (1913). *Interest and effort in education.* Boston: Riverside Press.

Eccles, J. S., Barber, B. L., Updegraff, K., & O'Brien, K. (1998). An expectancy-value model of achievement choices: The role of ability self-concepts, perceived task utility and interest in predicting activity choice and course enrollment. In L. Hoffmann, A. Krapp, K. A. Renninger, & J. Baumert (Eds.), *Interest and learning: Proceedings of the Seeon Conference on interest and gender* (pp. 267–279). Kiel, Germany: IPN.

Eccles, J. S., & Midgley, C. (1989). Stage/environment fit: Developmentally appropriate classrooms for early adolescents. In R. Ames & C. Ames (Eds.), *Research on motivation in education* (Vol. 3, pp. 139–181). New York: Academic Press.

Eccles, J. S., & Midgley, C. (1990). Changes in academic motivation and self-perceptions during early adolescence. In R. Montemayor, G. R. Adams, & T. P. Gullotta (Eds.), *Advances in adolescent development: From childhood to adolescence* (Vol. 2, pp. 134–155). Newbury Park, CA: Sage.

Eccles, J. S., Wigfield, A., & Schiefele, U. (1998). Motivation to succeed. In N. Eisenberg (Ed.), *Social, emotional, and personality development in handbook of child psychology* (Vol. 3, pp. 1017–1096). New York: Wiley.

Elsworth, G. R., Harvey-Beavis, A., Ainley, J. & Fabris, S. (1999). Generic interests and school subject choice. *Educational Research and Evaluation, 5,* 290–318.

Epstein, J. L., & McPartland, J. M. (1976). The concept and measurement of the quality of school life. *American Educational Research Journal, 13,* 15–30.

Erikson, E. (1959). Identity and the life-cycle. *Psychological Issues* (Monograph 1, No. 1). New York: International Universities Press.

Erikson, E. (1968). *Identity: Youth and crisis.* New York: Norton.

Fivush, R. (1998). Interest, gender and personal narrative: How children construct self-understanding. In L. Hoffmann, A. Krapp, K. A. Renninger, & J. Baumert (Eds.), *Interest and learning: Proceedings of the Seeon Conference on interest and gender* (pp. 58–73). Kiel, Germany: IPN.

Flum, H. (1994). Styles of identity formation in early and middle adolescence. *Genetic, Social, and General Psychology Monographs, 120,* 435–467.

Follings-Albers, M., & Hartinger, A. (1998). Interest of girls and boys in elementary school. In L. Hoffman, A. Krapp, K. Renninger, & J. Baumert (Eds.), *Interest and learning: Proceedings of the Seeon Conference on interest and gender* (pp. 175–183). Kiel, Germany: IPN.

Gardner, P. L. (1998). The development of males' and females' interests in science and technology. In L. Hoffman, A. Krapp, K. Renninger, & J. Baumert (Eds.), *Interest and learning: Proceedings of the Seeon Conference on interest and gender* (pp. 41–57). Kiel, Germany: IPN.

Ginzberg, E. (1972). Toward a theory of occupational choice: A restatement. *Vocational Guidance Quarterly, 20,* 169–176.

Ginzberg, E., Ginsburg, S. W., Axelrad, S., & Herma, J. L. (1966). *Occupational choice.* New York: Columbia University Press.

Guthrie, J. T., & Wigfield, A. (1999). Engagement and motivation in reading. In *Handbook of reading research III.* New York: Longman.

Haladyna, T., & Thomas, G. (1979). The attitudes of elementary school children toward school and subject matters. *Journal of Experimental Education, 48,* 18–23.

Hannover, B., & Kessels, U. (2001, August). *Girls' and boys' self-concept and interest in physics.* Paper presented at the meeting of the the European Association for Research on Learning and Instruction, Fribourg, Switzerland.

Harackiewicz, J. M., Barron, K. E., Tauer, J. M., Carter, S. M., & Elliot, A. J. (2000). Short-term and long-term consequences of achievement goals in college: Predicting continued interest and performance over time. *Journal of Educational Psychology, 92,* 316–330.

Harter, S. (1981). A new self-report scale of intrinsic versus extrinsic orientation in the classroom: Motivational and informational components. *Developmental Psychology, 17,* 300–312.

Harter, S. (1986). Cognitive-developmental processes in the integration of concepts about emotions and the self. *Social Cognition, 4,* 119–151.

Harter, S. (1990). Processes underlying adolescent self-concept formation. In R. Montemayor (Ed.), *Advances in adolescent development: From early childhood to adolescence* (Vol. 2, pp. 205–239). Beverly Hills, CA: Sage.

Haussler, P., & Hoffmann, L. (1998). Qualitative differences in students' interest in physics and the dependence on gender and age. In L. Hoffmann, A. Krapp, K. Renninger, & J. Baumert (Eds.), *Interest and learning: Proceedings of the Seeon Conference on interest and gender* (pp. 280–289). Kiel, Germany: IPN.

Haussler, P., Hoffmann, L., Langeheine, R., Rost, J., & Sievers, K. (1998). A typology of students' interest in physics and the distribution of gender and age within each type. *International Journal of Science Education, 20,* 223–238.

Herbart, J. F. (1906/1965). Allgemeine Pädagogik, aus dem Zweck der Erziehung abgeleitet. In J. F. Herbart, *Pädagogische Schriften* (Vol. 2, pp. 9–155). Düsseldorf, Germany: Küpper.

Hidi, S. (1990). Interest and its contribution as a mental resource for learning. *Review of Educational Research, 60,* 549–571.

Hidi, S. (2000). An interest researcher's perspective on the effects of extrinsic and intrinsic factors on motivation. In C. Sansone & J. M. Harackiewicz (Eds.), *Intrinsic and extrinsic motivation: The search for optimum motivation and performance* (pp. 309–339). New York: Academic Press.

Hidi S. (2001). Interest, reading, and learning: Theoretical and practical considerations. *Educational Psychology Review, 13,* 191–209.

Hidi, S., & Anderson, V. (1992). Situational interest and its impact on reading and expository writing. In K. A. Renninger, S. Hidi, & A. Krapp (Eds.), *The role of interest in learning and development* (pp. 215–238). Hillsdale, NJ: Erlbaum.

Hidi, S., & Baird, W. (1986). Interestingess: A neglected variable in discourse processing. *Cognitive Science, 10,* 179–194.

Hidi, S., & Berndorff, D. (1998). Situational interest and learning. In L. Hoffman, A. Krapp, K. Renninger, & J. Baumert (Eds.), *Interest and learning: Proceedings of the Seeon Conference on interest and gender* (pp. 74–90). Kiel, Germany: IPN.

Hidi, S., & Harackiewicz, J. (2000). Motivating the academically unmotivated: A critical issue for the 21st century. *Review of Educational Research, 70,* 151–179.

Hoffmann, L., & Haussler, P. (1998). An intervention project promoting girls' and boys' interest in physics. In L. Hoffman, A. Krapp, K. Renninger, & J. Baumert (Eds.), *Interest and learning: Proceedings of the Seeon Conference on interest and gender* (pp. 301–316). Kiel, Germany: IPN.

Holland, J. L. (1985). *Making vocational choices: A theory of vocational personalities and work environments* (2nd ed.) Englewood Cliffs, NJ: Prentice-Hall.

Holland, J. L. (1996). Exploring careers with a typology: What we have learned and some new directions. *American Psychologist, 51,* 397–406.

Hopkins, L. B. (1982). Assessment of identity status in college women using outer space and inner space interviews. *Sex Roles, 8,* 557–566.

Hunt, J. M. V. (1965). Intrinsic motivation and its role in psychological development. In D. Levine (Ed.), *Nebraska Symposium on Motivation* (Vol. 13, pp. 189–282). Lincoln: University of Nebraska Press.

Husman, J., & Lens, W. (1999). The role of the future in student motivation. *Educational Psychologist, 34,* 113–125.

Iran-Nejad, A. (1987). Cognitive and affective causes of interest and liking. *Journal of Educational Psychology, 7,* 120–130.

Jodl, K. M., Michael, A., Malanchuk, O., Eccles, J. S., & Sameroff, A. (2001). Parents' roles in shaping early adolescents' occupational aspirations. *Child Development, 72,* 1247–1265.

Kanfer, R. (1994). Motivation. In N. Nicholson (Ed.), *The Blackwell dictionary of organizational behavior.* Oxford, UK: Blackwell.

Kelso, G. I. (1986). An orientation to Holland's theory. In J. J. Lokan & K. F. Taylor (Eds.), *Holland in Australia: A vocational choice theory in research and practise.* Melbourne: ACER.

Kolhberg, L. (1967). A cognitive-developmental analysis of children's sex-role concepts and attitudes. In E. E. Maccoby (Ed.), *The development of sex differences* (pp. 82–173). Stanford, CA: Tavistock.

Krapp, A. (1999). Interest, motivation and learning: An educational-psychological perspective. *European Journal of Psychology in Education, 14,* 23–40.

Krapp, A. (2000). Interest and human development during adolescence: An educational psychological approach. In J. Heckhausen (Ed.), *Motivational psychology of human development* (pp. 109–128). Amsterdam: Elsevier.

Krapp, A. (2002). Structural and dynamic aspects of interest development: Theoretical considerations from an ontogenetic perspective. *Learning and Instruction.*

Krapp, A., & Fink, B. (1992). The development and function of interests during the critical transition from home to preschool. In K. A. Renninger, S. Hidi, & A. Krapp (Eds.), *The role of interest in learning and development* (pp. 397–431). Hillsdale, NJ: Erlbaum.

Krapp, A., Hidi, S., & Renninger, A. (1992). Interest, learning and development. In R. A. Renninger, S. Hidi, & A. Krapp (Eds.), *The role of interest in learning and development* (pp. 3–25). Hillsdale, NJ: Erlbaum.

Krietler, S., & Nussbaum, S. (1998) Cognitive orientation and interest: The motivational understructure for achievement in mathematics. In L. Hoffmann, A. Krapp, & K. A. Renninger (Eds.), *Interest and learning: Proceedings of the Seeon Conference on interest and gender* (pp. 377–386). Kiel, Germany: IPN.

Kroger, J. (2000a). *Identity development: Adolescence through adulthood.* Thousand Oaks, CA: Sage.

Kroger, J. (2000b). Ego identity status research in the new millennium. *International Journal of Behavioral Development, 24,* 145–148.

Kuder, G. F. (1948). *Kuder Preference Record—Form C (Vocational).* Chicago: Science Research Associates.

Lepper, M. R., & Cordova, D. I. (1992). A desire to be taught: Instructional consequences of intrinsic motivation. *Motivation and Emotion, 16,* 187–208.

Lepper, M. R., & Henderlong, J. (2000). Turning "play" into "work" and "work" into "play": 25 years of research on intrinsic versus extrinsic motivation and performance. In C. Sansone & J. M. Harackiewicz (Eds.), *Intrinsic and extrinsic motivation: The search for optimal motivation* (pp. 253–307). New York: Academic Press.

Maccoby, E. E. (2000). Perspectives on gender development. *International Journal of Behavioral Development, 24,* 398–406.

Maehr, M. L. & Midgley, C. (1996). *Transforming school cultures.* Boulder, CO: Westview Press.

Marcia, J. E. (1966). Development and validation of ego-identity status. *Journal of Personality and Social Psychology, 3,* 551–558.

Marcia, J. E., Waterman, A. S., Matteson, D. R., Archer, S. L., & Orlofsky, J. L. (1993). *Ego identity: A handbook for psychosocial research.* New York: Springer.

Markus, H., & Nurius, P. (1986). Possible selves. *American Psychologist, 41,* 954–969.

Marsh, H. (1989). Age and sex effects in multiple dimensions of self-concept: Preadolescence to early adulthood. *Journal of Educational Psychology, 81,* 417–430.

Mitchell, M. (1993). Situational interest: Its multifaceted structure in the secondary school mathematics classroom. *Journal of Educational Psychology, 85,* 424–436.

Murphy, P. K., & Alexander, P. (2000). A motivated exploration of motivation terminology. *Contemporary Educational Psychology, 25,* 3–53.

Naylor, F. D. (1993). The generality of interest themes. *Australian Psychologist, 28,* 1–7.

Nuttin, J. R., & Lens, W. (1984). *Motivation and future time perspective: Theory and research method.* Hillsdale, NJ: Erlbaum.

Osipow, S. H. (1983). *Theories of career development* (3rd ed.). Englewood Cliffs, NJ: Prentice-Hall.

Piaget, J. (1967). The mental development of the child. In D. Elkind (Ed.), *Six psychological studies.* New York: Random House.

Pintrich, P. (2000). An achievement goal theory perspective on issues in motivation terminology, theory and research. *Contemporary Educational Psychology, 25,* 92–104.

Renninger, K. A. (1992). Individual interest and development: Implications for theory and practice. In K. A. Renninger, S. Hidi, & A. Krapp (Eds.), *The role of interest in learning and development* (pp. 361–376). Hillsdale, NJ: Erlbaum.

Renninger, K. A. (1998). The roles of individual interest(s) and gender in learning: An overview of research on preschool and elementary school-aged children/students. In L. Hoffman, A. Krapp, K. Renninger, & J. Baumert (Eds.), *Interest and learning: Proceedings of the Seeon Conference on interest and gender* (pp. 165–175). Kiel, Germany: IPN.

Renninger, K. A. (2000). How might the development of individual interest contribute to the conceptualization of intrinsic motivation? In C. Sansone & J. M. Harackiewicz (Eds.), *Intrinsic and extrinsic motivation: The search for optimal motivation and performance.* New York: Academic Press.

Renninger, K. A., & Hidi, S. (2002). Student interest and achievement: Developmental issues raised by a case study. In A. Wigfield & J. Eccles (Ed.), *Development of achievement motivation* (pp. 173–195). San Diego, CA: Academic Press.

Renninger, K. A., & Wozniak, R. H. (1985). Effect of interest on attention shift, recognition, and recall in young children. *Developmental Psychology, 21,* 624–632.

Rudolph, K. D., Lambert, S. F., Clark, A. G., & Kurlakowsky, K. D. (2001). Negotiating the transition to middle school: The role of self-regulatory processes. *Child Development, 72,* 929–946.

Sansone, C., & Harackiewicz, J. M. (1996). "I don't feel like it": The function of interest in self-regulation. In L. L. Martin & A. Tesser (Eds.), *Striving and feeling: Interactions among goals, affect, and self-regulation* (pp. 203–228). Mahwah, NJ: Erlbaum.

Sansone, C., & Smith, J. L. (2000). Self-regulating interest: When, why and how. In C. Sansone & J. M. Harackiewicz (Eds.), *Intrinsic motivation: Controversies and new directions* (pp. 343–372). New York: Academic Press.

Schiefele, H., Hausser, K., & Schneider, G. (1979). "Interesse" als Ziel und Weg der Erziehung. Uberlegungen zu einem vernachlaBigten padagogischen Konzept. *Zeitschrift fur Padagogik, 25,* 1–20.

Schiefele, H., & Stocker, K. (1990). *Literaturinteresse* [Interest in literature]. Weinheim, Germany: Beltz.

Schiefele, U. (1998). Individual interest and learning: What we know and what we don't know. In L. Hoffmann, A. Krapp, & K. A. Renninger (Eds.), *Interest and learning: Proceedings of the Seeon Conference on interest and gender* (pp. 91–104). Kiel, Germany: IPN.

Schiefele, U. (2001). The role of interest in motivation and learning. In J. M. Collis & S. Messick (Eds.), *Intelligence and personality: Bridging the gap in theory and measurement* (pp. 163–194). Mahwah, NJ: Erlbaum.

Schiefele, U., & Krapp, A. (1996). Topic interest and free recall of expository text. *Learning and Individual Differences, 8,* 141–160.

Schraw, G., & Dennison, R. S. (1994). The effect of reader purpose on interest and recall. *Journal of Reading Behavior, 26,* 1–18.

Schraw, G., & Lehman, S. (in press). Situational interest: A review of the literature and directions for future research. *Educational Psychology Review.*

Shernoff, D., Schneider, B., & Csikszentmihalyi, M. (1999, April). *The quality of learning experiences in American classrooms: Toward a phenomenology of student engagement.* Paper presented at the meeting of the American Educational Research Association, Montreal.

Sorrentino, R. M. (1996). The role of conscious thought in a theory of motivation and cognition: The uncertainty orientation paradigm. In P. M. Gollwitzer & J. A. Bargh (Eds.), *The psychology of action: Linking cognition and motivation to behavior* (pp. 619–644). New York: Guilford Press.

Steinberg, L., & Morris, A. S. (2001). Adolescent development. *Annual Review of Psychology, 52,* 83–110.

Strong, E. K., Jr. (1943). *The vocational interests of men and women.* Stanford, CA: Stanford University Press.

Super, D. E. (1980). A lifespan, life space approach to career development. *Journal of Vocational Behavior, 13,* 282–298.

Tobias, S. (1994). Interest, prior knowledge, and learning. *Review of Educational Research, 64,* 37–54.

Todt, E., & Schreiber, S. (1998). Development of interests. In L. Hoffman, A. Krapp, K. Renninger, & J. Baumert (Eds.), *Interest and learning: Proceedings of the Seeon Conference on interest and gender* (pp. 25–40). Kiel, Germany: IPN.

Travers, R. M. (1978). *Children's interests.* Kalamazoo: Michigan State University.

Urdan, T. C., & Maehr, M. L. (1995). Beyond a two-goal theory of motivation and achievement: A case for social goals. *Review of Educational Research, 65,* 213–243.

Walker, J. M. T. (2001). *Age-related patterns in student motivation and strategy use during homework: Implications for research on self-regulated learning.* Unpublished manuscript.

Wegge, J. (2001). Motivation, information processing and performance: Effects of goal setting on basic cognitive processes. In A. Efklides, J. Kuhl, & R. M. Sorrentino (Eds.), *Trends and prospects in motivation research* (pp. 269–296). New York: Klewer Academic.

Wigfield, A., & Eccles, J. S. (1992). The development of achievement task values: A theoretical analysis. *Developmental Review, 12,* 265–310.

Zimmerman, B. J. (1989). A social-cognitive view of self-regulated learning. *Journal of Educational Psychology, 81,* 329–339.

Zimmerman, B. J., & Kitsantas, A. (1999). Acquiring writing revision skill: Shifting from process to outcome self-regulatory goals. *Journal of Educational Psychology, 91,* 1–10.

CHAPTER 10

SOCIAL DETERMINANTS OF PUBLIC BEHAVIOR OF MIDDLE SCHOOL YOUTH

Perceived Peer Norms and Need to be Accepted

Jaana Juvonen
RAND
R. Jean Cadigan
UCLA

Middle school years are often portrayed as the most difficult phase of young people's lives. Parents and teachers report that students' academic motivation declines and disciplinary problems increase (Eccles & Midgley, 1990). Such problems are often attributed to changes in young teens' attitudes and values. Yet there are a number of studies that document youth endorsing attitudes and values that are consistent with those of most adults in our society. For example, adolescents believe that education is important to get ahead in society (Allen, Weissberg, & Hawkins,1989; Steinberg, Dornbusch, & Brown, 1992). But this belief does not seem to relate to, or explain, the public behavior of young adolescents in school, where they appear unmotivated and at times rebellious, challenging school rules and "causing trouble." Thus, there appears to be a disparity between adolescents' personal values or beliefs and their public behavior.

277

Social scientists have provided various interpretations for this disconnection between personal beliefs (cf. values, attitudes) and behavior. Our goal is to integrate some of the interpretations provided by social and developmental psychologists as well as sociologists and anthropologists. We focus our analysis on social norms and specifically perceived values of school-based peer groups. The chapter is designed to provide insights into why and how perceived peer group values, in contrast to personal values, might be critical determinants of public behavior in middle school. In our analysis, we review studies that cover a range of behaviors that are relevant for young teens, including health-compromising behaviors as well as achievement-related and social behaviors.

To provide examples of some of the main conceptual points, we rely on past research as well as include excerpts from a recently completed ethnographic study of social relations and peer culture in a large, urban middle school called Fernwood (Cadigan, 2002). Each year, approximately 450 sixth graders enter Fernwood from five different elementary schools. From October 2000 through June 2001, over 100 days of observations and over 50 interviews were conducted with a group of 27 ethnically and socioeconomically diverse sixth graders (16 girls, 11 boys), all members of one physical education (PE) class. Additionally, several naturally occurring conversations were tape recorded and analyzed to examine how social norms and values were created and maintained through conversation. Participant observations occurred during PE class, lunch, before and after school, and at various social functions outside the normal school day. The PE class was chosen as a research site because it afforded an opportunity to observe a relatively small group of students interacting in a more social manner. Rules surrounding behavior in PE class are typically lax and group activities predominate.

All students were given the option of being interviewed alone or with one or two friends from the PE class. While most interviews were structured, less formal interviews took place when several students attended the session. All interviews explored themes documented in observations. The main interview questions concerned changes in peer group norms during the transition from elementary to middle school, academic achievement, conflict and harassment among peers, and social status and popularity in middle school. The interview transcripts were analyzed and coded for themes relating to the wider goals of the study—to understand the development and maintenance of peer culture.

DISCONNECTION BETWEEN PERSONAL
BELIEFS AND BEHAVIOR

Allen and colleagues (1989) found that students in Grades 7 and 8 condemned "getting drunk," and instead endorsed values, such as "doing well on tests" and "volunteering answers in class." Although we do not know how representative their sample was, we want to presume the sample was representative for the sake of the following argument: The very behaviors these youth condemned are prevalent among their age group, whereas those that they reported valuing are rare. About half of seventh- and eighth-grade students report using alcohol (Blum, Beuhring, & Reinehart, 2000). At the same time, teachers might have a hard time believing that most seventh and eighth graders think that academic success and high levels of class participation are important to more than a small minority of their students.

A great deal of social psychological research conducted with college students and older adults also demonstrates that the relations between personal attitudes (cf. values) and behavior are relatively weak (e.g., Eagly & Chaiken, 1993). Thus, the disconnection between personal values and behavior is not unique to young adolescents. Much of the social-psychological research on adults has been guided by the theory of reasoned action proposed by Fishbein and Ajzen (1975; see also Ajzen & Fishbein, 1980). Although Fishbein and Azjen proposed that an individual's behavior is determined by both (personal) attitudes and subjective norms, the latter construct has not received as much attention in empirical research as the former (e.g., Terry & Hogg, 1996). Fishbein and Ajzen maintain that the subjective norm is determined by perceived expectations of specific individuals or groups weighted by the motivation to comply with the expectations of the reference group. The first component (i.e., expectations of others) is typically operationalized as a person's perceptions of the degree to which significant others would disapprove of a particular behavior (e.g., "Do you think your parents/friends would be upset if you failed an important test?"). The latter part of the definition of subjective norm, that is, motivation to comply, is normally inferred rather than directly assessed. Because of the methodological challenges posed by the subjective norm construct, alternative and complementary conceptualizations of social normative influences have been proposed.

Grube, Morgan, and McGree (1986) proposed that in addition to subjective norm (cf. significant others' expectations about one's actions), the perceived behavior of significant others also affects the behavior of individuals (cf. Bandura, 1977). They labeled this construct behavioral norms and found that indeed the effects of the perceived prevalence of the behavior independently predicted both smoking intentions and smoking behavior among young adolescents. White, Terry, and Hogg (1994) further distinguished two components of perceived group norms: behavioral norms (i.e., whether peers engage in behavior) and perceived group attitudes (i.e., agreement among group members about the importance of the behavior). They showed that in addition to the predictions by personal attitudes and subjective norms, perceived group norms toward condom use predicted safer sex behaviors among young adults. Thus, in addition to perceptions regarding significant others' expectations, the mere prevalence of the behavior and the perceived attitudes among the members of an important reference group are critical motivators to consider.

For the sake of simplicity, we do not make a distinction here between behavioral norms and group attitudes. Rather, we prefer to use the term *perceived group values*, given that values can be reflected in group members' behavior, attitudes, or both. What is critical about this construct is that it is tapping a perception about the importance of behavior for the relevant group. But how well aware are young teens of the values of others?

PERCEIVED VALUES OF OTHERS AND SELF-PRESENTATION

When Cohen and Cohen (1996) studied developmental differences in the private values and perceived peer values of youth ranging from ages 10 to 17, they found minor differences across the age groups regarding admiration of conventional (i.e., friendly, helpful, getting good grades) and antisocial (i.e., being tough, defiant, or disobedient toward teachers) personal values. However, there were marked differences in perceived values of peers. Specifically, perceived peer admiration of antisocial values increased sharply up to about age 15 with no significant change thereafter, whereas peer admiration of conventional values declined to until age 12 and leveled thereafter. The difference between private and perceived peer values of antisocial and conventional behavior peaked around 13–15 years of age (i.e., during middle school years). Thus, young adolescents seem to be keenly aware of the distinction between what they value and what their peers value.

Research on impression management or self-presentation allows us to understand how the perceived values of others can affect behavior. The effect of perceived values of others on behavior can be best demonstrated by varying the "audience" using experimental procedures. In a series of school-related experiments, Juvonen and Murdock (1993, 1995) examined how students want to portray themselves to their teachers and peers in positive and negative achievement situations. The social motive was controlled in these experiments: Students were specifically told that they want to get along with the teacher or the popular peers. This was done in order to be able to examine whether youth can adjust their accounts to be consistent with the perceived values of others, not to study their preference to please one party more than the other.

In one of the studies (Juvonen & Murdock, 1995), age-related differences were examined in the public accounts provided for teachers versus popular classmates across Grades 4, 6, and 8 followed by successful and unsuccessful exam performance. In this case, only the eighth graders were in middle school, whereas both fourth and sixth graders resided in elementary settings. Across all three grade levels, the participants were likely to convey to their instructors that they did well in the exam because they had studied hard and were reluctant to say that they failed because of lack of effort. Whereas the youngest students wanted to portray themselves as diligent to both their teachers and peers, the eighth graders did not want to depict themselves as studious to the popular kids in their class. The students were not only reluctant to convey to these popular peers that they did well because they studied hard, but when they did poorly on the imaginary exam, they were eager to tell these peers that they failed because they did not study for the exam. Thus, these middle school youth did not want their peers to view them as studious.

In addition to examining self-presentational preferences, perceptions of the determinants of teacher and peer approval were also investigated with the same students (Juvonen & Murdock, 1995). The participants rated teacher liking and peer popularity of hypothetical students who varied in terms of their level of diligence or laziness. Whereas both fourth- and sixth-grade students thought that hard-working students are preferred over lazy ones by both teachers and peers, the eighth-grade students believed that studious behavior promotes teacher liking, but negatively impacts popularity among peers. Thus, the differentiations between their self-presentational preferences were consistent with the students' views of the discrepant determinants of teacher and peer approval.

The interview findings from Fernwood Middle School were consistent with the research described above, suggesting that early adolescents believe peers value more unconventional and antisocial behaviors than they do themselves. Students remarked that other "kids look up to people who have bad grades," although they themselves think that mentality is "stupid." The following excerpt from an interview with two boys, Nate and Thomas, suggest that the relation between perceived popularity and academic performance is rather complex.

> Interviewer: What about kids who get in trouble a lot? Are they cooler than other kids?
> Thomas: That makes them popular too.
> Interviewer: What about kids who get good grades?

Thomas: It depends.

...

Interviewer: So if I were a guy and I got really good grades, how would I go about still being popular?

Thomas: You'd still have to have your bad attitude. You have to act—it's just like a movie. You have to act. And then at home you're a regular kind of guy, you don't act mean or nothing. But when you're around your friends you have to be sharp and stuff like that, like push everybody around.

Interviewer: So, if I get good grades—if I'm in class and I'm always like, "Oooh, oooh, I know the answer, I know the answer"—

Nate: Then between periods, like in the hallways, you gotta act tough or something.

Interviewer: I see.

Thomas: Not when your friends are around, you can't say, "Oooh, oooh, I know the answer."

Interviewer: So if your friends are around, then you don't even answer the questions in class?

Nate & Thomas: [Nod their heads yes.]

These two boys are aware not only of the conflict between conventional school norms and peer group norms, but also recognize that public behavior at school is altered from "regular" behavior in the privacy of one's home. They also believe that students can be popular in spite of the fact that they get good grades as long as they present themselves as socially tough outside of the classroom. Thus, this excerpt indicates that adaptive self-presentation requires sophisticated understanding of not only the values of those whom one desires to please, but also of the right balance between various types (e.g., conventional and antisocial) of behaviors.

Taken together, young adolescents are indeed cognizant of the fact that their values are different from the values of others and that the values of various individuals and groups vary. Middle school youth also realize that they can facilitate the social relations between themselves and their target audience by behaving in ways that are consistent with the values of those with whom they interact. However, the fact that youth *can* alter their self-presentation across different parties does not mean that they do. In other words, we cannot presume that young adolescents desire to please everybody but that approval by certain individuals or groups is more critical than by others. Although there is little direct research evidence comparing social motives across various parties, there is strong evidence that peer approval becomes increasingly important for young adolescents (e.g.,

Adler & Adler, 1998; Coleman, 1974; Fine, 1981; Youniss & Smollar, 1985). Indeed, the concern for maintaining peer approval seems to peak starting in early adolescence and to diminish after mid-adolescence (Clasen & Brown, 1985). But why does the need for peer approval become so salient during early adolescence?

DEVELOPMENTAL AND CONTEXTUAL REASONS WHY PEERS BECOME MORE IMPORTANT

During early adolescence, youth start spending more of their time with peers than with their family (Savin-Williams & Berndt, 1993). This change in shared time should in part reflect shifting personal and social motives. We contend that both the desire to become more autonomous (or less dependent on adults) and the need for relatedness or belongingness (within a peer collective) play a part in this process. We assume that these desires and needs are heightened not only because of developmental changes, but especially during the time when youth are trying to fit in to a new middle school setting.

It is typically during early adolescence when youth desire to be less dependent on adults or authority figures (e.g., Buhrmester, 1996; Connolly & Goldberg, 1999). We propose that what is typically considered as a desire to become autonomous reflects more of a need to no longer be perceived as dependent on adult authority. Specifically, it is the desire not to be controlled by adults and the need to be *perceived* as not needing adult support that seem to matter for young teens.

One example of the contempt that heavy reliance on adults created at Fernwood involved a female student who had no close friends and was repeatedly victimized by her peers. Other students saw her as "childish" (a stigmatizing term used to refer to dependency on adults) because her mother reportedly came to school to have lunch with her and walk her to and from classes. Based on the observation and interview data, it was evident that this perception of the mother's presence at Fernwood made things worse for the student because it made others view the student as overly dependent on her mother. For example, one girl commented that "her mom comes up here sometimes and eat [sic] with her. I'd be so embarrassed . . . I'd be like, 'Mom, get out of here!'"

The observations and interviews of the sixth graders of the Fernwood Middle School youth also revealed that the young teens very much resented the fact that adults (e.g., teachers, parents) control their behavior (i.e., tell them how not to act or look). The sixth graders especially objected to the dress code. These adolescents saw the dress code as a way for adults to control their behavior in a manner that questioned their level of maturity. Students responded to the dress code by routinely pushing the rules' limits—girls, for example, would wear prohibited spaghetti-strap T-shirts underneath cardigan sweaters they could quickly remove or put on depending on whether an adult authority figure was present.

Resistance to school rules was also documented in a recent ethnographic study of another urban middle school where youth viewed enforcement of rules, such as dress code, as "arbitrary authority exercised by teachers or administrators" (Alvarez, 1993, p. 366). Resistance literature in general recognizes not only the influence of peer culture on adolescents' behavior in school toward adult authority figures, but also highlights the gap between the publicly expressed values and beliefs of peers versus adults (Alpert, 1991; Everhart, 1983; McLaren, 1986; Willis, 1981).

The desire for autonomy does not seem to be affected by adolescents' willingness to comply with perceived peer group norms, however. In other words, the behavioral changes associated with decreased dependence from authority figures do not signal a desire to be independent from peers—quite the contrary. We suspect that conformity to peer group norms is considered voluntary and relates to a complementary need of adolescents, namely to belong. Thus, perception of "free will" might be more critical here than absolute independence per se.

By relying on both qualitative and quantitative methods, several researchers have shown that conformity to peer group norms is more intense in early than in late adolescence (e.g., Berndt, 1979; Canaan, 1987; Clasen & Brown, 1985; Gavin & Furman, 1989). We presume that conformity is especially meaningful for young teens as they transfer to a new school where they are the youngest of the group. Changes in school structure, peer exposure, and changing relationships with teachers are all likely to affect social needs and behavior. Compared to elementary schools, middle schools are not only large but also much less structured—students are no longer taught in self-contained classrooms instructed by one primary classroom teacher (Eccles & Midgley, 1990). When youth do not know all their classmates or have one teacher who is very familiar with them, the need for being part of the group becomes increasingly important (Gavin & Furman, 1989).

In sum, the desire to be less dependent on authority figures (i.e., not wanting to appear dependent on or controlled by adults) and the need to fit in within the new peer collective in the new school environment can help us better understand the increased importance of peers. Although each of these factors can be considered as a step toward total independence or autonomy, we presume that these factors depict more of a need to develop a new social identity. Specifically, we expect that the contrasts between adult authority and peers reflect distinctions made between "us" and "them" (Harris, 1995). Thus, the development of social identity and in-group and out-group distinctions are integrally related.

SOCIAL IDENTITY DEVELOPMENT AND POLARIZATION OF IN-GROUPS AND OUT-GROUPS

Self-categorization theorists (e.g., Turner, 1982; Turner, Oakes, Haslam, & McGarty, 1994) maintain that social identities contribute to categorization of groups into in-groups and out-groups (cf. "us" and "them"). Whereas in-groups are favored, the out-groups are more likely to be negatively stereotyped (Tajfel & Turner, 1979). At times, the mere recognition of out-groups can increase the cohesiveness of the in-group.

We argue that for middle school students, the most basic group distinction pertains to defining peers separate from adults. The polarization of perceived values between these two groups therefore reinforces the distinction between peers and teachers. For example, the interviews of the sixth graders at Fernwood revealed that most students believed that the determinants of teacher and peer approval were in conflict. Much of this discussion involved the notion of coolness, a proxy for desirable peer group values, in relation to teacher expectations.

> Interviewer: Is it cool to talk back to a teacher in class?
> Thomas: [laughs] No. It affects your grade.
> Nate: No. It lowers it.
> Interviewer: But what do the other kids think when you do it?
> Thomas: They think it's cool.

Thus, the effects of "talking back" are perceived to have the opposite effects for teacher approval and peer group acceptance. We maintain that such a contrast between adults and peers underscores the distinction and distance between the two groups. Furthermore, it seems that by engaging in public behaviors that conflict with the perceived values of adult authority, the sixth-grade students stress (a) their independence from adult control and (b) their alliance with peers (i.e., the in-group).

Based on the observations and interviews at Fernwood, it was clear that students who act in ways that please the teachers run the risk of being called a teacher's pet—a socially detrimental label within the peer collective. The following excerpt partly speaks to the shift in loyalties between teachers and peers across elementary and middle school grades.

> Interviewer: What's so bad about being a teacher's pet?
>   Julia: Because you're always sucking up to a teacher. You're always helping her. You're always staying after or you're always doing things to make her be glad, when other people are just doing what they're supposed to do and not more.
> Interviewer: Was it always bad to be a teacher's pet—was it bad in elementary school?
>   Julia: Fifth grade it was, and fourth. Third, second, first, kindergarten, it wasn't bad.
> Interviewer: Why? What's the difference?
>   Julia: Little kids don't think about it that much. They always get good grades because they like school. And then grade by grade you get more interested in being cool.

Consistent with the previously discussed experiments regarding self-presentation, Julia appears to believe that the determinants of a teacher's favoritism are in conflict with those that make one cool or popular in middle school, but that in the lower grades in elementary school these two social forces were not in conflict. Behaving badly in class and going against a teacher's wishes seems to boost students' social standing also in other cultures. Despite the preconceived notion of strict academic discipline displayed by Japanese youth, young adolescent behavior that tests the boundaries of teacher control in the classroom confers social status among peers (Fukuzawa & LeTendre, 2001).

It appears that young adolescents believe that they cannot publicly make alliances both with peers and with teachers, but have to choose one or the other. We interpret the perception of exclusive group membership to underscore the need to separate the peer collective from the most obvious out-group, that is, teachers and other authority figures. In his discussion of resistance to adult authority in a junior high school, Everhart (1983) concluded that while peers may fight in school, "The underlying and ongoing conflict between the student and the teacher, in many respects the two prime antagonists in the conflict arena, was more pervasive than the conflicts between students."

Although the need for peer approval appears to be strong and instrumental in reinforcing a new social identity, and although there may be an exaggerated need to view the world as adults versus peers, these factors still do not explain why youth behave in ways that are not consistent with their personal values. Are young teens so desperate for peer approval that they do whatever it takes? We think that the answer is somewhat more complex than this. Social psychological research on pluralistic ignorance, a phenomenon that accounts for misperceived values of in-group members, can help us explain why perceived values of peers might be a stronger motivator of public behavior than one's own private values.

PLURALISTIC IGNORANCE: MISPERCEIVED PEER GROUP VALUES

Although individuals recognize that that their own public behavior does not correspond with their private beliefs, they falsely assume that other individuals' public behavior reflects their private attitudes and values (Miller & Prentice, 1994a, 1994b). Because of this bias, they come to incorrectly view the collective norm as a reflection of the average of the private values of its group members (Miller & Prentice 1994a; 1994b). This phenomenon, labeled as pluralist ignorance, hence arises when "the facades that ... individuals present to one another are so effective that everyone is convinced of their authenticity. Pretence becomes reality" (Miller & Prentice, 1994b, p. 542). Although this is true also with adults, we regard pluralistic ignorance as one of the ultimate ironies of early adolescence because it is during this particular developmental phase when peer group values are perceived to be most different from one's private values (Cohen & Cohen, 1996).

Given that young adolescents are cognizant of the difference between their own values and those presumed of their peers, the question is how they deal with this difference. Theories of cognitive dissonance (e.g., Festinger & Carlsmith, 1959) suggest that individuals strive for a balance. In situations of imbalance, people have two choices: to either alter their attitudes (cf. values) or to change their behavior. We propose that most young adolescents, and especially those who are new to middle school, change their public behavior, not their private values. Thus, young sixth graders do not turn into "bad students" who value antisocial behaviors. Rather, they desire to fit in with the peer group by publicly acting consistently with their perceptions of the group values and norms of the collective.

Ironically, the perceived group values do not reflect the private values of the members of the group, but represent an illusion. Hence, the desire not to be considered as a teacher's pet and a desire to be perceived as cool by one's peers may result in defiant behavior, which in turn encourages this behavior among others—although no individual student necessarily values defiance. From their research on juvenile delinquents, Miller and Prentice (1994b) conclude that "the façade of toughness ... created 'a system of shared misunderstandings...,' which in turn, led to a level of antisocial behavior that no individual member fully embraced" (p. 543). This phenomenon has also been referred to in basic developmental research as well. For example, Berndt (1996) concluded that "adolescents often behave the way they perceive their friends as behaving. Unfortunately, adolescents often perceive their friends as engaging in socially undesirable behaviors (e.g., using drugs) more often than the friends actually do" (p. 79).

Misperceptions of peer group norms have indeed been of particular interest and concern to researchers who study adolescent drug use. It has been well documented that adolescents tend to overestimate substance use among their peers (e.g., Sussman et al., 1988), and that such overestimates predict their subsequent drug use (e.g., Collins et al., 1987; Graham, Marks, & Hansen, 1991; Marks, Graham, & Hansen, 1992). In light of these findings, increased accuracy of peer substance use is now considered an important component in drug-abuse prevention for young adolescents (e.g., Botvin & Willis, 1985; Ellickson, Bell, & McGuigan, 1993).

But how do the illusory group norms get formed? Group norms can be conveyed and inferred not only by the behaviors of the group majority, but also by the group's high status members. Based on the ethnographic data from Fernwood, it is clear that perceived peer group values often reflect those of the most popular peers, as these students are often the most vocal and visible in the school setting, even though they are, in actuality, a minority group. For example, highly salient cool kids may, for example, "broadcast" their wild party behaviors, or endorse slacking off in school and getting bad grades. These very public endorsements can then become the collective norm if there is an illusion of majority support (Miller & Prentice, 1994b). Illusion of majority support is created by no group member expressing contrary beliefs. We believe that this type of collective lack of resistance or silence is very typical in contexts where the youngest or most recent members need to establish their status within the new group. The following excerpt illustrates a more active form of peer support for behavior that challenges norms set by the school or instructors.

> Interviewer: Are some kids more popular than other kids in your grade?
>
> Patty: Yeah. People who are—if you're bad and you're funny then everybody likes you.
>
> ...
>
> Carolina: Yeah. Like students who make fun of the teacher or something and then everybody laughs.

By laughing at misbehaving class clowns, students support the values that conflict with conventional norms (i.e., to be respectful of teachers).

In sum, among young adolescents, the influence of popular kids—those with the highest status—is substantial. These students establish and maintain the social norms through their prestige, although privately their lower-ranking peers describe them as arrogant (e.g., Eder, 1985, 1995). In spite of the fact that the behaviors of the popular kids are not representative of the group as a whole, youth wish to emulate their behavior in order to promote their acceptance and inclusion in the high-status crowd. Or is it that they want to conform to demonstrate their alliance with the cool kids in order to avoid peer rejection?

DESIRE TO BE INCLUDED VERSUS FEAR OF EXCLUSION AS THE MOTIVE FOR CONFORMITY?

Thus far, we have presumed that the need to belong to and identify with the new peer collective is a strong motivator underlying conformity to perceived peer group norms. Although this may be the case for many young teens, there is an alternative motive as well. Conformity may result from a fear of exclusion. Exclusion can manifest itself in the majority of the group members rejecting a person or in the ridicule and abuse by few high status members of the collective. At Fernwood Middle School, it is evident that youth wish to be friends with popular students in order to increase their own status, but at the same time the popular students are considered "stuck up" and "mean," a paradox found in other studies of early adolescents (Adler & Adler, 1998; Canaan, 1987; Eder, 1985; Merten, 1996). Indeed, students with the highest status (i.e., the popular students) were often physically, verbally, and indirectly aggressive both with each other and with their peers. In spite of their "mean" behavior, less popular students wanted to wear what popular kids wore and act the way they believed popular kids thought was cool. Again, this finding does not seem to be limited to Western adolescents. Even among Japanese middle school youth, those students who make up the highest status level "are powerful, informal forces whose decisions and opinions prevail even if they are in the minority" (Fukuzawa & LeTendre, 2001, p. 49).

Thus, it seems that conforming behavior at times has more to do with avoidance of exclusion than with an explicit desire to be part of the popular crowd. Furthermore, when students talked about their interest in being popular, they often explicitly stated that being popular is beneficial because it protects an individual from open ridicule by other students, as suggested by the following excerpt.

> Interviewer: How important is it to be popular?
> Nate: Really, really. The most.
> Thomas: 'Cause if you're popular, nobody messes with you.

Harassment was a daily reality for many students, but certain students were harassed more than others. Being seen in any way different (e.g., a teacher's pet, or as child-like) led to ridicule at Fernwood Middle School. However, students who faced the most ridicule were those who had few, if any, friends. These students, "loners," faced rejection and abuse on a daily basis. All students were keenly aware that loners were ridiculed, and not surprisingly, most youth said that while it would be nice to be popular, what they really desire is to avoid being labeled a loner. Thus, the ultimate motive for peer group conformity was to avoid ridicule and exclusion.

SUMMARY

In this chapter, we have attempted to challenge the widely held view that the behavioral changes associated with the onset of adolescence are due to changes in young teens' values. We argue that public behaviors do not necessarily reflect private values and review various developmental and social psychological research findings that can help us understand this apparent contradiction.

Social psychological literature supports the idea that an individual's behavior is affected by one's own attitudes (cf. values) as well as significant others' expectations, behavior, and perceived attitudes. Developmental research, in turn, shows that young teens are not only cognizant of the fact that their values differ from those of others, but that they need to vary the way they present themselves to various parties to facilitate their social approval. During early adolescence, peer approval becomes especially salient to youth. Hence, the public behavior of middle school students seems to be motivated by their desire to behave in ways that are consistent with perceived peer group norms.

The heightened need for peer approval, paired with the need to be seen as less dependent on adults, typically coincide with a transition to a middle school. In middle school settings, where there is more of a need to create a social structure due to the relative lack of institutional structure as compared to elementary school, young teens are especially likely to come to sort their social world into "us" versus "them." Although this simple categorization between an in-group and an out-group helps youth master their expanding social world, it also fosters a peer culture that is incompatible or in conflict with the values endorsed by the most likely out-group—authority figures, such as teachers. Hence, the perceptions of peer group norms—which unfortunately fail to reflect the average values of the group—combined with their need to belong to and identify with a new peer collective, guide the way young teens publicly conduct themselves, often despite a contradiction with their private values.

Our analysis of the young adolescents' behavior being determined by perceived peer group norms pertains only to *public* behavior. The distinction between how youth conduct themselves in public places, such as in school versus in the privacy of their homes, is critical. We suspect that public behaviors are often guided by self-presentational concerns and that these behaviors do not necessarily reflect their own values or "true self" (Harter, 1993). Thus, the fact that young teens seem to be unmotivated to do well in school does not mean that they undervalue academics. Unfortunately, however, public behaviors affect how people treat a person. For example, it may be hard for a student with a reputation of a "slacker" to convince teachers that he indeed studies hard and tries to excel in school. Thus, in some cases, the social reputation that is created to boost peer popularity may become too real and inadvertently compromise the school career of a young teen.

In this chapter, we have focused our analyses on young teens who are acclimating to the new social environment of their middle school. We have depicted a rather homogeneous peer culture, one in contrast to the formal school culture endorsed by instructors. This portrayal is an oversimplification of the social structures and dynamics prevailing in middle school. However, we believe that social categorization begins with a dichotomous in-group–out-group distinction, which gets more complex over time. Both the social systems as well as youth's understanding of such systems get more complex later on in middle school, and by high school various peer crowds defined by a different set of attitudes, values, and behavior can be identified (Brown, 1993).

Taken together, we have argued that simply claiming that young teens are immoral and have questionable or antisocial values that contribute to their increasingly problematic behavior in school is missing a larger point. Rather than blaming teens, we should be asking ourselves whether these undesirable behavioral changes are inevitable or whether any of these social dynamics can be altered by changing middle school structures, policies, and practices to be more adolescent friendly. Could we, for example, create environments where teachers are not considered as an obvious out-group but as allies? Or could we manipulate the social dynamics so that young teens can come to believe that their peers value prosocial rather than antisocial values?

REDUCING REACTIVITY TO AUTHORITY-IMPOSED NORMS

To change the public behavior of young adolescents in middle school to be less "difficult" and more proachievement, one would need to change youngsters' perceptions of teachers as out-group members based on the analysis presented in this chapter. The goal should be to decrease the stark in-group–out-group distinctions (or the perceived polarization of values) between peers and adult authority figures or at least to diminish the out-group resentment that many middle school students feel toward school staff.

Based on ethnographic data, it is clear that adult authority elicits negative reactions from young adolescents because youth view authorities to control their behavior at a time when they seek to be less dependent on adults. Thus, there is a particularly poor match between the developmental needs of adolescents and their new school environment (Eccles & Midgley, 1990). It seems that authority control will in fact elicit resentment and rebellious responses, thereby contributing to the development of (rather than the reduction of) antisocial behavior. We suspect that this is most likely to happen in large schools where teachers do not know their students personally. In such settings, teachers are controlling because they think that is the only way to manage young adolescents, while young adolescents react to their high level of control by challenging the rules and regulations set by the school staff.

We contend that teaching young adolescents should be viewed more like parenting of young adolescents: behavioral control should be co-negotiated rather than dictated. As Steinberg (1993) states, "transformation of the relationship from one of unilateral authority to one of cooperative negotiation is necessary for the adolescent's social and psychological development to proceed on course…" (p. 265). If students have more input in the establishment of behavioral rules regarding their conduct, and if they can work together with their teachers, who know them, the need to view teachers as out-group members will probably be diminished. Teachers play an integral role in the moderating and shaping of rules and norms and by doing that, they can be perceived as less of an out-group member. Ability to negotiate with students and yet maintain ultimate control over the activities should be the goal of a middle school teacher. But would the less authoritarian teacher behavior also promote more prosocial and less antisocial social norms among students?

Although peer group norms seem to develop in part as a reaction to the heavy-handed authoritarianism prevalent in middle schools, this doesn't explain the unkind and harsh social interactions among students. The ethnographic data from Fernwood reveal that peer group norms are shaped in large part by the vocal and highly salient "cool" kids whose minority power is maintained, on one hand, by the misperceived group consensus or lack of resistance, and on the other hand, by the fear of exclusion or ridicule. Thus, the question is whether such in-group dynamics can be altered.

FOSTERING PROSOCIAL PEER GROUP NORMS

Just like the power of the adult authority, so should the power of dominant peers be diminished to create a more prosocial school environment. As a first step toward such a goal, young adolescents need a chance to step back and see what is happening within their peer collective. While some students are aware of the power dynamics involved, many of them have not necessarily thought about what factors contribute to the social dominance of the few. This can be best accomplished with discussion based on analyses of other places and people rather than one's own school.

Social awareness or empathy training using real-life examples has been successfully implemented in the context of comprehensive, school-wide anti-harassment programs developed in Scandinavian countries (e.g., Olweus, 1993). The goal of these programs is to reduce bullying by changing the prevailing norms that support and maintain dominance by the means of hostility. Youth are shown videotapes of typical peer harassment incidents where one of two bullies can be identified harassing one particular victim. The videos depict all of the situations in ways that highlight the role of bystanders or what might be called the "silent minority." The role of the subtle support and the lack of resistance of the larger peer group in maintaining and reinforcing bullying behaviors by the few dominant individuals become very apparent. The scenarios provide a safe and an engaging context for discussion of the topic that otherwise might be too sensitive, abstract, or difficult to engage in. Furthermore, the public recognition of the problem of harassment provides an impetus for change. In addition, the goal to resist the power of bullies must be supported by school staff who portray themselves not as the adult authority who regulate students' behavior, but as allies who help youth defend their own rights as well as other people's rights to fear-free schooling.

FINAL CONCLUSION

We conclude our analysis of the public behavior of young adolescents by providing two concrete ways in which behavioral changes could be moderated. Environments in which young teens feel that they are listened to and cared about—not merely controlled—and environments where social interactions are part of the explicit curriculum (i.e., topic of common discussion) should alleviate the need to appear tougher and rougher than one is. These changes involve reduction of the distinctions between the most salient in-groups and out-groups (i.e., peers vs. teachers) and reduction of in-group social hierarchies. We hope that our analyses of the behavior, and possible behavior change, of middle school youth convey how much educators could benefit from learning about research and how important it is for researchers to convey their knowledge to teachers and school administrators to help them see alternative explanations underlying the challenging behaviors of young teens.

REFERENCES

Adler, P. A., & Adler, P. (1998). *Peer power: Preadolescent culture and identity.* New Brunswick, NJ: Rutgers University Press.

Ajzen, I., & Fishbein, M. (1980). *Understanding attitudes and predicting social behavior.* Englewood Cliffs, NJ: Prentice-Hall.

Allen, J. P., Weissberg, R. P., & Hawkins, J. A. (1989). The relation between values and social competence in early adolescence. *Developmental Psychology, 25,* 458–464.

Alpert, B. (1991). Students' resistance in the classroom. *Anthropology and Education Quarterly, 22,* 350–366.

Alvarez, A. A. (1993). *An ethnographic study of student resistance in a predominantly Chicano public school.* Unpublished doctoral dissertation, University of California, Los Angeles.

Bandura, A. (1977). *Social learning theory.* Englewood Cliffs, NJ: Prentice-Hall.

Berndt, T. J. (1979). Developmental changes in conformity to peers and parents. *Developmental Psychology, 15,* 608–616.

Berndt, T. J. (1996). Transitions in friendship and friends' influence. In J.A. Graber, J. Brooks-Gunn, et al. (Eds.), *Transitions through adolescence: Interpersonal domains and context* (pp. 57–84). Hillsdale, NJ: Erlbaum.

Blum, R.W., Beuhring, T., Rinehart, P. M., (2000). *Protecting teens: Beyond race, income, and family structure.* Center for Adolescent Health, University of Minnesota.

Botvin, G. J., & Wills, T. A. (1985). Personal and social skills training: Cognitive-behavioral approaches to substance abuse prevention. *NIDA Research Monograph Series 63.*

Brown, B. B. (1993). Peer groups and peer cultures. In S. S. Feldman & G. R. Elliott (Eds.), *At the threshold: The developing adolescent* (pp. 171–198). Cambridge, MA: Harvard University Press.

Buhrmester, D. (1996). Need fulfillment, interpersonal competence, and the developmental contexts of early adolescent friendship. In W.M. Bukowski, A.F. Newcomb, et al. (Eds.), *The company they keep: Friendship in childhood and adolescence* (pp. 158–185). New York: Cambridge University Press.

Cadigan, R. J. (2002). *An ethnographic study of peer culture and harassment in an urban middle school.* Unpublished doctoral dissertation, University of California, Los Angeles.

Canaan, J. (1987). A comparative analysis of American suburban middle class, middle school, and high school teenage cliques. In G. Spindler & L. Spindler (Eds.), *Interpretive ethnography of education: At home and abroad* (pp. 385–406). Hillsdale, NJ: Erlbaum.

Clasen, D. R., & Brown, B. B. (1985). The multidimensionality of peer pressure in adolescence. *Journal of Youth and Adolescence, 14*, 451–468.

Cohen, P., & Cohen, J. (1996). *Life values and adolescent mental health.* Mahwah, NJ: Erlbaum.

Coleman, J. C. (1974). *Relationships in adolescence.* London: Routledge & Kegan Paul.

Collins, L. M., Sussman, S., Rauch, J. M., Dent, C. W., Johnson, C. A., Hansen, W. B., & Flay, B. R. (1987). Psychosocial predictors of young adolescent cigarette smoking: A sixteen-month, three-wave longitudinal study. *Journal of Applied Social Psychology, 17*, 554–573.

Connolly, J., & Goldberg, A. (1999). Romantic relationships in adolescence: The role of friends and peers in their emergence and development. In W. Furman, B. Bradford Brown, & Feiring (Eds.), *The development of romantic relationships in adolescence* (pp. 266–290). Cambridge, UK: Cambridge University Press.

Eagly, A. H., & Chaiken, S. (1993). *The psychology of attitudes.* Forth Worth, TX: Harcourt Brace Jovanovich.

Eccles, J. S., & Midgley, C. (1990). Changes in academic motivation and self-perception during early adolescence. In R. Montemayor & G.R. Adams (Eds.), *From childhood to adolescence: A transitional period?* (pp. 134–155). Thousand Oaks, CA: Sage.

Eder, D. (1985). The cycle of popularity: Interpersonal relations among female adolescents. *Sociology of Education, 58*, 154–165.

Eder, D. (1995). *School talk: Gender and adolescent school culture.* Mahwah, NJ: Erlbaum.

Ellickson, P. L., Bell, R. M., & McGuigan, K. (1993). Preventing adolescent drug use: Long-term results of a junior high program. *American Journal of Public Health, 83*, 856–861.

Everhart, R. B. (1983). *Reading, writing and resistance: Adolescence and labor in a junior high school.* Boston: Routledge & Kegan Paul.

Festinger, L., & Carlsmith, J. M. (1959). Cognitive consequences of forced compliance. *Journal of Abnormal and Social Psychology, 58*, 203–210.

Fine, G. A. (1981). Friends, impression management, and preadolescent behavior. In S. R. Asher & J. M. Gottman (Eds.), *The development of children's friendships* (pp. 29–52). Cambridge, UK: Cambridge University Press.

Fishbein, M., & Ajzen, I. (1975). *Belief, attitude, intention, and behavior: An introduction to theory and research.* Reading, MA: Addison-Wesley.

Fukuzawa, R. E., & LeTendre, G. K. (2001). *Intense years: How Japanese adolescents balance school, family, and friends.* New York: RoutledgeFalmer.

Gavin, L. A., & Furman, W. (1989). Age differences in adolescents' perceptions of their peer groups. *Developmental Psychology, 25*, 827–834.

Graham, J. W., Marks, G., & Hansen, W. B. (1991). Social influence processes affecting adolescent substance use. *Journal of Applied Psychology, 76*, 291–298.

Grube, J. W., Morgan, M., & McGree, S. T. (1986). Attitudes and normative beliefs as predictors of smoking intentions and behaviours: A test of three models. *British Journal of Social Psychology, 25*, 81–93.

Harris, J. R. (1995). Where is the child's environment? A group socialization theory of development. *Psychological Review, 102*, 458–489.

Harter, S. (1993). Self and identity development. In S. S. Feldman & G. R. Elliott (Eds.), *At the threshold: The developing adolescent* (pp. 352–387). Cambridge, MA: Harvard University Press.

Juvonen, J., & Murdock, T. B. (1993). How to promote social approval: Effects of audience and achievement outcome on publicly communicated attributions. *Journal of Educational Psychology, 85,* 365–376.

Juvonen, J., & Murdock, T.B. (1995). Grade-level differences in the social value of effort: Implications for self-presentation tactics of early adolescents. *Child Development, 66,* 1694–1705.

Marks, G., Graham, J. W., & Hansen, W. B. (1992). Social projection and social conformity in adolescent alcohol use. *Personality and Social Psychology Bulletin, 18,* 96–101.

McLaren, P. (1986). *Schooling as a ritual performance: Towards a political economy of educational symbols and gestures.* London: Routledge & Kegan Paul.

Merten, D. E. (1996). Burnout as cheerleader: The cultural basis for prestige and privilege in junior high school. *Anthropology and Education Quarterly, 27,* 51–70.

Miller, D. T., & Prentice, D. A. (1994a). The self and the collective. *Personality and Social Psychology Bulletin, 20,* 451–453.

Miller, D. T., & Prentice, D. A. (1994b). Collective errors and errors about the collective. *Personality and Social Psychology Bulletin, 20,* 541–550.

Olweus, D. (1993). *Bullying at school: What we know and what we can do.* Oxford, UK: Blackwell.

Savin-Williams, R. C., & Berndt, T. J. (1993). Friendship and peer relations. In S. S. Feldman & G. R. Elliott (Eds.), *At the threshold: The developing adolescent* (pp. 277–307). Cambridge, MA: Harvard University Press.

Sussman, S., Dent, C. W., Mestel-Rauch, J., Johnson, C. A., Hansen, W. B., & Flay, B. R. (1988). Adolescent nonsmokers, triers, and regular smokers' estimates of cigarette smoking prevalence: When do overestimations occur and by whom? *Journal of Applied Psychology, 18,* 537–551.

Steinberg, L. (1993). Autonomy, conflict, and harmony in the family relationships. In S. S. Feldman & G. R. Elliott (Eds.), *At the threshold: The developing adolescent* (pp. 255–276). Cambridge, MA: Harvard University Press.

Steinberg, L., Dornbusch, S. M., & Brown, B. B. (1992). Ethnic differences in adolescent achievement: An ecological perspective. *American Psychologist, 47,* 723–729.

Tajfel, H., & Turner, J. C. (1979). An integrative theory of intergroup conflict. In W. G. Austin & S. Worchel (Eds.), *The social psychology of intergroup relations* (pp. 33–147). Pacific Grove, CA: Brooks/Cole.

Terry, D. J., & Hogg, M. A. (1996). Group norms and the attitude–behavior relationship: A role for group identification. *Personality and Social Psychology Bulletin, 22,* 776–793.

Turner, J. C. (1982). Towards a cognitive redefinition of the social group. In H. Tajfel (Ed.), *Social identity and intergroup relations* (pp.15–40). Cambridge, UK: Cambridge University Press.

Turner, J. C., Oakes, P. J., Haslam, S. A., & McGarty, C. (1994). Self and collective: cognition and social context. *Personality and Social Psychology Bulletin, 20,* 454–463.

White, K. M., Terry, D. J., & Hogg, M. A. (1994). Safer sex behavior: The role of attitudes, norms and control factors. *Journal of Applied Social Psychology, 24,* 2164–2192.

Willis, P. (1981). *Learning to labour: How working class kids get working class jobs.* New York: Columbia University Press.

Youniss, J., & Smollar, J. (1985). *Adolescents' relations with mothers, fathers, and friends.* Chicago: University of Chicago Press.

CHAPTER 11

THE DEVELOPMENT AND CONSEQUENCES OF STEREOTYPE VULNERABILITY IN ADOLESCENTS

Joshua Aronson
New York University
Catherine Good
Columbia University

Adolescence is often described as time of storm and stress. It is described this way by parents, teachers, the popular media, and by adolescents themselves. These accounts arise, in part, from the salience, intensity, and rapidity of the cognitive, social, and physical changes associated with this period in life. It is during adolescence, after all, when one is most likely to experience acne, depression, eating disorders, and thoughts of suicide (Birmaher, Ryan, Williamson, Brent, & Kaufman, 1996; Condit, 1990; Larson & Ham, 1993; Rutter & Garmezy, 1983). Research suggests the turmoil associated with adolescence is, to some degree, exaggerated (e.g., Holmbeck & Hill, 1988; Males, 1996). Yet it is quite clear that adolescents face many difficult challenges, arising not only from maturational changes but also from transitions to new and more difficult environments. Many such challenges have consequences for academic achievement. In this chapter we discuss what research findings suggest is a significant factor for minority adolescents and girls in many situations—contending with stereotypes that allege some sort of intellectual or academic inferiority.

During adolescence, students become increasingly vulnerable to academic underperformance caused by negative cognitive, behavioral, and emotional reactions to awareness of ability impugning stereotypes about one's group, a phenomenon known as "stereotype threat." By the time individuals reach late adolescence (ages 18 to 21), ability-related stereotypes, such as those about African American's intellectual skills and females' math skills, become meaningful enough to disrupt performance on standardized tests. The existing research—much of which is preliminary—suggests that stereotype-related underperformance can occur quite early in development. Yet it is during adolescence that it is seen most clearly, acutely, and consistently. This is due both to the development of social-cognitive and metacognitive abilities that occur during adolescence, coupled with the social climate that begins when young adolescents transition to middle or junior high school. These factors combine, we believe, to create an environment of unnerving expectations that for many minority students has long-term consequences for their educational outcomes and contribute to a depressing trend of underachievement for women in math and science domains, and for blacks and Latinos across the academic board. We turn now to a description of this trend.

ACADEMIC ACHIEVEMENT OF MINORITIES AND FEMALE STUDENTS

The academic underperformance of black and Latino students and the underrepresentation of girls and women in mathematics and science domains are long-standing concerns among developmental psychologists and anyone concerned with educational inequities. Each year, fresh statistics from statewide and national tests and national surveys replicate the troubling pattern of underachievement noted for as long as records have been kept. For example, black students underperform on most measures of achievement from grade school through college. Compared to white and Asian students, black students receive lower grades, obtain lower scores on tests of reading, math, and science, and have higher dropout rates (Jencks & Phillips, 1998; National Center for Education Statistics, 2000). Although the black–white gap has narrowed since the 1970s, the average Black student still scores below 75% of white students on most standardized tests (Jencks & Phillips, 1998). Hispanic students fare somewhat better, but their test and school performance tends also to lag substantially behind that of white and Asian students (see Romo & Falbo, 1995). What is more troubling is that these disparities persist even after differences in socioeconomic factors are taken into account (Warren, 1996).

A similar yet distinct pattern exists for girls and young women in the areas of math and science. Although most studies find no gender gap in math performance until about Grade 8 (National Center for Education Statistics, 2000), girls' enjoyment and confidence in math tends to be measurably lower than boys' as early as elementary school—despite equal performance. Over time in school, the gender gap in confidence increasingly is accompanied by actual performance differences. For example, scores on the Third International Mathematics and Science Study (TIMSS), an achievement test given to half a million students in Grades 4, 8, and 12 in 41 nations, reveals a gender gap that widens with age; by Grade 12, boys significantly outscore girls. Behavioral changes also become more pronounced over time, with girls being significantly less likely than boys to enroll in the more advanced math and science courses (American Association of University Women, 1992, 1998). Furthermore, girls who do pursue an advanced math course are more likely to drop out before finishing the course (Hanson, 1996; Stumpf & Stanley, 1996). Results of this trend are quite clear at the graduate and professional levels, where women received only 22% of the mathematics doctorates and a mere 9% of mathematics professorships.

Much psychological and educational research has examined the various factors presumed to underlie these gaps. For example, researchers have identified specific sociological processes that impede the achievement of Black students (e.g., Jencks & Phillips, 1998), of Hispanic students (e.g., Romo & Falbo, 1995; Valencia, 1997), and of girls and women in math and science (e.g., Congressional Hearing, 1994; Eccles & Jacobs, 1992; Sadker & Sadker, 1994). Recent research in social psychology has suggested the operation of a more general process that may systematically contribute to the underachievement of students in these groups (Aronson et al., 1999; Aronson, Quinn, & Spencer, 1998; Spencer, Steele, & Quinn, 1999; Steele, 1997; Steele & Aronson, 1995; Steele, Spencer, & Aronson, 2002). This research suggests that individuals suffer negative performance outcomes— lower test scores and less engagement with and less enjoyment of academics—because they are burdened by an uncomfortable awareness of cultural stereotypes impugning their intellectual and academic abilities. Steele and Aronson (1995) called this burden "stereotype threat," and established in their laboratory experiments with Black adolescents (college freshmen and sophomores) a link to substantial decrements in standardized test performance. Subsequent experimental work has established that stereotype threat also undermines the academic performance of students from low socioeconomic backgrounds (Croizet & Claire, 1998) and females in math (Inzlicht & Ben-Zeev, 2000; Spencer et al., 1999). The view emerging from this research is that underperformance occurs because stereotypes facilitate pejorative interpretations of failure or academic difficulty, suggesting low ability rather than surmountable challenges. This adds stress and self-doubt to the educational experience and uneasiness about not belonging in the academic arena. Ultimately, stereotype threat can undermine the degree to which students value academic achievement, an effect that appears to accumulate over time (Aronson et al., 2002; Osborne, 1995; Steele, 1997).

Researchers have learned much about the stereotype threat process as it affects adolescents in college (see Aronson, 2002; Steele et al., 2002, for reviews). Yet relatively little is known about the development of vulnerability to stereotype threat—when and under what conditions children and adolescents become meaningfully affected by ability-relevant stereotypes about the groups to which they belong. Although even young children are aware of and use stereotypes, the age that negative ability stereotypes influence performance has received little attention. Are children susceptible to negative stereotypes about their intellectual abilities? If so, at what age and under what circumstances does their awareness of negative ability stereotypes become disruptive to their achievement? Does the stereotype threat process work in the same way for children and early adolescents as it does for older adolescents?

STEREOTYPE THREAT IN LATE ADOLESCENCE

As Gordon Allport (1954) noted nearly 50 years ago, "one's reputation, whether true or false, cannot be hammered, hammered, hammered, into one's head without doing something to one's character" (p. 142). Although Allport was referring to the direct effects of stereotypes and prejudice on personality, research increasingly shows that stereotypes have consequences both for achievement and for academic self-concept. For example, the findings of Steele, Aronson, and their colleagues suggest that mere awareness of negative stereotypes in stereotype-relevant situations is sufficient to undermine the academic performance of individuals to whom the stereotype applies. Since the initial publication of studies on stereotype threat, researchers have examined many issues surrounding this important construct. For example, they have found that virtually any group to which ability stereotypes apply can experience stereotype threat. As noted, stereotype threat effects have been found among African American and Latino students, females on math tests, and students of low socioeconomic status on general achievement tests.

Researchers also have identified individual risk factors that increase one's vulnerability to stereotype threat—their "stereotype vulnerability" (Aronson, 2002). One clear factor—at least in laboratory research—is "domain identification," the degree to which one values achievement in a given academic domain as a personally defining construct. The higher the domain identification, the more one is bothered by implications of inferiority in that domain. And thus, underperformance due to stereotype-related stress is most pronounced for those who value and care about doing well in the stereotyped domain (Aronson et al., 1999; Aronson & Good, 2001). Other personal factors that influence stereotype vulnerability include racial or gender identification, expectations for being discriminated against, and beliefs about the nature of intelligence (see Aronson, 2002, for a review). These vulnerability factors, however, may be less influential than the situational factors that have been shown to induce stereotype threat—the evaluative scrutiny and racial or gender salience that arise in many academic situations.

Evaluative Scrutiny

Perhaps the most fundamental factor associated with vulnerability to stereotype threat is the predicament of having one's ability evaluated. Tests that purportedly measure intelligence create a situation in which low performance could indicate limited ability and thus verify the stereotype (Aronson et al., 1998; Steele & Aronson, 1995). Research has shown that under such "diagnostic" conditions, stereotyped individuals' performance suffers; under "nondiagnostic" conditions when ability evaluation is downplayed, their performance improves.

The classic example of how evaluative scrutiny undermines performance involves African American students solving verbal problems on a standardized test (Steele & Aronson, 1995). In these studies, African American and white college students took a difficult verbal test resembling the GRE under one of two conditions. Participants were told either that the test measured their intellectual abilities, or alternatively, that the test measured psychological processes involved in problem solving. Results showed that in the "diagnostic" condition, white participants outscored African Americans—a performance pattern resembling the SAT racial gap. However, in the "nondiagnostic" condition, the racial gap disappeared. In other words, African Americans performed far better when the threat of evaluation was lifted.

Steele and Aronson (1995) argued that the underperformance of African Americans occurred because stereotypes change the meaning and consequences of failure. All students face the risk of shame or discouragement if they perform poorly on a task. For stereotyped individuals, however, the normal risks of low performance that anyone feels taking a test escalate. A single failure on an evaluative task can raise the troubling possibility that the stereotype is true of one's self, or that it may appear to accurately characterize one's self in the eyes of others. Thus, although most people strive to do well on a diagnostic test, stereotyped individuals may become hypermotivated to perform well in order to disprove the stereotype (Aronson, 2002). This hypermotivated state appears to create an added level of stress and anxiety that inhibits the relaxed concentration optimal for high performance on complex cognitive tasks (Aronson, 2002; Osborne, 2001).

Steele and Aronson (1995) also found evidence to suggest that the diagnosticity of the exam aroused race-related and doubt-related thoughts among African Americans, presumably compounding their distraction and anxiety. In a similar study, Steele and Aronson manipulated test diagnosticity and then measured the cognitive activation of race-related constructs. African Americans in the diagnostic condition—that is, participants who thought they would have their abilities measured by an upcoming test—were more likely to be thinking about race. The specter of ability evaluation thus appears to be cognitively linked to racial stereotypes.

Group Identity Salience and Identification

Another significant situational precursor to stereotype threat is group identity salience: when one's stereotyped group status is made relevant or conspicuous by features of the situation. Such would be the case if a black student were taking a test in the presence of a group of white students, or if a female were asked to solve math problems in a male-dominated classroom. Steele and Aronson (1995) examined the effects of racial salience by having African American college students in one study indicate their race on a test booklet prior to taking a test. They found that merely asking participants to indicate their race on the test booklet (as is required by many official standardized tests) caused the anxiety of black students to increase and their test scores to drop, even though the test was presented as a nondiagnostic exercise.

Evaluative situations in which someone judges another person's competencies and abilities are understandably threatening for stereotyped individuals. And, as indicated by the study described above, any performance situation, explicitly evaluative or not, can disrupt performance if a person's stereotyped group membership is expressly brought to mind (Steele & Aronson, 1995). There is mounting evidence that identity salience can disrupt performance even when it is very subtly activated (Ambady, Shih, Kim, & Pittinsky, 2001; Shih, Pittinsky, & Ambady, 1999; Wheeler & Petty, in press). For example, Shih and her colleagues (1999) found that Asian females underperformed on a math test (relative to a control group) when their female identity had been subtly primed by a previously completed questionnaire. Interestingly, in a parallel condition in which the questionnaire primed their Asian identity, females performed *better* than did the control group, presumably because the Asian stereotype facilitates math performance. Thus, making one's stereotyped group membership salient (as in the Steele and Aronson study) can turn a nonevaluative performance situation into a threatening experience for stereotyped group members. But subtle activation of a stereotype can either impair or boost performance—without any detectable emotional reaction—depending on whether the stereotype predicts strength (e.g., Asians and math) or weakness (women in math) in a domain. These rather subtle stereotype effects, sometimes referred to as "stereotype susceptibility" effects (e.g., Ambady et al., 2001), are distinct from stereotype threat effects first identified by Steele and Aronson, in that they appear not to involve anxiety. Rather, they appear to be mediated by a simpler process, wherein one behaves automatically in line with a cognitively activated image (e.g., Bargh, Chen, & Burroughs, 1996; Wheeler & Petty, in press). As such, the performance deficits associated with susceptibility effects tend to be substantially smaller and occur significantly earlier in a child's development than stereotype threat effects—most likely because their operation seems to require little more than knowledge of stereotype content.

Importantly, the role of identity salience means that stereotype threat can arise in situations just by dint of a group's composition. Inzlicht and Ben-Zeev (2000) demonstrated that females taking a math test could experience stereotype threat due to the presence of a single male in a testing situation. In their study, the experimenters manipulated the gender composition of the groups taking a diagnostic math test. The three-person groups included three females, two females and one male, or one female and two males. Results showed that when females took an evaluative test without the presence of a male, their performance remained high. When even one male was introduced into the group, females' performance was impaired, and with every additional male, females' performance deteriorated proportionately. Inzlicht and Ben-Zeev argued that the male presence increased the salience of females' gender identities, and that the salient gender identities, in turn, evoked the negative stereotype about females' mathematics competencies. Thus, situations that increase the salience of one's racial or gender identity—either subtly or blatantly—can influence performance.

Some individuals appear to be more chronically vulnerable to stereotype threat for one of two reasons. For some, gender or ethnic identity remains at the forefront of their minds in almost any situation. These are people who feel deeply attached to their racial or gender group and highly identify with that aspect of their self. Preliminary research suggests that the more one is invested in one's racial or gender identity, the more one will be burdened by negative stereotypes suggesting limited ability (Schmader,

2002). A related vulnerability factor appears to be what Pinel (1999) calls "stigma consciousness," the chronic expectation that one will be discriminated against. For some individuals, past experience with or parental warnings about prejudice can breed a persistent vigilance, a cross-situational tendency to be on the lookout for bias (e.g., Hughes & Chen, 1999). Such individuals appear more likely to underperform in stereotype threat situations—that is, when their stigmatized status is activated (Brown et al., 2001). Both of these differences, either separately or in conjunction, can intensify the experience of stereotype threat.

To summarize, any person contending with negative stereotypes could potentially experience the debilitating effects of stereotype threat. And, as research shows, vulnerability to stereotype threat is most pronounced in situations that are evaluative or that direct conscious attention to one's stereotyped status. Importantly, these two conditions—evaluative scrutiny and identity salience—are characteristic of most testing environments in which adolescents find themselves, especially in high stakes situations such as Advanced Placement examinations, the SAT, the GRE, and so on. One's performance on these tests can have important implications for one's future in terms of college credit, scholarships, and school admissions. Furthermore, group salience is endemic to the testing situation, not only because students often indicate their race and gender prior to taking the test, but also because minority and female students take the tests in the presence of white students and males. It is these tests—those that hold the key to future opportunity—that not only show the greatest gaps in achievement between stereotyped and nonstereotyped students, but also contain the very variables so strongly related to stereotype threat, evaluative scrutiny, and identity salience.

THE DEVELOPMENT OF STEREOTYPE VULNERABILITY

That stereotype threat can affect academic achievement in late adolescence is clear. As researchers continue to study the phenomenon, they have gained greater understanding of the personal and situational factors that moderate stereotype threat, the processes that mediate it, and some useful tactics for reducing its impact on performance and engagement (see Aronson, 2002). This knowledge can serve as a useful guide in thinking about the development of stereotype vulnerability in younger adolescents, something that researchers have only begun to examine. When and under what conditions will young adolescents experience extra anxiety on evaluative tasks as a function of their stereotyped-group membership? It seems reasonable to assume that children must achieve a certain level of developmental maturity to be meaningfully affected by stereotypes about their group. Current knowledge suggests the following as necessary conditions: awareness of ethnic stereotyping, a sufficiently developed ethnic or gender identity, a well-formed conception of academic ability, and the cognitive skill necessary to consider and fully comprehend the implications that negative stereotypes have. The developmental literatures devoted to these constructs suggests the ages of 11 or 12 as a reasonable period to expect to see stereotype vulnerability in children, to see explicit evaluation of ability result in extra stress and apprehension among members of groups alleged to lack some intellectual ability.

The Development of Sex Stereotyping in Children

Stereotype Knowledge

The developmental literature on sex stereotyping in children suggests that children exhibit knowledge of gender stereotypes at a very early age. By the age of 2, children reliably discriminate between boys and girls (Huston, 1987). As their awareness of separate genders forms, so too does their gender-related knowledge and attitudes. For example, some research shows children expressing knowledge of sex-related stereotypes as early as 2 years old and, as children mature, their stereotype knowledge increases, plateauing by Grade 4, when their gender stereotypes resemble those of adults (Nadelman, 1974; Reiss & Wright, 1982; Ruble & Martin, 1998; Williams, Bennett, & Best, 1975).

Sex Stereotyping

Children also are able to apply stereotype knowledge at an early age. As preschool children grow and develop, their thinking about boys and girls becomes increasingly influenced by gender stereotypes (Signorella, Bigler, & Liben, 1993). For example, by age 5 or 6, both boys and girls make stereotype-consistent associations between personality traits and a doll's gender (Albert & Porter, 1983), and they judge boys and men as taller than girls and women (Biernat, 1993). Children at this age also express vocational aspirations rigidly aligned with societal sex stereotypes (Garrett, Ein, & Tremaine, 1977). During the elementary school years, however, gender stereotypes begin to become more flexibly applied in that older children make less stereotypical judgments than do younger children (Signorella et al., 1993). In sum, young children develop knowledge of gender stereotypes and, through ages 8 or 9, rigidly apply them. Although sex stereotyping plateaus and begins to become more flexible between the ages of 9 and 11, adolescence heralds an increase in social pressures to behave in gender-stereotypic ways (Alfieri, Ruble, & Higgins, 1996; Crouter, Manke, & McHale, 1995; Huston & Alvarez, 1990; Katz & Ksansnak, 1994).

Sex Stereotyping of Academic Abilities

Much of the research on sex stereotyping focuses on vocational beliefs (such as whether girls can be a firefighter versus a nurse), physical differences (such as height), and personality traits (such as aggressive or passive). Some sex stereotypes, however, refer more specifically to academic domains such as science and mathematics. Do these stereotypes develop in a fashion similar to the development of stereotypes about personality traits? Are children's stereotypic beliefs about math and science related to their achievement in those domains? There is some evidence that as early as age 6, math performance appears to be more relevant to the self-concept of boys than of girls (Entwisle, Alexander, Cardigan, & Pallas, 1987). Moreover, girls at this early age begin to believe that boys are better at math (Lummis & Stevenson, 1990). This early endorsement of the gender stereotype gathers force as students progress through schooling; by age 11, boys are more likely than are girls to see science as suitable for boys but not girls (Kelly & Smail, 1986) and to see math as a male domain (Fennema & Sherman, 1977).

These stereotypic beliefs have some consequences for performance, though the research often is contradictory. Although simple knowledge of sex stereotypes in general is not associated with performance on a spatial test for children in Grades 5 through 7 (Nash, 1975), endorsement of the math and science stereotype is. There is, moreover, some evidence to suggest that "sex-typed" girls, whose personalities, preferences, or behaviors resemble the traditional gender stereotype, perform less well on tests of science knowledge, spatial visualization, and mechanical reasoning, even after controlling for prior ability (Dwyer, 1974; Kelly & Smail, 1986). Conversely, girls who see themselves as more masculine perform better on spatial tasks (Nash, 1975). Thus, some research suggests that girls who endorse gender stereotypes about academic abilities or behave in stereotypical ways also perform less well on math and science tasks. Other research finds that endorsement of the gender stereotype does not affect math achievement, that girls' perception of math as a male domain is not strongly associated with math achievement (Sherman & Fennema, 1978). Thus, the picture is far from clear, pointing to a need for more research on gender stereotyping and mathematics-related performance among girls.

The Development of Racial Stereotyping in Children

The developmental literature paints a similar picture of racial stereotyping. Aboud's (1988) review of over 20 years of research in the field concludes that children demonstrate ethnic and racial awareness as young as 3 to 4 years of age. Furthermore, this work suggests that as children become aware of group differences, social attitudes begin to form about members of different ethnic groups.

Racial and ethnic awareness. Research findings show that children are able to identify people of different races at a very early age, usually between ages 3 and 5 (Aboud, 1988; Hirschfeld, 1996), and begin to accurately identify their own ethnicity as well (Aboud, 1988). This ethnic awareness increases from ages 4 to 6 or 7, at which time white children become almost 100% accurate at identifying their own ethnicity. Although slightly fewer black and Hispanic children can accurately identify their own ethnicity at age 4, these students also reach almost 100% accuracy in their ethnic self-awareness by the age of 6 or 7. Although almost all children can accurately identify their own and other's race by age 6, the concept of ethnic constancy does not develop until the ages of 8 or 9. For example, before this time, many children believe that one can easily change one's race through exposure to sunlight or even by changing one's clothes. It is not until around the ages of 8 or 9 that children become aware that ethnicity is a more internal, stable construct (Aboud, 1988). Although children become aware of skin color at a very young age, they do not yet understand that it will place them in a particular racial group (Semaj, 1985).

Racial and ethnic stereotyping. At the same time that ethnic awareness begins to develop, children begin to acquire attitudes toward their own and other racial groups (Aboud, 1988). For example, by the age of 3, white children display negative attitudes toward black children. These initial prejudicial attitudes become considerably more prevalent among 4 year olds and continue to increase through age 7. Negative attitudes toward black children are typically expressed as the black child being judged as "bad," as having negative qualities, or as being rated as the least preferred classmate. In addition to the negative attitudes they express toward other ethnic groups, white children also show a very strong preference for their own group from a very early age—around the age of 3 or 4.

Black and Hispanic students demonstrate ethnic awareness and attitudes by about the same age as do white students—around age 4 (Asher & Allen, 1969; Kircher & Furby, 1971). However, whereas white students exhibit bias toward other ethnic groups and a preference for their own group by the age of 3 or 4, the pattern of in-group attachment and out-group rejection is not found in black and Hispanic students until age 7 (Aboud, 1988). Until that time, many black and Hispanic students are initially more negative to their own ethnic group.

In addition, children at a very young age exhibit knowledge of racial stereotypes. For example, children as young as 5 years old are more likely to associate negative adjectives with pictures of black children and positive adjectives with pictures of white children (Augoustinos & Rosewarne, 2001). Around age 7 or 8, however, a fundamental shift occurs in both white and black students' ethnic attitudes, but not necessarily in their stereotype awareness. For example, children exhibit a decline in prejudicial attitudes, yet their knowledge of stereotypes remains high (Aboud, 1988; Augoustinos & Rosewarne, 2001).

Furthermore, the negative attitudes that white children express about other ethnic groups declines between the ages of 8 and 12, while at the same time the strong preference initially exhibited by white children for their own group begins to decrease. Although white children at this time continue to prefer their own group, the strength of this in-group attachment diminishes and at the same time, they become more positive toward other groups (Aboud & Mitchell, 1977). This trend continues through adolescence (Kalin, 1979). For black children, the negative attitudes initially expressed toward their own group begin to decrease around age 8. Furthermore, this in-group attachment that eventually develops does not moderate later in adolescence as it does with white children (Cross, 1980).

Aboud (1988) argues that the shift in attitudes evident around age 7 or 8 is attributable, in part, to the growth of cognitive flexibility and skill. However, the early bias exhibited by white children supports the notion that stereotypical attitudes and prejudice are rooted in children's memories even before they have the cognitive capacity to question them (Allport, 1954; Katz, 1976). It is not until children reach early adolescence that they become aware that racial and ethnic differences are linked to such things as social class and allocation of resources (Quintana, 1996). During late middle childhood and early adolescence, children begin to develop a more sophisticated understanding of social categories and to view them as meaningful constructs. This research is useful in helping us understand the age at which children become aware of racial groups and begin to form attitudes toward those groups, both of which may be important precursors to children's vulnerability to stereotype threat.

Identity Development

It is also important to consider developmental changes in how students think about their sense of self. Specifically, what significance does a child ascribe to being male or female, to being black or white? Although children may be aware of their sex and race at an early age, these constructs do not become an integrated part of their social identity until adolescence. As Tajfel and Turner's (1979, 1986) social identity theory contends, a person must internalize an identity and incorporate that identity into the self before significant hedonic consequences of group membership are felt. Applying this theory, simply being aware of one's racial or gender group membership should not predict vulnerability to stereotype threat. Similarly, the expression of stereotypical attitudes may not necessarily predict vulnerability, perhaps because early expressions of stereotypes may simply be a reflection of the prevalence of these stereotypes in society. Instead, a meaningful conception of one's identity that is integrated and coherent must be developed before stereotypes about one's group membership become capable of eliciting the anxiety associated with stereotype threat. Thus, researchers should consider the consequences of the development of one's social identity when investigating the age at which stereotype threat develops.

Prior to adolescence, one's identity is composed of disjointed pieces that have not been integrated (Harter, 1997). Not until adolescence does one have the mental capacity to integrate the various aspects that make up one's self and achieve a coherent sense of identity (Erikson, 1968; Livesley & Bromley, 1973). According to Erikson (1968), people enter a crisis of identity versus identity diffusion during adolescence. During this crisis, adolescents reflect on their place in society and on the ways that others view them. Because resolution of this conflict hinges on the adolescents' interactions with significant others and the reactions that others have to their actions, adolescents are more likely to be aware of other people's impressions of them (Elkind, 1967). Through the exploration of various behaviors, coupled with an increased awareness of and reflection on the consequences of those behaviors, adolescents develop a sense of who they are and what attributes they possess (Livesley & Bromley, 1973). Thus, identity formation is both a mental and a social process, resulting in the organization and integration of different aspects of their self-image into a logical, coherent whole (Harter, 1990; Marsh, 1989).

The development of ethnic identities is similar to identity development in general (Cross, 1978; Phinney, 1990). Adolescents move from a period of unquestioning acceptance of self to a crisis stage in which they attempt to understand their place within their racial or ethnic culture. Once the crisis has been resolved, individuals may experience a period of immersion in their ethnic group, preferring to associate predominantly with members of their own group and rejecting the white majority culture. Eventually, a coherent sense of personal identity emerges that includes an integrated sense of ethnic identity. Full integration of one's sense of ethnic identity with one's sense of personal identity typically occurs in late adolescence, although the process most likely begins earlier.

Gender is a critical component of one's social identity from an early age. Strong gender stereotypes prevail from childhood to adulthood and these stereotypes influence the development of one's gender identity early on. For example, although gender stereotypes become more flexible in adolescence, social forces pressure adolescents to behave in more gender-stereotypical terms (Alfieri et al., 1996).

Considering the developmental trends in gender and ethnic stereotyping, children could be vulnerable to stereotype threat as early as elementary school. As discussed previously, elementary school children have extensive knowledge of stereotypes and may actually buy into their negative messages. But although simple knowledge of stereotypes may be sufficient to influence performance via stereotype susceptibility, it does not appear to be the case that children experience stereotype-induced performance anxiety. As findings on identity formation suggest, for example, elementary school children may not have formed the coherent sense of self that is necessary for stereotypes to become personally meaningful. Thus, elementary school may be too early a time to anticipate the emergence of stereotype threat. Alternatively, the research on identity formation suggests that students may not be vulnerable to stereotype threat until adolescence. Theories of identity development imply that it is during adolescence that people become more aware of and attend more fully to others' impressions of them (Elkind, 1967). Because of this heightened concern about what others think that emerges in early adolescence, we believe that children at early adolescence may be more susceptible to stereotype threat than younger children.

The Development of Ability Conceptions

Because the problematic stereotypes refer specifically to cognitive abilities, it is reasonable to assume that children must develop a meaningful conception of ability to be bothered by the stereotype's ability-impugning messages. It is likely that they also must develop more advanced cognitive skills in order to process the social implications of the stereotype. As with the development of sex-stereotyping, children's conceptions about ability follow a developmental pattern. Ability conceptions develop throughout childhood, and, as Dweck (2002) argues, coalesce around Grade 5 into a meaningful framework that affects students' achievement motivation. In general, young children do not seem to have a coherent conception of ability. For example, young children maintain high perceptions of their competence despite actual performance (Stipek & Hoffman, 1980a, 1980b). Moreover, they are relatively unaffected by failure feedback. For example, after receiving failure feedback on a task, young children maintain high expectations for future achievement (Parsons & Ruble, 1972, 1977). Thus, young children appear to be blissfully resilient to the negative expectations that low performance often evokes. As children progress through school, however, this changes. Self-ratings of ability decline markedly—perhaps a reflection of their more accurate self-assessments (Stipek & Hoffman, 1980a, 1980b)—and they become increasingly responsive to failure and negative feedback (Eccles, 1984). Furthermore, perceptions of ability begin to become increasingly global and stable (Dweck & Elliott,

1983; Pomerantz & Ruble, 1997; Rholes & Ruble, 1984). For example, older children who experience failure on a specific task are more likely to view the failure feedback as indicative of their overall abilities, and they are more likely to use failure feedback as a predictor of their future success. An important change in ability conceptions occurs for 7- to 8-year-olds. Here, children's definitions of ability take shape and begin to influence the way they use ability information (Dweck, 2002). In the early years, although children do not infer future ability from current performance levels (Parsons & Ruble, 1972, 1977), they do associate ability with global ideas of goodness and badness. For example, they tend to associate success on a task with being a "good child" and failure with being a "bad child." By the time they are age 7 or 8, they begin to distinguish ability from social-moral qualities (Stipek & Daniels, 1990). Furthermore, at these ages, children change their ability definitions from more personal and mastery to more normative and based on social comparison (Frey & Ruble, 1985). That is, they rely more on social comparison information—on how well their peers are doing—to infer their own ability, and they begin to define smartness as outperforming others (see Ruble, Boggiano, Feldman, & Loebl, 1980.

Children's changing definitions of ability also affect the way they use information regarding their abilities. For example, they are more likely than are younger children to use success and failure feedback to assess their ability (Frey & Ruble, 1985; Ruble, 1987). In addition, 7- to 8-year-olds become less positive yet more accurate about their abilities (Wigfield & Eccles, 2000). This decline in unrealistic optimism may be due to their increased sensitivity to performance feedback. These changes continue until children become age 10 or 12, at which point they continue the trend of lower self-ratings of ability, higher accuracy in rating ability, and higher belief in the predictive power of performance feedback (Benenson & Dweck, 1986; Cain & Dweck, 1989; Nicholls & Miller, 1984; Ruble et al., 1980). Moreover, children at this time increasingly believe in ability as a stable trait and less in the effectiveness of effort to increase ability (Dweck & Sorich, 1999). Furthermore, these effort beliefs in turn begin to affect ability conceptions. For example, children age 10 to 12 are more likely than are younger children to agree that, given equal performance, less effort implies higher ability (Nicholls & Miller, 1984; Pomerantz & Ruble, 1997).

Although at first glance it may appear that ability conceptions do not change much between childhood and early adolescence, significant differences do exist. Most importantly, 10- to 12-year-olds exhibit a greater coherence of ability beliefs than do younger children, for whom ability conceptions appear to be a series of isolated beliefs with little relation to one another (Dweck, 2002). By the time children reach early adolescence, ability beliefs begin to affect other aspects of achievement. For example, whereas young children who admit they are poor at something will not devalue the task, early adolescents begin to devalue domains in which they have low perceived competence (Wigfield, Eccles, Yoon, & Harold, 1997).

For children at this stage, moreover, competence perceptions begin to predict attributions for success and failure. Children with high perceived competence tend to attribute their successes to high ability rather than luck or effort, and their failures to bad luck rather than low ability (Nicholls, 1979). Furthermore, older children's perceptions of ability as a relatively stable trait begin to predict a host of maladaptive beliefs. In particular, students at this age who believe that intelligence is a fixed trait also tend to believe that high effort implies low ability and that effort is an ineffective route to increased ability (Dweck & Sorich, 1999). In general, a stable view of intelligence relates to a belief system focused on traits rather than on effort. Although some young children may adopt a fixed view of intelligence, this perspective does not predict impairment in the face of failure until early adolescence (Cain & Dweck, 1995; Pomerantz & Ruble, 1997).

In addition to their changing ability conceptions, early adolescents also are increasingly concerned with self-evaluation (Butler, 1989a, 1989b; Ruble & Flett, 1988) and increasingly use peer progress inquiries as a method of social comparison (Frey & Ruble, 1985; Pomerantz, Ruble, Frey, & Greulich, 1995). For example, although young students recognize that inquiring about their peers' progress can provide social comparison information, they do not engage in these behaviors until around Grade 5. By the fifth grade, approximately 80% of students report engaging in this type of behavior, whereas fourth graders seldom make these types of inquiries, despite their earlier awareness of its utility for social comparison purposes (Pomerantz et al., 1995).

Social-Cognitive and Metacognitive Development

Another important factor in predicting when children may become vulnerable to negative stereotypes is the developmental change in social-cognitive and metacognitive capabilities that occurs during adolescence. Prior to adolescence, children lack the cognitive skills necessary to think abstractly or to reflect on their own thinking—skills that may be necessary for negative stereotypes to be meaningfully disruptive to performance.

Compared to younger children, adolescents are more able to think about possibilities, to think about abstract concepts, and to think about thinking (Elkind, 1974; Flavell, 1977; Inhelder & Piaget, 1958; Piaget, 1972). For example, whereas young children's thinking is limited to concrete events, adolescents are more capable not only of generating alternative possibilities but also of reasoning systematically about the consequences of different events. Facility with hypothetical thinking and thinking about abstract concepts also increases during adolescence, which permits adolescents to apply advanced reasoning and logical processes to social and ideological issues (Flavell, 1977). In other words, they are more able to engage in "social cognition." In addition, adolescents are more capable than younger children of thinking about their own thinking—to engage in metacognition. For example, they are more introspective, in that they think more about their own emotions, and they are more self-conscious in that they think more about what others think about them (Lively & Bromley, 1973). It is during adolescence that people develop an increased concern for the "imaginary audience," the heightened sense of self-consciousness that one's behavior is the focus of everyone's concern and attention (Elkind, 1967; Goossens, Seiffge-Krenke, & Marcoen, 1992; Quadrel, Fischoff, & Davis, 1993).

These gains in social-cognitive and metacognitive abilities confer numerous benefits. Compared to younger children, adolescents are more able to understand abstract math problems such as the Pythagorean theorem, to play devil's advocate in a discussion, and to understand higher-order abstract constructs such as puns, metaphors, and proverbs. But the increased facility in these cognitive skills also carries some negative consequences. The increased ability to think about an abstract concept, such as a stereotype, implies that adolescents develop a greater understanding that stereotypes, and people's perceptions of them based on these stereotypes, may have meaningful implications in their own personal lives. Furthermore, adolescents' greater ability to think hypothetically sets the stage for them to worry about possible consequences of their behaviors. They are more capable of envisioning consequences of poor academic performance. Consequently, some children pay a price for the increased cognitive abilities that develop during adolescence. Although beneficial in many ways, these abilities may set the stage for stereotype vulnerability because they enable an understanding of a stereotype's meaning, hypothesizing about consequences of their behavior, and concerns about what other people think.

RESEARCH EVIDENCE

The confluence of these developmental factors map quite consistently onto the achievement literature. Early adolescence is precisely when girls begin to lose ground in math performance and when ethnic minorities experience increased decrements in academic achievement (e.g., Eccles et al., 1993; Eccles, Lord, & Midgley, 1991; Harter, Whitesell, & Kowalski, 1992; Rosenberg, 1986; Simmons & Blyth, 1987). Our own recent research suggests that stereotype threat may play a role in this pattern of underperformance. For example, employing the evaluative scrutiny paradigm pioneered by Steele and Aronson (1995), Good and Aronson (2002) tested students from Grades 4 through 6. Results were remarkably clear. On a test comparing girls' and boys' standardized test performance, evaluative scrutiny had no discernable effect on performance until Grade 6, at which it resulted in significantly lower math performance among the girls relative to the boys. There was no corresponding difference in reading performance. Because no differences were found on girls' reading test performance under evaluative versus nonevaluative conditions, the differences found on the math test likely resulted from stereotype threat and not a general evaluation threat. Interestingly, this corresponded precisely to girls' questionnaire ratings indicating worry about their future math performance; they indicated no worries prior to Grade 6.

An additional study revealed another dimension to this vulnerability. Students in Grades 4, 5, and 6 took grade-appropriate math and reading tests under stereotype threat or nonthreat conditions. Before they took the tests, however, they were told that they would be taking a second test of both math and reading, but on this second test, they would get to choose the difficulty level of the problems. We then offered them a choice of five different problem-difficulty levels for reading and math. The difficulty levels included very easy, kind of easy, right at their level, kind of hard, or very hard. Results showed a clear effect of the stereotype threat manipulation for sixth-grade girls: under the stereotype threat condition, they selected easier problems than did the boys. Under nonevaluative (no stereotype threat) conditions, girls chose more difficult problems than did boys. And, as in the previous study, there was no difference between boys and girls on the verbal problems or prior to Grade 6.[1]

This last study suggests that one strategy students use to cope with stereotype threat may be to arrange things to avoid or reduce the risk of confirming the stereotype. When there is a clear choice between easy tasks with a high probability of success and more difficult tasks with a greater chance of failure, stereotype threat may lead people to play it safe and avoid the challenge. Because challenge is required for intellectual growth and for developing the skills and abilities needed for future success, evaluative settings may actually impede *learning*—not just their performances—of stereotyped individuals. The accumulated effect of years of reduced opportunities to strengthen and grow one's capabilities may eventually lead to the very differences in performance to which the stereotype refers. We replicated this study with Latino and white students taking a verbal test and choosing the difficulty level of verbal tasks under threat or no-threat conditions. The results paralleled those found for girls in math: under evaluative scrutiny, Latino students selected easier tasks. As with the girls, this pattern emerged only among the Grade 6 students.

Other researchers have found what appear to be stereotype threat effects in children at levels lower than Grade 6, though in substantially different contexts. For example, McKown and Weinstein (2000) investigated stereotype threat in minority children (African Americans and Latinos) between the ages of 6 and 11. They found that the most important predictor of children's vulnerability to stereotype threat was not their age, but their ability to report their awareness of stereotypes operating in the real world. To measure this ability, the researchers told the children a story about an imaginary land comprised of two groups of people, Greens and Blues. Children are told that in this land Greens think Blues are not smart. Then the researchers asked the children to describe any similarities between the imaginary land and the real world. The children's responses—the number of similarities each reported—comprised the measure of their ability to report stereotypes. After this measure, the children participated in a stereotype threat experiment in which they wrote the alphabet backward in 45 seconds under either diagnostic or nondiagnostic conditions. In the diagnostic condition, they were told that the task would show how good they were at different types of school problems. Thus the task purportedly measured general academic ability.

Results of the study showed that, among students who were developmentally advanced enough to draw parallels between the stereotypes in the story and those in real life, evaluative scrutiny undermined minority students' performance. In the diagnostic condition, white students outperformed minority students; however, in the nondiagnostic condition, the performance pattern reversed and minority students outperformed white students, even when controlling for prior ability. Students who could not report stereotypes did not exhibit evidence of stereotype threat. Because the researchers did not analyze the data by age, no conclusions can be drawn about the age at which stereotype threat undermines performance. The researchers argued, however, and we agree, that the ability to understand how intelligence stereotypes can be used against people in the world is a more valid predictor of stereotype threat than age alone. They added that children who report stereotypes are vulnerable to stereotype threat because they are developmentally advanced enough not only to be aware of stereotypes—which occurs very early in children (Aboud, 1988)—but also to attend to and care about the meaning of stereotypes about their group. Still, it is not altogether clear from this intriguing research what was being tapped by McKown and Weinstein's measure of stereotype vulnerability.

A study by Ambady and colleagues (2001) suggests that stereotypes can influence cognitive performance even earlier than our discussion suggests.

In their experiments, Asian American girls between kindergarten and Grade 8 completed a stereotype activation task designed to evoke either their gender identity or their ethnic identity. A control group also participated but did not respond to any manipulations making their gender or ethnic identity salient. The younger participants (kindergarten through Grade 2) either colored a picture of a girl holding a doll or of two Chinese people eating with chopsticks. The older participants (Grades 3 through 8) either answered gender-related questions or ethnicity-related questions. Participants then took a difficult math test appropriate for their grade level.

Results from this study show an interesting pattern of stereotype susceptibility that depends on grade level. Girls in the early elementary (Grades K through 2) and middle school (Grades 6 through 8) had the highest accuracy on the math test when their ethnic identity was made salient and the lowest accuracy when their gender identity was made salient. Interestingly, girls in upper elementary (Grades 3 through 5) showed the reverse pattern: girls were more accurate when their gender identity was made salient than when their ethnic identity was made salient. It is instructive to note that these experiments find very small differences in actual test performance, presumably because the subtle activation of stereotypes tends not to arouse anxiety. Thus, although they demonstrate that knowledge of stereotype content can influence performance—either positively or negatively—the process is quite distinct from the typical stereotype threat finding, which involves measurable apprehensiveness and a desire to disprove the stereotype rather than an "automaticity" effect (see Wheeler & Petty, in press, for a discussion). Indeed, as a recent study with college students demonstrated, if one makes the connection between the identity and the performance explicit rather than implicit, the process changes—either identity (Asian or female) induces performance pressure and undermines performance (Cheryan & Bodenhausen, 2000). Thus, the Ambady and colleagues (2001) research appears not to involve threat. In our own research (Good & Aronson, 2002), explicitly making gender or ethnicity salient shows no evidence of affecting performance until Grade 6. We believe that some critical factors—such as those we have discussed—need to develop for ability evaluation or identity salience to induce anxiety among girls and minorities, and, for most children, these do not develop before early adolescence.

Interestingly, although identification with the stereotyped domain is an important predictor of older adolescents' vulnerability to stereotype threat (see Aronson et al., 1999), researchers have not yet demonstrated a clear relationship between academic identification and vulnerability to stereotype threat in younger children. Because the participants in Good and Aronson (2002) all strongly identified with academics in general and with math achievement, they could not investigate whether children with low academic identification were vulnerable to stereotype threat. To date, researchers have not measured children's identification with academics and used it to predict stereotype vulnerability. Because of the importance of this variable in older adolescents' vulnerability to stereotype threat, there is clearly a need for more research investigating the relationship between domain identification and stereotype vulnerability in children and young adolescents. Yet it is important to note that, although students who are highly identified with academics show the most vulnerability to stereotype threat, this relationship has only been revealed in laboratory conditions—a decidedly low stakes situation for all but the most identified with academics. Clearly there are situations in which less serious students may be vulnerable to underperformance (see Aronson et al., 1999).

The Changing Academic Context

We believe that by the time children reach early adolescence they are developmentally ready to experience stereotype threat. The transition to middle and junior high school capitalizes on this readiness, producing what we believe are significant manifestations of stereotype threat—a significant decline for many students, particularly girls in math and minority students more generally. Several studies tend to report significantly more problems—suspensions, low academic performance, conflicts with parents, and so on—among black and Latino students than among white students making the transition to junior high, or from one school to another (e.g., Felner, Primavera, & Cauce, 1981; Simmons, Black, & Zhou, 1991). Why might this be? One possible reason is the "stereotype climate" that we hypothesize is engendered and reinforced by the middle school setting and the developmental stage in question. The transition confronts many students who attend public schools with the most intensive—if not the first—contact with youngsters from diverse ethnic backgrounds. In most cases, this will not be the "equal status" contact considered essential to minimizing prejudice. Rather, black and Latino children, because they tend to come from poorer school districts, are likely to be academically behind their white counterparts by as much as two grade levels (Gerard, 1983). Such preexisting differences may be underscored by the "ability grouping" (e.g., "tracking") prevalent in many middle and junior high schools (Eccles et al., 1993), which tends to racially stratify the classrooms (Romo & Falbo, 1995). Furthermore, the middle school or junior high setting is likely to be more competitive than the grade school setting (Harter et al., 1992), which may further encourage overt and covert racial stereotyping (Aronson & Patnoe, 1997). Thus, the existing stereotypes (e.g., "Blacks are not as smart as whites") may be confirmed and intensified by the type of contact afforded by the middle school or junior high structure.

Students' vulnerability to the stereotype climate may be magnified by the fact that, relative to those of grade school, middle and junior high school contexts tend to place a higher premium on social comparison. Peers and peer evaluations become powerful influences, making "fitting in" a high priority (e.g., Harter, 1990; Spencer & Dornbusch, 1990). Because stereotype threat stems to a great extent from concern about how one is viewed by others (e.g., peers, teachers), it seems reasonable to assume that the threat may be particularly acute, and, at this stage of development, particularly damaging to the formation of a healthy academic self-image. Eccles and her colleagues (see Eccles et al., 1991, 1993) have argued that the classroom environment in junior high school is much different than that in elementary school and that this change in environment may cause difficulty for some students. Middle school and junior high classrooms are often larger and more impersonal than elementary school classrooms. Furthermore, Midgley, Berman, and Hicks (1995) argued that junior high teachers hold different beliefs about students than do elementary school teachers. For example, junior high teachers are less likely to trust their students and more likely to emphasize control and discipline in their classrooms. More importantly, junior high teachers are more likely to believe that their students' abilities are fixed and less likely to believe that students can increase their abilities through instruction. And, as research is beginning to show, teachers who believe in fixed versus acquirable ability differ in their pedagogical theories and practices. For example, teachers who see abilities as fixed tend to judge students' abilities by comparing them to those of other students rather than by observing personal improvement (Butler, 2000; Lee, 1996; Plaks, Stroessner, Dweck, & Sherman, 2001). These different methods of evaluation have important implications, for it has been found that students of math teachers who emphasize normative evaluation rather than individual progress over time (in line with fixed ability perspective) come to value math less over time (Anderman, Eccles, Yoon, Roeser, Wigfield, & Blumenfeld, 2001). Moreover, as will be discussed in the next section, stereotype threat is exacerbated for students performing in a fixed-ability context; that is when they believe that the abilities that are being evaluated are thought not to be expandable (see Aronson, 2002). Because adolescence is the period during which students become more sophisticated in their understanding of societal stereotypes, the fixed ability beliefs held by junior high teachers may be particularly disruptive for minority students and for females in math and science. This confluence of developmental and structural factors suggests that even if black, Latino, and female students graduate from elementary school feeling competent and enjoying school as much as their counterparts, they may become demoralized not long after entering.

Reducing Stereotype Threat: The Role of Implicit Theories of Intelligence

How can the impact of stereotype threat be reduced during the storm and stress of adolescence and the transition to stereotype threatening schooling contexts? In addition to studying factors involved in evoking a stereotype threat response, researchers have been investigating factors that protect people from stereotype threat's debilitating effects. One obvious approach would be to change the existing stereotypes themselves, or to construct educational or testing situations such that evaluation or the salience of race or gender is minimal. Unfortunately, such approaches are rarely feasible. First, as much research has shown, stereotypes doggedly resist change. And reducing evaluation and racial salience are, almost by definition, impossible in integrated testing centers or classrooms. Instead, recent stereotype threat research has focused on more realistic approaches, capitalizing on lessons learned from research in achievement motivation. In particular, Dweck and her colleagues (e.g., Dweck, 1986, 1999; Dweck & Leggett, 1988; Hong, Chiu, & Dweck, 1995) have shown that students' beliefs about intelligence strongly affect their achievement motivation.

This research suggests that people's implicit theories about the nature of intelligence—as a fixed, stable trait (entity theory), or as something that increases with effort (incremental theory)—have important consequences for their academic achievement. And what the research consistently shows is that students with an incremental view of intelligence fare better than their entity-view counterparts, especially in the face of difficulty. For example, researchers have reported that students with an entity view of intelligence persist less in the face of challenge, view failures as indicative of future abilities, avoid challenging tasks, and believe effort to be an ineffective strategy for success. Their goal is to perform at a level that marks them as smart, capable students; thus, they prefer unchallenging tasks—those that ensure high performance. In contrast, incremental theorists persist longer when challenged, view failure as a signal to increase effort, and recognize challenging tasks as the route to increased knowledge. Their goal is to learn and increase their intelligence; thus, they prefer challenging tasks that increase their current understanding. Consequently, students' implicit theories of intelligence greatly influence academic achievement. How do implicit theories of intelligence relate to stereotype threat? Aronson, Freid, and Good (2002) reasoned that stereotyped individuals may find themselves in the same mindset as people who hold an entity view of intelligence, especially when faced with academic difficulty or the possibility of low performance. The very nature of the stereotype itself suggests that individuals, by virtue of their group membership, are inherently limited in their abilities. Thus, stereotyped individuals not only must contend with the expectation of low performance but also the suggestion that their abilities are fixed. The stereotype, with its implication of inborn and fixed traits, imposes an entity framework upon achievement situations. Consequently, stereotyped individuals may, at least temporarily, adopt an entity mindset, complete with all the trademark responses of entity thinking. If, however, stereotyped individuals can maintain an incremental mindset when faced with challenging academic tasks, perhaps they will be less vulnerable to the threat of ability-impugning stereotypes.

Recent laboratory and field research supports this reasoning. In one laboratory study, students' conceptions of ability as fixed versus expandable were manipulated to investigate the effects on subsequent test anxiety and performance (see Aronson, 2002). Participants (African American and white college students) took a challenging verbal test. One-third of the participants were told that the abilities being tested were highly expandable, one-third were told that the ability was fixed, and one-third simply were told that the test measured verbal ability. In the fixed ability condition, participants solved fewer items and reported more anxiety than participants in the control condition. When participants were led to believe that the ability being tested was malleable, they solved more items and reported less anxiety. These effects held for both the white and black participants. In the control group, performance correlated to the test-takers' own views of intellectual ability measured prior to the test: the more malleable they thought it was, the better their performance on the test.

In a recent field study, researchers wanted to see if encouraging an incremental theory of intelligence would affect students' academic engagement and achievement outside the laboratory (Aronson et al., 2002). Three groups of African American and white undergraduates participated in the study. One group participated in an intervention that used various attitude-change techniques designed to teach them, help them internalize, and make cognitively available the notion that intelligence is expandable (malleable condition). The attitudes and achievement outcomes for this group were compared to those of two control groups—one that participated in the same intervention with a different intelligence orientation, and a second group that did not participate in the intervention. The results of the intervention showed that teaching African American students that intelligence is malleable created an enduring and beneficial change in their own attitudes about intelligence. Furthermore, they reported enjoying and valuing academics more and they received higher grades than did African Americans in the other conditions.

Taken together, these studies provide clear evidence of the benefits of holding an incremental theory of intelligence—especially when faced with a stereotype suggesting limited ability. Thus, although stereotype threat undermines performance, "incrementalism" appears to provide an effective defense against its negative effects. Using this model, stereotyped individuals may protect themselves from the negative effects of stereotype threat by rejecting an entity view of intelligence and adopting an incremental view.

CONCLUSIONS

Stereotype threat is a predicament that can undermine the achievement of students from a wide range of stereotyped groups. Recently, researchers have investigated the age at which stereotypes become meaningfully disruptive to students' academic pursuits—that is, when stereotype vulnerability develops. We have learned that students are aware of and to some degree influenced by ability impugning stereotypes throughout their academic lives. However, it is not until early adolescence that children develop the cognitive abilities necessary for stereotypes to be meaningfully disruptive, that is, to arouse extra performance anxiety when abilities are under scrutiny. We believe this is the case because it is during adolescence that children begin to think about and pay greater attention to others' perceptions, because they have developed complex ways of thinking about cognitive abilities, and because of an increasing awareness and application of stereotypes. Finally, these advances in cognitive ability and coherence of self-perceptions occur in the context of junior high or middle schools, environments that appear to be breeding grounds for sensitivity to stereotype-based judgments of ability. The effects of this stereotype vulnerability appear to be compromised performance, learning, and engagement with academics. The good news is that the more that is learned about these processes, the more optimistic we are that, with wise, research-based interventions, we can help students cope with stereotype threats during this critical period in life.

NOTES

1.   One might argue that boys thrive on competitive situations, and thus, their eagerness to prove themselves resulted in their higher performance under evaluative scrutiny. Is it the case that boys are really going out of

their way to outperform others or is it the case that girls' performance is greatly debilitated under the specter of evaluative scrutiny? The answer seems to be both. A closer inspection of the pattern of means in this study showed that boys' performance increased when they thought they were being evaluated. At the same time, however, girls; performance decreased under evaluative conditions. It is interesting that at the exact time in which boys get a boost from evaluation—early adolescence—girls are debilitated, but only when the evaluation occurs in a stereotyped domain. It is also important to note that although we were evaluating the students' math abilities, we did not make normative comparisons between students. Thus, these results cannot be adequately explained by the research suggesting that boys prefer normative evaluation.

REFERENCES

Aboud, F. (1988). *Children and prejudice.* New York: Blackwell.

Aboud, F. E., & Mitchell, F. G. (1977). Ethnic role taking: The effects of preference and self-identification. *International Journal of Psychology, 12,* 1–17.

Albert, A. A., & Porter, J. R. (1983). Age patterns in the development of children's gender-role stereotypes. *Sex Roles, 9,* 59–67.

Alfieri, T., Ruble, D., & Higgins, E. (1996). Gender stereotypes during adolescence: Developmental changes and the transition to junior high school. *Developmental Psychology, 32,* 1129–1137.

Allport, G. (1954). *The nature of prejudice.* New York: Doubleday.

Ambady, N., Shih, M., Kim, A., & Pittinsky, T. L. (2001). Stereotype susceptibility in children: Effects of identity activation on quantitative performance. *Psychological Science, 12,* 385–390.

American Association of University Women. (1992). *How schools shortchange girls.* Washington, DC: Author.

American Association of University Women. (1998). *Gender gaps: Where schools still fail our children. Executive Summary.* Washington, DC: Author.

Anderman, E. M., Eccles, J. S., Yoon, K. S., Roeser, R., Wigfield, A., & Blumenfeld, P. (2001). Learning to value mathematics and reading: Relations to mastery and performance-oriented instructional practices. *Contemporary Educational Psychology, 26,* 76–95.

Aronson, E., & Patnoe, S. (1997). *The jigsaw classroom.* New York: Longman.

Aronson, J. (2002). Stereotype threat: Contending and coping with unnerving expectations. In J. Aronson (Ed.), *Improving academic achievement: Impact of psychological factors on education.* San Diego, CA: Academic Press.

Aronson, J., Freid, C., & Good, C. (2002). Reducing the effects of stereotype threat on African American college students by shaping theories of intelligence. *Journal of Experimental Social Psychology, 38*(2), 113–125.

Aronson, J., & Good, C. (2001). [The role of internal versus external stakes in stereotype threat]. Unpublished raw data, University of Texas, Austin.

Aronson, J., & Good, C. (2002). *Reducing vulnerability to stereotype threat in adolescents by shaping theories of intelligence.* Manuscript in preparation.

Aronson, J., Lustina, M. J., Good, C., Keough, K., Steele, C. M., & Brown, J. (1999). When White men can't do math: Necessary and sufficient factors in stereotype threat. *Journal of Experimental Social Psychology*, *35*(1), 29–46.

Aronson J., Quinn, D., & Spencer, S. (1998). Stereotype threat and the academic performance of minorities and women. In J. Swim & C. Stangor (Eds.), *Prejudice: The target's perspective*. San Diego, CA: Academic Press

Asher, S. R., & Allen, V. L. (1969). Racial preference and social comparison process. *Journal of Social Issues, 25*, 157–167.

Augoustinos, M., & Rosewarne, D. (2001). Stereotype knowledge and prejudice in children. *British Journal of Developmental Psychology, 19*, 143–156.

Bargh, J. A., Chen, M., & Burrows, L. (1996). Automaticity of social behavior: Direct effects of trait construct and stereotype priming on action. *Journal of Personality and Social Psychology, 71*, 230–244.

Benenson, J. F., & Dweck, C. S. (1986). The development of trait explanations and self-evaluations in the academic and social domains. *Child Development. 57*, 1179–1187.

Biernat, M. (1993). Gender and height: Developmental patterns in knowledge and use of an accurate stereotype. *Sex Roles, 29*, 691–713.

Birmaher, B., Ryan, N., Williamson, D., Brent, D., & Kaufman, J. (1996). Childhood and adolescent depression: A review of the past 10 years. Part II. *Journal of the American Academy of Child and Adolescent Psychiatry, 35*, 1575–1583.

Butler, R. (1989a). Interest in the task and interest in peers' work in competitive and non-competitive conditions: A developmental study. *Child Development, 60*, 562–570.

Butler, R. (1989b). Mastery versus ability appraisal: A developmental study of children's observations of peers' work. *Child Development, 60*, 1350–1361.

Butler, R. (2000). Making judgments about ability: The role of implicit theories of ability in moderating inferences from temporal and social comparison information. *Journal of Personality and Social Psychology, 78*, 965–978.

Cain, K. M., & Dweck, C. S. (1989). The development of children's conceptions of intelligence: A theoretical framework. In R. J. Sternberg, et al. (Ed.), *Advances in the psychology of human intelligence* (Vo. 5, pp. 47–82). Hillsdale, NJ: Erlbaum.

Cain, K. M. & Dweck, C. S. (1995). The relation between motivational patterns and achievement cognitions through the elementary school years. *Merrill-Palmer Quarterly, 41*(1), 25–52.

Cheryan, S., & Bodenhausen, G. V. (2000). When positive stereotypes threaten intellectual performance: The psychological hazards of "model minority" status. *Psychological Science, 11*, 399–402.

Condit, V. (1990). Anorexia nervosa: Levels of causation. *Human Nature, 1*, 391–413.

Congressional Hearing. (1994). *Women and K–12 mathematics education.* Hearing before the Subcommittee on Energy of the Committee on Science, Space, and Technology, United States House of Representatives, 103rd Congress, Second session, June 1994.

Croizet, J., & Claire, T. (1998). Extending the concept of stereotype and threat to social class: The intellectual underperformance of students from low socioeconomic backgrounds. *Personality and Social Psychology Bulletin, 24*, 588–594.

Cross, W. (1978). The Thomas and Cook models of psychological nigrescence: A literature review. *Journal of Black Psychology, 4,* 13–31.

Cross, W. (1980). Models of psychological nigrescence: A literature review. In R. L. Jones (Ed.), *Black psychology* (pp. 81–90). New York: Harper & Row.

Crouter, A., Manke, B., & McHale, S. (1995). The family context of gender intensification in early adolescence. *Child Development, 66,* 317–329.

Dweck, C. S. (1986). Motivational processes affecting learning. *American Psychologist, 41,* 1040–1048.

Dweck, C. (1999). *Self-theories: Their role in motivation, personality, and development.* Philadelphia: Psychology Press.

Dweck, C. S. (2002) The development of ability conceptions. In A. Wigfield & J. Eccles (Eds.), *The development of achievement motivation* (pp. 57–91). San Diego, CA: Academic Press.

Dweck, C. S., & Elliott, E. S. (1983). Achievement motivation. In P. Mussen & E. M. Hetherington (Eds.), *Handbook of child psychology* (pp. 643–692). New York: Wiley.

Dweck, C. S., & Leggett, E. L. (1988). A social-cognitive approach to motivation and personality. *Psychological Review, 95,* 256–273.

Dweck, C. S., & Sorich, L. (1999). Mastery-oriented thinking. In C.R. Snyder (Ed.), *Coping.* New York: Oxford University Press.

Eccles, J. S. (1984). Sex differences in achievement patterns. *Nebraska Symposium on Motivation, 32,* 97–132.

Eccles, J. S., & Jacobs, J. E. (1992). The impact of mothers' gender-role stereotypic beliefs on mothers' and children's ability perceptions. *Journal of Personality and Social Psychology, 63,* 932–944.

Eccles, J. S., Lord, S., & Midgley, C. (1991). What are we doing to early adolescents? The impact of educational contexts on early adolescents. *American Journal of Education, 99,* 521–542.

Eccles, J. S., Midgley, C., Wigfield, A., Buchanan, C., Reuman, D., Flanagan, C., & MacIver, D. (1993). Development during adolescence: The impact of stage-environment fit on young adolescents' experiences in schools and families. *American Psychologist, 48,* 90–101.

Elkind, D. (1967). Egocentrism in adolescence. *Child Development, 38,* 1025–1034.

Elkind, D. (1974). *Children and adolescents: Interpretive essays on Jean Piaget* (2nd ed.). New York: Oxford University Press.

Entwisle, D. R., Alexander, K. L., Cardigan, D., & Pallas, A. (1987). The emergent academic self-image of first graders: Its response to social structure. *Child Development, 58,* 1190–1206.

Erikson, E. (1968). *Identity: Youth and crisis.* New York: Norton.

Felner, R. D., Primavera, J., & Cauce, A. M. (1981). The impact of school transitions: A focus for preventive efforts. *American Journal of Community Psychology, 9,* 449–459.

Fennema, E., & Sherman, J. (1977). Sex-related differences in mathematics achievement, spatial visualization and affective factors. *American Educational Research Journal. 14,* 51–71.

Flavell, J. (1977). *Cognitive development.* Engelwood Cliffs, NJ: Prentice-Hall.

Frey, K. S., & Ruble, D. N. (1985). What children say when the teacher is not around: Conflicting goals in social comparison and performance assessment in the classroom. *Journal of Personality and Social Psychology, 48,* 550–562.

Garrett, C. S., Ein, P. L., & Tremaine, L. (1977). The development of gender stereotyping of adult occupations in elementary school children. *Child Development, 48,* 507–512.

Gerard, H. (1983). School desegregation: The social science role. *American Psychologist, 38,* 869–878.

Goossens, L., Seiffge-Krenke, I., & Marcoen, A. (1992, March). *The many faces of adolescent egocentrism: Two European replications.* Paper presented at the biennial meeting of the Society for Research on Adolescence, Washington, DC.

Hanson, S. (1996). Gender, family resources, and success in science. *Journal of Family Issues, 17,* 83–113.

Harter, S. (1990). Identity and self-development. In S. Feldman & G. Elliot (Eds.), *At the threshold: The developing adolescent* (pp. 352–387). Cambridge, MA: Harvard University Press.

Harter, S. (1997). The development of self-representations. In W. Damon (Series Ed.) & N. Eisenberg (Vol. Ed.), *Handbook of child psychology: Vol. 3. Social, emotional, and personality development* (5th ed.). New York: Wiley.

Harter, S., Whitesell, N. R., & Kowalski, P. (1992). Individual differences in the effects of educational transitions on young adolescent's perceptions of competence and motivational orientation. *American Educational Research Journal, 29,* 777–807.

Hirschfeld, L. (1996). *Race in the making: Cognition, culture, and the child's construction of human kinds.* Cambridge, MA: MIT Press.

Holmbeck, G., & Hill, J. (1988). Storm and stress beliefs about adolescence: Prevalence, self-reported antecedents, and effects of an undergraduate course. *Journal of Youth and Adolescence, 17,* 285–306.

Hong, Y., Chiu, C., & Dweck, C. S. (1995). Implicit theories of intelligence: Reconsidering the role of confidence in achievement motivation. In M. H. Kerns (Eds.), *Efficacy, agency, and self-esteem.* New York: Plenum Press.

Hughes, D., & Chen, L. (1999). The nature of parents' race-related communications to children: A developmental perspective. In L. Balter & C. S Tamis-LeMonda (Eds.), *Child psychology: A handbook of contemporary issues.* Philadelphia: Psychology Press.

Huston, A. (1987). The development of sex typing: Themes from recent research. In S. Chess & A. Thomas (Eds.), *Annual progress in child psychiatry and child development.* Philadelphia: Brunner/Mazel.

Huston, A., & Alvarez, M. (1990). The socialization context of gender role development in early adolescence. In R. Montemayor, G. Adams, & T. Gullotta (Eds.), *Advances in adolescent development, Vol. 2: The transition from childhood to adolescence* (pp. 156–179). Beverly Hills, CA: Sage.

Inzlicht, M., & Ben-Zeev, T. (2000). A threatening intellectual environment: Why females are susceptible to experiencing problem-solving deficits in the presence of males. *Psychological Science, 11,* 365–371.

Jencks, C., & Phillips, M. (1998). *The black–white test score gap.* Washington, DC: Brookings Institution Press.

Kalin, R., (1979). Ethnic and multicultural attitudes among children in a Canadian city. *Canadian Ethnic Studies, 11,* 69–81.

Katz, P. A. (1976). The acquisition of racial attitudes in children. In P. A. Katz (Ed.), *Towards the elimination of racism* (pp. 125–154). New York: Pergamon Press.

Katz, P., & Ksansnak, K. (1994). Developmental aspects of gender role flexibility and traditionality in middle childhood and adolescence. *Developmental Psychology, 30,* 272–282.

Kelly, A., & Smail, B. (1986). Sex-stereotypes and attitudes to science among eleven-year-old children. *British Journal of Educational Psychology, 56,* 158–168.

Kircher, M., & Furby, L. (1971). Racial preferences in young children. *Child Development, 42,* 2076–2078.

Larson, R., & Ham, M. (1993). Stress and "storm and stress" in early adolescence: The relationship of negative events with dysphoric affect. *Developmental Psychology, 29,* 130–140.

Lee, K. (1996). A study of teacher responses based on their conceptions of intelligence. *Journal of Classroom Interaction, 31,* 1–12.

Livesley, W., & Bromley, D. (1973). *Person perception in childhood and adolescence.* New York: Wiley.

Lummis, M., & Stevenson, H. W. (1990). Gender differences in beliefs and achievement: A cross-cultural study. *Developmental Psychology, 26,* 254–263.

Males, M. (1996). *The scapegoat generation: America's war on adolescents.* Monroe, ME: Common Courage Press.

Marsh, H. (1989). Age and sex effects in multiple dimensions of self-concept: Preadolescence to early adulthood. *Journal of Educational Psychology, 81,* 417–430.

McKown, C., & Weinstein, R. (2000). *The development and consequences of stereotype-consciousness in childhood.* Paper presented at the Society for the Psychological Study of Social Issues, Minneapolis, MN.

Nadelman, L. (1974). Sex identity in American children: Memory, knowledge, and preference tests. *Developmental Psychology, 10,* 413–417.

Nicholls, J. G. (1979). Development of perception of own attainment and causal attributions for success and failure in reading. *Journal of Educational Psychology, 71,* 94–99.

Nicholls, J. G., & Miller, A. T. (1984). Reasoning about the ability of self and others: A developmental study. *Child Development, 55,* 1990–1999.

Osborne, J. (2001). Testing stereotype threat: Does anxiety explain race and sex differences in achievement? *Contemporary Educational Psychology, 26,* 291–310.

Osborne, J. W. (1995). Academics, self-esteem, and race: A look at the underlying assumptions of the disidentification hypothesis. *Personality and Social Psychology Bulletin, 21,* 449–455.

Parsons, J., & Ruble, D. N. (1972). Attributional processes related to the development of achievement-related affect and expectancy. *Proceedings of the Annual Convention of the American Psychological Association, 7,* 105–106.

Parsons, J., & Ruble, D. N. (1977). The development of achievement-related expectancies. *Child Development, 48,* 1075–1079.

Phinney, J. (1990). Ethnic identity in adolescents and adults: A review of research. *Psychological Bulletin, 108,* 499–514.

Piaget, J. (1972). Intellectual evolution from adolescence to adulthood. *Human Development, 15,* 1–12.

Pinel, E. (1999). Stigma consciousness: The psychological legacy of social stereotypes. *Journal of Personality and Social Psychology, 76,* 114–128.

Plaks, J., Stroessner, S., Dweck, C. S., & Sherman, J. (2001). Person theories and attention allocation: Preference for stereotypic vs. counterstereotypic information. *Journal of Personality and Social Psychology, 80,* 876–893.

Pomerantz, E., & Ruble, D. (1997). Distinguishing multiple dimensions of conceptions of ability: Implications for self-evaluation. *Child Development, 68,* 1165–1180.

Pomerantz, E., Ruble, D., Frey, K., & Greulich, F. (1995). Meeting goals and confronting conflict: Children's changing perceptions of social comparison. *Child Development, 66,* 723–738.

Quadrel, M., Fischoff, B., & Davis, W. (1993). Adolescent (in)vulnerability. *American Psychologist, 48,* 102–116.

Reiss, H., & Wright, S. (1982). Knowledge of sex-role stereotypes in children aged 3 to 5. *Sex Roles, 8,* 1049–1056.

Rholes, W. S., & Ruble, D. N. (1984). Children's understanding of dispositional characteristics of others. *Child Development, 55,* 550–560.

Romo, H., & Falbo, T. (1995). *Latino high school graduation: defying the odds.* Austin, TX: University of Texas Press.

Ruble, D. N., Boggiano, A. K., Feldman, N. S. & Loebl, J. H. (1980. Developmental analysis of the role of social comparison in self-evaluation. *Developmental Psychology, 16,* 105–115.

Ruble, D., & Flett, G. (1988). Conflicting goals in self-evaluative information seeking: Developmental and ability level analyses. *Child Development, 59,* 97–106.

Ruble, D., & Martin, C. L. (1998). Gender development. *Handbook of Child Psychology, 3,* 933–1016.

Rutter, M., & Garmezy, N. (1983). Developmental psychopathology. In E. M. Hetherington (Ed.), *Handbook of child psychology, Vol IV: Socialization, personality, and social development.* New York: Wiley.

Sadker, M., & Sadker, D. (1994). *Failing at fairness: How our schools cheat girls.* New York: Touchstone.

Schmader, T. (2002). Gender identification moderates stereotype threat effects on women's math performance. *Journal of Experimental Social Psychology, 38,* 194–201.

Semaj, L. (1985). Afikanity, cognition and extended self-identity. In M. Spencer & G. Brookins (Eds.), *Beginnings: The social and affective development of black children* (pp. 173–183). Hillsdale: Erlbaum.

Shih, M., Pittinsky, T., & Ambady, N. (1999). Stereotype susceptibility: Identity salience and shifts in quantitative performance. *Psychological Science, 10,* 80–83.

Signorella, M., Bigler, R., & Liben, L. (1993). Developmental differences in children's gender schemata about others: A meta-analytic review. *Developmental Review, 13,* 147–183.

Simmons, R. G., Black, A., & Zhou, Y. (1991). African-American versus white children and the transition to junior high school. *American Journal of Education, 99,* 481–520.

Simmons, R. G., & Blyth, D. A. (1987). *Moving into adolescence: the impact of pubertal change and school context.* Hawthorn, NY: Aldine de Gruyter.

Spencer, M. B., & Dornbusch, S. M. (1990). Challenges in studying minority youth. In S. S. Feldman & G. R. Elliott (Eds.), *At the threshold: The developing adolescent* (pp. 352–387). Cambridge, MA: Harvard University Press.

Spencer, S., Steele, C. M., & Quinn, D. M. (1999). Stereotype threat and women's math performance. *Journal of Experimental Social Psychology, 35,* 4–28.

Steele, C. M. (1997). A threat in the air: How stereotypes shape intellectual identity and performance. *American Psychologist, 52,* 613–629.

Steele, C. M., & Aronson, J. (1995). Stereotype threat and the intellectual test performance of African-Americans. *Journal of Personality and Social Psychology 69,* 797–811.

Steele, C. M., Spencer, S., & Aronson, J. (2002). Contending with images of one's group: The psychology of stereotype and social identity threat. In M. Zanna (Ed.), *Advances in experimental social psychology.* Academic Press.

Stipek, D. J., & Daniels, D. H. (1990). Children's use of dispositional attributions in predicting the performance and behavior of classmates. *Journal of Applied Developmental Psychology, 11,* 13–28.

Stipek, D. J., & Hoffman, J. M. (1980a). Children's achievement-related expectancies as a function of academic performance histories and sex. *Journal of Educational Psychology, 72,* 861–865.

Stipek, D. J., & Hoffman, J. M. (1980b). Development of children's performance-related judgments. *Child Development, 51,* 912–914.

Stumpf, H., & Stanley, J. (1996). Gender-related differences on the College Board's Advanced Placement and Achievement tests, 1982–1992. *Journal of Educational Psychology, 88,* 353–364.

Valencia, R. R. (1997). Latinos and education: An overview of sociodemographic Characteristics and schooling conditions and outcomes. In M. Barrera-Yepes (Ed.), *Latino education issues: Conference proceedings.* Princeton, NJ: Educational Testing Service.

Warren, J. (1996). Educational inequality among white and Mexican-origin adolescents in the American Southwest: 1990. *Sociology of Education, 69,* 142–158.

Wheeler, S. C., & Petty, R. E. (in press). The effects of stereotype activation on behavior: A review of possible mechanisms. *Psychological Bulletin.*

Wigfield, A., & Eccles, J. (2000). Expectancy-value theory of achievement motivation. *Contemporary Educational Psychology, 25,* 68–81.

Wigfield, A., Eccles, J., Yoon, K., & Harold, R. (1997). Change in children's competence beliefs and subjective task values across the elementary school years: A 3-year study. *Journal of Educational Psychology, 89,* 451–469.

Williams, J., Bennett, S., & Best, D. (1975). Awareness and expression of sex stereotypes in young children. *Developmental Psychology, 11,* 635–642.

CHAPTER 12

STUDYING MOTIVATION TO LEARN DURING EARLY ADOLESCENCE: A HOLISTIC PERSPECTIVE

Robert W. Roeser and Mollie K. Galloway
Stanford University

The wholeness of life has, from of old, been made manifest in its parts…

—Lao Tzu

Lao Tzu, a sage reputed to have lived some 26 centuries ago in what is modern-day China, articulated an outlook on the phenomenal world that was in some ways remarkably prescient from the vantage point of science in the 21st century. He was reputed to have taught that "everything in the universe follows certain patterns and processes that escape precise definition" (McGreal, 1995, p. 9). This predisposition to see the phenomenal world in terms of probabilistic patterned processes rather than determinate discrete parts may be a feature of the Chinese way of perceiving and conceiving of reality that extends more or less from antiquity down to this very day (Nisbett, Peng, Choi, & Norenzayan, 2001). Such a worldview, one more holistic than reductionistic, more dynamic than static, is undoubtedly a powerful theoretical force at play today in the minds of scientists the world over who are concerned with understanding complex systems over time. Such systems include the evolution of the physiochemical universe and biological life on earth

(Capra, 1982; Schneider & Londer, 1984), as well as the biological, psychological, and social development of human beings in particular times, places, and cultural settings on the earth (Sameroff, 1983).

What is striking to us and what we address in this chapter is how the central concept of this contemporary zeitgeist of the sciences, that of *organization*, has attained some prominence theoretically in developmental and educational psychology, but is still rather neglected conceptually and analytically in contemporary research on adolescents' motivation to learn, achievement, and experience in the context of middle school. Organization refers to the tendency of complex dynamic systems to show holistic functioning within and across levels of analysis in a manner in which component "parts" take on meaning and functional significance through their relationship with the whole system. This organizational tendency is referred to in the oft-quoted phrase "The whole is greater than the sum of its parts."

The concept of organization is beginning to be applied to the study of human motivation and development by various scholars (e.g., Bergman, Cairns, Nilsson, & Nystedt, 2000; Cicchetti & Cohen, 1995; D. Ford & Lerner, 1992; M. Ford, 1992). In relation to the study of motivation, an organizational perspective draws attention to the patterning of multiple psychological processes that ready and direct human action in specific activity settings. Features of activity settings, social relationships in those settings, and the identity of the individual in those settings are the "wholes" that give meaning to the component processes termed "motivation" by researchers (Ford, 1992; Goodenow, 1992).

School environments too can be conceptualized in terms of patterns of organized social, institutional, and instructional processes (Talbert & McLaughlin, 1999; Zalatimo & Sleeman, 1975). The characteristics of the community in which schools sit, district policies and the culture and resources of a particular school, the nature of academic departments, and characteristics of school leaders and teachers all represent other "wholes" that give form and meaning to the classroom settings, sets of relationships, and activities in which and through which students exhibit motivation to learn or not. Thus, the study of motivation to learn in school, from a holistic vantage point, includes a simultaneous focus on the patterning of intrapersonal psychological factors, social relationships, and extrapersonal school factors among subgroups of youth who manifest differential patterns of behavioral investment, participation, and achievement in school.

THE NEED FOR A HOLISTIC OUTLOOK

Despite the increasing appeal of systems perspectives in the sciences generally and in the developmental sciences in particular, we believe that in the main, contemporary researchers interested in early adolescents' motivation to learn and achievement behavior in middle school settings have neglected the concept of holistic organization in their work. In essence, we see this body of research as primarily one in which the parts are privileged over the whole. This privileging of the parts over the whole occurs in three ways: (a) through a limiting of investigations primarily to psychological processes and behavioral outcomes linked to the academic domain rather than to the overall organization of adolescents' psychosocial identity and behavior that includes but transcends the academic domain; (b) through a lack of theoretical integration; and (c) through a continued reliance on variable-centered analytic techniques in which the relations between variables across all persons are the focus, rather than on pattern-centered analytic techniques in which the relations among variables within subgroups of individuals are the focus (Magnusson & Bergmann, 1988). On the other hand, with respect to the study of how the school context can affect early adolescents' motivation to learn and achievement behavior during these years, we believe motivational researchers interested in early adolescence have tended to privilege the whole over the parts too much. Specifically, we mean that in many studies, including our own, researchers conceive of the middle school environment as a relatively uniform social sphere that is experienced similarly by all students in the school, with analytic strategies flowing from this implicit assumption (e.g., Roeser, Midgley, & Urdan, 1996). This stands in contrast to a view in which schools are recognized as institutions that both provide, and are experienced as providing, a differentiated set of social and academic opportunities to different subgroups of the student body (Lee, Bryk, & Smith, 1993; Oakes, Gamoran, & Page, 1992).

The purpose of this chapter is to outline why a holistic theoretical and analytic perspective on early adolescents' motivation to learn, behavior, and experience in the context of middle school, a perspective in which the concept of organization is central, can advance this field of study in the next generation of scholarship by addressing these aforementioned issues. In the first part of this chapter, we describe several ways in which the concept of organization has been influential and has been neglected in research on motivation and education during adolescence. Second, we describe how research on motivation to learn during adolescence points toward an organizational perspective in which a focus on subgroups of individuals is central. In the third part of the chapter, we describe the core concepts of an organizational, systems approach to human development and three principles derived from these concepts that we have used to guide our own research into adolescents' lives in school contexts. In the fourth section of the chapter, we provide an illustration of how we have instantiated the core principles of systems thinking in our own research using pattern-centered analytic techniques with cross-sectional and longitudinal data. We conclude with some thoughts on the utility of pattern-centered approaches for future research on adolescents' academic motivation.

WHEN THE SUM OF THE PARTS IS
LESS THAN THE WHOLE

The most basic feature of a holistic outlook on human motivation, behavior, and development is a conceptual shift from focusing on individual motivational processes, achievement behaviors, school experiences, and their interrelations across all individuals in a sample to thinking about the patterning or *organization* of multiple psychological processes, behaviors, and school experiences among different subgroups of individuals. Theoretically, researchers interested in academic motivation and achievement in school settings during adolescence have made important advances in a manner consistent with a holistic, systems worldview in which the concept of organization is central. These advances include (a) a conceptualization of young people as active agents in their own learning and development (e.g., a focus on self-organization); (b) the definition of motivation as a series of fluxional, goal-oriented cognitive and emotional states rather than as a set of fixed, mechanistic needs or personality traits (e.g., a focus on process dynamics or dynamic processes); and (c) a concern with how features of the environment, in conjunction with characteristics of individuals, co-contribute to variation in individuals' behavioral investment in or divestment from learning situations in and over time (e.g., a focus on the organization of behavior-in-context; see Boekaerts, Pintrich, & Zeidner, 2000; Eccles, Wigfield, & Schiefele, 1998; Lazarus, 1991). Despite these advances, however, we believe this work could be extended in at least four fruitful directions.

Beyond the Academic Domain

First, motivational researchers continue to be rather parochial in the kinds of psychological processes and behavioral outcomes they examine. Despite mounting evidence that indicators of psychological and behavioral competence or maladjustment, including but transcending academic motivation and achievement, "cluster" together during childhood and adolescence, educational psychologists rarely examine nonacademic outcomes in their research. For instance, many children who fail academically during elementary school not only have maladaptive academic motivational styles (e.g., Dweck, 1986), but also externalizing problems associated with impulsivity, hyperactivity, and difficulties with peers (e.g., Hinshaw, 1992) or internalizing problems associated with depression (Nolen-Hoeksema, Girgus, & Seligman, 1986). During secondary school, researchers have identified a syndrome of academic failure, relationships with peers who engage in antisocial behavior, and engagement in various problem behaviors outside of school among a considerable minority of young people (Dryfoos, 1990); and another syndrome of academic success, prosocial behavior, and abstention from problem behavior involvement among others (Ollendick, Greene, Weist, & Oswald, 1990). By broadening the focus of motivation research to include aspects of mental health, social motivation, peer relationships, and behavioral conduct in and outside of school, such research could make significant contributions to the broader study of developmental competence and psychopathology (e.g., Juvonen & Wentzel, 1996; Masten & Coatsworth, 1998).

Toward Theoretical Integration

Motivational researchers evidence a second form of parochialism in that they tend to concentrate on a subset of variables derived from a single theory rather than the network of motivational processes known to guide, direct, and energize achievement behavior that emerge from the field as a whole (see Ford, 1992, for argument). This theoretical parochialism occurs despite the empirical evidence on academic motivational processes that discloses a spectrum of cognitive and emotional processes, including goals; efficacy and competence-related beliefs; and feelings, moods, and values that contribute to "motivating" achievement behavior in school settings (Eccles et al., 1998). Calls for more intertheoretical perspectives are largely ignored (e.g., Eccles et al., 1998; Ford, 1992). Although we do not believe that researchers should haphazardly pick and choose constructs from different traditions without some particular goals in mind, we do see utility in including various constructs from different theories in the same study such that (a) variables could be assessed in terms of their statistical independence or higher order dependence; (b) variables could be compared in terms of their multivariate associations with specific educational outcomes; (c) variables could be examined in terms of their patterning within different subgroups of young people; and ultimately (d) "higher order" constructs, patterns, and theories of motivation could be forthcoming.

Toward Patterns and Pathways of Development

Another area that is underdeveloped in motivational research is the use of pattern-centered techniques in which configurations of variables within subgroups of individuals at one point in time, or over time, are the focal units of analysis. For instance, several researchers have advanced the field a great deal by showing how single indicators of academic motivation—whether in terms of competence beliefs, values, goal orientations, or intrinsic versus extrinsic motivational orientations—change over time during the transition from elementary to middle to high school (see Eccles et al., 1998, for review). What is needed now is a more focused assessment of how patterns of motivational variables change among various theoretically interesting subgroups of children and adolescents as they move through school and toward different developmental endpoints (e.g., high school graduation, school withdrawal, two-year college, four-year college; pregnancy or legal trouble; Roeser, Peck, Eccles, & Sameroff, 1999, 2000, 2001). In this way, linkages between patterns of motivation and pathways of educational achievement and attainments can be understood.

Harter (1996), for example, has examined differential patterns of changes in perceived competence and intrinsic–extrinsic motivational orientations among subgroups of students as they transition into middle school. She contends that reassessments of scholastic competence following the middle school transition precipitate changes in motivational orientations. Furthermore, she suggests that such reassessments are a function of (a) increases in the size of the student body in middle school and therefore the size of the reference group against whom youth judge their intellectual competence; and (b) increases in teachers' use of socially comparative practices. This work is exemplary in that it represents the natural evolution from variable-centered insights gained at the sample level (motivational shifts from intrinsic to extrinsic with increasing grade; Harter, 1981) to pattern-centered insights gained at the subgroup level (but only for youth who reassess their scholastic competence after a school transition and feel less competent) to causal explanations (because of new social reference groups and comparative teacher practices; Harter, 1996).

We see great utility value in this kind of research in which the focus is on the patterning of multiple motivational variables and outcomes within practically interesting or theoretically derived subgroups of youth. Furthermore, we believe that the marriage of such pattern-centered work with a focus on multiple developmental outcomes, previous histories of functioning, and social experiences including but extending beyond the academic domain and the context of school would do much to advance our understanding of the organization of behavioral competence or psychopathology. Such advances would address behavior not just within a particular domain of functioning but across domains; not just within a particular developmental stage but across time; not just within the individual but in terms of individuals and their social spheres of experience. For instance, in the Harter work, we wonder if the youth who reassessed their competence after transitioning to middle school and found themselves wanting also were more likely to get involved in problem behavior in and outside of school. Did such youth have a history of educational placements that would have forecast such changes in early adolescence? What academic "tracks" were such youth in; who were their classmates, and who were their friends? Studying patterns and pathways of school functioning with a focus on subgroups and broader outcomes and contexts of human development is another area into which motivational research could extend in the future.

Into Schools

A final area in which we see opportunities for the next generation of motivation research concerns the conceptualization of the differentiated environment of the secondary school. Developmentalists have rarely studied schools as central contexts of human development Ie.g., Eccles & Roeser, 1999), and some have argued psychologists in general have never adequately addressed schools and their problems (Sarason, 2001). This is especially true in relation to secondary schools, where sociologists have conducted the most research (Eccles et al., 1998). What psychologists interested in motivation to learn have to offer in this area is a rather sophisticated set of ideas about how schools, as complex organizations characterized by multiple levels of instructional, interpersonal, and organizational processes, shape meanings, motivations, and behaviors among their inhabitants; and how at the same time different subgroups of young people, based on their academic history, race, class, and gender, develop differential orientations toward investment in school (e.g., Eccles & Roeser, 1999; Maehr & Midgley, 1991). Integrating this work with the sociological literature on how schools, through sorting mechanisms, staffing decisions, curricular offerings, and aspects of the school culture, provide different sets of experiences to different subgroups of young people (e.g., Lee et al., 1993) could advance both the psychological and sociological study of student functioning in middle and high school settings.

Summary

In sum, we believe that the next generation of scholarship on motivation to learn during adolescence could make significant advances by focusing holistically on (a) the relations between motivation and achievement in school and aspects of identity and behavioral outcomes transcending the academic domain of functioning; (b) the common and unique insights into differential patterns of investment, participation, and achievement offered by different theoretical approaches; (c) patterns and pathways of functioning among subgroups of youth using pattern-centered analytic techniques; and (d) the ways in which secondary school environments provide and are experienced as providing different academic and social opportunities to different subgroups of youth. Early adolescence, with all of its characteristic biological, psychological, and social changes, offers a unique time in the lifecourse in which to address these important issues.

EDUCATION AND DEVELOPMENT DURING EARLY ADOLESCENCE

Research on early adolescents' motivation to learn highlights the need for greater attention conceptually and analytically to the concept of organization in order to gain a greater understanding of how and why different subgroups of youth show diverging patterns of academic engagement and success during this particular period in the lifespan. Many studies have now documented, for instance, that early adolescents' academic motivation and achievement, at the aggregate level, decline, whereas levels of school truancy, school violence, and absenteeism increase during these years (see Eccles, Lord, & Roeser, 1996; Simmons & Blyth, 1987). Furthermore, changes in academic motivation and achievement in early adolescence have been linked to longer-term developmental sequelae. Adolescents who are disengaged from school in early adolescence are much more likely to experience a host of "downstream" problems during late adolescence including curtailed educational attainments and school withdrawal, teenage pregnancy, abuse of substances, engagement in antisocial behavior, and contact with the legal system (Dryfoos, 1990; Roderick, 1993). On the other hand, adolescents who are engaged with school during these years are more likely to stay on track toward high school graduation and enrollment in college and to avoid the major problems that curtail future opportunities (Eccles et al., 1997; Roeser, Galloway, Watson, Casey-Cannon, & Keller, 2001). The question of why some adolescents do well in school and some do not during this period is complex and likely reflects a diversity of factors. Many different explanations focused on individual-developmental, and social-environmental factors have been offered to explain individual or subgroup differences in the nature of academic functioning during this period.

Theories of Why Academic Motivation Changes in Early Adolescence

Some attribute general declines in academic motivation in early adolescence to the fact that pubertal maturation, concerns with physical appearance, and concomitant interests in potential romantic partners all combine to cause a shift in motivational energies from the academic to the social domain. That is, as concern with one's physical appearance, social relationships, and one's romantic potential become more important to one's overall sense of well-being, individuals shift their focus away from school toward these consequential life domains (Harter, 1990).

Others have highlighted potential role conflicts that can arise for certain youth during the identity formation processes initiated by puberty in early adolescence. As one example, some females may be confronted with a conflict between their desire to fulfill cultural gender roles in which a woman is supposed to be romantically appealing, well-liked, cooperative, and demure, and their desires to be high achievers who are outstanding, outspoken, and competitive with others (Maccoby, 1998). Role conflicts have also been explored in relation to why disproportionate numbers of minority youth from historically targeted groups disengage from school during these years (Ogbu, 1978).

Still others have focused on the developmental roots of academic disengagement and failure in adolescence. In this work, attention is directed toward the developmental precursors of disengagement from school in adolescence in terms of childhood difficulties in addressing lifetasks associated with trust, autonomy, and academic or social competence (Erikson, 1950). The basic notion here is that adaptational failures in the earlier period set young people on psychosocial and contextual trajectories that make school failure during adolescence probabilistically more likely (Cairns, Cairns, & Neckerman, 1989; Carlson et al., 1999; Roeser, Eccles, & Freedman-Doan, 1999). A different version of this developmental orientation focuses on how early educational decisions such as grade retention or special education placements, appropriately made or not, place disproportionately high numbers of poor and minority youth on trajectories toward academic disengagement and failure during adolescence (Entwistle & Alexander, 1993).

Other theorists have focused more on the nature of the social experiences young people are going through during early adolescence to explain negative motivational and achievement patterns. For instance, Simmons and Blyth (1987) described how the sheer number of simultaneous life changes in early adolescence, including puberty, school change, entry into dating, family transitions, and so on, can tax the adaptational resources of some young people, diminish their capacity to cope with the challenges confronting them, and lead to academic problems. In their work, white females were found to be particularly at risk for school problems due to a build-up of simultaneous life changes.

Finally, others have focused not on the number, but on the nature of the social experiential changes that occur in early adolescence. For instance, Eccles and Midgley (1989) suggested that a "developmental mismatch" between the emerging needs of adolescents and the nature of the affordances they experience at home and in school is an important factor in explaining motivational and achievement declines during these years. Just as adolescents are in need of noncomparative, autonomy-supportive, and caring contexts in which to develop their academic capabilities, these authors note that schools become more comparative, controlling, and anonymous in character. In reaction to this mismatch of needs and opportunities, young people's motivation and achievement are diminished (Eccles & Midgley, 1989). Similar processes have been described in relation to the family environment (Lord, Eccles, & McCarthy, 1994).

What is interesting and perhaps obvious from both a practical policy and a scientific perspective is that the reasons for changes in motivation and achievement during adolescence are as diverse as the student body and the social experiences that characterize their lives. As this brief theoretical overview shows, the reasons for negative changes in indices of academic functioning differ among different subgroups of individuals—subgroups that vary with respect to issues of physical maturation; focal identity issues related to gender, race, and class; developmental histories of academic failure or success; and social experiences in the home and school. Focusing on this diversity among subgroups of young people and drawing together different theoretical insights to do so seems important in the next generation of scholarship in this area. Systems approaches to human development, in which the concept of organization plays a central role, provide a set of research principles and analytic strategies by which researchers can directly examine the diverse patterns of academic functioning and pathways of educational development that characterize different subgroups of youth.

WHEN THE WHOLE IS GREATER
THAN THE SUM OF THE PARTS

Although numerous theorists have articulated different aspects of holistic systems thinking as interpreted and practiced by scientists in the physical, life, and developmental sciences, at the heart of all systems thinking are four central foci (Capra, 1996). These foci include attention to (a) holistic patterns of organization among constituent phenomena, (b) dynamic processes, (c) the multilevel contexts in which phenomena exist, and (d) change and continuity in patterns of organization over time. In this section, we overview the central concepts of systems thinking and highlight their relevance to studies of motivation to learn among early adolescents in school settings.

From Parts to Patterns

The foundational aspect of systems thinking is a fundamental perceptual, conceptual, and analytic shift from the parts of given phenomena to their holistic patterning within and across levels of analysis (a focus on multivariate, multilevel phenomena). The notion of holism does not imply that researchers need to attend to everything at once, because in nature complex systems are characterized by componentization and hierarchic organization in which specialized functions are elaborated into semi-autonomous subsystems that are buffered from, but interrelated with, other parts of the whole in which they are embedded (Ford & Ford, 1987).

For example, the motivational subsystem that includes cognitive and emotional processes that help individuals evaluate situations (e.g., expectancies), frame courses of action (intentions), and energize such actions (emotions) can be seen as distinct from but related to the ability subsystem that includes an individual's repertoire of mental abilities, knowledge, and strategies that allow intentions to be carried toward fruition in action (Ford, 1992; Snow, Corno, & Jackson, 1996). These subsystems, in turn, can be seen as distinct from but orchestrated by "higher-order" self-regulatory systems. Such higher order systems are the means by which individuals volitionally self-monitor and protect their intentions from competing demands or pressures as a means of ensuring "good enough" execution of them in favorable situations (Kuhl, 1984). Though buffered from one another and separated by special function, these subsystems nonetheless, from a systems perspective, act in conjunction with one another and the situational (system of) affordances and constraints to produce complex, observable behaviors such as learning or test performance (Ford, 1992; Snow, 1994). The entire set of psychological systems that motivate and enact achievement behaviors, in turn, can be seen as embedded within the broader context of the person's identity, such that doing well or failing academically takes on meaning only in relation to their broader sense of self in relation to that activity. The person, in turn, can be seen as embedded within particular social group affiliations, which give meaning to their scholastic identity (Steele, 1997). Understanding and attending to the multilevel patterns of processes that contribute to emergent behaviors such as school achievement is at the heart of a holistic approach.

Process Thinking

Systems thinking is also characterized by a fundamental perceptual, conceptual, and analytic shift from defining phenomena in static terms to defining them in terms of patterned, dynamic processes (or process dynamics). For instance, from such a perspective, motivation is viewed as fluxional patterns of cognitive and emotional processes (states) that ready individuals to act in relation to specific goals and contexts rather than as a set of stable drives or personality traits (Ford, 1992). Process thinking moves one from a focus on presumed static properties of individuals—their traits, sex, or race, toward a focus on dynamic processes such as situational states, sex role beliefs, ethnic identities, and so on (Bronfenbrenner, 1999).

A second, correlated notion of process thinking is that manifest phenomena such as achievement behaviors are seen as emerging from a pattern of underlying and overarching processes. Said another way, behavior reflects both the organization of and is the emergent property of a set of underlying and overarching intra-, inter-, and extrapersonal processes. In the example given above, one could say that performance on an achievement test emerges from a pattern of underlying psychological (e.g., test-related beliefs, feelings, strategies), social (e.g., social stigmas and stereotypes in a society), and instructional (e.g., cognitive task demands of tests) processes. Modeling the configurations of these multilevel processes in relation to specific outcomes becomes a basic goal from a holistic perspective.

Third, process thinking involves a consideration of not only the patterning but also the dynamic relations between aspects of a patterned phenomena. For instance, at the level of the personality, achievement behavior can be viewed not only as a function of a pattern of identity beliefs predisposing one to invest or divest from learning activities, but also with reference to the dynamic relations among different aspects of identity—relations characterized by consistency, coherence, or conflict (Pervin, 2000). For instance, individuals who are highly competent academically may still not apply themselves in the classroom if they view such behavior as in conflict with their reputation as being "cool" in the eyes of peers. In this instance, their in-class behavior is probabilistically predicted, at the psychological level of analysis, by the patterning of identity elements (e.g., competent student and cool) and the dynamic relation between them (e.g., conflict between being smart and being cool). We cannot say that their behavior was a function of one of these identity elements or the other in isolation; rather, it emerges from the interdependence between them.

The same is true of more task-related motivational processes. Oftentimes, perhaps always, it is in the patterning and dynamic relations among relevant goals, feelings, and beliefs of various kinds that behavior is forged. For instance, a person can be interested in learning something like calculus but may nonetheless elect not to take an AP math class if failure is antic- ipated. In this instance, the behavior, at the psychological level of analysis, is probabilistically predicted by a pattern of emotions (interest and fear), goals (approach mastery, avoid failure), and beliefs about attaining each goal (uncertain about ability to master calculus, certain one could avoid failure by not taking class). It is in the dynamic relations among these con- flicting motivational processes that behavioral choices are forged. Is one's fear of failure and the desire to avoid it functionally more potent, though at odds with, the person's task interest and desire to master it, thereby lead- ing to behavioral avoidance? In the management (or failure to do so) of conflicting desires and identities is perhaps where the motivational spice of life is found in most of us most of the time.

Moving from the intrapsychic to the interpersonal level of functioning, there is a fourth implication of process thinking at the level of the person-in- context. Specifically, process thinking suggests the possibility that behavior can be viewed as a function of the dynamic relations between the person and the situation—relations sometimes characterized by attunement or asyn- chrony, fit or mismatch (Eccles & Midgley, 1989). For instance, an individual may be motivated to take initiative on a project, but fail to engage with the project due to a lack of contextual affordances for autonomy. In this case, we might say the lack of attunement between the need for autonomy in the per- son and support for autonomy in the context "caused" the lack of behavioral engagement. Here, motivation itself begins to be seen as an emergent prop- erty of the relation between the person and the environment, rather than solely a property of the individual. Motivational theories in which implicit underlying needs and their corresponding overarching social affordances are central, in general, tend to view beliefs, emotions, and related behavior as "emergent" (Connell & Wellborn, 1991; Deci & Ryan, 1985).

Contextual Thinking

Another central hallmark of systems thinking is a shift from seeing phenom- ena as field independent to field interdependent (contextualism). In terms of motivation to learn, this suggests that motivational processes be viewed within the broader contexts of various intra-, inter-, and extrapersonal envi- ronments such as the self, social relationships, and activity settings such as the classroom. By definition, an accounting of these various contexts that transcend but include each other requires a cross-fertilization between theo- ries of motivation and self, social relationships, and social institutions. Per- haps most importantly, contextual thinking requires one to develop rather sophisticated theories of the multilevel subcontexts of social environments such as schools in relation to the psychological functioning of individuals who inhabit those settings. As we describe below, in middle level schools these multilevel subcontexts include tasks, classroom environments, and teachers, academic tracks, peer groups and the school as a whole organization, community characteristics, and so on (see Figure 12.1).

In sum, systems thinking is contextual thinking and draws attention to the embedded intra-, inter-, and extrapersonal contexts within which any phenomena exists. Individual motives exist within whole personalities; whole persons exist within sets of relationships with others; human relationships occur in specific activity settings such as the classroom; classrooms are situated within school organizations; schools exist within governance structures and communities; and so on up the ecological ladder. To address the complex, multilevel nature of social reality, researchers need to parsimoniously attend to work in the fields of education, sociology, public policy, history, and anthropology that deal with these larger frames of reference and social contexts that envelop the scholastic development of young people in schools (e.g., Jessor, 1993).

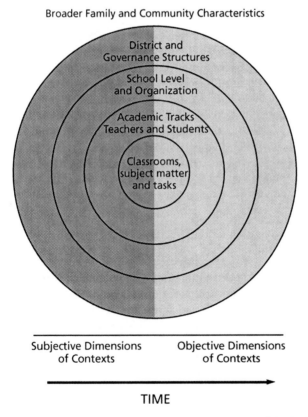

Figure 12.1.   Descriptive embedded contexts model of school.

Developmental Thinking

A final aspect of all systems thinking is its developmental orientation. Patterned phenomena exist in time and show change and continuity in organization over time. Indeed, one definition of development (and learning) refers to qualitative, enduring changes in the organization of functioning between people and their social contexts over time that tend to increase the structural and functional diversity of the individual and/or produce new steady states of behavioral functioning (D. Ford & Lerner, 1992).

One way to conceptualize such changes in the organization of individual functioning over time is in terms of a single line of development, for instance, physical or intellectual development, or a single line of identity development, for instance, scholastic identity. Motivational theorists are often concerned with continuities and discontinuities in perceived scholastic competence or valuing of education over time (see Eccles et al., 1998).

Another way to conceptualize development is in terms of intrapersonal patterns of organization of functioning across different domains. Masten and her colleagues (1995), for instance, examined correlational patterns across individuals in academic, social, and behavioral functioning during childhood and adolescence. They found that academic achievement shows a different relation with peer competence in childhood than it does in adolescence at the aggregate sample level. In childhood, academic achievement is strongly linked to peer competence—doing well in school and making friends go together, perhaps because school success brings social status. In adolescence, however, academic achievement and peer competence were uncorrelated. From a pattern-centered perspective, this set of findings is likely explained by the existence of two different subgroups in the sample, subgroups that would be explicitly examined and documented empirically. These subgroups probably include one consisting of adolescents who do well in school and make friends who presumably also do well in school, and another of adolescents who are failing in school but who are still good at making friends, presumably with those who are also failing in school (Berndt & Keefe, 1995). The combination of these two different subgroups of individuals, one in which high achievement goes with peer competence and one in which low achievement goes with peer competence, could result in a net relation of zero at the full sample level using correlations.

This example demonstrates how variable-centered analyses can provide important information at one level—the relation between achievement and peer competence changes over time—and yet at the same time obscure important insights at the subgroup level in terms of holistic patterns of functioning within subgroups. Using both types of analyses together can yield greater overall understanding of the organization of functioning generally and within specific subgroups (e.g., Roeser, Eccles, & Sameroff, 1998). The same is true for longitudinal studies in which average, sample-level trends are the focus. Such analyses reveal important sample-level trends, but also tend to obscure the significant variation in patterns of change and continuity that exist among different subgroups (e.g., Roeser et al., 1999). Thus, pattern-centered techniques become useful adjuncts to variable-centered techniques, especially when one is interested in identifying and studying subgroups of individuals who display specific patterns of functioning across domains within time or within lines of development over time that diverge from statistically average trends.

Summary

Taking these four focal concepts as a whole, one could say that systems thinking is multivariate and multilevel, process oriented, contextual, and developmental in outlook. Manifest phenomena at any given level of analysis are viewed as "emerging" from a pattern of underlying and overarching processes that exist at different levels of analysis within and over time. In the next section, we attempt to use these core concepts of systems thinking to explicate three principles that may prove useful for guiding the next generation of scholarship on early adolescents' motivation to learn and achievement in school from a holistic vantage point.

FROM HOLISTIC CONCEPTS TO RESEARCH PRINCIPLES

From the core concepts of systems thinking that we have just reviewed, we have derived three specific principles that have guided our scholarship on early adolescents' motivation to learn in middle school. We have named these the "whole person principle," the "lifespace principle," and the "lifespan developmental principle." In the most general sense, these three principles are founded on the proposition that early adolescents' evolving sense of self and contemporary social experiences that bear on their behavior in school are the *fundamental psychological and social contexts* within which to consider the patterned, multivariate, multilevel *processes* that motivate patterns of engagement or disengagement, participation or nonparticipation, and achievement or failure in different subgroups of early adolescents in middle school. Additionally, these principles are founded on the systems idea that the quality of early adolescents' prior academic and social functioning in childhood, as well as their future educational and social aspirations for themselves in adulthood, form the *fundamental temporal contexts of the overall lifespan* within which to examine their motivation and behavior in school during adolescence. By situating the study of adolescents' motivation to learn within these contexts of self, social environment, and time, we believe motivational research could be more fully aligned with systems principles and could address complex questions that require researchers to go beyond average statistical trends and variable relations. Below, we elaborate these principles in more detail and then provide one example of how we have tried to actualize them in our own research.

The Whole Person Principle

From a systems perspective on human behavior and development, the whole person is viewed as the organizing principle of the person's own experience. Human beings are "self-organizing" insofar as they actively anticipate and co-create their experiences in and their experiences of the world (Magnusson, 2000). In a psychological sense, the self is the inner context and active center from which whole persons organize their experience. It is from the self that individuals psychologically *extend* themselves in activity and social relationships, and it is the self that is *informed* by activities and people (Ryan, 1992). Thus, the self is the intrapsychological context in which to study the motivational processes by which individuals prepare for and then extend themselves in specific relationships and activities, and also the context within which to consider the functional significance of relationships and activities for an individual's behavior (Deci & Ryan, 1985). Individuals' senses of self are often intimately related to their biological characteristics (e.g., sex and stage of physical maturation) as well as their sociological statuses (race, social class, religion, etc.). Thus, these become important variables as well in the study of the intrapsychological context of motivational processes related to learning. In our view, there are two different ways of "situating" motivational processes within the broader context of the self that are relevant for researchers of motivation in school settings.

The Organization of Behavior in the Classroom

One way to think about the person holistically in motivational research is to focus on the pattern of the person's motivation and behavior in relation to a particular activity and its demands, for instance, learning in a classroom. This is the most common approach in motivational research on adolescence today. In this case, it is the proximal activity setting that provides the analytic frame for assessing holistic patterns of achievement behavior (Ford, 1992). The task here is to identify different subgroups of young people who show patterns of behavioral investment in or divestment from learning in the classroom, and then to relate such behavioral patterns to underlying sets of task-specific psychological processes that energize and

direct behavior in classroom and school settings. Such motivational processes include goals, capability-related beliefs, and emotions (Ford, 1992).
The construct of a goal in particular, defined as an end that guides behavioral investment in a particular situation, provides a rather specific means
of linking psychological and behavioral processes of individuals to the particular demand characteristics of learning activities in formal settings like
the classroom (e.g., Ames, 1992; Dweck, 1996; Ford, 1992). Thus, goals
become fundamental to defining situation-specific motivational patterns.
An important consideration is how young people coordinate or manage
conflict among multiple goals, feelings, and beliefs that may be activated in
the setting of middle school or a particular classroom environment within
the school (e.g., Pintrich, 2000). We have assumed that in any given sample
of early adolescents, there exist a finite variety of goal-directed psychologi-
cal-behavioral patterns of school investment (e.g., intrinsic or extrinsic
forms of motivation to learn and achievement) and divestment (e.g., withdrawn or aggressive forms of alienation and failure). Patterns already identified in the educational and developmental literatures include those of
the competitive student, the intrinsically motivated student, the student
motivated by both extrinsic and intrinsic goals, the anxious-helpless student, and the aggressive student (see Dweck & Leggett, 1988; Pintrich,
2000; Roeser & Eccles, 2000).

The Organization of School Identities

A second way of thinking about the person as the central unit of analysis
in motivational research in schools is to focus on the holistic patterning of
individuals' sense of identity across multiple social roles that are salient in
the context of school. These roles include, but transcend, the student role.
Other salient dimensions of adolescents' school-based identities include
that of peer group member, potential romantic partner, friend, athlete, art-
ist, and so on. In this case, it is assumed that the salient identities of the
person as a whole in school provide the analytic frame for assessing patterns of achievement behavior, and that such behavior emerges from both
the patterning and dynamics among multiple aspects of a person's identity.

School-Relevant Social Identities

Several nonstudent roles interact dynamically to produce different patterns of achievement behavior in middle school—roles associated with
physical attractiveness and gender, popularity and being cool, ethnicity
and race, and so on. Conflict between roles may cause either academic disengagement or heightened stress, whereas consistency among roles should
be related to engagement and well-being. For instance, that the student
role is often defined in schools in the United States by competitive striving,
self-assertion, and independence may make it more difficult for some ado-

lescents from cultural backgrounds in which different values such as cooperation and interdependence are emphasized to adopt such a role into
their sense of self without reframing it somehow (Bernal, Saenz, & Knight,
1995; Olsen, 1997). In such instances, adolescents may experience significant stress or distress as they attempt to navigate the sociocultural borders
between a home environment where cooperation is emphasized and a
school culture where competition is emphasized (Davidson & Phelan,
1999). Similarly, some females may experience difficulty coordinating
achievement and affiliation-related pursuits if the former leads to standing
out and away from others and the latter leads toward cultural gender role
fulfillment, intimacy, and interdependence (Maccoby, 1998).

As another example, some have conjectured that ethnic or racial identity (group membership roles) can also influence the ease with which certain adolescents identify with the student role and the institution of school.
Ogbu (1978) suggests that what he calls "caste-like minorities," such as Afri-
can- and Mexican-Americans, can experience difficulty adopting the student role and valuing school as a consequence of their group's historical
devaluation by the White majority. He argues that such groups develop
"oppositional identities" in which the behaviors and frame of reference of
whites, which he believes include working hard for good grades at school,
are rejected as a means of repudiating the dominant group, its oppression,
and its institutions. In this case, we would expect ethnically identified individuals from these groups to resist the student role because of the conflicts
it presents to their sense of ethnic loyalty and identification. Others have
found evidence that early adolescent African Americans who are strongly
ethnically identified are actually *more*, not less, likely to identify with school
and the student role (Wong & Eccles, 1996). This work with African Americans from a broad range of socioeconomic backgrounds contrasts with
that of Fordham and Ogbu (1986) with primarily poor African Americans
in which evidence for oppositional identities in relation to school were
found. Thus, how one's role as a member of a particular ethnic or racial
group is associated with identification with the student role is no simple
matter. It seems to depend on the intersection of race, class, and gender
identities among different subgroups of individuals, among other things.

Mental Health

One implication that flows from this more identity-level focus on motivation to learn in school is that the maintenance and enhancement of
one's overall emotional and social sense of self is dynamically related to
one's ability to enact the student role. Concerns for physical, emotional,
and social safety and well-being in school may in fact assume organismic
priority over concerns for mastery of academic material among certain
subgroups of adolescents, especially during the many physical and social

changes of early adolescence (e.g., Boekaerts & Niemivirta, 2000). Thus, in addition to considering the interrelations among multiple roles in different subgroups of youth, one can think about how motivation to learn and aspects of mental health (e.g., felt safety, social belonging, and well-being) are configured and related to one another in certain subgroups of individuals.

In sum, a second way to take a whole person perspective on motivational processes in school is to focus on how different patterns of achievement behavior among different subgroups of early adolescents emerge from how well the student role fits or does not fit with other valued aspects of their identity. We have assumed that in any given sample of early adolescents, there exist a finite variety of self patterns in which being a good student is seen as a central part of oneself (e.g., the all-American teenager, the nerd, the quiet, conscientious student) and others in which it is not (e.g., the social butterfly, the troubled adolescent, the iconoclast). The essence of the whole person principle is to focus on the one who is motivated or not in terms of the fullness of their in-school identities, whatever they may be, rather than simply in terms of the student role as defined by the institution.

The Lifespace Principle: Adding Contextual Features

As noted earlier, systems thinking is characterized by a shift from seeing phenomena as field independent to field interdependent. Just as goals and the overall configurations of psychological processes of which they are a part, and roles and the overall self of which they are a part, form the fundamental intrapersonal contexts within which to frame questions about motivation, so too do the tasks, people, and culture of classrooms and schools form fundamental inter- and extrapersonal contexts within which to situate these "lower level" psychological processes. From a pattern-centered perspective, the "lifespace principle" draws attention to the fact that variations in achievement behavior can be conceptualized as a function of various configurations of motivational and identity processes, subjective school experiences, and the objective tasks, people, and practices that inform subjective experiences. In short, the lifespace principle draws attention to the fact that the person-in-context becomes the focal unit of analysis (Lewin, 1936).

The research problem in making the person-in-context the focal unit of analysis is twofold. First, one must link subjective experiences of school to patterns of motivation and behavior among different subgroups of individuals. Second, one must attempt to identify the inter- and extra-personal features of the school environment that inform adolescents' subjective experiences of school. In order to address these twin challenges, we have found it necessary to develop a descriptive taxonomy of the multilevel, embedded contexts that constitute the "middle school environment" from a third-person, non-subjective perspective. We have then attempted to marry this taxonomy with a prescriptive model in which different aspects of the school context as experienced in the first-person, subjective sense are related theoretically to motivational, mental health, and behavioral outcomes through their hypothetical "fit" or "mismatch" with the fundamental needs of early adolescents (Eccles & Midgley, 1989). We describe these interdependent heuristic models below.

Descriptive model

To organize our understanding of the tasks, people, and practices that form the subcontexts of school, we have conceived of middle school environments as a series of embedded, organized hierarchical contexts moving out from the student to the level of the communities in which the school is embedded. Figure 12.1 depicts these various levels, which include the curricula of different subject matters; the informal curriculum of the classroom, the person of the teacher and his or her pedagogy; the academic track and associated students in which specific classes are embedded; the culture of the school as a whole; the grade span of the institution (Grades K–8, 6–8, 7–9); school governance structures and sector (public or private school); and the families and communities that the school serves. Factors at each of these levels of the secondary school environment have been linked to aspects of adolescents' academic engagement and achievement (see Eccles & Roeser, 1999, and Lee et al., 1993, for full reviews).

Each level of the school environment, as perceived from the student position, can be characterized by both "objective," third-person and "subjective," first-person features. For instance, we have depicted a "right-hand, objective dimension" of these contexts to denote the explicit features of each level such as the curricular content of the different subject matters; the age, gender, and ethnic composition of the teaching staff; the social class backgrounds of students in different tracked classes; the size and resources of the school, district, state; and federal educational policies; and the socioeconomic characteristics of the community of the school (Talbert & McLaughlin, 1993, 1999). These right-hand dimensions can be assessed from an outsider, "etic" perspective.

Each of the right-hand dimensions is assumed to have a corresponding left-hand, subjective dimension. These dimensions are implicit and include things like the challenge level and meaningfulness of the tasks and the sequence and scope of the different subject matter curricula; the classroom norms and rules; the beliefs, values, and pedagogical outlook of the teachers; the motivational attitudes and mental health of students and peer groups in "high" and "low" track classes; the culture of the school in terms of norms, roles, and rules; the culture of the district; and the values of parents and the community (e.g., Lee et al., 1993; Maehr & Midgley, 1991; Stodolsky & Gross-man, 1995). The left-hand dimensions are not readily apparent to outsiders and are usually assessed via the perceptions of students, teachers, parents, and educational leaders who inhabit these settings on a daily basis (e.g., an "emic" perspective). It is these "left-hand" dimensions that have the most functional significance for inhabitants' behavior.

One important assumption from a psychological perspective is that con-siderable variation in perceptions of the environment may exist among inhabitants of the same setting. In addition, we assume that students who go to the same physical school do not necessarily experience the school environment in similar ways or even get exposed to the same kinds of sub-contexts within the school. This assumption is based upon several different factors. First, young people can differ in the physical location and size of the organizational unit in which they go to school, and in their exposure to different teachers, peers, and kinds of curricula and teaching even within the same school. Some students in a school may be in portable trailers, which may or may not have adequate heat, whereas others may be in heated classrooms. Some may move into a "school within a school" that is located in a specific wing of the school, whereas others may have to traverse large areas and numbers of people as they transition from class to class. Furthermore, because differentiation practices intensify in public schools as youth move into the middle grades (Braddock & McPartland, 1992), students of different ability levels get exposed to different kinds of tasks, classmates, teachers, and teaching methods (Lee et al., 1993; Oakes et al., 1992). Status hierarchies based upon physical size, class, race and immigration status, involvement in school athletics or other activities, and peer groups generally are potent forces in secondary schools (Eckert, 1989; Epstein, 1983; Olsen, 1997). Thus, one's group memberships can likely have a profound impact on how one experiences school on a daily basis— whether one is in power or afraid, whether one is recognized or ignored, whether one feels a sense of belonging or alienation. Finally, different ado-lescents arrive at school with different educational histories and place-ments, and such experiences can shape their perceptions of schooling in the contemporary moment. Attending to how students may differ in their school experiences requires attention to both the "objective" and "subjec-tive" dimensions of their contemporary experience, as well as their educa-tional histories. Some factors such as track placement and classroom composition can be assessed from an etic perspective; others such as per-ceived treatment by teachers or curricular meaningfulness can only be assessed via first-person, emic reports.

Prescriptive model

We have found it useful in our own work to integrate this heuristic model of the tasks, people, and practices of school with a theory that prescribes how these various features of the environment will, theoretically, through early adolescents' subjective experience of them, affect their motivation and consequent patterns of behavior investment or divestment, participation or nonparticipation, achievement or failure in school. Rather than viewing young people as passive recipients of "educational treatments," motivational theories assume that adolescents are actively making meaning of the environment and having their self and school-related beliefs and feelings influenced by the meaning they derive there. These beliefs and feelings, in turn, are thought to "motivate" in-school behavior. In this sense, motivational theories stress that individuals are, in part, organizing their own development.

In one approach that has guided our work, Eccles and Midgley (1989) hypothesized that early adolescents have certain developmental needs. Specifically, they suggested that early adolescents want to feel that they are competent at various activities, and that they are especially sensitive to instances where their incompetence, relative to peers, is highlighted. In addition, they suggested that puberty and cognitive development herald new desires for autonomy; early adolescents want to exercise some choice and control over aspects of their activities. Finally, physical, cognitive, and emotional development in early adolescence is thought to lead to a need for developing intimate friendships with peers who are experiencing similar changes and to mentor-like relationships with nonparental adults who can guide youth as they move through the normative process of emotional individuation from parents.

Logically, Eccles and Midgley (1989) then concluded that young people attend to the specific environmental affordances in the home, at school, or in any environment that either provide opportunities for them to fulfill these stage-specific needs, or that tend to frustrate such need fulfillment (see also Lazarus, 1991). In relation to school, Eccles and Midgley (1989) hypothesized that potentially fulfilling afforances would include (a) a relatively noncomparative, noncompetitive but challenging learning environment for developing emerging competencies; (b) opportunities for decision making in the classroom and for connecting what is being learned with personal interests and experiences during this age of identity exploration; (c) extended contact with classmates during a time when young people are trying to find their social niche; and (d) extended contact with and respectful support from teachers during a time when adolescents are striving for emotional autonomy from parents and therefore have a need for nonparental role models. Eccles and colleagues (1993) have shown that junior high school settings that provide such affordances do seem to positively influence early adolescents' motivation to learn and consequently, their achievement behavior. Such a situation is depicted graphically in Figure 12.2. On the other hand, socially comparative practices in school, lack of meaningful work or opportunities for choice or personal expression, and unsupportive relationships have been related to the opposite outcomes—low perceived academic competence, poor valuing of school, poor mental health, and, as a consequence, poor achievement and in-school behavior (Eccles et al., 1993; Roeser et al., 1998). Assessing the dynamic relation between developmental needs and school contextual affordances, *as perceived by adolescents' themselves*, provides a parsimonious and prescriptive way to link various objective features of the school environment to patterns of motivation and behavior at the individual level.

In sum, the "lifespace principle" draws attention to the fact that variations in achievement behavior can be conceptualized not only as a function of individual differences in motivational processes and the various intrapsychological contexts of which they form a part (e.g., the self), but also as a function of the dynamic relation between individual's needs and the inter- and extrapersonal contexts that characterize their lives. Here, the person functioning in context becomes the focal unit of analysis; and behavior is seen as emerging from how well environmental opportunities "fit" or are "mismatched" with salient developmental needs of the individual. Coordinating both etic and emic perspectives on specific features of the school environment and their implicit "fit" or "mismatch" with the salient developmental needs of individuals becomes the twofold task of assessing the lifespace among subgroups of individuals—individuals who may be afforded differential opportunities in a specific context, and who may also experience opportunities differentially based on their social group memberships, educational history, and so on.

The Lifespan Principle: Adding Time

A third principle we have found useful in instantiating systems concept in our work is what we have termed "the lifespan principle." The lifespan principle is simply the notion that development during any given period is influenced by the developmental periods directly preceding and succeeding it (Lerner, 1987). Adolescents' motivation to learn in school, for example, reflects a developmental process that is more or less continuous from childhood, and that stretches out toward adulthood roles and statuses. In terms of the past, behavior at any given moment reflects not only the immediate configuration of person-by-context interactions and transactions, but also the entire history of such interactions and transactions in the developmental past that are relevant to present functioning (Lewin,

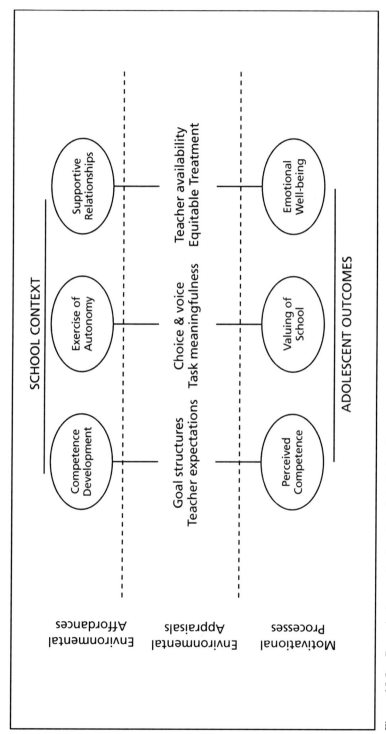

Figure 12.2.   Prescriptive motivational model of school context.

1936; Sameroff, 1983). The past history of an individual's academic performance, for example, "appears" in the present moment in terms of the person's academic motivation, knowledge, and abilities that are relevant to contemporaneous academic tasks and demands. In a very real way, the past is present in that it conditions how individuals approach or avoid new situations that are similar to those encountered in the past (Ford, 1992). Thus, individuals' history of academic performance and their educational placements (e.g., special education or gifted and talented programs) represent the developmental foundations that probabilistically forecast their motivation to learn during adolescence. It appears, for instance, that the evidence for declining motivation to learn among early adolescents is a reflection of at least two subgroups: those with long-term educational difficulties traced to the middle childhood years (Cairns et al., 1989; Roeser et al., 1999), and those who experience more proximal difficulties with the transition to junior high or middle school in early adolescence (Eccles et al., 1993; Simmons & Blyth, 1987).

From a motivational perspective in which anticipatory processes that ready individuals to act (or not act) are the focus, it is important to note that not only past encounters in childhood but also anticipated future ends in adulthood can influence present functioning (e.g., Markus & Nurius, 1986). This is especially true during adolescence, when one of the fundamental life tasks confronting adolescents is the linking of their past with a viable future (Erikson, 1968). Thus, another aspect to the lifespan principle is the idea that in studying motivation to learn among adolescents, we must not only account for present functioning and its link to individuals' educational histories, we must also account for where different individuals feel they are going educationally and occupationally. Perceptions of future opportunities and hoped for and feared selves all become important motivators of present functioning. Hopes and fears can "pull" present functioning in certain desired directions as much as past experiences can "push" behavior toward certain habitual, probabilistic ends. Currently, the integration of multiple time periods using longitudinal data, and multiple time perspectives using assessments of various short- and long-term goals in studies of adolescents' motivation, are not widespread.

In the next section, we endeavor to show how these three principles, the whole person, lifespace, and lifespan principles, have guided our own thinking about how to study motivational processes and schooling during adolescence. Through the presentation of one empirical example from our own research, we describe how we have tried to match our theoretical appreciation for the notion of organization within the person and between the person and the school context with data analytic techniques in which the pattern is the main unit of analysis.

AN EMPIRICAL ILLUSTRATION OF THE WHOLE PERSON, LIFESPACE, AND LIFESPAN PRINCIPLES

Recently, we completed a study using pattern-centered analyses in which we examined the organization of school identities and their linkages to school experiences among different subgroups of early adolescents (Roeser, Eccles, & Sameroff, 1998, 2000). This study is briefly described here as a means of illustrating how we have instantiated the "whole person," "lifespan," and "lifespace" principles described earlier in our own research. The goals of this study were to (a) describe subgroups of early adolescents who showed different patterns of academic motivation and social-emotional functioning; (b) link such patterns to consequential developmental outcomes that included but extended beyond the academic domain; (c) investigate the overarching organizational, instructional, and interpersonal processes that might explain these different patterns of functioning using stage-environment fit theory (Eccles & Midgley, 1989); and (d) examine how patterns of functioning in middle school among the different subgroups were related to subsequent educational attainments at the end of high school.

We began this study pragmatically. We wondered if we could identify subgroups of early adolescents who were characterized by patterns of functioning not adequately captured in aggregate-level trends that were well described in the literature: declining motivation and achievement and increased mental health problems. Did the same young people who experienced success or difficulty in one domain (the academic or the social-emotional) necessarily experience success or difficulty in the other? Synthesizing disparate bodies of research (see Eccles et al., 1996; Roeser et al., 1998, 1999), we assumed we could identify not only a "high-risk" group of youth who showed co-occurring academic and social-emotional problems, but also a group who were sad or angry but who nonetheless remained engaged in school and stayed away from bad peer influences—a group of young people we would call "academically resilient" because in the face of emotional adversity, they nonetheless stayed on track academically. Conversely, we assumed we could identify a group of adolescents who seemed free of emotional distress but who nonetheless felt psychologically disengaged from learning in school, perhaps due to the nature of their middle school environment (e.g., Eccles et al., 1993). Finally, contrary to prevailing stereotypes about adolescents in the wider culture, we assumed we would find that a majority of youth were characterized by multiple assets—positive motivation, good grades, no mental health problems, and avoidance of peers involved in problem behaviors (e.g., Dryfoos, 1998).

Theoretically, our interest was in exploring how these hypothesized patterns of school and social-emotional functioning among different subgroups of early adolescents might be explained, in part, by their pattern of experiences in school. Specifically, we were interested to see if youth with more positive academic motivation and behavior, mental health, or both reported the kinds of school experiences hypothesized to "fit" with their developmental needs. In contrast, we wondered if those who were disengaged academically, social-emotionally, or both might report more developmentally inappropriate school experiences. To test these ideas, we conducted a longitudinal investigation with a sample that included approximately 1,000 primarily African American and white families with an adolescent child these families began the study when the adolescent was in seventh grade and remained in the study for the next six years (J. Eccles & A.J. Sameroff are the study's principal investigators). Adolescents attended one of 23 middle schools in a large, county-wide school district. A portion of the research done within the context of this larger study is described here in four phases for purposes of illustrating some ways of conducting pattern-centered research.

Phase I: Identifying Subgroups

Person-centered, cluster analytic techniques were used to define subgroups of early adolescents. Such techniques assess the interdependence among variables within persons and thereby classify persons into relatively homogenous groups based upon their similarity across a series of measures (Magnusson & Bergmann, 1988). In this case, we clustered adolescents into subgroups based upon their pattern of self-reported academic competence, academic value, and emotional distress during the beginning of Grade 7. The four clusters that emerged and were retained for analyses are depicted in the graph portion of Figure 12.3. The clusters were named "multiple assets," "poor school value," "poor mental health," and "multiple problems," respectively. These empirically derived clusters matched our intuitions about plausible subgroups, and, as expected, the largest group was characterized by multiple assets (41% of the sample).

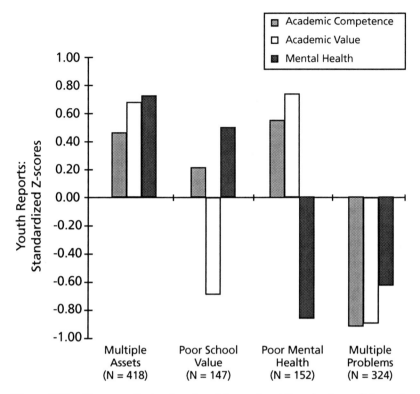

Figure 12.3.   Patterns of school and social-emotional functioning at 7th grade: Teacher, parent, and youth reports of academic and social behavior.

Table 12.1.   Adolescent Functioning

	Multiple Assets (N = 418)	Poor School Value (N = 147)	Poor Mental Health (N = 152)	Multiple Problems (N = 324)
Teachers: GPA 7th Grade	0.21[a]	0.21[a]	0.10[a]	−0.39[b]
Parent: Percent failing a class	13%[a]	20%[a]	20%[a]	39%[b]
Parent: Youth distress	−.027[a]	−0.06[b]	0.02[b]	0.35[c]
Youth: Anti-social friends	−0.27[a]	0.00[b]	0.00[b]	0.27[c]

All group comparisons showed significant F-values. Student Newman-Keuls post-hoc comparisons were used to test the nature of specific between-group differences. Different superscripts for a particular variable across clusters indicates a significant mean difference at the $p \leq .05$ level. All of these variables in the table, with the exception of parent reports of whether or not their adolescent failed or did very poorly in a class during the last two years, are expressed in standardized, z-score units.

Phase II: Subgroup Differences in Multiple Behaviors

In the next phase, we examined group differences in variables not used to create the subgroups. These included teacher-reported grades, parent reports of their child's academic failure and mental health, and youth self-reports of engaging in problem behaviors in school (cheating, getting in fights, etc.) and associating with peers who engage in such problem behaviors. In the table portion at the bottom of Figure 12.3, one can see how the groups differed across these varied consequential behaviors.

Several findings are noteworthy. First, academically, we found that it was only the "multiple problems" youth who are different—they got poorer grades and were more likely to have done poorly in or failed a class in school compared to the youth in the other three subgroups. These three groups, in turn, did not differ from one another in terms of their achievement behavior. However, the middle two groups were not "risk free"—their parents reported poorer emotional functioning than parents of the multiple assets youth; and these adolescents themselves reported average levels of hanging out with friends who engaged in minor delinquent acts such as cheating in school, stealing something worth less than $50, trying drugs, and so on. The multiple assets youth, in contrast, did well in school, avoided peers who engaged in these problem behaviors, and were seen as more emotionally healthy by their parents compared to youth in each of the other subgroups.

A second form of cluster description undertaken at this phase concerned the demographic characteristics of the clusters. Two group differences were noteworthy. First, White boys who came from relatively well-educated and wealthy families were overrepresented in the poor school value group. Second, white girls and African American boys were overrepresented in the poor mental health group. These findings are discussed briefly below (see Roeser et al., 1998, 2000, for further discussion).

Phase III: Lifespace Analysis

In the next stage of this study, we made the assumption that youth would show stability in their pattern of school and social-emotional functioning throughout middle school. The graph portion at the top of Figure 12.4 plots the means of youths' Grade 8 self-reported academic competence, academic value, and mental health by Grade 7 subgroup. As one can see, the assumption of continuity was borne out insofar as the between-group differences are still significant on these measures, albeit attenuated (see Roeser et al., 1998).

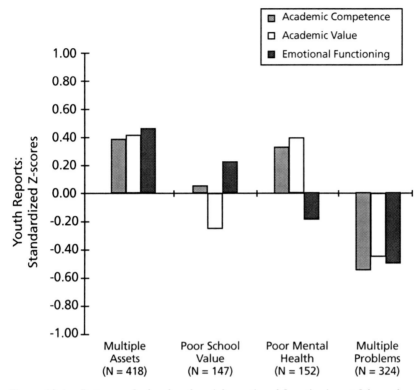

Figure 12.4.   Patterns of school and social-emotional functioning at 8th grade: Youth reports of school experiences.

Table 12.2.   Subjective School Percepions

	Multiple Assets (N = 418)	Poor School Value (N = 147)	Poor Mental Health (N = 152)	Multiple Problems (N = 324)
School ability goal structure	-0.24^a	0.07^{bc}	-0.05^{ab}	0.29^c
School mastery goal structure	0.18^a	-0.21^b	0.17^a	-0.18^b
Positive teacher regard	0.24^a	0.12^a	0.02^a	-0.35^b
Meaningful cuuricula	0.20^a	-0.23^b	0.25^a	-0.24^b
Classroom autonomy provisions	0.14^a	-0.16^b	0.20^a	-0.18^b
Teacher emotional support	0.19^a	-0.30^b	0.17^a	-0.18^b
Inequitable treatment by race	-0.19^a	-0.17^a	0.03^b	0.25^b
Inequitable treatment by sex	-0.23^a	-0.14^a	0.18^b	0.25^b

All group comparisons showed significant F-values. Student Newman-Keuls post-hoc comparisons were used to test the nature of specific between-group differences. Different superscripts for a particular variable across clusters indicates a significant mean difference at the $p \leq .05$ level. All of these variables in the table are expressed in standardized, z-score units.

Next, we compared the subgroups on a series of measures that assessed their school environments—both subjectively and objectively. The first series of measures was designed to tap developmentally appropriate and regressive school experiences—measures described in Figure 12.2 that included a socially comparative (school ability goal structure) or mastery-oriented (school mastery goal structure) school culture, teacher expectations, meaningful curricula and opportunities for voice and choice in the classroom, emotionally available teachers, and (in)equitable treatment of the sexes and those from different racial groups. Results assessing group differences in students' subjective school perceptions are presented in the table portion at the bottom of Figure 12.4.

The results provided a rather differentiated, theoretically predicted portrait of how certain school experiences are linked to certain patterns of motivation, mental health, and behavior among different subgroups of adolescents. First, note that the multiple assets group reported a consistent pattern of developmentally appropriate school affordances, as did the youth in the poor mental health group for the most part. These results are consistent with the notion that developmentally appropriate environments are associated with positive educational outcomes in youth, even among youth perhaps who are otherwise struggling with emotional problems. In contrast, the multiple problems youth reported the most developmentally regressive school experiences. Based upon parent reports of their child's course-taking patterns, we also found that disproportionate numbers of these multiple problem youth were in what could be considered low track or remedial classes in school. These findings are in keeping with the idea that school practices that are mismatched with adolescents' needs are associated with academic and emotional difficulties, and that low track classrooms are places where the most developmentally regressive pedagogical practices are likely to occur (Oakes et al., 1992). Of course, with this data and a pattern-centered approach, we can clearly see configurations of these theoretically consistent factors, but cannot make claims about the causal direction of influence between the motivational, behavioral, and contextual variables that comprise these configurations.

Perhaps of most interest are the factors that differentiate the two middle groups from the others. The poor school value youth are differentiated by precisely those variables we would most expect to affect poor valuing of school—less of an emphasis on task mastery, less meaningful curricula, fewer provisions for autonomy, and less emotionally available teachers. At the same time, these young people say their teachers think they are good students, they do fine academically, and they do not feel mistreated by teachers. In effect, they seem bored by the work, controlled by the teacher, and perhaps a little uncared for emotionally. The only factor that differentiated the poor mental health youth was perceived inequitable treatment by teachers predicated on sex, and to a lesser degree, race. It is interesting that white girls and African American boys were overrepresented in this group. They both felt that teachers were less likely to call on them, more likely to grade them harder, and less likely to think they are smart. We are currently pursuing a better understanding of what might be behind this finding in an interview study (Roeser, Galloway, Watson, Casey-Cannon, & Keller, 2001).

Finally, we compared the subgroups of objective measures of schools derived from data gathered from school officials and published government reports—the percentage of students on reduced or free lunch, the racial composition of the student body, the percentage of Grade 8 students taking algebra, and the aggregate standardized test scores and grade point averages of the student body in the school. Generally, we found no differences between groups on the objective school measures. We did find that those in the poor school valuing group (of whom white, relatively wealthy boys were overrepresented) tended to go to schools with higher aggregate mathematics and reading test scores, a higher proportion of white students, and a lower proportion of students on free lunch compared to those in the multiple problems group. These latter youth tended to be in slightly poorer, lower achieving schools, though the differences were not great. Taken as a whole, demographic factors seemed to most differentiate adolescents who were members of the poor school valuing group—they appear to be average achieving, academically disengaged white boys attending middle class schools. Socioeconomic variables did not seem to be a defining feature in any of the three other subgroups, whereas psychological and social contextual process measures did.

Phase IV: Lifespan Analysis

In the last analysis, we examined how subgroup patterns in Grade 7 were related to educational outcomes for the adolescents for whom we had data six years later (Roeser et al., 2000, 2001). At this point in time, youth who were college bound and on track educationally would have graduated from high school and been in their first year in college. What we found is perhaps not surprising—the multiple assets youth were overrepresented in the category of those who graduated from high school and went on to college, and underrepresented among those who graduated from high school but did not go on to college. On the other hand, the multiple problems were more likely to have dropped out of high school or completed high school and not gone on to college, and less likely to have graduated and gone on to college than predicted by chance. From a pattern-centered perspective, what is interesting in this analysis is the fact that six students in the multiple assets group did in fact drop out, and 93 students in the multiple problems group did go on to college. Exploring these "off-trajectory" youth based on their earlier patterns is another interesting use of pattern-centered data analytic techniques.

Implications

This study illustrates some of the insights that can be gained when using pattern-centered data analytic techniques to address motivational questions. First, the study began with an interesting practical question that necessarily focused on subgroups: Do youth necessarily show consistent success or difficulty in the academic and social-emotional domains of functioning? We chose indicators of motivation and mental health to form the subgroups, and then assessed a series of contextual factors derived from stage-environment fit theory (Eccles & Midgley, 1989) that might be useful in differentiating subgroups and thereby providing some explanation for why youth were characterized by different patterns of promise or problem. We assumed those who reported experiences that better "fit" adolescent needs, based on theory, would show more optimal patterns of functioning, whereas those who reported experiences mismatched with needs would show worse patterns of functioning.[1]

Second, this study presented one way of deriving subgroups. Specifically, they were based on youth self-reports of motivation and mental health that were cluster analyzed. Emergent subgroups were then compared on teacher, parent, and youth reports of various behaviors. Using multiple informants, when possible, is a powerful way to differentiate different subgroups of individuals in practically and theoretically meaningful ways. A key element in this latter illustration was showing how patterns of motivation and mental health are not only associated with achievement, but also school problem behavior and peer affiliations during adolescence. Developmental assets and risks "cluster" during this period (Dryfoos, 1990), and addressing this in motivational research by going beyond the academic domain is important. For instance, we suggest that the low track placement of the multiple problems youth likely exposes them differentially to peers who are similarly disengaged from school, potentiating perhaps their own misconduct, failure, and alienation from school (Dishion, Patterson, Stoolmiller, & Skinner, 1991).

Third, and perhaps most importantly, we showed how indicators of the lifespace of school, derived from both first-person, subjective reports and third-person sources, could be combined with different patterns of motivation, mental health, and behavior in theoretically meaningful ways. Indeed, what we created is what Lewin (1936) meant by a "lifespace configuration"—a pattern of motivational processes and perceptions of the environment that energize and give direction to behavior in that environment. As Lewin noted and our results showed, understanding the subjectively experienced environment is essential for understanding the functional significance of that environment for an individual's behavior. The "objective" measures of the school that we examined were much less differentiating of the subgroups than were the subjective measures.

Finally, the results of this study highlight the utility of pattern-centered techniques for illuminating the diversity of patterns and pathways that can eventuate in unique or common developmental outcomes. In the first instance, we found three patterns and pathways linked to a common set of outcomes: positive achievement, high school graduation, and college enrollment. One such pattern among middle school students was characterized by positive motivation and mental health, another was characterized by positive academic motivation despite poor mental health, and still another was characterized by "good enough" school functioning (e.g., poor school valuing group). These results highlight the diversity of ways of attaining positive educational outcomes among different youth. On the other hand, we found one pathway to academic problems and dropping out—the multiple problems pattern. Consistent with other studies, these were the youth who showed externalizing problems, grade retention, and academic failure much earlier in elementary school (Cairns et al., 1989). Again, these results highlight the need for a lifespan approach in the study of motivation during adolescence.

CONCLUSIONS

Although it is perhaps true that the wholeness of life has from of old been made manifest in its parts, it may also be true that everything in the universe follows certain patterns and processes. Although the future is the hardest to predict, it appears that it may once again be time for educational and developmental psychologists to take a holistic approach to the mystery that is a human life in progress. Seeing holistically and appreciating the phenomenal world in its process-oriented and patterned splendor is, if nothing else, the fast-approaching scientific future.

The use of pattern-centered techniques are the analytic analogue to the theoretical concept of organization that permeated each section of this chapter. Such techniques, whether based on mathematical algorithms, multi-informant nominations, or some other method, have several underutilized advantages. First, they take the researcher beyond statistically average trends in data analysis and focus on (hopefully) substantive or theoretically interesting subgroups whose functioning may not be represented by average trends at all. Second, they allow for an examination of configurations of multiple "predictor" and "outcome" variables at the same time. This seems to bode well for studying the kinds of clustering of developmental outcomes that occur during adolescence. Implicit in pattern-centered approaches is a direct examination of higher-order interactions among many variables. Third, and perhaps most importantly, such techniques make the person as the focal unit of analysis and are consistent with many of the tenets of modern developmental theory in which the person is seen as the organizing principle of their own development (Magnusson, 2000). Pattern-centered techniques allow for direct examinations of patterns and pathways of functioning in ways that may, given the focus on holistic patterning of variables within subgroups, speak to the "case-like" reasoning of practitioners in educational and clinical settings. Such techniques, when married with the assumptions of contemporary systems thinking, provide a powerful complement to existing research on academic motivation and schooling during adolescence, and also a rich set of possibilities for future research on the diversity of motives, selfways, educational pathways, and in-school experiences that characterize different subgroups of adolescents in U.S. schools today.

NOTES

1.   We have already examined, using variable-centered analytic techniques, the question of causal influence as best we could with correlational, longitudinal data to see if perceptions of context were accounted for primarily by the state of the individual. Time and again we found that after controlling for sociodemographic factors and prior measures of motivation, mental health, and achievement, perceptions of school still contributed additional variance to outcomes measures of motivation, mental health, and achievement (Roeser, 1996; Roeser et al., 1998, 2000). Thus, though such configurations may simply reflect the "state" of the individual youth, we believe that the specific patterns in the data and their consistency with theory suggest something more substantive is reflected in with these findings.

REFERENCES

Ames, C. (1992). Achievement goals and the classroom motivational climate. In D.H. Schunk & J. L. Meece (Eds.), *Student perceptions in the classroom* (pp. 327–348). Hillsdale, NJ: Erlbaum.

Bergman, L. (2001). A person approach in research on adolescence: Some methodological considerations. *Journal of Adolescent Research, 16*, 28–53.

Bergman, L. R., Cairns, R. B., Nilsson, L., & Nystedt, L. (2000). *Developmental science and the holistic approach.* Mahwah, NJ: Erlbaum.

Bernal, M. E., Saenz, D. S., & Knight, G. P. (1995). Ethnic identity and adaptation of Mexican-American youths in school settings. In. A. Padilla (Ed.), *Hispanic psychology: Critical issues in theory and research* (pp. 71–88). Thousand Oaks, CA: Sage.

Berndt, T. J., & Keefe, K. (1995). Friends influence on adolescents' adjustment to school. *Child Development, 66,* 1312–1329.

Boekaerts, M., & Niemivirta, M. (2000). Self-regulated learning: Finding a balance between learning goals and ego-protective goals. In M. Boekaerts, P.R. Pintrich, & M. Zeidner (Eds.), *Handbook of self-regulation* (pp. 417–450). San Diego, CA: Academic Press.

Boekaerts, M., Pintrich, P. R., & Zeidner, M. (Eds.). (2000). *Handbook of self-regulation.* San Diego, CA: Academic Press.

Braddock II, J. H., & McPartland, J. M. (1993). *Education of early adolescents.* In L. Darling-Hammond (Ed.), *Review of research in education* (Vol. 19, pp. 135–170). Washington, DC: American Educational Research Association.

Bronfenbrenner, U. (1999). Environments in developmental perspective: Theoretical and operational models. In S. L Friedman & T. D. Wachs (Eds.), *Measuring environment across the life span: Emerging methods and concepts* (pp. 3–28). Washington, DC: American Psychological Association.

Cairns, R. B., Cairns, B. D., & Neckerman, H. J. (1989). Early school dropout: Configurations and determinants. *Child Development, 60,* 1437–1452.

Capra, F. (1982). *The turning point: Science, society, and rising culture.* Toronto: Bantam Books.

Capra, F. (1996). *The web of life: A new scientific understanding of living systems.* New York: Anchor Books.

Cicchetti, D., & Cohen, D. J. (1995). *Developmental psychopathology* (Vols. 1 & 2). New York: Wiley.

Connell, J. P., & Wellborn, J. G. (1991). Competence, autonomy and relatedness: A motivational analysis of self-system processes. In M. Gunnar & A. Sroufe (Eds.), *Minnesota Symposium on Child Psychology* (Vol. 23, pp. 43–77). Hillsdale, NJ: Erlbaum.

Davidson, A. L., & Phelan, P. (1999). Students' multiple worlds: An anthropological approach to understanding students' engagement with school (pp. 233–272). In T. C. Urdan (Ed.), *Advances in motivation* (Vol. 11). Stamford, CT: JAI Press.

Deci, E., & Ryan, R. (1985). *Intrinsic motivation and self-determination in human behavior.* New York: Academic Press.

Dishion, T. J., Patterson, G. R., Stoolmiller, M., & Skinner, M. L. (1991). Family, school, and behavioral antecedents to early adolescent involvement with antisocial peers. *Developmental Psychology, 27,* 172–180.

Donovan, J. E., & Jessor, R. (1985). Structure of problem behavior in adolescence and young adulthood. *Journal of Consulting and Clinical Psychology, 53,* 890–904.

Dryfoos, J. G. (1990). *Adolescents at risk: Prevalence and prevention.* New York: Oxford University Press.

Dryfoos, J. G. (1998). *Safe passage: Making it through adolescence in a risky society.* New York: Cambridge University Press.

Dweck, C. S. (1986). Motivational processes affecting learning. *American Psychologist, 40,* 1040–1048.

Dweck, C. S. (1996). Social motivation: Goals and social-cognitive processes. A comment. In J. Juvonen & K. R. Wentzel (Eds.), *Social motivation: Understanding children's school adjustment* (pp. 181–195). New York: Cambridge University Press.

Eccles, J. S., Lord, S., & Roeser, R. W. (1996). Round holes, square pegs, rocky roads, and sore feet: A discussion of stage-environment fit theory applied to families and school. In D. Cicchetti & S. L. Toth (Eds.), *Rochester Symposium on Developmental Psychopathology, Volume VII. Adolescence: Opportunities and challenges* (pp. 47–92). Rochester, NY: University of Rochester Press.

Eccles, J. S., Lord, S., & Roeser, R. W., Barber, B., & Hernandez-Jozefowicz, D. (1997). The association of school transitions in early adolescence with developmental trajectories through high school. In J. Schulenberg, J. Maggs, & K. Hurrelmann (Eds.), *Health risks and developmental transitions during adolescence* (pp. 283–320). New York: Cambridge University Press.

Eccles, J. S., & Midgley, C. (1989). Stage-environment fit: Developmentally appropriate classrooms for young adolescents. In C. Ames & R. Ames (Eds.), *Research on motivation in education: Goals and cognitions* (Vol. 3, pp. 13–44). New York: Academic Press.

Eccles, J. S., Midgley, C., Wigfield, A., Buchanan, C. M., Reuman, D., Flanagan, C. & MacIver, D. (1993). Development during adolescence: The impact of stage-environment fit on adolescents' experiences in schools and families. *American Psychologist, 48*, 90–101.

Eccles. J. S., & Roeser, R. W. (1999). School and community influences on human development. In M. H. Boorstein & M.E. Lamb (Eds.), *Developmental psychology: An advanced textbook* (2nd ed., pp. 503–554). Hillsdale, NJ: Erlbaum.

Eccles, J. S., Wigfield, A., & Schiefele, U. (1998). Motivation. In N. Eisenberg (Ed.), *Handbook of child psychology* (Vol. 3, pp. 1017–1095). New York: Wiley.

Eckert, P. (1989). *Jocks and burnouts: Social categories and identity in the high school.* New York: Teachers College Press.

Entwistle, D. R., & Alexander, K. L., (1993). Entry into school: The beginning school transition and educational stratification in the United States. *Annual Review of Sociology 19*, 401–423.

Epstein, J. L. (1983). The influence of friends on achievement and affective outcomes. In J. L. Epstein & N. L. Karweit (Eds.), *Friends in school* (pp. 177–200). New York: McGraw-Hill.

Erikson, E. H. (1950). *Childhood and society.* New York: Norton.

Erikson, E. H. (1968). *Identity, youth and crisis.* New York: Norton.

Ford, D. H. & Ford, M. E. (1987). Humans as self-constructing living systems: An overview. In M. E. Ford & D. H. Ford (Eds.), *Humans as self-constructing living systems: Putting the framework to the test* (pp. 1–46). Hillsdale, NJ: Erlbaum.

Ford, D. H., & Lerner, R. M. (1992). *Developmental systems theory: An integrative approach.* Newbury Park, CA: Sage.

Ford, M. E. (1992). *Motivating humans: Goals, emotions, and personal agency beliefs.* Newbury Park, CA: Sage.

Fordham, S., & Ogbu, J. U. (1986). Black students' school success: Coping with the "Burden of 'Acting White.'" *The Urban Review, 18*, 176–206.

Goodenow, C. (1992). Strengthening the links between educational psychology and the study of social contexts. Educational Psychologist, 27, 177–196.

Harter, S. (1981). A new self-report scale of intrinsic versus extrinsic orientation in the classroom: Motivational and informational components. *Developmental Psychology, 17*, 300–312.

Harter, S. (1990). Self and identity development. In S. S. Feldman & G. R. Elliott (Eds.), *At the threshold: The developing adolescent* (pp. 352–368). Cambridge, MA: Harvard University Press.

Harter, S. (1996). Teacher and classmate influences on scholastic motivation, self-esteem, and level of voice in adolescents. In J. Juvonen & K. R. Wentzel (Eds.), *Social motivation:_Understanding children's school adjustment* (pp. 11–42). New York: Cambridge University Press.

Hinshaw, S. P. (1992). Externalizing behavior problems and academic under-achievement in childhood and adolescence: Causal relationships and underlying mechanisms. *Psychological Bulletin, 111*, 127–155.

Jessor, R. (1993). Successful adolescent development among youth in high-risk settings. *American Psychologist, 48*, 117–126.

Juvonen, J., & Wentzel, K. R., (1996). *Social motivation: Understanding children's school adjustment.* New York: Cambridge University Press.

Kuhl, J. (1984). Volitional aspects of achievement motivation and learned helplessness: Toward a comprehensive theory of action-control. In B. A. Maher (Ed.), *Progress in experimental personality research* (Vol. 13, pp. 99–171). New York: Academic Press.

Lazarus, R. S. (1991). *Emotion and adaptation.* New York: Oxford University Press.

Lee, V. E., Bryk, A. S., & Smith, J. B. (1993). The organization of effective secondary schools. In L. Darling-Hammond (Ed.), *Review of research in education* (Vol. 19, pp. 171–267). Washington DC: American Educational Research Association.

Lerner, R. M. (1987). A life-span perspective for early adolescence. In R. M. Lerner & T. T. Foch (Eds.), *Biological-psychosocial interactions in early adolescence* (pp. 9–34). Hillsdale, NJ: Erlbaum.

Lewin, K. (1936). *Principles of a topological psychology.* New York: McGraw-Hill.

Maccoby, E., (1998). *The two sexes: Growing up apart, coming together.* Cambridge, MA: Harvard University Press.

Maehr, M. L., & Midgley, C. (1991). Enhancing student motivation: A school-wide approach. *Educational Psychologist, 26*, 399–427.

Magnusson, D. (2000). The individual as the organizing principle in psychological inquiry: A holistic approach. In L. R. Bergman, R. B. Cairns, L. Nilsson, & L. Nystedt (Eds.), *Developmental science and the holistic approach* (pp. 33–48). Mahwah, NJ: Erlbaum.

Magnusson, D., & Bergmann, L.R. (1988). Individual and variable-based approaches to longitudinal research on early risk factors. In M. Rutter (Ed.), *Studies of psychosocial risk: The power of longitudinal data* (pp. 45–61). New York: Cambridge University Press.

Markus, H. R., & Nurius, P. (1986). Possible selves. *American Psychologist, 41*, 954–969.

Masten, A. S., & Coatsworth, J. D. (1998). The development of competence in favorable and unfavorable environments: Lessons from research on successful children. *American Psychologist, 53*, 205–220.

Masten, A. S., Coatsworth, J. D., Neemann, J., Gest, S. D., Tellegen, A., & Garmezy, N. (1995). The structure and coherence of competence from childhood to adolescence. *Child Development, 66,* 1635–1659.

McGreal, I. P. (1995). *Great thinkers of the Eastern World.* New York: HarperCollins.

Nisbett, R. E., Peng, K., Choi, I., & Norenzayan, A. (2001). Culture and systems of thought: Holistic versus analytic cognition. *Psychological Review, 108,* 291–310.

Nolen-Hoeksema, S., Girgus, J. S., & Seligman, M. E. P. (1986). Learned helplessness in children: A longitudinal study of depression, achievement, and explanatory style. *Journal of Personality and Social Psychology, 51,* 435–442.

Oakes, J., Gamoran, A., & Page, R. N. (1992). Curriculum differentiation: Opportunities, outcomes, and meanings. In P. Jackson (Ed.), *Handbook of research on curriculum* (pp. 570–608). New York: MacMillan.

Ogbu, J. U. (1978). *Minority education and caste.* New York: Academic Press.

Ollendick, T. H., Greene, R. W., Weist, M. D., & Oswald, D. P. (1990). The predictive validity of teacher nominations: A five year follow-up of at-risk youth. *Journal of Abnormal Child Psychology, 18,* 699–713.

Olsen, L. (1997). *Made in America : Immigrant students in our public schools.* New York: New Press.

Parker, J. G., & Asher, S. R. (1987). Peer relations and later personal adjustment: Are low-accepted children at risk? Psychological Bulletin, 102, 357–389.

Pervin, L. A. (2000). The four c's of personality: Context, consistency, conflict, and coherence. In L. R. Bergman, R. B. Cairns, L. Nilsson, & L. Nystedt (Eds.), *Developmental science and the holistic approach* (pp. 251–264). Mahwah, NJ: Erlbaum.

Pintrich, P. R. (2000). Multiple goals, multiple pathways: The role of goal orientation in learning and achievement. *Journal of Educational Psychology, 92,* 544–555.

Roderick, M. (1993). *The path to dropping out: Evidence for intervention.* Westport, CT: Auburn House.

Roderick, M. (1994). Grade retention and school dropout: Investigating the association. *American Educational Research Journal, 31,* 729–759.

Roeser, R. W. (1996). Unfolding and enfolding youth: Studies in middle school experience, academic motivation, and psychological adjustment during adolescence. Unpublished doctoral dissertation, University of Michigan, Ann Arbor.

Roeser, R. W., Eccles, J. S., & Freedman-Doan, C. (1999). Academic and emotional functioning in middle adolescence: Patterns, progressions, and routes from childhood. *Journal of Adolescent Research, 14,* 135–174.

Roeser, R. W., Eccles, J. S., & Sameroff, A. J. (1998). Academic and emotional functioning in early adolescence. Longitudinal relations, patterns, and prediction by experience in middle school. *Development and Psychopathology, 10,* 321–352.

Roeser, R. W., Galloway, M., Watson, C. M., Casey-Cannon, S., & Keller, L. (2001, August). *Exploring academic resilience and relational status among early adolescent females.* Paper presented at the annual meeting of the American Psychological Association, San Francisco.

Roeser, R. W., Midgley, C. M., & Urdan, T. C. (1996). Perceptions of the school psychological environment and early adolescents' psychological and behavioral functioning in school: The mediating role of goals and belonging. *Journal of Educational Psychology, 88,* 408–422.

Roeser, R. W., Peck, S. C., Eccles, J. S., & Sameroff, A.J. (1999, April). *Pathways of academic and emotional functioning from 7th to 11th grade: Personality and school contextual predictors.* Paper presented at the biennial meeting of the Society for Research on Child Development, Albuquerque, NM.

Roeser, R. W., Peck, S. C., Eccles, J. S., & Sameroff, A. J. (2000, April). *On life space configurations in the prediction of adolescents' educational attainments and mental health.* Paper presented at the Biennial Meeting of the Society for Research on Adolescence, Chicago.

Roeser, R. W., Peck, S. C., Eccles, J. S., & Sameroff, A. J. (2001, April). *Studying adolescents' educational trajectories, in context, over time: Problems and promises of pattern-centered techniques.* Paper presented at the biennial meeting of the Society for Research on Child Development, Minneapolis.

Ryan, R. M. (1992). Agency and organization: Intrinsic motivation, autonomy, and the self in psychological development. In J. E. Jacobs (Series Ed.), *Nebraska Symposium on Motivation: Developmental perspectives on motivation* (pp. 1–56). Lincoln: University of Nebraska Press.

Sameroff, A. (1983). Developmental systems: Contexts and evolution. In W. Kessen (Ed.) & P.H. Mussen (Series Ed.), *Handbook of child psychology: Vol. 1: History, theory, and methods* (pp. 237–294). New York: Wiley.

Sarason, S. B. (2001). *American psychology and schools: A critique.* New York: Teachers College Press.

Schneider, S. H., & Londer, R. (1984). *The coevolution of climate and life.* San Francisco: Sierra Club Books.

Simmons, R. G., & Blyth, D. A. (1987). *Moving into adolescence: The impact of pubertal change and school context.* Hawthorn, NY: Aldine de Gruyler.

Snow, R. E. (1994). Abilities in academic tasks. In R. J. Sternberg & R. K. Wagner (Eds.), *Mind in context: Interactionist perspectives on human intelligence* (pp. 3–37). New York: Cambridge University Press.

Snow, R. E., Corno, L., & Jackson, D. (1996). Individual differences in affective and conative functions. In D. C. Berliner & R. C. Calfee (Eds.), *Handbook of educational psychology* (pp. 243–310). New York: Simon & Schuster Macmillan.

Steele, C. M. (1997). A threat in the air: How stereotypes shape intellectual identity and performance. *American Psychologist, 52,* 613–629.

Stodolsky S. S., & Grossman, P. L. (1995). The impact of subject matter on curricular activity: An analysis of five academic subjects. *American Educational Research Journal, 32,* 227–249.

Talbert J. E., & McLaughlin, M. W. (1993). Understanding teaching in context. In D. Cohen, M. W. McLaughlin, & J. E. Talbert (Eds.), *Teaching for understanding: Challenges for policy and practice* (pp. 167–206). San Francisco: Jossey-Bass.

Talbert. J. E., & McLaughlin, M. W. (1999). Assessing the school environment: Embedded contexts and bottom-up research strategies. In American Psychological Association (Ed.), *Measuring environment across the life span: Emerging methods and concepts* (pp. 197–227). Washington DC: American Psychological Association.

Wentzel, K. R., & Asher, S. R. (1995). The academic lives of neglected, rejected, popular, and controversial children. *Child Development, 66,* 754–763.
Zalatimo, S. D., & Sleeman, P. J. (1975). *A systems approach to learning environments.* Pleasantville, NY: Redgrave.

Printed in the United States
200786BV00007B/22/A